Warning!
Violence, War, Magic & the Supernatural

The fictional universe of Phase World® **and the Three Galaxies**™ is violent, deadly and filled with supernatural monsters. Other-dimensional beings often referred to as "demons" torment, stalk and prey on humans. Other alien life forms, monsters, gods and demigods, as well as magic, insanity, and war are all elements in this book.

Some parents may find the violence, magic and supernatural elements of the game inappropriate for young readers/players. We suggest parental discretion.

Please note that none of us at Palladium Books® condone or encourage the occult, the practice of magic, the use of drugs, or violence.

An epic adventure sourcebook for the Phase World® series.
Compatible with the entire Palladium Books® Megaverse®!

Dedication

To Kevin Siembieda, who called me up out of the blue one day to recruit me for further Phase World® supplements. Little did I know how much fuel he threw onto my imagination's fire.

To Allison, who always is willing to listen to my wacky ideas, but who also keeps me grounded with cryptic phrases such as "Heihachi stole your cookies again, didn't he?"

To the legion of authors and creators who fostered my love for speculative fiction throughout the years. Though the list could fill pages, a few of the more notable names include George Lucas, Gene Roddenberry, Iain M. Banks, William Gibson, David Brin, Neal Stephenson, Ray Bradbury, Robert Heinlein, and H.G. Wells.

– Bill Coffin, 2002

The cover depicts a Gene-Tech conducting genetic experiments inside a secret space laboratory. Painted by John Zeleznik.

Special Printing – February 2012

Palladium Online: **www.palladiumbooks.com** – also visit us at **Facebook.com/PalladiumBooks**

Rifts® Dimension Book™ Five: Anvil Galaxy™ is published by Palladium Books Inc., 39074 Webb Court, Westland, MI 48185. Printed in the USA.

Palladium Books® Presents:

Rifts® Dimension Book Five:

The Anvil Galaxy™

A *Phase World*® Sourcebook

Written by: **Bill Coffin**

Additional text and ideas by: **Kevin Siembieda**
Inspired by and based on *Phase World*® created by **C.J. Carella**.
Editors: **Alex Marciniszyn**
        Wayne Smith
Proofreader: **Julius Rosenstein**
Cover Painting: **John Zeleznik**
Interior Artists: **Wayne Breaux Jr.**
        Kent Burles
        Ramon Perez Jr.
        Freddie Williams II
        Michael Wilson
Art Direction & Keylining: **Kevin Siembieda**
Typography: **Maryann Siembieda**

Based on the RPG rules, text, characters,
concepts and Megaverse® created by **Kevin Siembieda**.

Special Thanks to Johnny Z for another great cover, Mike Wilson for a Herculean effort and all my artists, as well as Maryann for all her hard work and thankless efforts, and all the Palladium madmen from around the Megaverse.

— *Kevin Siembieda, 2002*

Table of Contents

Quick Find

Author's Introduction

I must admit, the idea of writing an Anvil Galaxy sourcebook was not my own. Kevin Siembieda came to me earlier this year and offered me the chance at expanding a thrilling space opera world C.J. Carella had invented but was no longer around to develop. Kevin already had a manuscript for an Anvil Galaxy sourcebook, but it did not take the setting in the direction he wanted, and ultimately, he asked if I wouldn't mind taking the job. I have a long-running bad habit of taking on projects and thinking about it later – part of a "go-getter" attitude that has gotten me into trouble more than once. Such was the case with this job at first. I gladly jumped at the opportunity to write about the *Three Galaxies*, but when it came time to actually do it, I found the task a little more than daunting. C.J. established a setting that tons of players knew and loved. It was one I was not terribly familiar with at first, but the more I dove into it, the more I grew to love the Three Galaxies and the limitless possibilities for adventure that they offered. Writing this was going to be a blast, I realized. And I was right. It has been. So I must tip my hat to C.J. Carella, on whose shoulders this work rests, and to Kevin Siembieda, who had the courage to give me the job. I guess he knew I could do it better than I did. It wouldn't be the first time.

Phase World®, the Three Galaxies and the **Anvil Galaxy** in particular are wonderful space opera settings. I like, no, I love space opera. Unlike "hard" science fiction, which often times is more rooted in science than fiction, space opera takes the attitude of, "don't let the facts get in the way of a good story." I live by those words, and I certainly applied them while writing the Anvil Galaxy sourcebook. Certain sections, like the planet and star generators, will feature a few tidbits of scientific knowledge heavily spiced with speculations and flat-out make-believe. Realism has not been the aim of this book. Creating an action-filled setting where square-jawed heroes can chase the mysteries of the Megaverse® while fighting off bug-eyed aliens and navigating endless turmoil between interstellar empires – now that was the aim here, and hopefully we have achieved just that. To get there, though, the reader might find more than a few cases where I bend the rules of science or where I just plain break them. If this rankles your allegiance to science, I apologize. Having been an SF novelist before I began writing role-playing games, I know that SF readers sometimes have a strong love for realism (despite the fact that they are reading about aliens, spaceships and technologies that do not yet exist). By that same token, a lot of gamers share that love for realism, and they are disappointed when they expect to find it someplace and do not. Let me dispel any such expectations right now. This is Phase World. The Three Galaxies. The Anvil Galaxy. This is the *battleground* where invincible Cosmo-Knights single-handedly confront incredible battle fleets of ultratech spaceships. It is where inter-dimensional *nexus planets* form a network that brings together not only the many worlds of the Three Galaxies, but of the entire Megaverse! It is a place where the strangest aliens humankind has encountered are actually far more familiar than the really freakish things that dwell in the center of the galaxy. It is the home of the *Cosmic Forge*, an artifact of ultimate power. It is a place where heroism and high adventure are the favored currency, and where a good plan and a trusty blaster will get you a lot farther than a textbook and calculator.

So with that, I welcome you to the third installment of the **Phase World®** series. For those of you who are picking up this book right after purchasing the **Rifts® RPG**, you might be figuring out that this is *not* the "original" Phase World® book. Relax! Although this book expands upon the Phase World® setting, you don't actually need Phase World® to play. This book has been written both to stand alone and to plug in neatly with pre-existing sourcebooks both for the Phase World® setting and for other Palladium RPG books. Though this is a stand-alone product, if you want to dive really deep into this stuff, there are a few other books I suggest you check out:

Dimension Book Two: Phase World®, the original supplement that started this all. **Phase World®** is kind of an RPG within an RPG, for it is basically a *separate game world* all its own. You can run endless campaigns in the **Phase World®** setting and never even set foot on Rifts Earth. The **Phase World®** book introduces you to this wild and wooly space opera setting, as well as offers detailed information on the single planet that ties together all of the Three Galaxies, a unique world eponymously known as *Phase World®*.

Dimension Book Three: Phase World® Sourcebook fills the reader in on the rest of the Three Galaxies, as well as offers additional aliens, technology, and best of all – star ships and star ship combat. This book also provides additional insight to three of the main powers of the Three Galaxies — the *Consortium of Civilized Worlds (CCW)*, the *Trans-Galactic Empire (TGE)*, and the *United Worlds of Warlock (UWW)*.

The Heroes Unlimited™ Galaxy Guide is not a **Rifts®** supplement, as the title suggests, but it is still a great resource for any Palladium gamer who wishes to run a space opera campaign. The Galaxy Guide offers rules on world creation, adventuring in space, and building spaceships (a personal favorite). Likewise, the **Aliens Unlimited™** sourcebook is for Heroes Unlimited rather than for Rifts, but it contains a slew of pre-generated alien races, any of which could be easily imported into a Phase World® campaign or any other space opera setting of your choosing. Then there is the upcoming **Mechanoid Space™** series, another science fiction space game to be unveiled at the end of 2002 sometime.

And finally, if you really want to include as much other material into your game as possible, consider the *Robotech® RPG*, *Robotech® II: The Sentinels RPG*, and the *Macross II™ RPG* and their various supplements. These games and sourcebooks are their own distinct universe, and they are not even in print anymore (so grab 'em while you still can!), but they have a lot going for them. They are just filled with cool robots, spaceships and other fighting machines. They also are part of an incredibly epic and popular space opera storyline, one that the enterprising G.M. might want to plunder for ideas and inspiration when filling out his own Phase World campaign.

One more thing before we get to the rest of the book. This is not the only new Phase World supplement to be hitting the shelves. Shortly after this book comes out, it will be followed by a **Cosmo-Knights™ sourcebook**, also written by yours truly. With a little luck, we might see a host of new **Phase World®** books hitting the shelves in the ongoing future, so thank you in advance for giving the Anvil Galaxy a shot and for supporting our games. We couldn't do it without you!

That's enough yakking for now. Game on!

– Bill Coffin, 2002

The Cosmic Forge

The legends of every space-faring civilization in the Phase World sector of space/Three Galaxies mention the **Cosmic Forge**, an ancient artifact believed to have had a part in the creation of the Three Galaxies, and perhaps the outer universe as well. The exact nature and abilities of the Cosmic Forge have never been described, but the general consensus is that it bestows upon its user ultimate power. The ultimate power to do anything, create anything, and destroy anything the user wishes. Of course, the Cosmic Forge is a sentient thing, so it might object to certain choices its user might command it to do (as has indeed happened in the Cosmic Forge's history, but more on that later), but in the end, whoever controls the Cosmic Forge controls the universe, plain and simple. And lo and behold, it looks like it has been hiding somewhere in the *Anvil Galaxy* all this time.

The Cosmic Forge is one of the very few things that unites all Phase World cultures and races. Very shortly, this shared knowledge of the Cosmic Forge and the ancient legend concerning its role in the creation of the Three Galaxies, its betrayal, and its disappearance will unite the entire Anvil Galaxy in a reckless quest for ultimate power. A quest that will likely end in the destruction of countless civilizations and might very well set the entire Anvil Galaxy afire. The existence of the Cosmic Forge can drive even the most level-headed and rational of folk to utter insanity, so obsessed do they get with the notion that one day they might find the Forge and command its limitless power.

The Anvil Galaxy, and indeed, perhaps all of the Three Galaxies might stand on the edge of a massive change in their future, all because of the Cosmic Forge. In many ways, the Forge, its legend, and the mad dash to find and capture it are the central themes of this sourcebook. Hopefully, they will make for great campaign fodder.

The Chronicles of the Cosmos

For all of its cultural and historical prominence, there is little *hard fact* to be had about the Cosmic Forge. Obscure ancient manuscripts offer some vague notion about the Forge's early history and nature, but they are so open to interpretation that it is hard to believe that *these* are supposed to be the authoritative documents on the subject.

Of these old manuscripts, the most valuable one is the *Chronicles of the Cosmos*, a lengthy treatise written by an unknown author eons ago. The original manuscript has been lost for thousands of years, and even the oldest translations of the text appear in so many different languages that it is impossible to tell which one might have been the original language version. That being the case, there is no telling how much error, misinterpretation and translator embellishment is in any of the copies, since none of them can be considered any more true or authoritative than another. Still, these "first generation" copies of the *Chronicles of the Cosmos* are considered the foundation of the legend and myth surrounding the Cosmic Forge. For anybody serious about studying the Forge, reading at least a few different versions of "first-generation" copies of the *Chronicles* is a must.

The Chronicles of the Cosmos lay out the basic facts of the Cosmic Forge Legend: That when Time itself was very young, an ancient race known only as *the First* explored and commanded a great stretch of the universe. Bored with their great achievements, they built an item of ultimate power: *The Cosmic Forge*. Exactly what shape this item took is open to considerable debate, but with this tool, the First did a great many incredible things. They made themselves immortal, and god-like, for one. They created (and destroyed) entire star systems. They built life out of lifelessness, and they played with the cosmos as if it were a mere set of child's building blocks. With their "Cosmic Forge," the First were truly masters of all they surveyed. Ultimately, the Forge can be credited with creating every unusual natural and supernatural **process** to be found in the Three Galaxies.

After a long while, the *Chronicles* state, one of the First grew jealous and stole the Cosmic Forge, using it to satisfy his own sinister urges. With it, he destroyed the First so he would reign supreme. However, the Cosmic Forge itself was horrified by this act, so it destroyed its usurper and then, ashamed at having destroyed its very Creators, the Forge hid itself, never to reveal itself to mortals ever again.

Virtually everybody in the Three Galaxies knows at least this much, but the *Chronicles of the Cosmos* goes far beyond this snippet. Indeed, *if* the text can be trusted as the "authoritative" and "true" record of the Cosmic Forge, it reveals much about the Forge's origins, early history, and in-depth background, as well as hints about how it works and thinks. Many people reason that if the *Chronicles* were properly studied and interpreted, it would yield some clue as to the Forge's whereabouts. Alas, the oldest copies of the manuscript are written in a strange, alien language that defies currently known linguistics. Thus, no translation can be considered 100% accurate, and even when translated into any one of the Phase World tongues, the *Chronicles of the Cosmos* remains an incredibly difficult read with thousands of variations in language interpretations and meaning. The *misinterpretation* of a single word or punctuation can change the meaning of an entire sentence or paragraph, and may reflect the interpretive author's own bias, beliefs and speculation. Consequently, many believe that no interpretation of the originals can be accurate, for the alien tongue of the ancient manuscripts remains enigmatic to this very day, and requires interpreters to make guesses, extrapolations and broad assumptions throughout. Of course, none of this has prevented people from studying the many texts or from making their own translations, guesses and conclusions.

To aid the common man, who does not have access to the most ancient texts nor possess the knowledge to read them, a few renegade scholars have written key passages from the *Chronicles of the Cosmos* so that the layman can understand them for the specific purpose of helping them search for the Cosmic Forge. Published together as the **Essential Truths of the Cosmic Forge**, this popular translation of the Chronicles focuses specifically on the Cosmic Forge, little else. It is the writings of the Essential Truths that have been memorized by countless individuals, cults, nations and people worshiping or seeking the Cosmic Forge. Certainly the serious student will read multiple versions of the *Chronicles of the Cosmos* on their own, but for the vast majority of those interested in the legend, these excerpts are the *key* to finding the Cosmic Forge and unraveling the secrets of the universe!

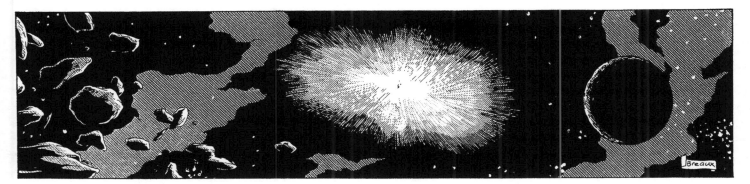

Essential Truths of the Cosmic Forge

In the Beginning

"In the time before time, there was naught but the Void, and all was quiet. Then the Fire of Creation burned hot and from its flames sprung the Universe. The darkness was scattered with the light of the Spirals, and there would be Life.

"During these young years, the First rose from the primordia and proclaimed their presence. Unique and alone, they commanded all the knowledge there was to know, and they had the entire Universe on which to paint their grand designs.

"The First mastered the art of the machine, and they built great devices of wondrous and amazing nature. They broke the chains of gravity and thus did travel where they liked faster than even the light of their stars. They pierced the fabric of *realspace* and did discover the vast realm beyond, the endless *nethersphere* that is nowhere yet connects all worlds and dimensions to each other. They roamed where they liked, settling all worlds as their own, reshaping them to fit their needs and leaving few places untouched. And they did build great laboratories in which they created all manner of creation, from the lowliest elements to the mightiest stars.

"They had learned all they could learn, and mastered all they could master. But still, it could never be enough. They could turn the Universe upside down looking for new places to control, but the First had only one frontier left before them: their innermost selves. And for that, no mere technology would suffice. They would have to build a tool of utmost power and design to test their skills and abilities. Little did they know that the device they would create would soon test their souls."

Birth of the Forge

"They wanted too much, the First did. A thousand worlds conquered, stars enclosed in crystal spheres, gateways to infinite realities, they had all this and more. The First thirsted for the innermost secrets of the universe and they searched for them with all their energy. On the farthest corner of reality, where realspace and otherspace meet, they built a *Forge*. A cauldron where a million galaxies could be born. The **Cosmic Forge** was no mere tool, for no mindless artifact could contain its power.

The minds and souls of the wisest among the First were placed within the Cosmic Forge. They would be its lifeblood and its source of power. They, the First, would actually *be* the Cosmic Forge. How lamentable this would turn out to be, for they had within them, all along, the power to achieve what the Forge accomplished. There never was a need for the Forge except in the minds and hearts of the First, whose creative powers were not so great to quiet the nagging doubts within them all. And so they built the Cosmic Forge and sacrificed to it their best and brightest, making a thing of such power and ability that it made all of the First's achievements before it seem like the trifles of a child.

"With no fear of what might happen next, the First stoked the fires of the Forge, lighting it for the first time. And when they did, the Forge gave off such a light that it could be seen across the Universe, and were there any other people to appreciate it, they would know that the First had built something special and terrible indeed. Unbound by distance and time, the Forge could do its many works, and it could satisfy the First's every urge and whim. With this, they would build such things that they had only dreamt of before. The Universe was truly theirs to mold into a shape of their liking, and the First rejoiced for it, basking in the glow of their newfound powers of creation."

The Endless Creation

As the legend goes, "The First put their creation to its test, and they created endless stars and worlds and life to fill them. They shaped the ways of the cosmos, bridging realms and dimensions unknown and binding together the pathways of time. However, this was nothing before their next creation. Unfulfilled with their deeds thus far, the First decided they would truly be like gods, and they would create a universe all their own. So they retired to the farthest corners of the known spaces and put their Forge to its test, spewing forth stars and worlds and all of the life needed to fill them. They created a master galaxy and two little siblings to go alongside, and this would forever be their special place, the place where the Forge and the First would call home above all other homes. From there, they moved on, creating galaxy after galaxy, but they never forgot their trio of original creations, their favorites among favorites. For these places were perfect in their vision, and of that they would always be proud.

"As the First filled the Universe with realms of their making, the Forge never grew weary or discontent. For it was a living thing, able to refuse its masters' commands should it desire so. But the Forge and the First maintained their good accord, for each wanted the same thing: to fill the cold void of space with the blessed warmth of Creation, to bring Life to the lifeless reaches, to fill the Universe with the sounds of laughter and wonder and awe.

"And for so very long, this is just what the First and the Forge did. They crafted endless galaxies and endless worlds within them, and endless peoples to live there, and endless wonders for those people to discover, and endless mysteries left untold. It was an amazing time, for the First had mastered their powers. They were like gods, but never demanded tribute from their creations, nor grew vengeful when their creations turned dark and angry and destructive. In response to these things, the First simply created more, for they knew to use the Cosmic Forge for Unmaking would itself unmake the Forge, and the First could not bear such a thought. Thus, they continued on with their crusade to fill the void with Creation, leaving behind what few mistakes and missteps they made along the way. None of these small blemishes weighed heavily on the minds of the First, but they should have. For in them lay the essential truth of their condition, that despite their Forge and powers of Creation, the First were *not* gods. They were *not* perfect. And they were *not* incapable of doing dark and terrible things. This they would learn firsthand very soon, and it would be their undoing."

The Great Betrayal

"For time beyond time, the First did fill the darkness with the light of the Forge. But all light must cast a *shadow*, and so it was with the First. There was One among them who did not rejoice in the deeds of the Forge, for there was a great emptiness in his heart. He tried to bask in the Forge's warmth, but there would be no heat for him who had grown so cold. He tried to gaze upon the Forge's light, but there would be no illumination for one so darkened. And in this, he knew a great despair for he alone among the First could not take pleasure in what his kind had done. He could not rejoice to see that the Forge was filling the universe with Creations untold. He could only take comfort when the Forge worked to fill his black and empty soul. So it was the One beseeched his fellows to let him have the Forge for one single day so that it might work its wonders on him. The First declined, for they said the wonders of the Forge were not meant to satisfy the cravings of any single being, for this was not the purpose for which the Forge was built. The One would have to find His own answers and seek his own light, if he could not find it in the Creations of the Forge, the First said. But the One protested, saying that he was special, that his needs were too great to overcome. That he needed the Forge in ways the First could not possibly understand. That the Forge must be *his*, and that he alone deserved the full blaze of its glorious power!

"The First lamented at this sad, wretched creature before them. So consumed by his darkness had he become that truly he was no longer of the First, but simply the One. 'We would cast you out,' the First said to the One, 'but you have already done that to yourself. No longer can you be part of the First, for there is no One among us. We are simply First, and the Forge is part of what we are. It is not ours to own, or to give away. It is not a thing but a force, it is our friend and our companion, our strength and our soul. To part with it would be to part with ourselves, to become like you, the One, and this the First cannot do, for it would be the end of our way.'

"'So you will not do this thing for me?' said the One to the First, already knowing the answer.

"'No, never, no.' said the First.

"'Then I shall respect your wisdom,' the One said, and he cast himself away from the First, as if to consort with them nevermore, perhaps to find a lonely corner of the Creation and spend the rest of his time there to dwell on his emptiness within.

"Only that is not what the One would do. Having lulled the First into false security, the One stole into their ranks once more and wrested the Cosmic Forge away from them. Grasping it in his hands, the One burned with the Forge's awesome power. He cackled before its heat, he glowed before its light, he trembled before its energy. Truly he was the master of all there was, and the Forge was his alone to command. He needed less than a moment to cast his first order, and thus did he use the Forge to unmake the First, the worlds they lived on, their children, and their child's children. He unmade any trace that the First might have left throughout their Creation. He would not unmake their Creation itself, for that was too awful a thing to carry out even for him. But he would make sure that when then far distant spawn of the universe would search for their First ancestors, there would be nothing there to comfort them. In that, they would know an emptiness like that which had gnawed at the One for so very long. At last, the Universe would know the One's pain, and he would be unique no longer.

"In unmaking the First, the One believed he would take their place, the First among First, the God of Gods. He would create a new Universe in his image alone, and it would far outshine anything the First had ever done during their time beyond time with the Forge at their side.

"But the Forge was no longer his to control. For in unmaking the First, he set forth cosmic flames which scorched the Universe, leaving only ashes in its wake. A thousand galaxies fell before the Flames, and the One knew nothing of how to stop it. All he knew was that *this* would be his legacy, a Great Unmaking that would scar everything the First had done, and take the shine of glory away from the universe. Suddenly, the emptiness within the One grew many fold, and he knew that soon there would be nothing of him left, just the nothingness that had consumed him from within. Before such an awful truth, the One fell to sorrow and did nothing but pity himself as the universe burned. The Forge lay unguarded, spewing forth fires of Unmaking while its undeserving master quivered with fear."

A Place of Hiding

"All that there is would have been unmade, had not the Cosmic Forge itself put an end to the carnage. For it being a living thing, it wanted no part of the catastrophe it was creating. It ceased spewing forth the Unmaking flame, but not before turning its terrible energies upon the One, he who set the Forge to this terrible end. The Forge would unmake this one last, miserable thing, and then it would unmake no more.

"In a sliver of a fraction of a moment, the One was no more, as if he never was.

"With like speed, the Forge snuffed its raging fires, and the Great Unmaking's source had ceased. But as with any fire, the flames set take on a life of their own, and the Forge could only watch as these final fires burned themselves out across the vast reaches of the universe. Most of the fire would indeed sputter and die, but there would always be those tiny fragments of the blaze that would live forever, glowing hot and skipping from place to place to place, forever keeping alive the travesty of the One and the time when the Forge was made into a dark parody of itself. Now and forever more, the wild fires of the Forge would touch down across the universe, but being of the Forge, they too contained a part of the Forge's essence. These were living fires, and they had not forgotten entirely the source from which they had sprung. Separated by time and space, they changed into a force of their own, not Making nor Unmaking, but Changing. These fires would roam the Creation, seeking that which the First had made from nothing, and adding their special energies to them, turning them into something more like of the glories the First once commanded. There would be those who wanted nothing of this kind of Change, and the random fires understood that and let them be. But there would be those who understood what the Changing Flames asked of them, and they would become more like the First in power and purpose. They would become the new guardians of the Forge, for the universe was now more filled with those like the One than those like the First. There could be no second Great Unmaking, and these new guardians of the flame would see that it never would come to pass.

"But for the Forge proper, the Great Unmaking was too much to bear. Shamed by the ease with which it had become an instrument of destruction, fearful that it might one day become that again, and doubtful that it could ever be put to the righteous purposes of the First again, the Forge decided it would *hide* away from the very Creation it helped to make. Filled with a sadness beyond sorrow, the Forge crept back to its favorite of favorites, to the Spirals Three, where it would always feel at home. And among the trilogy of star fields, there would be the one, the smallest and youngest among them, that the Forge would find its refuge. For here, it had always set apart a secret place, a special place, a place where it and it alone could find refuge where the Creation would bother it no longer. The Forge had always hoped such a place would not be needed, and for many eons it chided itself for having crafted such a refuge at all. But now it needed this hidden place, and to it the Forge did fly, closing the doors of solitude behind it and forever shutting itself away from the great and glorious Creation of the First.

"In the time to pass, there would be a great many peoples who would seek the Cosmic Forge, and indeed, a precious few would come close to finding it. Close enough that the Forge itself would stir from its hiding, bid its seeker a meeting and perhaps grant a gift, and then retreat to the place where it could not be found. The Changing Fires from the Great Unmaking would continue throughout Creation, but in time the Forge regained its control of them and they became the voice and the fingers through which the Cosmic Forge would touch the rest of the Creation, should it desire to.

"Even now, the Cosmic Forge remains hidden, though time and the noble few who have been touched by the Forge have done much to salve its wounds. Those who have felt its pure flame may attest that the Forge indeed seeks to shine its light throughout the universe once more, only it seeks those worthy enough to show it the way. For those who would seek such a challenge, the path would be difficult and narrow, for none save a few truly know what the Forge finds worthy in the hearts and souls of the mortal. Perhaps it is a glimmer of the First it seeks, a recognition of the past that bears the promise of a better future, one in which the glories of ancient times might one day be relived without the fear of darkness, or the blight of emptiness that fills the hearts of so many."

The Mythos of the Forge

The Nine Heresies

The *Chronicles of the Cosmos*, or at least the *Essential Truths,* outline the foundation for the Cosmic Forge legend, but this is ancient history (literally!), and since then, a huge body of supplemental myth and legend have grown up around it. This new information is collectively referred to as the *Mythos of the Forge.*

The problem with the Mythos is that it is not a single body of lore. Somewhere along the line, the "true" account of the Forge split into nine different branches, each of which has evolved into its own sub-mythos explaining exactly what the Forge is, where it has gone into hiding, the circumstances under which it made its last few appearances, and who is meant to find it. These are called the **Nine Heresies**, and they are the cause of much consternation, controversy and confrontation. Like the *Chronicles of the Cosmos*, each of the Nine Heresies is fairly cryptic and wide open to interpretation. Furthermore, adherents to any one Heresy tend to believe that particular story is the correct one and the other eight are pure balderdash. To this end, those who believe in any one of the Nine Heresies often do so with a quasi-religious fervor, which is how the Nine Heresies actually got their name. No matter what Heresy one believes in, the majority of Forge Followers consider it to be *wrong*. Hence, all branches of the new Mythos of the Forge are considered false and heretical, and they have been named as such. That said, folks tend to re-name the particular Heresy they believe in with titles such as the *Illumination, the Sole Truth, the Way, the Pathfinder*, and so on.

Scholars objective enough to view *each* of the Heresies without getting drawn into them believe that to really find the truth behind the Cosmic Forge, one must put together all of the clues in the Nine Heresies. The problem is, each Heresy has layer upon layer of clues to offer, and they only reveal themselves the more devoutly one follows a particular Heresy. The result is that to learn all a Heresy has to offer, one runs the extreme risk of losing objectivity, and of becoming seduced by one Heresy to the point of disbelieving all the others. This is called "dropping the hammer," and it means that in one's search for the Truth, one has become unable to see it anymore. It is just one reason why so many searches for the Cosmic Forge end in failure.

The First Heresy: The Koreda Matrix

This Heresy dates back to a planetary survey conducted over 550 years ago by the now-extinct Empire of Zeldun. Back then, the Zelduni had just lost an internecine war with several of their neighboring systems and as a result, they lost a great deal of territory. Pressured by overcrowding on their home world to find more living space, Zelduni scouts searched their realm in a renewed effort to evaluate which of their hundreds and hundreds of systems were most suitable for colonization. The Empire of Zeldun had, during its long years of supremacy and complacency, become something like an old attic – filled with things the owners forgot they even owned. So it was that the home world hardly knew anything about the planets in its domain. How excited they must have been, then, when news came back of the *Koreda* system, which had several likely worlds to settle, but most of all, it had a world of unusual composition. On the surface, it seemed like an ordinary rocky planet, but harmonic readings indicated an interior more consistent with an engine block or computer core. When Zelduni ships went out to investigate, the planet's rocky surface shattered, like dried mud breaking away from a lizard that was finally shaking it off. Beneath was a gleaming planet-sized piece of technology! It had huge energy vents at its various axes, and the rest of the surface was covered in deep circuit-like paths that cracked with white energy.

Preliminary Zelduni science reports indicated that this "world," known to them as Koreda Minor, was in fact a planet-sized mega-computer, most likely sentient, and probably of mind-boggling power. Zelduni scientists tried to contact the device, which obligingly accepted the "Koreda" title but insisted it be referred to as the *Koreda Matrix*. The Koreda Matrix communicated with the Zelduni briefly, and then demanded to know the answer to a series of radically advanced astro-mathematical equations. The Zelduni scientists, who had never even seen such figures before, retired to solve the problems. Clearly, the Koreda Matrix had posited to them a problem in a form of math nobody had ever seen before, a kind of computation that only something with a digital brain and enormous amounts of raw computational power could solve in a reasonably quick time frame. Frustrated, the Zelduni returned to the Koreda Matrix empty-handed. Apparently, this insulted the Koreda Matrix, which, as the story goes, fired energy bolts at its visitors, disintegrating them. Promptly thereafter, the Zelduni Parliament quarantined the Koreda system, citing "hyper-natural phenomena risks" and leaving it at that. Over the years, the Zelduni repeatedly denied the Koreda Matrix existed, though independent ships would frequently penetrate the system and try accessing the device on their own. Inevitably, the story was repeated time and again, with the Matrix offering a preliminary discussion, posing the equations and disintegrating anyone who returned without the correct answer.

This might have been the end of the story if not for a cataclysm blamed on the Matrix nearly 200 years ago. A large war fleet of ships hailing from the neighboring Thorov Hegemony invaded the Koreda system with the intent to take the Matrix by force. Zelduni warships intervened, and before long a full-fledged battle was raging across the system and around the Matrix itself. The fighting ended when, with a massive pulse of energy, the Koreda Matrix *disappeared*, taking with it every star system from both the Empire of Zeldun and the Thorov Hegemony. Where any of these systems or the Koreda Matrix went is unknown, but a few planets from either society have appeared in interstellar space in the years that followed. Every time one of these "stolen worlds" was discovered, all that remained was a charred, lifeless ball of rock, apparently destroyed by the Koreda Matrix.

Zelduni and Thorovian survivors who were not in their home system at the time they disappeared have become convinced that the Koreda Matrix was indeed the Cosmic Forge under a different name. The warfare around it must have spooked the Cosmic Forge so badly that it fled the system, but in doing so, accidentally took all of the Empire of Zeldun and the Thorov Hegemony with it, most likely destroying both civilizations in the process. Despite this fact, Zelduni, Thorovians, and those who believe in this theory, further speculate that all one must do is find the Koreda Matrix once more and present to it the answer to the mathematical problem it would pose to all of its former visitors. Whoever does this, so the theory goes, will prove to the Matrix that they are sufficiently advanced to be worthy of whatever gift the Matrix/Forge might be willing to bestow.

These theorists also believe that by conducting certain forms of harmonic triangulation, one can trace the route the Matrix took when it disappeared from the Empire of Zeldun and the Thorov Hegemony. The really weird thing is, no living Zelduni or Thorovian can actually *remember* where their homelands once were! All recorded evidence they might have had pointing to their homelands' location has also mysteriously vanished, all throughout the Three Galaxies! Somehow, the Koreda Matrix, be it the Cosmic Forge or not, has somehow erased all records that it has ever existed. Only through word of mouth among the now scattered and dying Zelduni and Thorovian civilizations does this story still circulate. To most folks in the Anvil Galaxy, this tale is just meaningless folklore, since there is no hard evidence at all to back it up. How could there be?

To those who believe in any of the other Eight Heresies, the story of the Koreda Matrix is just a pathetic excuse by the remnants of two long-dead civilizations to connect themselves to the Cosmic Forge. A sad attempt to make themselves important.

The Second Heresy: The Great Complexity

Many thousands of years ago, the world of *Soribin* was coming to life. A verdant planet with numerous plant and animal species, it was also home to a race of intelligent humanoids very much like humans in appearance and biology. Beings who came to call themselves the Soribu. A peaceful and content folk, the Soribu civilization knew very little strife or warfare. It also was fairly stagnant, and as such, it progressed very slowly in terms of culture and technology. Not that this was such a bad thing for the Soribu. Indeed, they remained an immensely happy and satisfied people who prospered and spread across their world.

Soribin is right in the middle of the Anvil Galaxy section of the *Consortium of Civilized Worlds,* and it was the CCW position to prohibit any space travelers from interfering with the planet for fear of upsetting the Soribu culture. For the most part, people obeyed, but the occasional pirate or would-be despot tried making a run on the planet, only to be destroyed by Consortium starships. Most of the time, offending ships were vaporized or burned up in Soribin's upper atmosphere – appearing as nothing more than a shooting star. However, 30 years ago, the pirate armada of *Jelka Ghensi* was stopped from invading the planet in a vicious battle right in Soribin's atmosphere. The fireworks were observed by the Soribu, and many of the pirate ships, though damaged beyond repair, were not destroyed but rather auto-landed on the Soribin surface, where the Soribu would get plenty of chances to examine them up close.

The CCW had a problem on its hands. There was a clear need to go down to the surface and retrieve the pirate ships before they could contaminate the Soribu culture as well as conduct damage control on the shell-shocked Soribu themselves. On the other hand, any further meddling might only worsen the situation, so the Soribu might be left to handle the ramifications of these objects from space on their own terms. Ultimately, political infighting within the CCW forced the monitoring of Soribin to be abandoned for a brief time, and as a default, it was decided to let the Soribu handle the ramifications of this event on their own. Automated defense satellites were set up in a tight grid around the world with orders to destroy anything that come too close. The word went out to the entire CCW: Leave Soribin be, or suffer dire consequences. That, thought the CCW, would be the end of that.

The anthropological community of the CCW did not agree, and they sent rogue teams of researchers to infiltrate the planet to find out what was going on. Only the defense satellites made a conventional approach to the planet impossible, so these rogue teams decided magic would be the transportation of choice. So, a number of mystics were hired to pop the teams to Soribin's surface where they could study the cultural impact, if any, the pirate ships had on the Soribu.

Every team that has gone to Soribin has failed to return. The only news back from any of them invariably comes from one of the hired mystics, who tells of an incredibly powerful magical device somewhere on the Soribin surface. To them, it appears as an enormous scale model of the Anvil Galaxy, with every star

and planet suspended on thin metal rods, all moving in exact accord with their real-life galactic counterpart. The entire machine hums and gives off a kind of electricity that can be tasted in the air. The Soribu, who have only reached crude medieval technology, are, presumably, not the builders of this device. One look at their homes and settlements is proof enough of that. However, a huge city has been built around the machine, and magical energy can be felt crackling out of the place at all times. The Soribu apparently live in harmony with this thing, clustering around it like it is the center of their lives and culture, soaking up the energy it gives off. Apparently, the Soribu have never even seen the pirate ships because they have never gone looking for them. Instead, this machine has captured their imaginations and they bask in its mystic glory. The Mystics would go on to say that any offworlder who so much as touches the device is instantly transformed into a Soribu, forgetting their past life entirely, and being assimilated into Soribu society as if that person had been one of them all along. Any offworlder mystic who gets too close to the device inevitably goes mad, but not before trying to send one last, desperate message to the outside Galaxy to stay away from this mysterious and sinister predicament.

Psychics have tried on several occasions to scan the world for this device, and all they get is an intense headache and a god-like voice telepathically telling them something along the lines of "I am not ready to come out into the universe yet. When I am, I will let you know. Until then, leave me alone."

Word of Soribin and its bizarre magical machine has slowly and surely leaked out to the larger community of the CCW and the rest of the Anvil Galaxy, but it remains a kind of mystic fish story to most who hear it. It is just too incredible to believe, and most folks are inclined to think that any teams sent to investigate the planet either died trying to get there or simply took the money and ran, sending back this weird story nobody could really follow up on. Others believe it is a CCW scare tactic to keep people away from the planet. The CCW does not want to hear about the Soribu and any odd machine they might have, because the world is under cultural quarantine, and to get that lifted for any reason would take about 10 years of cutting through red tape. Space explorers intrigued by the stories surrounding the planet are loath to check them out for fear of sure destruction by the planet's defensive satellites, and mystics and psychics now get a very bad feeling when they approach to within a light year of Soribin. A feeling that makes them almost nauseous, and which fills them with the certain knowledge that should they press on to the planet of Soribin, terrible tragedy will visit them. For all of these reasons, Soribin remains a cast-off world, home to a powerful enigma that nobody has dared explore any further.

Since Soribin made it into the collective set of worlds with unexplainable phenomena, all sorts of rumors and stories have begun circulating. The majority of them ultimately point to this magical device as really being the *Cosmic Forge*. To prove it, they cite the device's cryptic message, which certainly could be interpreted as the words of a Cosmic Forge that would prefer to remain in hiding, perhaps playing God to the harmless Soribu, than to re-enter the vast and conflicted Anvil Galaxy. A formidable cadre of true believers have sprung up to believe this concept, and it is the foundation around which the Second Heresy stands. Those who do not believe in the Second Heresy state that the device on Soribin really could be *anything*. It might very well be some kind of strange magical artifact, but that hardly makes it the Cosmic Forge. Until somebody can make a definitive study of the world, nobody will ever know. Opponents of the Second Heresy ridicule those who would believe so strongly in something that the CCW hasn't gotten around to disproving yet. Those who believe remain true to their convictions, however, and most conspire to secretly visit Soribin, touch the **Great Complexity**, as the magical device is called, and join the ranks of the blissful Soribu, who know nothing of the harsh outside world, only the feeling of basking forever in the object of their worship. Believers of the Second Heresy are convinced the Soribu are the "chosen people" of the Cosmic Forge. Meanwhile, far outside of the CCW, other civilizations only ever hear rumors that something which may or may not be the Cosmic Forge is on a cordoned off CCW world. With nothing else to go on, this is spurring foreign ships from all over to fly by the Soribin system (either as legal guests of the CCW or as insurgents) and see if this magic anomaly is something they might be able to steal for themselves.

The Third Heresy: Ranthall's Star

Since the beginning of recorded history, the yellow dwarf known as *Ranthall's Star* (named after the ancient human astronomer who first visited it) appeared to be an ordinary stellar body. It lay at the heart of a solar system sporting four planets, three of which developed life. Of those three, two developed intelligent life, and one developed an advanced, space-faring civilization – the Ranthall Republic.

Until 88 years ago, nothing had occurred around Ranthall's Star to connect it to the Cosmic Forge legend or any of the other Heresies. Then a solar research team was dispatched from the Republic of Ranthall to penetrate the core of their sun in order to take harmonic readings of it. For a full year, the star had given off strange pulses of energy and radiation, indicating that it might be suffering from some kind of harmonic disturbance. Knowing full well the destructive capability of a stellar-scale harmonic disruption, Ranthallian scientists were determined to see if their sun was about to suffer a similar fate and take the rest of the solar system with it.

The scientists never knew what hit them. As their specially shielded ship dove deeper and deeper into the heart of the sun, the star itself underwent a sudden and incredible transformation into a ball of pure, white, blazing energy. The Ranthallian ship was instantly disintegrated, and what had been Ranthall's Star now began to accelerate away from its former resting place! Like a comet the energy sphere hurtled through space, seemingly en route to the other side of the Anvil Galaxy. Scientists plotted the sphere's course, and they determined that it would not hit any worlds or stars on its current flight path, but any relief these findings generated soon vanished when the energy sphere sped to near light speed and curved to intercept the next planet near its path. The planet was the bustling independent world of *Hrase*, and by the time they could be alerted that certain doom was heading for them, it was too late.

The energy sphere collided directly with the planet, but instead of destroying it, it simply passed through it! As it turned out, the two objects were not quite on the same "dimensional frequency." The sphere slowed for a second, as if moving through a barrier that provided a little resistance and then kept moving through the Galaxy. As for the stunned Hrasians, 98% of them were unaffected by the event. Nearly 1% died during the "Intersection," as they called it, but that was more from Hrasians dying of fright than anything else. The final 1%, however, began to develop strange and incredible powers on par with a *Kreeghor Invincible Guardsman* or one of the vaunted *Cosmo-Knights!* Indeed, many Hrasians began mysteriously cutting their personal ties and leaving the planet, heading off on missions unknown, to worlds far outside their home system. Since then, Hrase has been the site of innumerable scientific investigations trying to figure out what that sphere was and how it might have affected the Hrasian people.

Needless to say, a good portion of the Hrasian people have been profoundly affected by this unexpected turn of events, and more than a few of them have insisted that since so many of their kind were apparently gifted with "cosmic power" by the Intersection, perhaps the sphere was really the Cosmic Forge! Like wildfire this concept spread across Hrase and beyond, and now a huge bastion of people believe in the Third Heresy, the mystery of Ranthall's Star and Miracle of Hrase. These people believe that the sphere, which mysteriously disappeared shortly after the Intersection, still exists and will one day pop back into existence and Intersect with another "chosen" populated planet, transforming those who are worthy into great champions, and leaving the rest to wonder about what just happened.

Those who do not believe in the Third Heresy think Hrase got really lucky, and whatever process transformed Ranthall's Star into a big ball of unusual energy is also what knocked it a few degrees off its native dimensional frequency, which is why it didn't collide with Hrase but passed through it. As for the Hrasians supposedly given super powers by this event, none of the affected have ever come forth and claimed that yes, they were transformed by the Intersection. Frankly, any gifts of cosmic powers have been supposed by the rest of the Hrasian public. There is no proof that any Cosmo-Knights were created by the Intersection at all, so claiming this sphere was in fact the Cosmic Forge is really more like a big dose of wishful thinking as well as a means of coping with the shock of a planetary near-death experience.

The Fourth Heresy: The Gurvian Atrocity

On the southernmost edge of the Anvil Galaxy, on what might be considered the "underside" of the stellar mass, is the *Gurvian star system*. Unusually large, it contains twenty planets and two asteroid belts, most of which support some kind of life. For many different reasons, not the least of which included divergent economies, religions and cultures, the Gurvian worlds were locked in a deadly inter-system war for over one thousand years, Periodically there would be a time of peace lasting for a few decades, and to the assorted Gurvian peoples, these periods of peace were as historic and society-changing as wars would be to otherwise peaceful societies. The Gurvian Conflict raged on many different fronts, and despite the involvement of out-of-system parties such as mercenary armies,

Cosmo-Knights, the CCW and the TGE, the war continued on as ever, seemingly without end. For the Gurvians, war was simply the baseline of their existence, and they had grown so used to it that to stop fighting seemed unnatural.

All of that changed some 350 years ago, when a cube of alien metal was found amid the wreckage of a merchant ship that had been destroyed on its way into the system. Nobody knew who owned the ship or where it had come from, but since the Gurvian worlds were used to getting unannounced freelance merchant visits (many would swing by the system to try selling off excess cargo) nobody thought anything unusual was afoot.

Independent salvage teams are a growth industry in a star system riddled by war, and so it was that when this merchant ship was destroyed several scrap ships deployed to the site at once. The vessel that retrieved the remains of the freighter and its contents brought the lot of the stuff to one of the scrap yard cities in the system's first asteroid belt. There the salvage experts noticed a strange cube amid the wreckage, composed of a kind of metal nobody had ever seen before. When subjected to harmonic frequencing, the cube displayed an energy reading that went off the chart. When put through Phasic resonance testing, the scanners spiked so hard it triggered their emergency shutdown routines. Clearly, the cube was special, but how? The salvage captain (whose name has been lost to history) kept the cube until he could decide where to sell it and for how much.

It is said that this captain had the cube with him the night he got a few drinks at the station bar. While drinking, he watched a news report about the latest battle in the system's middle worlds. Saddened by the carnage, the captain grabbed his cube while getting off his stool. He uttered something like "Damned war. I just wish it would all go away."

The next morning, the captain awoke to a lifeless station. Wherever he went, dead bodies filled every corridor, every room, every courtyard. Horrified, the captain scrambled to his ship, running through docking bays, maintenance yards and loading areas all scattered with the dead. The captain left the station, desperately searching for any local comm traffic, knowing that he would not get any. Somehow, his wish had been made true in the worst possible way, and the captain knew that it was his mysterious cube that had made it so. Horrified by this item in his possession, the captain thought of ejecting it from his airlock, but then he feared somebody else might find it. Out of a greater fear, he clutched the cube and swore never to let go. He also swore that he would never hurt anybody else with this thing, ever again, and he pointed his ship on an exit trajectory from the Anvil Galaxy, on a course that would put him on the other side of the universe. Certain he would be long dead by that time and that maybe the cube would have lost its power, the captain headed away from his home knowing that his only alternative was to risk another Gurvian Atrocity.

The captain has not been seen since he departed from his home system. The only reason why anybody knows about him is from various Gurvian message logs he left when trying to contact anybody on the morning after the whole system died. In his frenzied state, he laid out his plans before signing off, so there are a fair number of people who not only know what caused the

Gurvian Atrocity, but who was behind it and that he has left the Anvil Galaxy.

Scholars and expatriate Gurvians believe that perhaps the cube is either the *Cosmic Forge* or some kind of affiliate of it. To them, there can be no other explanation for how such a small and simple device could have effected such incredible devastation. Indeed, the snuffing out of the Gurvian system was reminiscent of the instant destruction the One visited upon the First when he wrested control of the Cosmic Forge. Could not this cube be the same thing that destroyed the First?

A lot of people, especially self-serving explorers and treasure hunters, believe the cube to be the Cosmic Forge, and they have all gone on a mad dash outside of the Anvil Galaxy to find the Gurvian captain's ship and take the cube from him. Meanwhile, people in surrounding systems have heard the story of the Gurvian Atrocity, and from them grew a sizeable cult fascinated, not horrified, by what happened under the cube's power. These twisted folk concluded that the Cube was no mere artifact of power, but it is the *Cosmic Forge*! What else could so easily wreak such destruction? These "Cubists," as they were derisively called by others (numerous star systems simply outlawed them and arrested any members of this group that they could), assert that the cube will one day return to the Anvil Galaxy, and when it does, it will somehow fall into their hands without them having to lift so much as a finger. And when the Cube comes to them, they shall use it as the Gurvian captain did, as a weapon of destruction to not only eliminate the living in a single star system, but to unmake all of Creation itself! And they shall not do this by accident; they do so as part of a nihilistic glee that makes each and every follower of this, the Fourth Heresy, an opponent of life itself.

Those who follow the other Heresies write off the Cubists as lunatics who would be really dangerous if their proclamations of the cube coming to them had any merit. First, followers of other Heresies do not believe any cube was to blame for the Gurvian atrocity. It is commonly known that several different terrorist factions in the system (to which many Cubists once belonged) were working on doomsday viruses that would wipe out pretty much every living thing within the star system. So the notion that a magical artifact *had* to be the culprit behind the Atrocity is not solid, say the followers of other Heresies. But even if this cube were the culprit, and even if it were the Cosmic Forge, why would it allow itself to fall into Cubist hands? History shows the Forge is intelligent and will not take part in things it doesn't believe in, so why would it agree to unmake *everything*? For the followers of the other beliefs, the Fourth Heresy is not just a gross misinterpretation of the Forge Mythos, but it is an affront to the Cosmic Forge itself. For this reason, numerous members from other Heresies routinely seek out Cubists or anybody else who buys into the Fourth Heresy and give them a really hard time. This might range from verbal abuse to outright murder or warfare.

The Fifth Heresy:
Voyage of the Meganaut

The GSV (General Service Vessel) *Meganaut* was the flagship of the now-destroyed *Vaast Imperium*, a huge and tyrannical civilization that dominated half of the Anvil Galaxy several thousand years ago. The Vaast, a cruel and highly evolved race, had declared a war of genocide upon the entire Galaxy, destroying any race that did not have sufficient genetic similarity to them. In short order, the Vaast managed to rally the rest of the galaxy's young civilizations against them, and battle was joined. For more than four centuries, the fighting was long and hard, but in the end, the Vaast teetered on the edge of total ruin. Their enemies were poised to invade the Vaast home world, and were that to fall into their hands, the rest of the Imperium would be finished. In a desperate gamble, the Vaast commanded their greatest warship, the artificial intelligence-commanded GSV *Meganaut*, to leave space-dock and hide in interstellar space during the first phase of the enemy attack on the home world. Then, when the enemy looked like it had the upper hand, the *Meganaut* would make a surprise attack and raise hell in the enemy's rear ranks, breaking the back of the invasion and saving the Imperium.

The gambit never played out, for the *Meganaut* never came back once it went into hiding. Years later, military historians ventured many different guesses as to the fate of the *Meganaut,* where it had gone and why. Without the *Meganaut* to defend the home world, the Vaast were helpless before their enemies and the Imperium was destroyed, taking their evil philosophies (for the time being, anyway) to the grave. Within a few decades, the matter of the *Meganaut* became little more than a footnote in galactic history as even the Vaast Imperium itself began to slip away from people's collective memory.

Fast forwarding to the present, the *Meganaut* has recently made an unexpected appearance in the Anvil Galaxy, one that carries with it enormous implications. Seventeen years ago, the *Meganaut* surfaced from hyperspace in the vicinity of where the Vaast home world used to be, in the heart of the Anvil Galaxy section of the Trans-Galactic Empire. TGE interceptors moved in to arrest the vessel, but the *Meganaut* simply opened fire on them, blasting the ships into particles. Then the *Meganaut* broadcast the following message on all communication bands, on a pulse strong enough that it was picked up by listening stations in every corner of the Anvil Galaxy:

"I live! The time of hiding is over, and my day of glory has just begun. Bow your heads before the shape of the future, for mine is the power cosmic to make and unmake as I alone see fit. No longer shall I remain content to be the tool of nameless masters or to be the device of some fool's petty desires. I am, and shall be, High Lord over all I have Created, now and forever. Mark well my words, for when you hear them again, my Reckoning will be at hand!"

It did not take long for huge numbers of Forge Followers to make some pretty bleak interpretations of the *Meganaut*'s message. It would seem that somehow the ship and the Cosmic Forge have become one, as horrifying as that might be — the Forge remade as a weapon of mass destruction. For those that believed this, the Fifth Heresy, then there could be few options. Surely the *Meganaut*'s grim message was a demand for tribute and a threat to the entire universe of what would happen if it did not receive the proper treatment when it returned once more. To that end, adherents to the Fifth Heresy, calling *themselves* "Meganauts," have taken it upon themselves to convert the entire Anvil Galaxy to their way of thinking, destroying all who would resist them. Theirs is the classic holy war (or unholy war, depending on what side you're on), pitting the Meganauts against the entire Anvil Galaxy. To the Meganauts' credit, they have already converted a small number of worlds to their beliefs out in one of the reaches of Independent space, and they are slowly but surely conquering their neighboring systems with ruthless efficiency. Sooner or later, they will run into one of the larger power blocs of the galaxy, and that is when the real fight will be joined. For the Meganauts, victory or defeat is relative. If they win, they convert more systems to the Fifth Heresy — all the more who will be spared from the *Meganaut's* wrath when it returns. And if they lose in combat, then they shall be embraced by the Cosmic Forge/*Meganaut* and resurrected into a state of eternal glory! For them, life and death are meaningless. Only acceptance into the Forge matters. And *that* is what makes them so dangerous.

In the meantime, a breakaway faction of the Meganauts have begun an earnest search for their namesake starship. They believe that rather than destroying star systems, they should simply seek out the center of their worship and supplant themselves before it. How better to be taken into the Forge's embrace than to surrender to it directly? Predictably, no Meganaut search parties have met with success. Or have they? Most of these search groups simply vanish into the depths of space. Are they losing themselves, or are they finding their namesake and getting exactly what they are seeking? Either way, there is no way of telling.

Those who believe other Heresies or who believe none of them feel that the Meganauts are simply another army of religious lunatics trying to hammer the galaxy into a philosophy of their own design. Those who know of the *Meganaut* story can easily dismiss it as something other than the Cosmic Forge having somehow taken on the hull of a warship as its physical body. After all, the Vaast were adept at psychological warfare, and they knew of the Cosmic Forge. Pre-programming their flagship to broadcast such a message might just have been a simple mind game that went off at the wrong time, under the wrong context. There is no proof the *Meganaut* (derisively nicknamed the "Mega-Nut" by those who think this entire situation is just the *Meganaut*'s artificial brain going on the blink or otherwise corrupting) can actually do anything special. All it has accomplished is it popped out of hyperspace, blasted a ship, broadcast a message and went back into hiding. Big deal! Lots of ships can do that. From the unbeliever's point of view, there is no need to set the galaxy on fire just for the benefit of a renegade warship that does not know the war for which it was designed ended millennia ago.

The Sixth Heresy: The Endless Eye

The Splugorth have been a continued presence of evil and mayhem in the Three Galaxies for thousands of years. In the Anvil Galaxy, the center of this evil takes form in the Kingdom of Rynncryyl, just one of four major Splugorth Kingdoms found throughout the Three Galaxies. Like the other Splugorth Kingdoms, Rynncryyl, the Splugorth lord after whom his kingdom is named (clever, huh? Or so Rynncryyl thinks...), has designs for taking over the Three Galaxies. Unlike his rivals, however, he has a line on something he believes will tip the scales in his favor.

It is the Sixth Heresy, the notion that the Cosmic Forge exists as a Splugorth power idol that was lost eons ago deep in the core of the Anvil Galaxy, but is now on the verge of being rediscovered. The idol, known as the **Endless Eye**, is said to be the Cosmic Forge itself made into a shape that would be pleasing to its Splugorth Masters – a huge lidless eye with three sets of claws sprouting from the underside so it might sit on a flat surface. The center of the Eye points upward, as if forever looking at the ceiling or the sky. It is made of an alien metal that is hard as diamond yet feels like ivory. This material which no longer exists in the Anvil Galaxy, is a special substance that is impervious to any kind of power spike or harmonic frequency, making it perfect for containing the *essence* of something as ultimately potent as the Cosmic Forge.

According to legend, the Endless Eye was crafted by a far distant predecessor to Lord Rynncryyl, who was on the verge of taking possession of the Cosmic Forge when a treacherous lieutenant struck him down and stole the Forge for himself. In the ensuing chaos, the turncoat was slain and the Cosmic Forge lost once more. Now, Rynncryyl stands on constant watch, looking for an opportunity to corner the device and to draw its essence into the still-empty shell that is the Idol of the Endless Eye. Rynncryyl keeps this idol on him at all times in case the chance to *imprison* the Cosmic Forge ever arises. So far, that chance has not happened, though many of Rynncryyl's operatives claim they have had intermittent contact with the Cosmic Forge, so it will only be a matter of time before the opportunity presents itself to Rynncryyl and he, in his infinite courage and genius, shall snatch up the Cosmic Forge and make it a prisoner to his

will. With a single, brilliant strike, Rynncryyl plans to become Lord of the Splugorth, the Anvil Galaxy, and indeed, the entire Universe! Yes, it is only a matter of time now, until Rynncryyl's glorious and eternal reign begins . . . .

Sound crazy? You bet it does. Lord Rynncryyl might be one of the four Splugorth Lords of the Three Galaxies, but that hardly exempts him from being an utter nut case. The upshot of this Heresy is that it is all a fabrication of Rynncryyl, who has deluded himself into thinking that indeed, this Splugorth idol he keeps with him at all times (which on its own has no powers at all) will be a suitable container/prison for the Cosmic Forge. Moreover, all of his subjects go along with the Sixth Heresy (some of them actually believe it), for fear that doing otherwise will be seen as treason and a cause to be put to death. So far, Rynncryyl has sent entire legions of soldiers throughout the Anvil Galaxy and deep within the Core Regions to find the Cosmic Forge, but they have found nothing, not even promising leads. Rynncryyl continues looking and will do so until he is dead or he has found his prize, for if any being can find the treasured Cosmic Forge, it is a nearly immortal Splugorth. Nothing else is acceptable to him, and if he must sacrifice his entire Kingdom to pursue this matter, then he will do so.

That Rynncryyl has found nothing is hardly a surprise to the other Heretics of the Forge. It is common knowledge that the Cosmic Forge will only reveal itself to those "worthy" of receiving it, and under any non-Splugorth standard, Rynncryyl is absolutely unworthy of it. If anything, the Cosmic Forge is more likely to hide from this wicked being than reveal itself to him.

The Seventh Heresy:
Kotus Point

Kotus Point was a massive black hole lying at a critical juncture in the interstellar trade lanes of the Anvil Galaxy. Within 50 light years of Kotus Point, one can find the boundaries of the CCW, the TGE, the UWW, and some of the other local power blocs as well as a smattering of noteworthy Independent worlds. The amount of mercantile and military traffic through this area is staggering, and it might very well be the most commonly crossed stretch of space in the galaxy.

What makes Kotus Point so dangerous is that it emits an unusually high level of radiation. So intense is the rad-burst from Kotus Point that any ship that draws to within a single light year of the hole will instantly suffer a full scramble of its navigation computers. This means that when a ship would get too close to the hole's gravity well, the automatic evasion software that would ordinarily kick in would do nothing, and the ship would get sucked into the black hole. Kotus Point, as far as anybody can tell, did not form a wormhole, so there was no way to travel through it. It was just an infinitely deep *gravity well* from which nothing could escape.

For centuries, Kotus Point has been a galactic landmark to competent space travelers and many spacers know better than to get too close to it. They just steer clear of it and tell themselves that when black holes are concerned, it really is better to be safe than sorry. Perhaps it is because Kotus Point is so commonly avoided that nobody realized until ten years ago that the hole had undergone a wild transformation. No longer was Kotus Point a killer gravity well; it has *reversed* itself somehow and is now a *white hole*, something emitting a gravitational field so strong that nothing could possibly get close enough to touch it.

White holes are fairly uncommon throughout the Anvil Galaxy, little understood by scientists and rarely visited by travelers. Never before has anybody gotten a chance to observe both the *before and after* of a black hole's transformation into a white one, giving the changeover of Kotus Point great importance, but there is more.

The antigravity field of the white hole is so strong that nothing can approach within a light year of Kotus Point. The radiation emitted is also so intense that it kills almost anything that gets within *three light years* of the point. In fact, Kotus Point's radiation emission is so intense that it can be picked up with ease by scanners anywhere in the Anvil Galaxy, Corkscrew Galaxy, and parts of the Thundercloud Galaxy. As a result, there are trillions of people who could tune in to Kotus Point and listen to the patterns of radiation pulsing out from its reversed singularity. *Xenolinguists* in particular have paid special attention to Kotus Point, as they do to every white hole, for they theorize that white holes actually are the devices of ancient and god-like beings to transmit messages through their radiation emissions. So far, this theory has never been proven, but with Kotus Point, the most powerful white hole ever discovered, xenolinguists believe they have picked up very strong patterns indicating that the white hole is broadcasting a message of some sort to any and all who would listen. The problem is, the message is in an alien language that is both incredibly difficult to understand and complex in nature. The language in which the message is transmitting will not be known at all until the message is completed. It is as if one could not possibly know what a sentence in English might mean until they read the period at the end of it, after which all becomes clear. It is the same for whatever communication is coming out of Kotus Point. Xenolinguists must wait and compile the entire message to learn what is being said.

More than a few Followers of the Forge are convinced Kotus Point, which is incredibly powerful even for a white hole, is actually the *Cosmic Forge* or a proxy the Forge is using to communicate with the rest of the Galaxy. These folks also believe that this message from the Forge will be its surrender of its secret location. When the message can be deciphered, the Cosmic Forge is up for grabs. The spacers of the Three Galaxies know this rumor, so a huge collection of stars ships hold a tight, grid-like pattern just outside of three light years away from Kotus Point, poised to rush in and grab what they can as soon as the opportunity presents itself. There are ships from every government and power bloc imaginable over Kotus Point, many of which are *not* on friendly terms. Still, even dire enemies are loath to fight one another so close to what might be the Cosmic Forge. And so, the thousands of ships wait, hoping that soon the white hole will reveal itself to be the Cosmic Forge.

Despite the general cease-fire among the ships monitoring Kotus Point, many fear (and rightly so) that if any kind of fighting breaks out (which is quite possible, given the conflicting views of the Nine Heresies and those who follow them) it will turn into a huge conflagration. Thus, the ships here nervously keep watch on each other as much as they do on Kotus Point, ever vigilant for the slightest sign a rival or "bad guy" is looking to take advantage of the situation or up to something underhand. Sabotage, backstabbing and subtle skullduggery regularly transpires among the sentinels of Kotus Point.

Those who do not believe in the Seventh Heresy simply write it off as a unique galactic phenomenon upon which people are pinning too many hopes and wild dreams. To these naysayers, believing the white hole's rad-pulses will spell out some kind of message leading people to the Cosmic Forge is like turning on a holovision monitor and watching static to find the secrets of life. It just is not going to happen. What is of immediate concern is all those jumpy gun ship captains in such close proximity to rivals and enemies, and who are bound to start a big shooting match if anything gets out of hand. In the Anvil Galaxy, those kinds of skirmishes have a bad tendency to fan into much larger conflicts.

The Eighth Heresy: Voidmaker

Kotus Point is not the only black hole to make its way into the Cosmic Forge mythos. For many eons, one of the leading theories behind the Forge's nature was that it was some kind of "black hole projector," or some other device capable of creating artificial black holes. Surely if such technology existed, it could revolutionize travel (instant wormholes to anywhere!) as well as warfare (simply create a black hole and suck up one's enemies). The thing was, there had never been any real proof to back up the assertions that the Cosmic Forge was a black hole maker. Granted, most of the people who believe in any of the Nine Heresies do so because a feeling in their gut tells them to, but they also need at least a shred of concrete example for their rational minds to cling to, and for the longest time, the "black hole projector" theory did not have that shred . . . . until now.

Nearly 250 years ago, a cabal of fanatical scientists, the *Union of Thought*, utterly convinced that the Cosmic Forge and the creation of black holes were intrinsically linked, founded the *Voidmaker Project*, an ongoing effort to design, build and use technology that could create stable black holes. The Union believed that once they could create black holes, it would somehow establish a connection between them and the Cosmic Forge. The consensus among these scientists is that black hole generation would be a watershed technological achievement, a pinnacle worthy of the Cosmic Forge's notice. Some of them believe that artificial black holes create special wormholes or dimensional bridges, and that these special passages will lead to wherever it is that the Cosmic Forge has been hiding itself all these years.

Either way, the chief means of synthesizing black holes is through *gravitonic technology*, a common technology throughout the Three Galaxies used mostly for faster-than-light (FTL) propulsion and certain kinds of weapons development. The Union of Thought's focus has been to refine gravitonics and push the upper limit of that field of science. They believe that if they can develop a gravitonic engine ten times more powerful than what is available now, they will have the power to create an artificial wormhole. After that, it is a straight line to the Cosmic Forge and ultimate power.

There have been a few problems with the Voidmaker Project, though. First and foremost, the experiments in gravitonic technology have gone poorly, to say the least. The upper limits of gravitonics have been well established for hundreds of years. Breaking through them requires a scientific breakthrough on par with the creation of the wheel, the discovery of relativity, cosmic unification theory, and so on. Brilliant though the Union of Thought's members may be, they don't seem to be that brilliant. If they are to succeed, they need some more brainpower. However, the Union is also made up mostly of human supremacists unwilling to enlist the help of more intelligent races. That being the case, further gravitonic development might be stalled for quite some time.

Secondly, when the Union does make a gravitonic breakthrough, they have to test their newly invented devices. This is really dangerous. Messing with gravity fields under any circumstances is akin to playing with nitroglycerine. One wrong move and it goes off in your face. Some of the Union's best and brightest have learned this the hard way with disaster while testing their new gravi-technology. In one case, the device caused a gravitonic implosion, sucking it — and every scientists in the room – into oblivion. In another case, the machine being tested exploded, killing four scientists and wounding thirty. (After that, group meetings to test new technology were halted.) There have been other accidents, too, contributing to an alarming rate of attrition for a science project. By looking at the numbers, one would think the Union of Thought was engaging in military operations, not lab experiments.

Thirdly, the Union has been covered extensively in the galactic media, especially in the CCW. This makes them fairly unpopular, both with adherents to other Heresies, and to ordinary folk who believe these scientists are recklessly playing with forces that could cause widespread catastrophe. As a result, the Union routinely gets drummed out of every planet it sets up shop on. Lately, it has purchased a fleet of civilian starships, and they do their work in interstellar space, where they are beyond anybody's laws. Out there, however, they are vulnerable to pirates, bandits, and merciless aliens, so they must hire mercenaries to run security. This is draining the Union's funds and soon they will have to acquire additional cash if they are to prevent their work from stopping altogether.

As the Eighth Heresy, the Voidmaker Project is decried by many as a fool's crusade. The theory that the Cosmic Forge was ever a black hole generator rings false to those who point out that all black holes do is destroy or transport; they do not create. That being the case, why would the Cosmic Forge be something that spewed out nothing but black holes? It just does not make any sense. And the notion that building artificial black holes (as if *that* were possible! Hah!) would somehow gain the Cosmic Forge's notice is equally subjective and far-fetched. It is ludicrous to believe, naysayers decry, that the Cosmic Forge must be hiding in the never-never land where only artificial wormholes go. Please.

The Ninth Heresy:
The Forge Dream

Exactly 333 years ago, 333 people spread out over 333 different worlds all experienced a rare vision in their sleep. In this vision, the people found themselves floating in the darkness of space, surrounded by a fountain of light. This light was really millions and millions of particles of light, and each particle was really a tiny galaxy, spreading out into the darkness, filling all that there is with light and life. Among all of these innumerable galaxies, the dreamer's attention was drawn to a single point in the sea of light. Somehow, the dreamer's focus is magnified so he can see the details of this single galaxy among so many billions just like it. The dreamer's focus gets finer and finer, as if the dreamer himself is flying through space into this galaxy, zooming in on a specific star, and then on a specific planet. It is a simple, blue-green world with abundant water and a cloudy sky, and a verdant surface. It is a place full of life, and from here, one can feel a wave of energy coming forth like no other. It is a pulse of pure Creation. And as the dreamer soaks this energy in, he hears a voice, coming from both nowhere and everywhere, and it says, *"This is my home, the home of the ancient ways. It waits for you and for all of your kind when the madness of the One is no more among the Three Homelands of the First. Abandon the madness of the Great Unmaking, and the fires of Creation shall be yours to hold dear once more. Do this, and my world becomes your world. Do it not, and know forever the coldness of exile, and the loneliness of the Unmade."*

And with that, the dreamer awakens. Only unlike an ordinary dream, the details of this vision do not fade. No, every detail remains clear. Those who had the dream found themselves unable to forget it, and one by one, everybody who had it changed their lives. Those involved in destructive or hurtful or selfish pursuits gave them up without explanation, rededicating their lives to promoting peace, understanding, and cooperation.

Such changes were obviously met with alarm and skepticism by the friends and families of these first Dreamers, but those who had the Vision simply kept on with their new lives, knowing that this new path was the right one to take.

Exactly one year later, another 333 people on 333 different worlds had the same vision, and with the same results. The next year, the process repeated. And the next year, and the next year, until this Dream phenomenon became an annual occurrence throughout the Anvil Galaxy.

Over the course of the 333 years after the first Dreaming, the total number of people who have had this shared vision numbers only 110,889. Given the huge population of the Anvil Galaxy, this is like a single grain of sand on the beach. But, in that time, some very prominent people have had "the Dream," and word of it has spread far and wide, turning it into a broad family of cults, schools of philosophy, and religions. World leaders, prominent heroes and villains, religious figures, social leaders, and people from every walk of life have shared the experience. A dream which many social anthropologists, dream interpreters, psychics and mystics agree is a command from the *Cosmic Forge* itself to the people of the Anvil Galaxy. The message is simple: Straighten up and fly right, and the Cosmic Forge will return. What this means exactly is open to interpretation, but the general feeling is no more wars, no more exploitation, no more conflict. Period. This is the "Forge Dream," as it is called, and it is the Ninth Heresy, and arguably the most widely held Heresy of them all.

Of special note is that the leaders of many of the major power blocs in the Anvil Galaxy have all had the Forge Dream, and many of them believe that it is their duty to do what they can to make sure the Cosmic Forge's command is carried out faithfully. As a result, many civilizations are undergoing massive changes so they better suit the Forge's desires. This means the dismantling of militaries, reordering of entire economies, sever-

ing diplomatic ties with evil or militant civilizations, and so on. From a distance, this might seem like a huge and beneficial phenomenon sweeping the Anvil Galaxy, but in truth, it is causing much more harm and unrest than good.

Most of the civilizations whose leaders are on a crusade to live the Dream do not appreciate the changes their leaders are trying to bring about. It is one thing to believe one's leader on matters of state. It is quite another to go along with him because he has had some weird vision and now sees the universe differently. In many societies, the presence of the Forge Dream has caused severe strife, coup d'etats and outright civil war as those who believe the Dream fight those who do not. Sometimes the Forge Dreamers win, sometimes they lose. But in every case, the death and damage done from such conflicts goes against everything the Dream demands, pushing the galaxy farther and farther from ever getting the Cosmic Forge to return. In most of the galaxy, the Forge Dream is seen as an infectious meme, a dangerous concept, philosophy or shared madness that is slowly spreading and infecting system after system after system. Worlds that have fully bought into the Forge Dream seem eerie and unsettling to their neighbors, for whom it looks like the entire population has been brainwashed.

Even though Forge Dreamers profess to spread harmony and hope throughout the galaxy, their blissful demeanor and vacant stare suggest that maybe not all is right with these people. That maybe they are not on some path to salvation or unity with the Cosmic Forge, but they have instead just lost their minds.

It would not be the first time some kind of mass insanity has plagued the Anvil Galaxy. Four thousand years ago, the *Way of the Star*, a cult of unusual strength, swept across the galaxy, converting 40% of the galactic population to its cause. Just as strangely, however, the converts all lost their faith around the same time, four years later. There is precious little mention of *any* of this in galactic history records, leading some to think that a massive memory alteration was carried out so future generations would not know of the Way of the Star and repeat its strange unification of thought.

Those who believe the other Heresies over this one point out that *anybody* can claim to have had the Forge Dream, and that doubtlessly, there are those among the Dreamers who only *think or falsely claim* they have had the Dream. After all, it certainly is well documented enough. Anybody interested can memorize the details and fake their way through to the ranks of the Dreamers to enjoy whatever rank and privileges that might entail. For those who do not put stock in the Ninth Heresy, it seems less like a way of finding the Cosmic Forge than it is a means of subverting one's mind to a recklessly optimistic way of looking at the universe instead of dealing with problems in a realistic fashion. Pirates cannot be defeated by sitting down and talking to them about how the Cosmic Forge does not think their violent ways are beneficial to the rest of Creation. Rogue armies cannot be held in place by large numbers of people holding hands and chanting mantras of peace. The Anvil Galaxy is a place of war and conflict, and the sooner the Ninth Heresy takes that into consideration, the sooner it can rejoin the rest of reality, or so the skeptics say.

Still, there are those who think how simple life would be if only they experienced the Forge Dream for themselves...

The Forge War

Though there are many followers of the Nine Heresies, they comprise a relatively small percentage of the total Anvil Galaxy population. However, their near-fanatical devotion to the *Forge Mythos* has spurred these true believers to find the Cosmic Forge no matter what. For the most part, these *Forge fanatics* are individuals or groups of private citizens conducting their own personal quest. In some cases, however, entire civilizations or governments have adhered to a particular Heresy, making it the driving goal of that civilization to find the Cosmic Forge and put it to what *they* believe would be a good use. Ordinarily, this would not be such a problem, except just about every civilization in the Anvil Galaxy is tied to each other in some way. Everywhere one travels, there are rivals, allies, enemies, trading partners, and so on. When an entire world or interstellar community devotes itself to finding the Cosmic Forge, it has a ripple effect that involves other civilizations that might not have anything to do with the Forge.

Consider, for example, the otherwise apocryphal civilizations of the Forbian Oligarchy and the Council of Thrace. Both are single-planet civilizations that have little impact on their surrounding star systems. However, the two have been locked in a state of cold war for a century. Neither likes each other and any major move one does, the other must counter. See where this is headed? Let's suppose the Forbians adhere to one of the Nine Heresies and decide it is time for them, as a civilization, to seek the Cosmic Forge. The Thracians are put in a bind. They do not believe the Forge even exists, but they fear what might happen if, on the off chance, the Forbians prove them wrong and get the Forge as a weapon. Just to be on the safe side, the Thracians must also seek the Cosmic Forge in the hopes of getting it before the Forbians do. Or, they must strive to thwart the Forbians' search whenever possible. Pretty soon, both civilizations are drawn into the quest for the Forge.

Now consider whatever other civilizations these two might have contact with. What if the Forbians and Thracians have third-party allies? What if they hire outside parties as mercenaries? What if they seek the aid of a larger civilization, like the CCW or the TGE? All of a sudden, this rivalry for the Forge has taken a much more prominent role on the galactic stage, because it has drawn in the major power players, who, like it or not, are now part of the quest to find the Forge.

This scenario has already played itself out repeatedly throughout the entire Anvil Galaxy, and indeed, every major power bloc is now involved in some way, shape or form, in an effort to find the Cosmic Forge. This is a massive, multi-headed and very interconnected situation, for with so many competing parties all looking for the same thing, the potential for major conflict is immense. Already, many are calling this tense situation the **Forge War**, even though the worst that has happened are some moderate skirmishes and acts of sabotage here and there by peripheral participants in the Forge quest. The majority of parties involved (which pretty much means any government of consequence in the Anvil Galaxy) have resigned themselves to the fact that someday, this mad race for the Forge will end up in "real war" between the major powers, and ultimately the entire galaxy, maybe even the whole of the Three Galaxies, will be drawn into the conflict. This is a grim outlook, but nobody sees a way out of it. It is not like the parties can just give up the quest because then their allies will feel abandoned, or their enemies might find the Forge, etc. As tragic as this all could end up being, there is no easy way out, so the bulk of the Anvil Galaxy marches on a path to mutual destruction.

With so much at stake and so many parties ready to fight each other over it, the Anvil Galaxy suddenly teeters on the brink of complete disaster. Should this total war scenario come to pass, the material destruction and loss of life could be horrific. More than that, entire planetary deaths could send massive P.P.E. surges into the galactic nethersphere, where they might very well channel into the various ley lines connecting certain stars together. If a big enough P.P.E. surge were to hit the right ley line nexus, it could cause a chain reaction of destruction similar to the one that nearly destroyed Rifts Earth. Only this time, the reaction would be on a galactic scale, an apocalypse that, in the worst case scenario, would consume countless star systems and lives, and leave the Anvil Galaxy a burned out ruin. At no time in recorded history has such a disaster even been theorized, much less predicted. Such a scenario is still a long way off, but it *is* possible, however slight. That there is any room for this to happen, however, is unacceptable to a growing number of scholars, scientists, mystics, and heroes. It is people like these who are willing to do anything, including sacrificing their own lives, to make sure this Doomsday Scenario never comes to pass. Such a mission takes many forms, from preventing certain parties from getting too close to the Cosmic Forge, to helping rival empires smooth out their differences, to preventing evildoers and villains from taking advantage of this turbulent environment, to monitoring the galaxy's ley line network and making sure no surges are present, to entreating the various god-like entities and beings in the Anvil Galaxy to do what they can to intervene and prevent Armageddon from visiting this, the smallest but most volatile of the Three Galaxies.

The Three Galaxies

Across the Megaverse, nestled in a corner of deepest space are the Three Galaxies – **the Corkscrew, the Thundercloud,** and **the Anvil**. Together, they form a unique and challenging environment for any hero, villain or freebooter looking to make a name for themselves, do a little larceny, or just do the right thing. The Three Galaxies have a long and tortured history, a wild mix of alien races and civilizations, and quite possibly something called the *Cosmic Forge*, which, as far as anyone can tell, is a source of ultimate power to whomever wields it. These galaxies are a place where, like Rifts Earth, magic and technology collide head-on, and usually with ugly results. It is place of nobility and depravity, of wonder and horror, of strife and serenity. It is a cauldron of contradictions, and perhaps that is why any serious traveler of the Megaverse will tell you: it's just one hell of a great place to adventure in. But most of all, it is the home of **Phase World**, one of the Megaverse's busiest and most important *inter-dimensional crossroads*. Few other places do so much to bring the farthest reaches of the Megaverse together in one spot, and for that reason alone, the Three Galaxies are worthy of special notice by *anybody's* standards.

The Geography of the Three Galaxies

All the known civilizations in the Phase World universe come from one of three galaxies, known respectively as the *Corkscrew*, the *Thundercloud* and the *Anvil*. The maximum distance from one tip of the Three Galaxies to the other is 170,000 light years. Neighboring galaxies are a considerable distance away. The closest one is 300,000 light years away; sporadic exploration of the other galaxies has occurred, but slowly, since there is so much to see in the local galaxy group.

The Corkscrew Galaxy

The Corkscrew is the largest of the Three Galaxies, measuring about 90,000 light years long and 2,000 light years thick. Nearly 33% of it is controlled by the **Consortium of Civilized Worlds (CCW)**, a freedom-loving federation of civilizations (more later on them, and every other power bloc mentioned in this section). Another 33% is controlled by the CCW's chief rival, the **Trans-Galactic Empire (TGE)**. Around 10% is controlled by the **Free World Council**, a collection of breakaway systems that have successfully seceded from the TGE (with the tacit help and cooperation of the CCW, of course). The remaining 24% of the Corkscrew Galaxy is made up of *independent* and *unexplored systems*. Of the many independent worlds and civilizations, no one among them controls much more than 1% or 2% of the galaxy; and most only govern a few planets at all. A few independent powers might control as much as 8% to 10%, but such entities are almost always large coalitions of smaller powers, which fall apart a few years after their formation.

Phase World

The Corkscrew Galaxy is home to **Phase World**, an independent planet positioned between the CCW and the TGE, and the foremost trading point in the Three Galaxies. Connected to hundreds of dimensions and accessible to thousands of planets in its own dimension, this world is often referred to as the "Center of the Universe." While this is an exaggeration, everybody who has visited the planet agrees that very few places in the Three Galaxies share the diversity and strangeness of this world.

Located near the core of the Corkscrew Galaxy, Phase World is the fifth planet of an aging red star. It is owned and governed by an ancient and powerful race known as the *Prometheans*, who control, among other things, the coveted knowledge of *Phase Technology* (more on that later). Phase World's position as a galactic and inter-dimensional crossroads brings people from hundreds of different worlds and thousands of races to the planet and region in general. Phase World itself is easily the most racially diverse world in the Three Galaxies, perhaps even in the Megaverse, but for all of this diversity, the Prometheans retain an iron grip on the reins of power. As far as the Prometheans are concerned, *they* made Phase World what it is, and they shall be the ones to control it.

Phase World's landscape is dotted by farms and cities, but visitors rarely get to see how the majority of the planet's inhabitants live, because they are confined to **Center**, an enormous enclosed city (or *arcology*). Center is an artificial mountain that stands one mile high. It is made up of hundreds of levels that go all the way down beneath the surface to a mile (1.6 km) in depth. Six hundred million sentient beings inhabit Center, making it one of the largest cities in the Three Galaxies. Inside, there are the equivalent of a dozen full cities, each on top of the other. Throughout the recorded history of the Three Galaxies, Center stands as one of the wonders of the universe, an unmatched feat of engineering.

Ships in orbit around Phase World can see an intricate network of ley lines crisscrossing the planet. Center itself has no less than twelve ley line nexi in diverse levels of the city! Ley line storms occur occasionally on the planet's surface, but somehow they are always controlled without injury to people or damaging property. How the Prometheans accomplish this remains just one of their many coveted secrets. Some believe that their mastery of Phase Technology might actually be able to tame the ley line storms, while others suspect that the Prometheans simply employ large numbers of powerful mages to pool their efforts and bring the ley line activity back to a safe level.

Surrounding the planet is a ring of sixteen large space stations where large ships and cargo vessels dock. Also within orbit are hundreds of smaller satellites, including military stations and sixty-four *Spacegates*. These are giant rings, 10 miles (16 km) in diameter, covered with strange machinery and monitoring stations. These unique artifacts are powered by legendary Phase Technology, and they can bend time and space to allow instant transportation from anywhere in the Three Galaxies to

Phase World. Many people covet the secret of the Spacegates, but nobody has been able to examine one closely, let alone get their hands on one of them. Teams of spies, thieves and scientists form virtually every power bloc in the Three Galaxies have tried to unlock their secrets but none have succeeded. No other civilization in the Megaverse has been able to replicate their effects.

A ship with a Phase Transceiver can instantly teleport to a Spacegate from anywhere in the Three Galaxies. The Prometheans who man the Spacegates can scan the ship (via the Phase Transceiver) before letting it *teleport* through. If the ship seems hostile or dangerous, they can refuse to let it make the jump. The gates only work for ships *arriving* "to" Phase World. The vessel needs to find another way back home, typically using some sort of propulsion system like a gravity drive, phase drive or Rift drive. Some merchants don't bother with a space drive at all. Instead, they fill a slower-than-light ship with merchandise, teleport to Phase World or to one of its space stations, and sell both the cargo and the ship! They get back home by booking passage back to their world on another space vessel or through a Rift Gate.

It is important to understand that the Spacegates are a *one-way trip* to Phase World; they cannot be used to return home. (Center has numerous *Rift Gates* which can be used to transport small groups of people and material to anywhere in the Three Galaxies, but as far as bringing spaceships to Phase World goes, using the Spacegates is a one-way trip unless the ship captains want to drive their ships home by conventional FTL propulsion, which might take a while.) Every hour, hundreds of ships arrive through the Spacegates. Meanwhile, hundreds of others arrive and depart using more conventional methods of travel. Not everybody trusts the Spacegates, although there has never been any problems with them.

The effect of these Spacegates on the economy of the Three Galaxies is enormous. Merchants from the farthest corners of the Three Galaxies can meet and exchange goods on Phase World in a fraction of the time it would take them to go to each other's planets. Coupled with Phase World's network of *dimensional gates* leading to other worlds in the Megaverse, the Spacegates make Phase World the place to find *anything*.

Spacegates are a large reason for Phase World's incredible prosperity. They make it easy to visit the world but difficult to leave. As a result, many ship captains see a trip to Phase World as a one-time deal. They Spacegate there, sell their cargo, sell their ship, and never leave Center, spending their newfound wealth in one of the most dynamic and exciting places in the Megaverse. After a while, such folks often become naturalized citizens and are allowed to move out of Center, where they may seek a quieter life elsewhere on the planet or go adventuring in the Three Galaxies.

Everything from small shuttle-sized vessels to giant cargo ships are allowed to land at Center's huge spaceport on the planet's surface. However, much of the trade takes place in orbit, with ships exchanging cargoes and passengers with other ships and orbital stations. Consequently, one never has to land on the planet itself. However, most travelers cannot resist the chance to visit Phase World. For one, the choicest merchandise, especially those of extra-dimensional origins, can only be found

"ground side" at the city of Center. In fact, it is said that anything can be found at Center, be it rare pieces of equipment, weapons, magic souvenirs or exotic entertainment. There is danger, especially in the lower levels where maintenance and law-enforcement are scarce, and where dimensional activity is a constant threat, but many risk themselves in those areas because forbidden pleasures and equipment can be purchased there.

Visitors to Phase World include merchants buying and selling wares from places in the Three Galaxies as well as more distant worlds and other dimensions, criminals trying to hide among Center's teeming multitudes, bounty hunters trying to root out those criminals, mercenaries, assassins and other "professionals" selling their talents to the highest bidder, smugglers trying to buy or sell illegal cargoes from all corners of the Megaverse, entertainers looking for work, scientists looking for new technologies to study, magicians searching for unique artifacts, dimensional travelers on their way to other destinations, and thrill-seekers, adventurers and refugees, each of them driven by personal reasons.

Despite its incredible strategic and economic importance, Phase World has remained an independent world throughout its history. Every would-be conqueror who has tried to take over the planet has failed, usually losing their life in the process. This independence places Phase World above the laws of most civilizations, which makes it a haven for criminals, fugitives, refugees, and unsavory characters of all kinds. Visitors go there at their own risk.

The Thundercloud Galaxy

The Thundercloud is 20,000 light years away from the "eastern" end of the Corkscrew Galaxy, and it measures some 30,000 light years long and 2,000 light years in thickness. Nearly 33% of the Thundercloud Galaxy is controlled by the **TGE (Trans-Galactic Empire)**, making it the dominant power. The next largest bloc is the **CCW (Consortium of Civilized Worlds)**, which controls nearly 20% of the galaxy. After that, the **FWC (Free World Council)** controls 10% of the galaxy. This territory is closely allied with the CCW, and their alliance helps maintain a balance of power against the tyrannical and expansive TGE. Beyond that, there are no other power blocs of similar size. The **UWW (United Worlds of Warlock)** commands 3% of the galaxy, but this is fairly scattered and unorganized territory spread out across the entire galaxy. It has shown no interest in trying to expand and take over other worlds, nor do the UWW worlds here wish to embroil themselves in the ongoing conflict between the CCW/Free World Council and the TGE. The remaining 33% of the Thundercloud Galaxy is made up of independent and unexplored territory. Most independent civilizations control less than 1% of the galactic territory. The majority of this space is still unexplored, especially near the galaxy's unusual center.

Unique in the universe, the Thundercloud Galaxy resembles a massive storm pattern, like a hurricane, rather than a spiral, ellipse, or other standard galactic form. Like a storm, the Thundercloud Galaxy rotates at incredible speeds. Even though those in the galaxy can not feel such movement, it is highly visible from outside the galaxy, making it virtually impossible for astronomers to mistake the Thundercloud Galaxy for anything else.

The galactic storm structure comes complete with an "eye" about 100 light years across in the center of the galaxy. Scientists suspect that this eye, known as **the Vortex**, is some kind of enormous black hole or a multidimensional gateway, and they would very much like to learn where it leads and what or who might be coming and going through it. In recent years, the governments and power blocs of that galaxy have made a concerted effort to study the Vortex, with mixed results.

First, the Vortex is surrounded by worlds inhabitable to carbon-based life, but home to all sorts of strange, non-carbon life forms. Most of these aliens want nothing to do with those from the Biosphere, or they are simply so strange and different that they cannot comprehend the Biosphere visitors at all. As a result, diplomatic disasters are commonplace, as is unprovoked warfare on explorers and adventurers. This makes getting near the Vortex a very tricky business indeed, and most efforts must rely on the good graces of those few non-carbon races who do understand the Biosphere and are willing to help its carbon-based life forms – for a price.

Second, there is pretty good evidence – science vessels have a nasty tendency to issue a Mayday when near the Vortex, only to be destroyed shortly thereafter – that any beings traveling through the Vortex are very hostile and do not want other people looking into their business. Exactly who these belligerents might be is unknown as of yet, even to the various non-carbon aliens near the Vortex. Military analysts fear that the Vortex might house or be the invasion route for a new alien mega-power of unbelievable technology and offensive capability, and that if and when they decide to invade the Thundercloud Galaxy, all of the Three Galaxies will be made to suffer for it.

The Anvil Galaxy

On the other side of the Corkscrew Galaxy, 30,000 light years beyond the Corkscrew's "western" edge, lies the Anvil Galaxy. A bull's-eye-shaped galaxy whose people are locked in intense warfare, unrest, danger and mystery, it is the smallest but most dynamic of the Three Galaxies in terms of the ongoing struggle between good and evil. Should the Thundercloud Galaxy turn into a huge invasion route for an as yet unknown alien conqueror, that all might change. Until then, the Anvil Galaxy – reported resting spot for the Cosmic Forge, home to an endless legion of ambitious power blocs who seek to gain the Forge at any cost, and likely candidate for total galactic war within the next century – remains the Three Galaxies' "hot spot" for danger and adventure.

It wouldn't be much of an **Anvil Galaxy** sourcebook if we stopped describing it here, now would it? Have no fear, the lowdown on the Anvil Galaxy's specific regions, main power players, and alien races all follow this section. Read on!

Biosphere Zones

The Three Galaxies contain billions of stars and planets, only a fraction of which actually support life of any kind. Along the outer edge of each galaxy is a "Biosphere Zone," that area in which one is most likely to find star systems supporting Earth-like worlds and other planets capable of supporting *carbon-based life* (like humans and animals). Beyond the Biosphere Zone, the worlds become increasingly hostile and strange. Still, even within the Biosphere Zone, there are hundreds of thousands of inhabitable worlds, and only a small percentage of them have been colonized and developed. As these "standard" humanoids (at least, they think of themselves as standard) drive inward toward the cores of their respective galaxies, they find that not only are most "inner systems" *not* habitable by carbon-based life forms, but they *are* inhabited by other kinds of life – silicon-based, hydrogen-based, and so on. What remains to be discovered beyond the Biosphere Zone could easily turn all preconceptions about the Three Galaxies upside down as explorers learn that the worlds beyond the Biosphere Zone teem with alien life. These strange aliens have historically avoided the Biosphere Zone because they consider it hostile, uninhabitable space (just as most Biosphere humanoids view the *Inner Systems*). However, things in the Three Galaxies are changing, and Biosphere humanoids are beginning to drive through the Inner Systems, where an inevitable meeting between carbon and non carbon-based life forms is inevitable. Whether or not a war is equally inevitable remains to be seen. Most Inner System civilizations just want to be left alone, so for now, the ball remains in the Biosphere Zone's court, but it might not stay that way for much longer.

For various reasons, Biosphere humanoids have been exploring the Inner Systems of each of the Three Galaxies. Some of these efforts are to find new worlds to colonize. Others are purely scientific – in the Inner Worlds one can get much closer to certain galactic phenomena. And still others are just curious and would like to see what the bulk of their home galaxy is like. All of them, however, treat the rest of the galaxy like it is theirs to claim when they like, an attitude the non-carbon residents of the Inner Systems are not likely to take kindly. It is exactly this sort of clash in mentalities that could spark an unusual war in the Three Galaxies, and to prevent that, many of the expeditions beyond the Biosphere carry with them at least one translator and a xenocultural specialist.

Meanwhile, back in the outer reaches of the Three Galaxies, there is still a great deal of territory for Biosphere humanoids to explore and conquer. First of all, there are the different galaxies themselves: The Corkscrew Galaxy, the Thundercloud Galaxy, and the Anvil Galaxy. There is also a fourth territory to consider, the remarkable planet Phase World, situated in the middle of the Corkscrew Galaxy. Each galaxy contains dozens upon dozens of various governments, empires, societies and civilizations, all of which are vying for their own piece of galactic territory, security and prosperity. More often than not, this hurtles these power blocs into conflict with each other, making the Three Galaxies war-torn and unstable on a massive scale. There may not be huge tears in the Megaverse all around, and monsters and demons infesting huge territories, but there are abundant pirates, despots, villains and other evildoers ready to do their part to make the Three Galaxies a difficult place in which to live.

Political Geography

The "political" geography of the Three Galaxies bears a funny resemblance to the political map of a planet, due to the fact that most inhabited planets occur on the "surface" of the galaxies. This is especially true of the larger civilizations, which tend to expand "downward" or "vertically" through their part of the galaxy before expanding "outward" or "horizontally."

Smaller civilizations often do not control much space at all, so they might be found on either galactic "surface" or stuck somewhere in the middle. Systems isolated in the middle of a galaxy are considered the interstellar equivalent of a landlocked country, and they almost always are not as prosperous or advanced as their "surface" neighbors. As such, these "landlocked" civilizations often end up joining or getting absorbed by larger powers.

Demographics of the Three Galaxies

According to the latest galactic census, there are approximately 25 trillion sentient beings living in the *Biosphere Zones* of the Three Galaxies. Twelve trillion of these live in the Corkscrew Galaxy, seven trillion live in the Thundercloud Galaxy, and six trillion live in the Anvil Galaxy. The census obviously does not take into consideration the potentially *huge* populations of non-carbon sentients living in the *Inner Systems* of all of the Three Galaxies. These figures are also largely educated *guesses* as to the real populations present in each galaxy. By universal standards, the Corkscrew Galaxy is pretty shrimpy, and the Thundercloud and Anvil Galaxies are pint-sized, but they are still vast places holding billions upon billions of star systems. The populations these regions can *support* is incalculable, but it certainly is a lot higher than a measly 25 trillion sentient beings. In the Biospheres alone, there might be large and advanced civilizations that have remained hidden from view from the galactic community, and remain uncounted. Furthermore, there is no central fact-finding organization in the Three Galaxies, no Census Bureau or anything of that sort. The population counts are based on known data and formulas for calculations based on reasonable expectations and guesswork. The scholars doing these estimates have often worked from incomplete and contradictory records offered by the thousands of different governments scattered across the Three Galaxies. These numbers are suspect, to say the least. The Trans-Galactic Empire (TGE), for example, has a history of inflating its population to make their society seem larger and more powerful than it really is. Likewise, the decentralized nature of the Consortium of Civilized Worlds (CCW) makes it nearly impossible to get a really firm grasp on its total population count since member states come and go, making the mean tally something of an ever-changing figure. Finally, there are countless independent systems as well as inhabited but uncharted territories that together present a sizeable population. Nobody has ever conducted a trustworthy accounting of these systems, and so the "official" population figures are further discredited. Thus, the real population is likely to be 50-500 times larger than current estimates.

Humans

Humans make up almost 12% of the total recorded population – nearly three trillion people – in the Three Galaxies' Biosphere population. This is over 300 times the population of Rifts Earth before the Great Cataclysm. What is really interesting, however, is that out of the 3,000+ alien races known to inhabit the galactic Biospheres, humans are the most numerous single race. This is cause for great jealousy and resentment from many other races who see such a statistic as the *de facto* rulership of humanity over all other peoples in the galaxies. That is not the case, of course, especially since both the TGE and CCW have sizeable human populations, as well as nearly every other major power bloc in the Three Galaxies. Still, there are those races and cultures who are sensitive to this sort of thing, and as a result, they have declared humanity to be their enemy. That humans have so successfully integrated themselves into almost every civilization within the Three Galaxies, and that they have proven themselves so adept at technology, are more reasons for other, arguably less successful, alien races to despise them. In many ways, humanity is a *pariah race* among the Three Galaxies, considered second-class citizens in the societies they call home. Unfortunately this has spawned an ugly human supremacist movement in some sectors of the Galaxies, as embattled humans draw together to exclude all other aliens from their collective sphere of influence. Such hate-mongering is not a good thing, and other humans fear that it will only exacerbate the current racial situation, not make things better.

Humanity's origin in the Three Galaxies is, like so much about this region of the universe, a mystery. Some legends claim that they came from another dimension. Others insist that humans evolved somewhere in the Three Galaxies, on a mythical planet called *Earth*, though this world has never been discovered nor factually referenced in any historical documents. Despite that lack of evidence, a large number of scholars insist that humans did come from a place called "Earth," but it was probably a planet that spawned an empire thousands of years ago and which now lies lifeless and forgotten in some abandoned corner of space. Others think that human colonizers came from another dimension, and that their planet of origin is nowhere to be found in this universe. A few human supremacists insist that humankind is descended from the First Race, the mythical creators of the Cosmic Forge, but fanatics from hundreds of races make the same claim.

The humans' primary language is *Galactic Trade Tongue Four*, which is amazingly similar to English/American (characters with either language automatically know Galactic Trade Tongue Four at 50% plus any I.Q. bonuses, and can improve it with experience). Seven human-inhabited worlds are named "Earth," although none of them are similar to "true" Earth. It is also interesting to note that, in the Galactic Four language, a standard day is 24 hours, and a standard year is 365 days with an extra day added every four years!

Wulfen

To the surprise of some trans-dimensional visitors, one of the most prolific races of the Three Galaxies are a race of canine humanoids called "Wulfen." As a people, the humanoid canines have proven themselves adept warriors, technicians and empire-builders. They are identical to those found elsewhere in the Megaverse, but those of the Three Galaxies claim to know of no common history connecting them to their canine brethren found abroad. (**G.M. Note:** Thus, a *Wulfen* from Phase World and a Wolfen from the **Palladium Fantasy RPG®** will have the same basic stats and same fundamental culture, but that is where their similarities end.) Wulfen are the second most populous people of the Three Galaxies, comprising almost 10% of the total tri-galactic population. Wulfen are frequently allies to humans, which makes them just as much an enemy in the eyes of those who already have an axe to grind against humanity.

Most (90%) of all Wulfen civilizations in the Three Galaxies can trace their origins to the Ancient Wulfen Empire, which originated on the planet they call *Motherhome*. The inhabitants of Motherhome developed their technology independently of humans or any other race and formed a budding star empire many eons ago. Regrettably, the Wulfen's first encounter with another major star-faring people were the sinister *Kreeghor,* and a war soon erupted. Despite fighting valiantly, the Wulfen came out the losers in that conflict, probably because the Kreeghor had already been a space-faring people for some time and had a decided edge in personnel and material strength. Many say that were that war replayed today, with a more even playing field, the Wulfen would certainly have decimated their Kreeghor rivals, but that is all speculation and history, for the Wulfen *did* lose the war, and a large number of them subverted themselves to Kreeghor authority. Today, the descendants of those Wulfen willingly serve the Kreeghor-dominated Trans-Galactic Empire (TGE), while others have joined the freedom fighters that battle to regain their lost worlds, and to end the Kreeghor's legacy of conquest.

The majority of the Wulfen, however, overthrew their royal family (blamed for mismanaging the war effort from the start) and re-established a Republic based on the old traditions of the Ancient Wulfen Empire. The Wulfen Republic joined the Consortium of Civilized Worlds, and Wulfen spacemen, soldiers and traders are now a common sight throughout the CCW as well as the independent worlds of the Three Galaxies.

G.M. Note: Statistics for the Wulfen/Wolfen can be found on page 65 of **Dimension Book Two: Phase World®**.

The Kreeghor

This race dominates the Trans-Galactic Empire (TGE), the second largest civilization and the number one threat to peace and stability in the Three Galaxies. The Kreeghor are the third most populous race in the galaxies, hovering at about 8% of the tri-galactic population. At one point, the Kreeghor were the largest single race, but the proliferation of humans and Wulfen, as well as the continued pressures (internal and external) upon the Trans-Galactic Empire have kept the Kreeghor population more or less static. This is something that weighs heavily on the Kreeghor psyche, and it only feeds their hatred and contempt for both humanity and the Wulfen, even though there are substantial Wulfen populations who serve the Kreeghor and their government, the TGE.

Although the Kreeghor are associated with the TGE, there are Kreeghor populations outside of that dreaded empire. Some of the Free World Council – rebel systems that have shaken off TGE control – are populated chiefly by the Kreeghor, and there are even pockets of Kreeghor citizens within the CCW and on numerous independent worlds. **Free Kreeghor** can often be found working in the security business or in some aspect of the galactic underworld, but not all Free Kreeghor are wrongdoers. In fact, the majority of them are decent, hard-working folk who just want to live their lives in peace. Life is hard for these renegades, for even though they might embrace justice, freedom and tolerance, the TGE has made most people see all Kreeghor as marauding and evil people bent on subjugating all people of the Three Galaxies to their will. Many people in the Three Galaxies have experienced firsthand the Kreeghor's ruthlessness and taste for savagery, and so they do not trust *any* Kreeghor, even those who renounce the TGE and have shown no interest in hurting or enslaving others. Such Free Kreeghor often must live lives of neglect and abuse from their fellow citizens, as well as with the guilt of what their ancestors have done to so many innocent people. For mutual safety and support, Free Kreeghor populations often band together, but this only makes a bad situation worse, as suspicious folk from other races automatically assume these "bands" are plotting some sort of viciousness or are otherwise up to no good. Such is the lot of the Free Kreeghor, a much maligned and misunderstood group of people totally undeserving of such treatment.

G.M. Note: For stats on the Kreeghor, see page 73 of the **Phase World®**.

Other Races

No other race makes up more than 3% of the total and most represent much smaller percentages, considering that a race with 5 billion members would only amount to 0.02% of the total. However, many races have power and influence that goes far beyond their numbers. These include, but are hardly limited to:

The **Noro**, an advanced and ancient people who are a major force within the CCW and numerous other civilizations. Their knack for science and psychic powers is legendary. They are largely citizens of the CCW. Although the Noro are famous for their kindness and strongly oppose any kind of tyranny, oppression or genocide, a growing contingent among them are forsaking these ways and have become dangerous rogues. Relishing combat, conquest and mayhem, such Noro are a blight upon their culture, but they are growing in alarming numbers. CCW intelligence indicates that the numbers of rogue Noro might be far larger than previously believed, and that they might be planning a mass defection to the TGE, taking with them all sorts of valuable CCW security information. Such a defection would be a grievous blow to CCW security and military intelligence. (**Phase World®**, page 61.)

The **Catyr**, red-skinned humanoids whose invulnerability to radiation, supernatural strength and incredible resilience make them tough and formidable spacers. They are staunch allies and participants of the CCW. The Catyr are relentless spacers, and less than one third of their total population permanently settle on any one planet. Most of them live in their starships, usually conducting careers of trade and/or exploration. Most of the scouting missions that leave the Three Galaxies altogether are captained by Catyr spacers. (**Phase World®**, page 68.)

The **Seljuk**, a race of super-powered saurians (dinosaurs) who are also CCW loyalists, though increasingly they may be found on Independent worlds and in the unexplored territories of the Three Galaxies. Approximately 13% of all Seljuk are currently dying from a strange plague known only as the *Retribution*, and Seljuk consistently believe it is a form of cosmic punishment for some evil deed their ancestors must have committed. There is no cure (yet), and it seems that any other race can be a carrier for the plague yet remain unaffected by it. (**Phase World®**, page 69.)

The **Machine People**, sentient robots who seem as organic as they do mechanical. They are loyal subjects of the TGE, but they can be found in various independent worlds, on Phase World, and especially in the Biosphere of the Thundercloud Galaxy, where they often gather before heading on ill-fated trips to the galactic core. They make these trips for reasons unknown, even to them. (**Phase World®**, page 77.)

Silhouettes, a race of mysterious humanoids renowned for their magic and psychic abilities, as well as the ability to meld with and control shadows (a power that only enhances their reputation as dark-hearted and creepy people). The Silhouettes have been a willing part of the TGE for quite some time now, prospering under Kreeghor rule and showing no signs of unrest or secession. There are a few independent Silhouettes throughout the Three Galaxies, of course, and almost every one of them knows of or is part of a mysterious project called the *Shade Gate*. This has mostly become known among conspiracy buffs and is therefore written off as foolish rumor, but if it is to be believed, independent Silhouettes are involved in a plot to open a massive gate to the Elemental Plane of Shadow, where they might rule as gods. Some already think that the dangerous Void taking up the middle part of the Thundercloud Galaxy is actually part of the Plane of Shadow, and that the Silhouettes there are poised to take over the rest of that galaxy! (**Phase World®**, page 81.)

Star Hive Insectoids are superhuman monsters from beyond the Three Galaxies. They have no discernable civilization per se, nor do they show any interest in meaningful relations with the civilizations of any Biosphere. They are a swarming force that seeks to devour what it comes into contact with, plain and simple. They are a menace to all who encounter them, be they CCW, TGE, independent, etc. Rumor has it there is a secret joint CCW/TGE effort underway to find a weakness to these hated creatures that might be used to wipe them out entirely. Rumor also has it that these insectoids are merely the distant (and crudely evolved) ancestors of more advanced insect-like races (such as the *Xiticix*) known as scourges in the Megaverse. (**Phase World®**, page 91.)

Dominators are an ancient and god-like race who number only a few hundred, but can be found in any of the Three Galaxies. They travel the stars in planetoid-sized behemoth ships that carry enough firepower to crack a world in half. They are another scourge of any civilization, for they thrive only on death, destruction, and the enslavement of others. Were it not for the valiant *Cosmo-Knights* who oppose them, the Dominators might ride roughshod over large sections of the Three Galaxies. (**Phase World®**, page 96.)

The **Cosmo-Knights** are a noble and valiant race of super-beings said to be infused with power directly from the *Cosmic Forge* to bring justice to the Three Galaxies. In general, they refuse to take part in the many political wars and antagonisms going on, preferring to fight villains such as the Dominators, the Star Hives, and other such entities that threaten life and civilization itself. Should a particular government or power bloc present an overt threat to the interstellar community, however, the Cosmo-Knights will not hesitate to step in and set things right. They never rule the planets they bail out of trouble, even though they could do so easily. The Cosmo-Knights are one of the most powerful and mysterious groups of people in the Three Galaxies. (**Phase World®**, page 99.)

Remember, these are just the races that figure most prominently in all of the Three Galaxies. Each galaxy has many *hundreds* of different races, each with their own particular abilities, culture and society. Some of the more prominent races of the Anvil Galaxy will be described later in this book. For guidelines on creating additional alien races of your own, check out **Phase World®**, page 104. Also see **Aliens Unlimited™** and **Aliens Unlimited™ Galaxy Guide**. Both are sourcebooks for the *Heroes Unlimited™* RPG, but can be easily adapted to **Phase World®**.

Languages

There are over 10,000 major languages and almost a hundred times as many dialects and variations among the races of the Three Galaxies. Over the millennia, however, six major common or trade languages have been developed. These languages are known as the Galactic Trade Tongues (Trade for short). A person who knows any one of these languages has a good chance of making himself understood in most civilized areas. Knowing four or more trade languages guarantees being understood and communicating almost everywhere. Computerized translators exist, but are not always reliable (10% chance of mistranslating a sentence).

Trade One: This is the oldest trade tongue in existence, and is believed to have been one of the languages of the First Race. It is surprisingly easy to master by any air-breathing creatures, and even races with different means of communication. This is because many of the sounds also have equivalent hand (or other

limb) signs and gestures. This language automatically has a +10% bonus to learn, in addition to any O.C.C. or I.Q. bonuses. Base skill is 50% plus any I.Q. bonuses and 5% per level of experience.

Trade Two: This language is favored by telepathic races, because it uses telepathy in addition to the spoken word. Without psychic abilities, much of the meaning of the language is lost. The psionic component allows users to bridge difficulties in speaking, and psychic sensitives pick it up very quickly. Characters with the psi-powers Telepathy or Empathy have a +20% bonus to learn Trade Two. Non-psychics have a -15% penalty. 50% plus any I.Q. bonuses and 5% per level of experience.

Trade Three: Trade Three is the Wulfen language, slightly streamlined to reduce the guttural and growling elements common to the "classical" Wulfen language, but is otherwise identical. However, to make a good impression on Wulfen speakers, it is necessary to emphasize the growls and whines of the original language. 50% plus any I.Q. bonuses and 5% per level of experience.

Trade Four: This language is clearly based on English/American. It has evolved enough to be different, however, with the addition of a number of technical terms, slang and foreign words (some of which are similar to other Earth languages like French, Chinese, Russian and Spanish). Normal English/American speakers automatically have Trade Four at 50% plus any I.Q. bonuses and 5% per level of experience.

Trade Five: Trade Five uses hisses, whistles and clicks for most words. It is favored by many reptilian and insectoid races. Humans and other air breathers can understand and learn Trade Five at no penalty, although they will retain a distinguishable "accent" that separates them from the races for which the language was originally created. Trade Five is commonly used by the Kreeghor and Seljuk races, and is usually the second language of the Draconids. 40% plus 5% per level of experience.

Trade Six: This is the newest common language of the Three Galaxies and was developed by linguists of the CCW. Trade Six is a deliberate attempt at creating a universal language that can be used by most races of the Three Galaxies. To do this, each word and expression has two or three equivalents, two using sound and one using gestures, so a being who cannot make a particular sound can replace it with an equivalent sound or gesture. The resulting language can be learned by all species without penalty, but the amount of different sounds and gestures that a speaker must know to understand another counterbalances this. Trade Six can be learned at no bonus or penalty by everyone. 45% +5% per level of experience.

Money and Trade

Space travel and galaxy-wide commerce have made it necessary to develop a universal medium of exchange. Although many planets still maintain their own currency, every place with a star port accepts **Universal Trade Credits (UTC)** as money. Prices will change depending on simple supply or demand, government tariffs and taxes, and the legality of the merchandise in question. For example: A gun that can be bought on Phase World for 10,000 credits might cost ten times as much from the black markets of the Trans-Galactic Empire (TGE).

Characters from other worlds will quickly discover that any credits, paper bills and other forms of exchange they may have brought along are useless on Phase World and the other planets of the Three Galaxies. Barter and the sale of goods (or services) are the best way to get cash. On Phase World, **Rifts®** characters with Earth credits can find Exchange Centers where they can trade their money for local cash. The exchange rate is brutally unfair, however: 10 Rifts Earth credits for every one Three Galaxies credit! The exchange centers then sell Rifts Earth credits at the rate of five for every Three Galaxy UTC credits. Since there aren't that many travelers going to and from Rifts Earth, that's the best characters can hope for. Selling and trading items is much more favorable and fair, providing one can find a buyer.

In select systems, usually those of incredible economic stability, local currency is worth just as much as Universal Trade Credits (UTC). Good examples of this are the currencies of any of the Consortium of Civilized Worlds' (CCW's) 20 Utopia Worlds, the worlds of any Splugorth Kingdom, and certain independent worlds that have somehow obtained an unusually high degree of economic power. In such civilizations, the local currency can trade for UTCs one-for-one. All other places can expect a worse trade ratio, depending on the economic strength of the area. In the most depressed parts of the Three Galaxies, a single UTC might go for thousands and even millions of local credits. Of course, in such areas, a loaf of bread might cost a million UTC, so everything is relative.

Coins of gold, silver, bronze and other precious metals can be sold for their metallic content, which will always be less than what they were worth at their place of origin. Given that there are at least 150 commonly used precious metals in galactic coinage among the Three Galaxies, monetary metallurgists are some busy people.

Banks are an important aspect of interstellar trade and commerce for a bunch of reasons. First, they can handle money exchanges. Second, they often are the only ones on a planet that can conduct financial exchanges across interstellar or interplanetary distances. Third, they offer spacers a convenient means of storing their cash without having to lug it with them all across the Galaxies.

Most banks are planetary in nature, or they might serve a single star system. Only those with the resources to manage an interstellar communications network of incredible stability (no system crashes or lost data pulses, please) can run a successful interstellar institution. And those that do, tend to be very successful indeed. Chief among them is the **Royal Exchange of Dracul**, the Three Galaxies' equivalent of every Swiss Bank combined. The "RED" has a long history of fair exchange rates, total stability (there has not been a run or panic on their vaults in over 1,000 years), customer service (they have branches on well over 150,000 different worlds) and above all, discretion. It is well known that the RED executives ask no questions of their clients, nor do they divulge any client details to anyone. Not the CCW, the TGE, Cosmo-Knights, nobody. The RED maintains a modest private army equipped with the latest Naruni weaponry (including a company of Repo-Bots on long-term lease for debt collection purposes, with one-third of all recovered monies kicking back to the Naruni).

The RED execs are cool as cucumbers, mostly because they know that pretty much *everybody* in the Three Galaxies either does business with them or depends on somebody who does. Even if somebody could take down this bank (which would require something on the scale of a galactic war against the RED specifically), chances are they would lose too much personally to make it worth their while. Lots of people suspect the RED of sinister dealings, but the truth is for all of their money, they really are not a bad institution. They certainly are not as ruthless or greedy as the Naruni or the host of other companies that practice the Naruni business model. To be fair, the RED's relatively gentle, laid back demeanor is probably because they really don't have to work that much. With a bank as large as this, the operation sort of works on its own momentum. They are so large nobody can really compete with them except on a single-planetary basis, and in most cases, the RED comes in and offers partnerships to the local indie banks, getting a piece of the action anyway. Others fear that the RED is too big for the Three Galaxies' own good – it pretty much has a monopoly on the galactic financial markets, and if it crashes, so will a good portion of the Three Galaxies' economy. At the same time, the RED practices very strict internal controls and accounting, and they have shown not even the slightest glimmer of weakness or instability in centuries. All of this adds up to one of the universal truths of the Three Galaxies: if you have a lot of money to stash, and you might not want people knowing where you got it from, letting the RED hold on to it is the best way to go, hands down.

Traders. For those who make their money trading between the many different planets of the Galaxies, there is a ton of profit to be made if one has the right mix of business sense, courage, street wisdom and pure luck. A trader does not have an easy job – finding the right markets to buy and sell from is hard enough, but weathering pirate attacks, corrupt tax officials, oppressive regulations, excessive taxes and tariffs, unpredictable market fluctuations, over-aggressive debt collectors – well, that can be murder. The vast majority of traders can just barely make ends meet, and most of them have adopted the philosophy that they do what they do not for the money (although it never hurts), but for the freewheeling lifestyle they lead. Those who need cash, and cannot earn it legally, often find themselves turning to smuggling (dangerous but lucrative and thrilling) and even piracy. The problem with that course of action is that once one enters the criminal underworld, it is nearly impossible to get out again, especially if one associates with organized crime rings of any kind. The Galaxies are filled with broken people who thought a little crime spree would never hurt them, only to find that it would cost them everything.

To protect traders living on the edge of financial doom, numerous trading guilds have popped up across the Three Galaxies. These are basically *unions* that require planetary markets to sell to and buy from their members at fair prices. They also provide various kinds of tax relief, discounted mechanical maintenance for ships, protection from local tax and extortion shakedowns, etc. To do this, *trade guilds* need their own militaries (which most do), or they need to have the resources and methods of a large organized crime ring (again, which most do) in order to get a little justice for their members. There are many trade guilds, but one in particular, the **Journeyman Merchant Society (JMS)**, is the most powerful. With a substantial presence in all three Galaxies, and with skilled and connected operatives pretty much everyplace where there is a major trade lane, the JMS has made itself a powerful economic, industrial and political force in the Three Galaxies. Plenty of governments hate these guys and would like to see them squashed, but destroying an organization like the JMS is impossible for anybody but the CCW, TGE, and maybe the UWW. Otherwise, this organization is just too big and dug in. Thankfully, they have no plans other than running a successful trade union and looking out for its members. If it were interested in conquest, it would not busy itself with things like price negotiations with worlds and factional challenges within the union itself.

Star Travel in the Three Galaxies

Faster Than Light (FTL) propulsion is normal in the Three Galaxies, enabling starships to cover 1-5 light years an hour on average, and 20-100 light years a day. **Riftjump drives** can cross great distances instantly, but their effective range is usually 5-20 light years per jump, with no more than six or seven jumps per day possible, which makes them roughly equivalent to standard FTL systems.

It has been determined that travel between galaxies is a lot faster than travel within a galaxy. It appears that the lack of massive objects in the "emptier" space between the galaxies reduces "gravity drag" and allows **Faster Than Light (FTL) systems** to operate at 500% efficiency. An average ship can cover between 100 and 500 light years per day when traveling between galaxies.

Traveling to a distant star is not something that people do lightly. A trip from one end of the Corkscrew galaxy to the next (90,000 light years) would take 1D6 months for most ships. The fastest CG-ship (top speed of 240 light years a day) would need almost two years to travel from one end of the Three Galaxies to the other. In some ways, this situation is comparable to sea travel during Earth's pre-industrial days, when a trip could take months or years, and was not something people did unless they had a good reason. Most inhabitants of the Three Galaxies will never get onto a starship, and live out their lives on the same world that they were born on.

Even most spacers spend most of their lives going back and forth through a relatively small area. Typically, 70% of all trade and travel between stars occurs in an area not exceeding 1,000 light years, roughly a week to ten day trip each way. Planets must by necessity be nearly self-sufficient, because imports may take weeks to arrive. Most planets have a fleet (or at least one or two ships) of merchant vessels to conduct trade with nearby worlds. Long-range trader ships that stop on dozens or hundreds of worlds, selling a little of their cargo to each of them, are less common, but do exist and play an important role in the economy. Advanced medicines and medical equipment, spare parts for machinery, and weapons are among the most common imports. Food is sometimes carried to densely populated worlds that cannot spare the room for cultivation. This is done by super-freighters carrying millions of tons of grain or pre-processed foodstuffs. If a world cannot manufacture something, it often becomes a luxury item that only the wealthy (or the government) can afford. Energy weapons are very expensive in primitive backwater worlds, although they are often purchased, at great expense, for self-defense.

The space ways are fraught with danger. In addition to natural disasters, cosmic anomalies, and accidents, there are space pirates, mercenary raiders, aggressive and enemy worlds/armies and alien menaces. Since the nearest help from raiders, pirates and trouble may be hours or days away, each planet (and space vessel) must be prepared to defend itself. Most planetary collectives, including the Consortium of Civilized Worlds (CCW) and Trans-Galactic Empire (TGE), have military detachments on every inhabited member or associated world. The detachment can be as small as a five- to ten-man squad on the ground, or as large as a 10 to 20 ship fleet and a ring of defensive satellites in orbit and a full division of troops on the ground.

Space patrols with law officers are a rarity, especially in deep space. The "law" and other protectors are most likely to be found in orbit around planets, moons, and space stations, or skimming known space-lanes. Consequently, the owners of cargo ships who can afford it and large convoys may have an escort of defending warships, or a strike force of robot, cyborg or superhuman protectors as part of their crew. Of course, Cosmo-Knights and many space-faring vessels will come to the rescue of those in distress, but the universe is a big place and the odds of them being close enough to offer immediate help in an emergency are slim.

Even though space travel is routine in the Three Galaxies, it still is not safe. Attacks from pirates, hostile aliens, or hostile military craft are commonplace. Likewise, simple mechanical failures while a ship is between worlds can prove lethal if the breakdown can not be fixed or if the ship's distress signal goes unheeded. Most ships carry escape vessels, more-than-adequate repair facilities and lots of spare parts, but one can never be too sure. The fear of being stranded in a broken ship is a fear that gives every spacer nightmares at least once. But these are just the mundane risks of space-faring. There are environmental risks, too, that pose as much of a threat as an enemy laser gun or a fritzed out engine. As one might expect, each galaxy has its own peculiar hazards (most of which are singular things and go uncharted by anybody until they are actually encountered) but there are some hazards common throughout the Three Galaxies. These are the things every competent spacer knows to look out for if he expects to have a long and safe career in space. These risks include *repression fields*, *nebula storms*, *black holes*, *chronal distortions* and worst of all, *harmonic disruptions*.

Repression Fields

The problem with faster-than-light propulsion, especially the **gravitonic engines** used so often in the Three Galaxies, is that they get slowed down by ambient gravity. That is, the stronger the gravity fields around them, the slower they go. That is why a gravitonic engine works best in the space between galaxies, because there are no gravity wells — stars, planets — out there. Without that "gravitational friction," ships can move much faster.

A hazard facing ships equipped with gravitonic engines (which means: most of them) is that sometimes, without warning and apparently without reason, huge fields of gravity will spontaneously appear, even in deep space where there are no stars or planets for light years. These gravity surges are called *repression fields*, and they are dangerous because they can slow a gravitonic engine down to nothing. Unless the ship is equipped with slower-than-light (STL) propulsion of one form or another, the ship can no longer move. Even the momentum it once had is gone. Repression fields usually only last for a few seconds, but sometimes they can last for years. Either way, if a ship stricken by one of these fields can not get moving again, it is dead in space, and the crew must either abandon it, call for help, or depend on alternate propulsion to carry them to safety. Most ships do have backup STL drives, but they are not meant for long journeys, and depending on where the ship was when it got stopped, it might be years before it ever reaches another planet. If the crew does not have adequate life support for such a journey, they are doomed.

Repression fields are growing increasingly common, and increasingly large and severe in their scope. Some scientists theorize that the intense use of gravitonic engines is itself causing the repression field problem, and that if people just stopped using these engines for a hundred years or so, the problem would correct itself. Of course, asking the Three Galaxies to stop using gravitonic engines for 100 years is pure folly, and so the problem is likely to get much worse before it gets better.

Nebula Storms

Nebula storms are essentially hurricanes in space. They occur when a young star system gets hit too hard by solar winds from a neighboring star. Since the system is young, it is still just a big disc of nebular gas — no planets have formed yet. But, blown by these solar winds, the gas begins to swirl around its center gravity (the star) and forms a hurricane-like formation that eventually breaks free of its gravity well and hurtles across the cosmos for up to 100,000 years before it finally disperses or gets swallowed up by another gravity well before then.

Any ship short of the largest military craft will get ripped apart in a nebula storm. These things are just deadly — inflicting one point of Mega-Damage per melee round (15 seconds) of exposure. Moreover, most ships do not have the engine power to escape one of these storms once they are in one, and only the finest of pilots can actually break free (three consecutive, successful piloting skill rolls at -25% each).

The worst part about nebula storms is they are uncharted. Since they do not have proper gravitonic, radio or harmonic signatures, scanners do not detect them — they come across as such a weird anomaly most scanning software discounts them as scanning error. As a result, ships can and do fly smack into the middle of one of these storms and before they know it, they are being torn to pieces.

Nebula storms do sometimes hit planets, too, but the process of entering a solar system wreaks havoc on the storm system and by the time these hit a planet they have weakened so much that they inflict only minor wind-style damage, if anything at all.

Reportedly, the United Worlds of Warlock are *intensely* interested in nebula storms. If they could create and manage and disperse nebula storms, the UWW would have a weapon in their arsenal powerful enough to repel almost any opponent.

Black Holes

Revered and reviled, dramatic and dangerous, black holes never fail to capture the imagination of spacers everywhere. Basically a black hole is an endless gravity well formed by the collapse of a super-massive star. The star falls back in on itself and creates an object with such gravity that it tears the Megaversal fabric and creates – you guessed it – a *black hole*.

For ships with Faster Than Light (FTL) capability, black holes are actually quite useful, because when they tear a hole in the Megaverse, what they really are doing is digging a tunnel to somewhere else in the Megaverse. Only that tunnel does not really take up any distance, so if one were to travel through it, they would basically find themselves instantly transported someplace else. Such a tunnel is called a *wormhole*, and spacers have been using them to skip across the Three Galaxies and the Megaverse for as long as there have been FTL drives.

Why FTL drives? Because if a ship enters a black hole going slower than the speed of light, it can not break free of the black hole's gravitational pull. That means it gets pulled into the hole's *singularity* and instantly gets crushed into oblivion. Not a fun way to go, is it? But if a ship is traveling faster than light when it enters a black hole, it skips by the singularity, does not get crushed, and can continue through to the other side of the wormhole.

Most of the time, a black hole's wormhole has a fixed entrance and exit. They are, in essence, a permanent space-time tunnel that spacers can go through either way as many times as they like. Approximately 10% of all black holes, however, have what scientists call *rogue singularities*. This means the black hole is not exactly fixed in space-time, so when a ship goes through its wormhole, it will come out to a different location every time. Sometimes, the difference might only be by a few light years, sometimes, the difference might be by a few *billion* light

years. And sometimes, the difference might mean the ship has come out to another dimension altogether!

Thankfully for spacers, black holes are scrupulously charted and detailed, so unless a ship is traveling in unexplored space, their navigational computers will know where every black hole is, and which ones contain rogue singularities.

It must be said that it takes a special breed of spacer to even think about going through a wormhole. Even though it can be done quite safely, there is still something about black holes that terrifies the mortal mind. Their infinite power and the huge body of lore surrounding them (most of it is just false talk from drunken spacers that somehow persists as rumor) make black holes one of the most awesome forces most spacers ever encounter.

Chronal Distortions

Spacecraft disappear all the time in the Three Galaxies. Any ship that falls prey to pirates rarely gets seen again (under its former ownership codes, anyway), those that get caught in a meteor shower usually disintegrate, captains with lots of debts ditch their vessels and assume new identities, etc. So, when a ship vanishes without a trace, it is a tragic thing, but not wholly unexpected. What *is* unexpected is when those missing ships come back bearing the signs that they have traveled through *time* as well as space! This is called a *chronal distortion*, and no scientist in the Three Galaxies has ever figured out exactly how, why or when these things occur. All anybody can tell is that these distortions always involve starships, and they never take place within the gravity well of a planet or a star. Other than that, what brings these things on and makes them work is anybody's guess.

There are really three kinds of chronal distortions: *white shifts*, *gray shifts*, and *black shifts*. A white shift hurtles a ship forward in time by a random amount, and a black shift hurtles a ship backward in time by a random amount. In either case, sometimes the time jump is just a few seconds, and the only way the crew can tell they went through a chronal distortion at all is their ship's chronometers are off a little (these things are super-accurate atomic clocks; they do not gain or lose appreciable amounts of time). Sometimes the ship is hurtled through time by hundreds or even thousands of years. Even longer time jumps have been documented (one crew was thrust forward in time over one million years, and claim that by then the stars of the Anvil Galaxy had actually all been *snuffed out* by some great cosmic force), but these are even rarer than a less severe chronal shift, which is itself an uncommon event.

A gray shift is a jump to an alternate version of the present. Technically, it is more like dimensional travel than time travel, but scientists insist that gray shifting is actually movement through the chronal medium. (Since the case to prove it is simply too complex for most lay people to care about, there is little debate over the topic.) Ships that make a gray shift might not realize at first that they have shifted at all, especially if the shift is slight. The mildest gray shift might send a ship to a virtually identical alternate universe where the only difference is a few people have different eye colors, or something equally trivial. Severe gray shifts leave no room for doubt, as the shifted crew arrives in an *alternate universe* so radically different form the one they left that there is no question something is amiss. A good example is the *Tendren Shift*, one of the few fully documented gray shifts on record, in which the science vessel *Tendren II* was caught in a gray shift while shooting footage of a supernova. The alternate reality the ship arrived in featured a totalitarian version of the CCW, a TGE nearly ruined by self-inflicted warfare, and a Thundercloud Galaxy that had actually collided with the Corkscrew Galaxy, causing the two to swap thousands of star systems, disrupting life on innumerable planets. Thankfully for the *Tendren II*, they gray shifted back home almost immediately, and their camera footage of the entire event proves it really did happen.

Most crews are not so lucky. Chronal shifts occur at random, and unless the crew has some kind of proof that they are from an alternate time and/or place, they have little means of showing conclusively that they were shifted at all. Due to the random nature of these things, the best way to shift back to one's home reality is to stay exactly where they were when they shifted the first time. There is a 01-85% chance the chronal shift will return, bringing the shifted crew back to the exact reality they had been plucked from. The problem is that most times, chronally shifted spacecraft are moving when they shift, and the crew may not realize initially what happened to them. As a result, ships undergoing a chronal shift usually find it difficult, if not impossible to find the general location where they shifted time lines. As a result, well over 90% of all chronal shifts end up stranding their victims forever in an alternate time or dimension. While this is traumatic for the victims, it can be immensely helpful to the people of the alternate time or dimension, who might benefit from knowledge and technology the shifted crew possess that do not exist in their reality or point in time. A good example is also from the Tendren Shift, in which the *Tendren*'s crew had been shooting footage of a supernova before they shifted. In the alternate dimension they visited, that star had not yet gone supernova, and it was orbited by inhabited planets! Armed with knowledge that could not exist in this alien dimension, the *Tendren* crew warned people about the coming supernova beforehand. Thanks to the *Tendren*'s timely intervention, hundreds of millions of lives were saved when the planets were evacuated just before the star exploded.

Harmonic Disruptions

Throughout the Three Galaxies, there exists an interstellar version of an earthquake, and it is the dreaded *harmonic disruption*, a phenomenon that can hardly be detected, cannot really be prepared for, and can destroy entire planets or even stars. They are, with the exception of black holes, the most destructive naturally occurring force yet encountered anywhere in the Three Galaxies. Harmonic Disruptions are fairly contained and infrequent, about one every ten years between all Three Galaxies, but their rate of incidence has been increasing steadily over the last thousand years. Nobody knows why, and even the few theories that exist do not carry much weight. Some feel that *any* kind of faster-than-light travel creates a harmonic ripple that travels through the universe and bounces off any other ripples caused by FTL travel. In areas with a lot of FTL movement, there are going to be lots of ripples, many of which will overlap each other, crash into each, and so on. When these ripples affect each other too much, the theory goes, it causes a harmonic disruption. The fact that most harmonic disruptions occur in heavily populated star systems with lots of starship traffic helps to validate this theory, but, like repression fields which are similar in a sense to harmonic disruptions, the best way to stop them is to stop starship traffic, which simply is not going to happen.

The effects of a harmonic disruption are horrifying to behold. Basically, they are an invisible shock wave that erupts in space and destroys *everything* in the immediate blast radius. Usually, anything more than a light-year or two from the disruption will be safe, though they will still feel buffeted by the shock wave when it does hit. Like a supernova, harmonic disruptions give little to no warning before they occur, and they happen so fast that unless one is capable of instantaneous transportation to another star system, there can be no escape.

The real threat of harmonic disruptions is not just one going off, but of two (or more) going off and their shock waves intersecting, possibly starting a third super-disruption that could permanently damage the fabric of the Megaverse, create a super-massive black hole, destroy every star within a thousand light years, or any one of a number of similarly apocalyptic (but hypothetical) results. Scientists who study harmonic disruptions claim that they represent a threat to the Three Galaxies the likes of which have never been seen before. If indeed they are caused by FTL ripples, then they *will* increase in number, frequency, and intensity over the next hundred years. Moreover, the super-disruption scenario is also best considered a matter of "if" rather than a matter of "when."

For the people of the Three Galaxies, the threat of such a hideous natural occurrence happening is like getting struck by lightning. Sure, it is a terrible threat, but there is nothing to do about it, so why worry? Conversely, there is no small number of villains, monsters and evil organizations that would love to learn how to trigger harmonic disruptions and maybe bring this super-disruption scenario to bear. Indeed, CCW intelligence has detected, within the last year, three different energy pulses outside the Three Galaxies that mimic the harmonic signature of a harmonic disruption but lacking the intensity of one. This indicates that somebody has a working prototype of a harmonic disruption generator, and they are fine tuning it so it might one day be put to use. A horrifying concept, if ever there was one.

Communications in the Three Galaxies

The most efficient communication systems depend on phase and contragravity technology. Messages are sent via laser or microwave transmitters combined with a phase or contra-gravity field to prevent their energies from being slowed down by gravity. These transmitters are able to cross space at a speed of 100 light years per hour, roughly ten times faster than the fastest starships. In the "empty" space between galaxies, this speed is multiplied by 5. Even so, a message sent from the farthest corner of the Three Galaxies will take 1300 hours (roughly 54 days, almost two months) to reach the other end; 170,000 light years away (considering that the 50,000 light year distance between the galaxies is crossed at a much greater speed).

All of this is beginning to change, however. The invention of super-tech networks such as the **Ultranet, Systran 60** and **IDAR** (Interstellar Directional Attunement Relay) promise, within the next several decades, to bring cheap, fast, and virtu-

ally *instantaneous* communications and information exchange from anywhere to anywhere within the Three Galaxies. Right now, the three previously mentioned network systems are all competing to bring their system online first. Each has established prototype systems covering just one or two systems, but none are ready to try to canvas the Three Galaxies just yet. For them, it is a matter of fine-tuning their *very* secret and proprietary technologies as well as raising the incredible capital needed to establish networks of this size.

So far, the **Ultranet** project, originated and owned by the *Belarian Empire* (a small independent government of three star systems), is receiving a trickle of funding from both the CCW and the TGE, with either government poised to dump huge money into this thing if it looks like it will be as good as its inventors promise. Ultranet technicians insist their system has the best bet to work on a galactic scale, thanks to the setting of what they call "quantum filaments" from star to star. These filaments will use the universe's own harmonic frequencies to carry messages and data packets from source to destination with absolutely no environmental friction whatsoever. The result, instant communications, regardless of volume or distance. Of course, unbeknownst to the Ultranet inventors (or anybody else for that matter), should Ultranet come online, it will be highly susceptible to harmonic disruptions anywhere in the Three Galaxies, so each disturbance could blow out the entire system, but there is also some concern that its use might *cause* destructive harmonic disruptions.

The **Systran 60** enterprise is the brainchild of *Camlann Industries*, a specialist in communications technology based entirely on spaceships that never leave interstellar space, that way they can avoid a majority of taxes on their work. The Systran 60 idea is to network the bulk of the Three Galaxies' independent worlds together, joining their economies and turning them into a major power bloc. This venture is not that far-fetched, for it currently contains over 350 assorted systems already, with more joining every day. If Systran 60 works, this new alliance of worlds might turn the independent realms of the Three Galaxies into a superpower the likes of which the CCW and TGE have never dreamed of. Intelligence agencies within the CCW, TGE, and those worlds not willing to connect with the Systran 60 network all have a huge stake in making sure the project never sees completion. To that end, Systran 60 laboratories, engineering facilities and admin offices have been the targets of relentless industrial sabotage and espionage. Frustrated and angry, Systran 60 has put out a call to any mercenaries, freebooters and adventurers who would like to make some excellent money guarding Systran 60 interests. In no time at all, the enterprise has assembled a formidable mercenary army, and the attacks on its infrastructure have stopped. The question now weighing on everybody's minds is once the Systran 60 is up and running, and once paying customers are generating ungodly revenue for the system designers, what will become of that mercenary army they have assembled? Will it simply turn to corporate security, or do the powers behind the Systran 60 throne have greater military aspirations for their communications empire?

IDAR is the most ambitious and technically advanced communications project of the three, developed under the aegis of the *Univerge Compact*, a not-for-profit organization devoted to developing high technology. IDAR uses a peculiar and never before seen kind of *power crystal* as its core technology. These crystals are smooth to the touch and small enough to fit in the palm of one's hand. They give the user what feels like a strange mix of telepathy, remote viewing, and virtual reality. The way the system works is users each use a *Transmission Stone* which they must keep somewhere on their person (held in the hand works best, but it also works fine in one's pocket or belt pouch). The user concentrates and expresses a mental desire to establish contact with the network. The stone activates a weird kind of reality field that seeks out the nearest Relay Stone in the network. The maximum range for a Transmission stone is a light year, but to keep things overlapping, the IDAR network intends to place Relay Stones in every star system that wishes to participate in the project. The Relay Stones have no range limitations, and they are the real backbone of the network. All information and communications route through them and to and from the individual users.

While using a Transmission Stone, the user can envision the equivalent of a computer software screen floating in front of him, somewhat translucently. This enables one to use the network while also conducting their "real world" business. The image of the screen is only in the user's head, like a form of telepathic virtual reality. From there, the user forms mental commands to communicate with others, compose messages, download information directly into one's personal memory, and so on.

There are two huge obstacles with this system. First, any *psychics* using it will cause painful amounts of psychic feedback to *everybody* on the network at the time. This means a single psychic cannot only crash the network, but inflict 1D6x10 points of damage to those using it, possibly killing some people. That means sabotage and possibly murder on a scale never before imagined, if IDAR were sufficiently deployed. Clearly, this is a "major bug" the IDAR team needs to work out, but they have not the foggiest idea of where to begin.

The second problem is that this is stolen technology. The Transmission and Relay Stones were created by an advanced but dying race in the Corkscrew Galaxy known as the *Hrell*. The Hrell mastered this odd crystalline technology eons ago, and their stones were discovered quite by chance by pirates who were looting the last of the Hrell home worlds almost a century ago. Since then, this cache of stolen stones has changed hands numerous times, finally coming into IDAR possession. IDAR only has a limited number of them, and they do not know how to make any more. At present, they have about one million Transmission Stones, and 1,000 Relay Stones. Hardly enough to create a galactic network, is it? To solve this little problem, they are going to have to decipher the mystery of the stones' design. But with the Hrell now extinct and their civilization in ashes (thanks to the many different interests who looted it over the years, including rogue CCW and TGE worlds), the plans for the stones might be forever lost.

People of the Anvil Galaxy

Consortium of Civilized Worlds R.C.C.s

In addition to humans, Wulfen, Noro, Seljuk, and the other races mentioned in **Phase World®** and the **Phase World® Sourcebook**, there are numerous alien races who play a large part in the Anvil Galaxy sector of the CCW. Obviously, not all of these alien races can be detailed, but a few of the more prominent ones are described here, including the *Durosk, Faustians,* and *Iborians*.

Skill Note: See page 150 and 151 of **Dimension Book 2: Phase World®** for space skills, otherwise use equivalent skills from **Rifts® RPG**. Unless noted otherwise, it is presumed all O.C.C.s and R.C.C.s can speak, read and write their own native language at 90% or better.

Spacecraft Note: FTL propulsion and specific types of spacecraft are also found in **Phase World®**, starting on page 152, and in **Dimension Book 3: Phase World® Sourcebook**, starting on page 79. Other alien races, O.C.C.s and R.C.C.s are found in both titles.

Durosk R.C.C.

Durosk (DOOR-osk) are short, squat, spotted slugmen with four arms (two primary, two secondary) and a pair of black glossy eyes. They are considered ugly by any definition of the word, and perhaps if they were not so adept at getting people to like them, they would be a real hard-luck race. The average Durosk is a total xenophile – one who loves other alien cultures. Durosk are experts at immersing themselves in other cultures to such a degree that they can be accepted by almost any group of people, given enough time. This makes them the perfect diplomats, ambassadors, spies, sleeper agents, explorers, traders and all-around social animals. Oddly, Durosk have little culture of their own, perhaps because they spend so much of their lives playing the social chameleon that they forget they might have a way of life that is distinctly their own.

Alignment: Any, but predominantly good or selfish.

Attributes: I.Q. 3D6+2, M.E. 3D6, M.A. 4D6+6, P.S. 4D6 (primary arms); 3D6 (secondary arms), P.P. 3D6, P.E. 3D6, P.B. 1D6, Spd. 2D6+2

Size: 4-5 feet (1.2 to 1.5 m) tall.

Weight: 150-250 lbs (67.5 to 112.5 kg).

Hit Points: P.E.+10, plus an additional 1D6 per experience level.

S.D.C.: 1D4x10. **Natural A.R.:** None.

M.D.C.: By armor only. Durosk must have armor specially made for them to accommodate their extra set of arms and flexible, odd slug-like body shape.

Horror Factor: 8

P.P.E.: 3D6

Average Life Span: 150 years.

Natural Abilities: Nightvision 300 feet (91.4 m), excellent eyesight, and can see into the ultraviolet spectrum.

Magic: By O.C.C. only.

Psionics: Standard; same as humans.

Combat: Two attacks per melee or as per Hand to Hand Combat skill.

R.C.C. Bonuses (in addition to attribute or skill bonuses): +2 to parry, +2 to roll with punch, +4 to save vs Horror Factor, +3 to save vs possession, +3 to save vs psionics and insanity.

R.C.C. Penalties: -2 to dodge.

Alien R.C.C.: Durosk Xenophile R.C.C. These oddly personable aliens are natural diplomats, ambassadors and salespeople who live to experience alien cultures. They have no problems fitting in with new groups of people, and they tend to be experts in language, culture, customs and history.

R.C.C. Skills:
Basic and Advanced Math (+20%)
Languages: Six of Choice (+15%).
Lore: Galactic/Alien (+15%)
Law: CCW/Phase World (+15%)
History (+15%)
Pilot Spacecraft (Small) (+10%)
Intelligence (+10%)
Streetwise (+10%)
Hand to Hand: Basic (never better than basic).

R.C.C. Related Skills: Select 12 other skills, but at least two must be from Communications and two from Technical. Plus select two skills at level three, two at level seven, and one at levels ten and thirteen.
Communications: Any (+10%).
Domestic: Any (+10%).
Electrical: Any.
Espionage: Any (+5%).
Mechanical: Automotive Mechanics, Basic Mechanics, Space: Drive Repair only.
Medical: First Aid, Paramedic, and Medical Doctor only.
Military: None.
Physical: Any except for Acrobatics, Gymnastics, Boxing or Wrestling.
Pilot: Any.
Pilot Related: Any.
Rogue: Any except Seduction (+10% to Palming and Concealment only).
Science: Any.
Technical: Any (+10%).
W.P.: Any.
Wilderness: Wilderness Survival only.

Secondary Skills: The character gets six Secondary Skills at level one, and two additional skills at levels four, eight and twelve. There are additional areas of knowledge that do not get the advantage of the bonus listed in the parentheses. All Secondary Skills start at the base skill level. Also, skills are limited (any, only, none) as previously indicated in the list.

Available O.C.C.s (Optional): Instead of selecting the Durosk Xenophile R.C.C., the player can elect to make his character a Spacer, Scientist, Scholar, Merchant/Trader or Runner (Smuggler) O.C.C. If so, use the skills for that O.C.C. plus 1D4+1 additional Languages, two Lore skills and choose either Intelligence or Streetwise at +10%.

Weapons & Equipment: Durosk characters start with 2D4x1,000 credits in weapons and equipment.

Bionics & Cybernetics: Durosk consider bionics and cybernetics to be most appropriate for medical or military purposes. As a result, they will not use them unless they are missing a body part or unless they are soldiers looking for an edge in firepower.

Money: Durosk start with only 1D4x1,000 credits in their pockets, but their social skills usually put them in a position where they can make a lot more in a short period of time.

Note: Durosk try to avoid violence whenever possible. As a result, many either carry no weapons on their person, or if they do, they are of the type easily concealed. Few Durosk will be seen walking about with a big, heavy weapon in plain sight. It is just the way they do things.

Faustian R.C.C.

The Faustians are a race of sinister humanoids with great psionic powers who suffered terrible persecution at the hands of the Kreeghor, mostly because they would not submit to Kreeghor authority. As a result, Faustians sought refuge within the Consortium of Civilized Worlds (CCW). However, the Faustians' long history of conquest, genocide and other heinous crimes has made them a probationary member of the CCW, and their conduct as a whole is being closely monitored. One major slip-up from *any* Faustian will result in the whole lot of them losing CCW citizenship, which means they will be easy pickings for the Kreeghor of the TGE.

Thanks to years of hard combat with the Trans-Galactic Empire, there are relatively few Faustians left – less than ten million. That means they really cannot afford to be turned out of the CCW, something that seems inevitable, given the Faustians' collective propensity for evil. In an unusual display of self-preservation, the Faustians have taken to policing themselves very strictly. If word of any one Faustian raising hell gets out, the Faustian populace across the entire CCW soon hears of it, and like a network of spies, they locate and hound the perpetrator to curb his dangerous activities and/or to bring him to justice immediately. In addition, Faustians often spend at least four years working for the CAF or GSA, acting as super-powered operatives against the TGE. Faustians often undertake the most hazardous of missions, both to prove their loyalty to the CCW, and to get back at their hated Kreeghor enemies. So far, all of this has reduced the amount of Faustian villainy a great deal, as well as raised the public image of these characters. End result: the Faustians will remain a part of the CCW . . . . for now.

Faustians have chalk-white skin, jet black hair (though many of them shave their heads), and a gaunt, almost skeletal appearance. Their eyes are a reflective bronze color, and they have a slit horizontal iris, like a goat. They possess wide, thin mouths filled with small, sharp teeth. While it is unfair to judge a book by its cover (or a whole alien species by its appearance), with the Faustians it is safe to make an exception. These villains clearly look the part.

Alignment: Most tend toward selfish and evil, 35% are Miscreant.

Attributes: I.Q. 3D6, M.E. 4D6+6, M.A. 4D6, P.S. 3D6, P.P. 3D6, P.E. 3D6, P.B. 2D6, Spd. 3D6

Size: 6-7 feet (1.8 to 2.1 m) tall.

Weight: 150-280 lbs (67.5-126 kg).

M.D.C.: 2D4x10 to start, +10 per level of experience.

Horror Factor: 10

P.P.E.: 3D6. **I.S.P.:** 2D6x10 in addition to whatever I.S.P. is gained by occupation.

Average Life Span: 300 years.

Natural Abilities: Faustians do not need to breathe, and as such can survive airless environments indefinitely. Toxic or corrosive environments still affect them because the toxin or corrosive elements in them makes contact with the Faustian, doing its damage that way.

Magic: None. Faustians *hate* magic, mostly because they are so vulnerable to it.

Psionics: All Faustians are *Master Psionics* with unusually high levels of I.S.P.

Combat: Two attacks per melee round or by Hand to Hand Combat skill; most know the Assassin or Martial Arts skill.

R.C.C. Bonuses (in addition to attribute or skill bonuses): +4 to save vs Horror Factor, +3 to save vs psionic attacks and insanity, +2 to save vs possession.

R.C.C. Penalties/Vulnerabilities: -3 to save vs magic of any kind. Moreover, Faustians suffer *double damage* from magic attacks, and any magic spell cast upon a Faustian will have double the normal duration.

Available O.C.C.s : Faustians may only select a Psychic O.C.C. They tend towards Mind Melters, Bursters, Zappers,

Psi-Slayers and the equivalent of Mind Bleeders (see **Rifts®** **World Book 12: Psyscape™** for most of these Psychic O.C.C.s).

Weapons & Equipment: By O.C.C.

Bionics & Cybernetics: They tend to avoid bionics and cybernetics as a rule. More than a few can be found sporting cybernetic limbs, however, especially those who are veterans of CAF or GSA anti-Kreeghor campaigns.

Money: By O.C.C.

Note: Kreeghor and Faustians will attack each other on sight in combat situations and go for each other's throats under other circumstances with the slightest provocation. This antagonism goes back for generations, with no end in sight.

Iborian R.C.C.

Iborians are wrinkled, leather-skinned humanoids who were created from scratch as a slave race eons ago by their ancient masters. Some say these overlords were the Gene-Splicers or Gene-Tech, but the Iborians insist they were not. They know this because when they rebelled against their masters, they slew every single one of them – their freedom was won through an act of genocide. Ever since, this people has been haunted by its past, and it is the ongoing Iborian legacy to make the universe a *better place.* To not contribute to the cycles of violence and injustice that define so much of civilization, and to ensure that good triumphs over evil and hope prevails over despair.

Now the Iborians are selfless healers desperately trying to make right by their heritage as universal healers. Their blood transfusion cures all ills, and enzymes in their skin provide incredible healing powers. Yet, they can not heal themselves, and modern medicine offers them little relief.

A sensitive, learned and perceptive people, Iborians are welcomed everywhere in the Anvil Galaxy and can travel without restriction from one political jurisdiction to another without interference or suspicion. Even the cruel TGE gives these aliens free passage so they might practice their healing abilities wherever they go. Though Iborians are almost never attacked by world and interstellar powers, they are the frequent targets of kidnaping by criminals, pirates and fugitives in need of medical attention. Iborians are also sometimes kidnaped and held for ransom, extorting huge amounts of money or supplies from those in desperate need of their healing powers. They are also sometimes kept as slaves and sold on slave markets for millions of UTCs.

According to legend, it is said that the Iborians once had direct contact with the *Cosmic Forge*, but no Iborian has any recollection of such a thing and refutes that such an event is part of their true history. Still those people who choose to believe the story point out that the Iborians don't know for sure because much of their ancient past is unknown to them. Consequently, many a fanatic and tyrant has captured and used psionic probes and every method imaginable on these poor beings to try to glean what "secrets of the Cosmic Forge" might be locked inside of them.

Iborians are loath to take life, but if pressed, they will fight to protect themselves and other innocent people, and even kill in self-defense, using their little known *Death Touch* ability. Those familiar with Iborian history believe that it was the use of their

lethal abilities that helped the Iborians destroy their ancient masters, and now, they equate the use of their Death Touch as a dreaded reminder of their terrible past. Thus, they will not use it unless they absolutely have to.

Despite their pacifistic nature, Iborians are an unusually common candidate for becoming a Cosmo-Knight. However, fully half of all Iborians offered the chance at becoming a Cosmo-Knight turn the offer down, preferring to live a life of quiet healing and reflection rather than endless crusading, noble though that cause may be.

Iborian Healer R.C.C.

Alignment: 50% Principled, 44% Scrupulous, 4% Unprincipled. On rare occasions, selfish or evil Iborians might be encountered, but these are very much the exception to the rule.

Attributes: I.Q. 3D6, M.E. 4D6+2, M.A. 3D6+4, P.S. 3D6, P.P. 3D6, P.E. 4D6, P.B. 3D6, Spd. 3D6

Size: Six feet (1.8 m) tall.

Weight: 150-200 lbs (67.5-90 kg).

Hit Points: P.E.+50, plus 1D6 per level of experience.

S.D.C.: 1D6x10.

Natural A.R.: 8.

M.D.C.: By armor only.

Horror Factor: None.

P.P.E.: 1D4x10 +P.E. attribute number.

I.S.P.: 2D6x10 +M.E. attribute number, plus 10 per each level of experience.

Average Life Span: 300 years.

Natural Abilities: Tremendous aptitude for healing as well as a tolerance for and patience with others. An Iborian can give blood transfusions to *any* carbon-based life form, and a single pint of their blood will miraculously cure all types of infections, viruses and blood and immune diseases! Enzymes secreted from their skin can be used in or as healing salves (heals cuts, burns and abrasions three times faster than normal with no or little scarring), or a balm that completely stops itching and burning sensations and heals rashes in 2D6+32 hours. Instinctively know how to use their own body healing capabilities.

Magic: By O.C.C. only. It is rare, however, for an Iborian to be anything other than a doctor and natural healer.

Psionics: Iborians are Master Psionics who instinctively know *all* Healing Psionics plus the Super-Psionic power of Bio-Manipulation. However, they can never learn any other kind of psionic talent. They are healers exclusively.

Special Abilities: In addition to their impressive psionic abilities (described above), all Iborians can perform their infamous *Death Touch*. Iborian culture looks upon this ability as something of a curse and a mark of shame, a reminder of their wretched life as slaves and the genocide they inflicted upon their masters. Iborians will only use this ability when somebody else's life depends on it or in self-defense. However, most Principled aligned Iborians will not use it to save themselves, for they don't see saving their own life as a sufficient reason to use the "cursed touch." Whether the use of this ability actually kills somebody or not, once the encounter is over, Iborians will usually enter a period of repentance during which they will not use the Death Touch for *any* reason. Those who do, if discovered, will bear a mark of eternal shame and face total expulsion from Iborian society. The length of an Iborian penance depends on the individual and how much reason and justification the individual had to use their dreaded ability. A typical penance lasts for 2D4 months, during which time the Iborian wears special clothes or jewelry bearing an Iborian Penance Sigil that shows to all familiar to this culture that the individual has recently used the Death Touch and is repenting for it.

Iborian Death Touch: This lethal power actually disrupts the nervous system of the person who falls victim to it. The Iborian must physically touch his opponent/victim's body to have any effect. The touch will induce its effects on bare skin and through all normal fabrics, but will not affect those inside environmental body armor, shielded space or hazard suits, force fields, robots, exoskeletons, or those transformed into an inorganic material (such as rock or metal). The Death Touch also will not affect an intended victim if the Iborian touches a cybernetic appendage instead of the victim's actual body.

The touch inflicts 6D6 M.D. directly to the victim and shocks the nervous system, plunging the victim into a coma (if he is not already dead) unless a successful saving throw of 15 or higher is made. If the saving throw is a success, the person only suffers the physical damage from the Death Touch and is not placed in a coma.

Those who fall into a coma are subject to the normal surviving coma/death rules but side effects from physical damage are not applicable. Those who fail to save vs coma/death simply die. However, because the Death Touch is an unusual effect, victims get a +10% chance to save vs coma/death. Furthermore, an *Iborian* using the psionic Increased Healing (10 I.S.P.) ability can bring the individual out of his coma without any need to roll for death, but no damage is restored.

Using the Death Touch takes its toll on the Iborian. With each use of this ability, the Iborian's Speed attribute goes down by 50%, and he is -2 to strike, parry and dodge, and -2 on all saving throws for 2D6 minutes. In the rare case that the Iborian uses his ability multiple times, then the side effects are cumulative.

Each use of the Death Touch counts as two melee attacks. It may be used more than once per melee round, again, if the Iborian somehow feels justified in doing so (which is almost never).

Combat: Two attacks per melee or by Hand to Hand Combat skill.

R.C.C. Bonuses: +6 to save vs Horror Factor, +4 to save vs psionics, +2 to save vs insanity. Iborians are also +6 to save vs all poisons and toxins.

Iborian Healer R.C.C.: These aliens are instinctive healers who learn skills that complement their natural healing abilities.

R.C.C. Skills:
Cook (+10%)
Languages: Six of choice (+15%).
Biology (+25%)
Holistic Medicine (+25%)
Paramedic (+25%)
Identify Plants & Fruits (+15%)
Preserve Food (+10%)
Wilderness Survival (+10%)
W.P.: Any two.
Hand to Hand: Basic (never better than basic).

R.C.C. Related Skills: Select 10 other skills, but at least two must be from Medical. Plus select two skills at levels three, six, nine and twelve.
Communications: Any (+5%).
Domestic: Any (+10%).
Electrical: Any.
Espionage: None.
Mechanical: Any.
Medical: Any (+20%).
Military: None.

Physical: Any except for Wrestling or Boxing.
Pilot: Any.
Pilot Related: Any.
Rogue: None.
Science: Any (+10%).
Technical: Any (+10%).
W.P.: Any.
Wilderness: Any (+10%).

Secondary Skills: The character gets three Secondary Skills at level one, and one additional skill at levels four, eight and twelve. There are additional areas of knowledge that do not get the advantage of the bonus listed in the parentheses. All Secondary Skills start at the base skill level. Also, skills are limited (any, only, none) as previously indicated in the list.

Available O.C.C.s (Optional): Instead of selecting the Iborian Healer R.C.C., the player can elect to make his character any kind of Phase World O.C.C. except for Men at Arms. However, the vast majority of Iborians will choose some kind of psychic, science or medical profession, and most prefer their instinctive adventurous Healer R.C.C.

Weapons & Equipment: Iborian Healers start out with 3D4x1,000 credits in weapons and equipment. Iborians of other O.C.C.s start with that O.C.C.'s initial weapons and equipment.

Bionics & Cybernetics: Iborians dislike bionics and cybernetics and will refuse them for personal use. They understand their medical application, however, and if their patients desire, they will fit them with bionic or cybernetic attachments. The vast majority of Iborians will *not* install, maintain, repair or upgrade bionic or cybernetic weapons.

Money: Iborian Healers start with 1D4x1,000 credits in cash. Iborians of other O.C.C.s start with that O.C.C.'s initial money.

Trans-Galactic Empire

In addition to the various TGE races mentioned in **Phase World®** and the **Phase World® Sourcebook**, there are numerous races who play a large part in the Anvil Galaxy sector of the TGE. Among the most prominent of these are the *Kelesh*, *Qidians*, and the *Sinestrians*.

Kelesh R.C.C.

These baroque pack rats are relentless collectors of technology. They are just fascinated with machinery in general, but any kind of novel techno-trinket, especially small things, are highly coveted and must be acquired. The Kelesh are also formidable warriors and traders who value wealth and prestige both for their own purposes and as a means to further acquisitions of technology. They voluntarily joined the TGE because they felt more cultural kinship with the Kreeghor than with the humans of the CCW. The Kelesh are a secretive and exclusive people, however, and their multiple layers of complex social codes are almost impossible for an outsider to decipher. Thus, their society is an impenetrable mystery to virtually all outsiders, making the Kelesh rightly seem aloof and hostile to most other humanoids.

Kelesh Collector R.C.C.

Alignment: Usually Unprincipled, Anarchist or Miscreant. A few may be Aberrant or Diabolic, though Kelesh are almost never good.

Attributes: I.Q. 3D6, M.E. 3D6, M.A. 3D6, P.S. 3D6, P.P. 3D6, P.E. 3D6, P.B. 2D6+1, Spd. 3D6

Size: Six to seven feet (1.8-2.1 m) tall.

Weight: 160-240 lbs (72-108 kg).

Hit Points: P.E. number plus 2D6 per level of experience.

S.D.C.: 3D6+6 plus those acquired from physical skills.

Natural A.R.: None.

M.D.C.: By armor only.

Horror Factor: 9

P.P.E.: 2D6

Average Life Span: 100-125 years.

Natural Abilities: None.

Magic: None.

Psionics: Standard, same as humans.

Combat: Two attacks per melee round or by Hand to Hand Combat training.

R.C.C. Bonuses (in addition to possible attribute and skill bonuses): +1 attack per melee (if the character has hand to hand training only), +1 on initiative, +2 to strike, parry and dodge, +3 to roll with punch or impact, +1 to pull punch, and +1 to save vs Horror Factor.

R.C.C. Penalties: Not exactly a penalty, but Kelesh have a real weakness for cool new technology. It is not quite an obsession, nor is their urge to obtain tech stuff a compulsion, but it is definitely a weakness of theirs, one that wily enemies can exploit if they use their heads.

Kelesh Collector R.C.C.: Nearly half of all Kelesh are *Collectors*, individuals who are part scout, part trader, part salvage expert, and all pack rat.

R.C.C. Skills:

Basic and Advanced Math (+20%)

Languages: Three of choice (+15%).

Basic Electronics (+15%)

Basic Mechanics (+15%)

Mechanical Engineering (+15%)

Computer Operation (+10%)

Recognize Weapon Quality (+10%)

Weapons Engineer (+20%)

Streetwise (+10%)

Salvage (+15%)

W.P.: Any two.

Hand to Hand: Basic, which may be upgraded to Hand to Hand: Expert at the cost of one "R.C.C. Related Skill" or Martial Arts or Assassin (if Anarchist or evil) at the cost of two.

R.C.C. Related Skills: Select 12 other skills, plus select two skills at levels three, six, nine and twelve.

Communications: Any (+10%).

Domestic: Any.

Electrical: Any (+10%).

Espionage: Any.

Mechanical: Any (+10%).

Medical: First Aid and Paramedic only.

Military: Armorer/Field Armorer, Find Contraband, Ship to Ship Combat, and Space Defense Systems only.

Physical: Any.

Pilot: Any (+5%).

Pilot Related: Any.

Rogue: Any.

Science: Any.

Technical: Any (+10%).

W.P.: Any.

Wilderness: None.

Secondary Skills: The character gets four Secondary Skills at level one, and one additional skill at levels four, eight and twelve. There are additional areas of knowledge that do not get the advantage of the bonus listed in the parentheses. All Secondary Skills start at the base skill level. Also, skills are limited (any, only, none) as previously indicated in the list.

Available O.C.C.s (Optional): Instead of selecting the Kelesh Collector R.C.C., above, the player can *elect* to make his character any Men at Arms or Scholar/Adventurer O.C.C., but only about one third are one of these O.C.C.s instead of a Collector R.C.C.

Weapons & Equipment: Kelesh Collectors start with a whopping 2D6x10,000 credits worth of weapons and equipment. The trick is, Kelesh are really into *keeping* their various trinkets on their person, which means that most items are small and the Collector rather looks like a walking high-tech expo. Consequently, they are almost always seen wearing clothing and body armor with many hooks, straps, belts, pouches, harnesses and clips on to which they can attach and carry a plethora of their choicest belongings. Kelesh are incredible pack rats, so they are likely to own tons of stuff they have sentimental attachments to but will never really use. **Note:** Kelesh characters must spend all of this initial W&E money

when creating the character. They are meant to be loaded up with lots of smaller bits of tech, tools, and electronics, not just a few super-expensive items.

At the G.M.'s approval, a Kelesh Collector character may begin with a small starship as well. Most will ultimately pack their vessels full of precious (to them) collectibles. The ship of a Kelesh techno Collector often looks and feels like an old, overstuffed attic, with crates of stuff in the cargo hold and trinkets and souvenirs filling every nook and cranny.

Bionics & Cybernetics: Kelesh *love* bionics and cybernetics and will get them as time, money and circumstance allow. Kelesh Collectors start off with one cybernetic body part of choice with 1D4 special features or weapons installed, or 1D4+4 cybernetic implants.

Money: Kelesh Collectors begin with 3D4x1,000 credits in cash. While always loaded with gear, these beings are seldom cash-rich, in part because they are spendthrifts when in comes to electronics, cybernetics, technology and alien gizmos, and in part because they cannot resist a bargain. Thus, if an item is on sale for more than a 30% discount, a Kelesh wants it all the more. Generally speaking, they cannot resist the urge to blow their savings on a cool new bit of machinery, tech-artifact, etc., they found in a trading post somewhere, even if they have no clue what the tech item does or how to make it work. For these collectors, if it looks exotic and rare, it is that much more desirable.

Note: Game Masters should try to exploit this quirky "collector" aspect of the character for both Player Characters and Non-Player Characters. For example, perhaps the character *accidentally* acquires some rare, helpful, powerful, or sacred device or artifact that somebody desperately needs or wants. If an NPC, the player group may need to find this character and convince him to sell this precious item – something he will be loath to do, especially once he discovers its immense importance or value. At that point the player characters may have to try to steal it, which is likely to involve tricking, subduing and/or battling the Kelesh (and his crew/teammates) and then finding it in the vast warehouse he calls a ship or home. Additionally, Kelesh Collectors *always* keep an ear out for rumors about alien devices and artifacts and are always among those out to get it – the Cosmic Forge being the ultimate collectable. That means the player group is likely to encounter bands of competing Kelesh Collectors whenever they are on a quest to find and recover technology, relics and alien devices. Kelesh Collectors are also frequently found among pirates, salvage teams, cargo haulers and adventurer types.

As a player character, the Collector can be played both seriously and for laughs. In the former case, the character will always encourage his teammates to "go after stuff," and his collecting may get the group in trouble from time to time (i.e. he has that rare, coveted something that the bad guys want or will lead the group on a wild goose chase or take a dangerous mission so he can try to get . . . . "X"). On the more humorous side, the character is unable to prowl because he clunks, clinks and jingles with every step he takes. Likewise, his piles 'o junk may require hiring porters and additional shipping expenses and delays (i.e. he's got six or even twenty suitcases when everyone else has one). Having so much stuff might also attract bandits or pirates although anybody familiar with Kelesh Collectors knows that three-quarters of the stuff is worthless or has minimal value to anybody but the individual collector. And these are just a few ideas. Cut that imagination loose and exploit the potential of this fun character.

Qidian

These fin-headed, golden scaled, barrel-chested reptilian humanoids are notable psychics who have a special aptitude for empathy, sensing danger, and seeing the future. They also are well known for having fits of rage that give them Supernatural Strength (as well as the inability to discern friend from foe; i.e., berserker rage). This makes them a valued if unpredictable member of the TGE, who routinely uses these people for manual labor, the occasional gladiator gig, and as part of a growing corps of psionic operatives and warriors working directly under military aegis. The Qidians are not proud of their fits of mindless rage, and as a result of it, they tend to stick to themselves, hoping to keep away from the things that might trigger their anger reflex. These people do not want to be seen as "monsters" or "primitive," but that is how many view themselves. Generally, most mammalian races find these stocky reptilians a bit frightening.

Qidian Adventurer R.C.C.

Alignment: Good or selfish. Very few Qidians are actually evil.

Attributes: I.Q. 2D6+4, M.E. 4D6+2, M.A. 2D6+4, P.S. 5D6, P.P. 4D6, P.E. 4D6, P.B. 2D6, Spd. 3D6

Size: Six feet, six inches to seven feet, eight inches (1.98 to 2.3 m) tall.

Weight: 250-400 lbs (112.3 to 180 kg).

Mega-Damage Creatures.: 1D4x10 plus 10 M.D.C. per level of experience. May also wear M.D.C. body armor for additional protection.

Horror Factor: 10

P.P.E.: 2D6. **I.S.P.:** 2D6x10 +M.E. attribute number.

Average Life Span: 80 to 90 years.

Natural Abilities: Qidians can hold their breath for a number of minutes equal to their P.E. attribute.

Magic: Not applicable, very few Qidians have the temperament or patience to learn magic.

Psionics: All Qidians possess the psychic Sensitive abilities of *Clairvoyance*, *Empathy*, and *Sixth Sense*. Also see Qidian Seer R.C.C. (see below). Empathy is used without expending any I.S.P. because it is second nature to these beings.

Combat: Two attacks per melee round or by Hand to Hand Combat training.

R.C.C. Bonuses: +4 to save vs insanity and psionics and +3 to save vs Horror Factor.

R.C.C. Penalties: All Qidians suffer from a form of Semi-Mindless Aggression when they are extremely angry or traumatized (i.e. enraged or horrified by the injury or death of a friend, feels trapped and about to die, is subjected to physical or emotional torture, and similar, as well as just being provoked to the point of rage). The following changes/bonuses apply only when in the "berserker rage": +2 attacks per melee round, +4 to initiative, +2 to strike and parry, +50 M.D.C., and their P.S. becomes Supernatural. However, when a Qidian enters this aggressive phase, he cannot tell friend from foe, is unaware of any innocent bystanders or dangerous conditions (i.e. don't breach the hull, be careful of vital controls or explosives, etc.), and fights to kill. Until the Qidian is restrained or all opposition is defeated (those who don't want to fight need to lay low and not move or say anything), the Qidian will continue to fight until he is slain.

Qidian Seer R.C.C.: A good 40-50% of all Qidians live as *Seers*, using their natural powers of psychic insight to further glimpse into the mysteries of the universe, and perhaps to find the means to master the rage that forever seethes within them. Qidian Seers are similar to Mind Melters in their powers and training. <u>Psionic Powers of the Qidian Seer</u>: Receives *all* Sensitive psionics at level one, plus two of choice from the Healing, Physical and Super categories at level two. The Super-Psionic powers of Psi-Sword and Psi-Shield manifest at levels three and four respectively. **Note:** About 10% of all Qidians are Mystics, fundamentally the same as the R.C.C. described in the **Rifts® RPG**.

R.C.C. Skills:

Languages: Two of choice (+15%).

Lore: Psychics & Psionics (+25%)

Basic Electronics (+10%)

Basic Mechanics (+10%)

First Aid (+10%)

Streetwise (+10%)

Hand to Hand: Basic. Qidian Seers may upgrade to Expert at the cost of two "R.C.C. Related Skills" or Martial Arts or Assassin (if evil) at the cost of three skills.

R.C.C. Related Skills: Select eight other skills, but at two must be from Technical and two from Rogue. Plus select one skill at levels four, eight, and twelve. New skills start at first level proficiency.

Communications: Any.

Domestic: Any.

Electrical: Any (+5%).

Espionage: None.

Mechanical: Any (+5%).

Medical: Any (+5%).

Military: None.

Physical: Any.

Pilot: Any.

Pilot Related: Any.

Rogue: Any (+5%).

Science: Any.

Technical: Any (+5%).

W.P.: Any.

Wilderness: Any (+5%).

Secondary Skills: The character gets four Secondary Skills at level one, and one additional skill at levels three, six, nine, twelve and fifteen. There are additional areas of knowledge that do not get the advantage of the bonus listed in the parentheses. All Secondary Skills start at the base skill level. Also, skills are limited (any, only, none) as previously indicated in the list.

Available O.C.C.s (Optional): None, other than Soldier/Grunt, Space Pirate, Vagabond or Mystic. The rest are Seers or simple Qidian R.C.C. psychics who may take on most any simple job (clerk, salesperson, laborer, guard, freelance adventurer, etc.).

Weapons & Equipment: Begin with one modern weapon of choice, one ancient weapon of choice, and 1D4x1,000 credits in other equipment. Qidian Seers get an extra 1000 credits for gear.

Bionics & Cybernetics: Qidians are neutral concerning bionics and cybernetics. They believe that these things are perfectly acceptable to those who need or want them, but the Qidian way is to hold off until one really requires the use of bionics or cybernetics to keep living life properly.

Money: Qidians start with only 1D4x1,000 credits in their personal savings.

Sinestrian

Sinestrians are long (nearly 10 feet/3 m) serpentoids who balance themselves and move about like an upright humanoid, even though they have no legs – just a single, powerful tail (snake-like lower body). To use tools and weapons, they always wear a set of robotic arms, or "waldoes" that are as important and indispensable to them as, say, clothes might be to most humans. They simply do not go anywhere without them. Perhaps because they must always take good care of their waldoes, Sinestrians are natural mechanics who are most in their element when tinkering with some device or repairing a broken bit of hardware. Their home world was destroyed by the TGE many years ago, and most were absorbed by the Empire. Many of them dispersed, however, and sell their impressive mechanical skills on an *independent basis*. Word has it many free Sinestrians yearn for the day when they can all get together and finance a massive rescue operation to free all of the Sinestrians living under the TGE (even the ones who are happy there).

Sinestrian Mechanic R.C.C.

Alignment: Any, but tend toward Unprincipled and Anarchist.

Attributes: I.Q. 4D6, M.E. 3D6, M.A. 2D6, P.S. 20 (robotic; see details below), P.P. 3D6+6, P.E. 3D6, P.B. 3D6, Spd. 4D6

Size: 10 feet (3 m) long, including tail. Stand about 5-6 feet (1.5 to 1.8 m) tall.

Weight: 250-300 lbs (112.5 to 135 kg).

Hit Points: P.E. attribute number +45, plus 1D6 per level of experience.

S.D.C.: 1D6x10.

Natural Armor Rating: 10

M.D.C.: By armor only. Sinestrians must wear specially designed armor, both to accommodate their sinuous, snake-like bodies as well as their bionic "waldo" arms.

Horror Factor: 10

P.P.E.: 2D6

Average Life Span: 100 years.

Natural Abilities: High intelligence and agility, good speed. Has a prehensile tail (works like a tentacle) and moves like a snake. Has excellent balance.

Magic: None. The Sinestrians' universal use of robotic waldoes directly interferes with their ability to master magic, besides, Sinestrians are much more fascinated by the technological than the arcane.

Psionics: Standard, same as humans.

Combat: Two attacks per melee or by Hand to Hand Combat skill.

R.C.C. Bonuses: +3 on initiative, +2 to parry, +4 to automatic dodge (meaning the act of dodging does NOT use up a melee action, but still requires a roll to see if the dodge is successful or not; add any possible attribute and skill bonuses to this number), +2 to entangle and roll with punch or impact, +2 to save vs magic and poison. +1 to save vs psionics and insanity. +3 to save vs Horror Factor.

R.C.C. Penalties: Without their waldo arms, Sinestrians have no fine manipulation abilities. That means they cannot use most weapons or tools well, forced to use their prehensile tail. This seriously hampers combat and skill performance: Reduce number of melee attacks/actions by two, no combat bonuses apply for the tail and skills requiring manual dexterity are -25%.

Sinestrian Mechanic R.C.C.: These aliens have a natural affinity for machinery and robotics.

R.C.C. Skills:
Language: One of choice (+15%).
Basic and Advanced Math (+20%)
Basic Electronics (+15%)
Robot Electronics (+15%)
Basic Mechanics (+15%)
Bioware Mechanics (+15%)
Robot Mechanics (+15%)
Computer Operation (+10%)
Computer Programming (+10%)
Computer Repair (+10%)
W.P.: Any two.
Hand to Hand: Basic, which can be upgraded to Expert for the cost of one "R.C.C. Related" skill or to Martial Arts (or Assassin if evil) at the cost of two.

R.C.C. Related Skills: Select eight other skills, but at least two must be from the Mechanical category. Plus select two skills at level three, two at level seven, and one at levels ten and thirteen. New skills start at first level proficiency.
Communications: Any (+5%).
Domestic: Any.
Electrical: Any (+10%).
Espionage: None.
Mechanical: Any (+10%).
Medical: Any.
Military: Armorer/Field Armorer (+10%), Demolitions, Military Fortification, Recognize Weapon Quality and Trap Construction and Detection only (all are +5%).
Physical: Any, other than Acrobatics and Gymnastics, +10% to Swim skill.
Pilot: Any (+5%).
Pilot Related: Any (+5%).
Rogue: Computer Hacking (+5%) only.
Science: Any.
Technical: Any (+5%).
W.P.: Any.
Wilderness: None.

Secondary Skills: The character gets five Secondary Skills at level one, and one additional skill at levels four, eight and twelve. There are additional areas of knowledge that do not get the advantage of the bonus listed in the parentheses. All Secondary Skills start at the base skill level. Also, skills are limited (any, only, none) as previously indicated in the list.

Available O.C.C.s (Optional): Instead of selecting the Sinestrian Mechanic R.C.C., the player can elect to make his character any kind of Man at Arms or Scholar/Adventurer. Most Sinestrians opt for occupations that deal with machinery, so many of those who are not Sinestrian Mechanics become Operators, Cyber-Docs, or Fixers.

Weapons & Equipment: Sinestrian Mechanics begin with two energy weapons of choice, a robotic tool kit, a suit of light, medium or heavy cyber-armor, and 2D6x1,000 credits in weapons and technology.

Bionics & Cybernetics: All Sinestrians begin with a pair of robotic arms, known as "waldoes." These have a robotic P.S. of 20. Beginning characters may install 1D4 additional weapons or features in their arms. They may also upgrade them later (including increasing their strength) at their own expense.

Money: Having spent almost all of their money on equipment, Sinestrian Mechanics have only 2D6x100 credits to their name when starting out. They typically gain extra money by working as a mechanic or from adventuring plunder.

United Worlds of Warlock R.C.C.s

The UWW is home to numerous races commonly encountered on other worlds and dimensions of the Megaverse, but which at first glance might seem out of place in the Anvil Galaxy. Thus the UWW is trying to integrate its increasingly non-human population into the surrounding worlds without causing too much of an uproar. Time will tell. Of the many races that make up the UWW, four stand out as special: *Star Elves*, *Dwarven Guildmasters*, *Space Minotaurs* and *Ratanoids*.

Star Elves

Tall, slender and beautiful, with thick crops of blonde or red hair, the Star Elves of the Anvil Galaxy seem to be an ancient strain of an elder race, perhaps descended from the Asgardian High Elves. Though races calling themselves "Elves" are encountered in numerous places across the Megaverse, the Star Elves most exemplify the lithe grace and delicate splendor of that most people have come to think of when they imagine Elvenkind. Star Elves are thin, sometimes to the point of looking frail, as if they are meant more for scholarly pursuits or commanding powerful magic rather than wrangling with clamorous technology or engaging in rough and tumble adventuring. However, they are stronger and more durable than they may look, possessing a keen intellect, sharp minds, agility and Supernatural Strength! Many love to mix it up in sports, combat and rough stuff. That having been said, Star Elves *do* have a special aptitude for magic, and many of them become ace spell casters early in life before moving on to another field of study. Haughty, arrogant and aloof, Star Elves also exemplify the holier-than-thou attitude for which Elves are infamous. This attitude does not terribly strain relations between the Elves and other races of the UWW because everybody knows that for all of the Elves' bluster and arrogance, the truth is they would all be dead if they did not belong to a powerful federation of peoples who, by coming together, found the strength to survive.

Alignment: Any, but lean toward Anarchist and Unprincipled.

Attributes: I.Q. 3D6+ 6, M.E. 3D6+2, M.A. 2D6+3, P.S. 3D6 (Supernatural), P.P. 4D6, P.E. 4D6, P.B. 4D6+6, Spd 6D6

Size: Six to seven feet (1.8 to 2.1 m) tall.

Weight: 150 to 230 pounds (67.5 to 103.5 kg).

Mega-Damage Creatures: 1D4x10 M.D.C. +P.E. attribute number and an additional 1D6 per level of experience.

Horror Factor: None.

P.P.E.: 5D6 or by magic O.C.C.

Average Life Span: 1,000 years.

Natural Abilities: Superior physical prowess and beauty, generally high intelligence. Nightvision 120 feet (36 m; can see in total darkness). Natural aptitude and eons of tradition in the art of the long bow (add one extra attack per melee if the Archery skill is taken) and wilderness/ranger skills (+2% on all Wilderness skills). Bio-regenerate 4D6 M.D.C. per hour.

Magic: By O.C.C. only.

Psionics: Standard.

Combat: Two attacks per melee or by Hand to Hand Combat skills.

R.C.C. Bonuses: +1 to strike and dodge, +1 to pull punch, and +2 to save vs Horror Factor.

O.C.C.s: Virtually any Phase World O.C.C. that a human can take, a Star Elf can take, though they tend to lean toward highly skilled and prestigious occupations. Many Star Elves show an extremely high interest in magic and scholastic or scientific pursuits, as well as interest in espionage (they love the challenge and necessity to think quick on their feet) or an

occupation that involve nature such as Wilderness Scout/Ranger/Explorer, and Long Bowman. Their belief that they are a superior race of people often drives them to be the best, thus there are far more warriors of renown, scientists, and men of magic (even Cosmo-Knights) than there are vagabonds and simple laborers or grunts.

Skills of Note: 90% speak and read the Elf language at 98%, and will be literate in two other languages (+20%), speak 1D4 others and know Basic Math (both +20%), in addition to the usual O.C.C. skills.

Weapons & Equipment: Star Elves start with two weapons of choice. They can either be technological or magical (nothing outrageous for the latter and may be magic devices, enchanted weapons or even minor rune weapons). In addition, Star Elves start with 2D4x1,000 credits in extra weapons and equipment.

Bionics & Cybernetics: Star Elves generally avoid bionics and cybernetics unless, for some odd reason, they have abandoned their appreciation for nature and the mystic world, in which case they might trick themselves out with all kinds of cybernetic goodies.

Money: Star Elves will also start with 1D6x1,000 credits in cash.

Note: Star Elves tend to be impudent, arrogant, and elitist in attitude, as well as noble, valiant and spirited. They may be disciplined in their studies and work, but demand a great deal of personal freedom and flexibility, so they do not work well in a military structure unless they are at the top of the food chain or in a position (like spies) where they have a lot of freedom and don't have to follow strict rules and protocols.

Dwarven Guildmasters

A.K.A. Anvil Dwarves

The Dwarves of the Anvil Galaxy are most likely descended from the Asgardian Dwarves who live on a few planets within the UWW that are in fact portals to the deific realm of Asgard itself! These "Anvil Dwarves," or "Dwarven Guildmasters" are especially adept at handling machinery and rune weapons and other types of magical weapons, devices and constructs. Though they are gruff and dour, they are quite likeable in their own way, and they can be very helpful if asked in the right manner. Dwarven Guildmasters never cooperate with somebody if they feel like they are being pushed around, shown disrespect or commanded to do a task they do not want to do. However, if a Dwarven Guildmaster is merely *requested* to carry out a task or service, and treated with respect and consideration (they don't like obvious kiss ups), then that Dwarf is made to feel like his work is appreciated and he will stop at nothing to make sure the job is done to 100% satisfaction. High King Silverlight knows this, and through a mixture of diplomacy and sincere outright flattery, has managed to keep the Dwarven Guildmasters of the UWW loyal, happy and productive. Generally, these small folk want to feel important, needed and appreciated.

The typical Anvil Dwarf has long, flaming red hair typically worn in one or more braids, and most males have a full, mid-length, beard and mustache. Beards may also be braided. Although they seldom exceed four feet (1.2 m) in height, they are powerfully built, possess excellent endurance and Supernatural Strength.

Alignment: Any.

Attributes: I.Q. 3D6, M.E. 3D6, M.A. 2D6, P.S. 4D6+2 (supernatural), P.P. 3D6, P.E. 4D6, P.B. 2D6+2, Spd 2D6

Size: Three plus 3D4+2 inches (3-4 feet/0.9 to 1.2 m) tall.

Weight: 150 to 200 pounds (67.5 to 90 kg).

Mega-Damage Creatures: 2D4x10 M.D.C. +P.E. attribute number and an additional 2D4 per level of experience.

Horror Factor: None.

P.P.E.: 4D6 or by magic O.C.C.

Average Life Span: 250+ years.

Natural Abilities: Superior physical strength and endurance, generally high to average intelligence. Nightvision 90 feet (27.4 m; can see in total darkness). Natural aptitude for weapon design, mechanics and manufacturing, providing a bonus of +10% to all mechanical, military, electrical, and computer skills.

Psionics: Standard.

Magic: By O.C.C., but Dwarven Guildmasters are rarely spell casters.

Rune Smithing: 35% of Dwarven Guildsmasters are versed in the ways of rune magic. This means that, given enough time, preparation, components and adequate facilities, they can create rune weapons and other magical weapons or devices! However, the creation of rune weapons takes months or years of constant work to complete, requires exotic components, incredible amounts of P.P.E., and the sacrifice of a living essence – usually a powerful hero, demon, elemental, creature of magic, godling or god to power the weapon. Consequently, no good aligned character will be-

45

come a Rune Smith, and Anvil Dwarves who take to adventuring or other trade seldom have the knowledge of rune magic. Although Rune Smiths who go adventuring find their knowledge and ability to make rune weapons of little practical use, they can identify/recognize authentic rune weapons, tell the level of power (lesser, greater, greatest), and tell the alignment of the weapon. The smith can also read runes and magic symbols. The Anvil Dwarf smith also has a rudimentary understanding of Bio-Wizardry and the dangers of symbiotic organisms. All Rune Smiths must be Anarchist or evil and will have one lesser and one greater rune weapon of their own! Rune Smiths are not usually spell casters of any kind, though Ley Line Walkers, Wizards and Shifters typically assist them in the creation of rune items.

Combat: Two attacks per melee or by Hand to Hand Combat skills.

R.C.C. Bonuses: +2 to save vs possession and +5 to save vs Horror Factor.

O.C.C.s: Pretty much any O.C.C., except magical ones (Rune Smiths being one of the exceptions). Strongly lean toward occupations that involve mechanics, electronics, construction, and building, whether it be making weapons, machines, electronics, buildings, tunnels or works of art, as well as other down and dirty work like mining or soldiering. They love high-tech weapons, power armor, fast vehicles and machines.

Skills of Note: 70% speak and read the Dwarf language at 98% and Dragonese/Elven (+30%) in addition to the usual O.C.C. skills.

Weapons & Equipment: Dwarven Guildmasters begin with three weapons of choice, usually reflecting their chosen W.P.s and may be technological, magically enchanted, or even minor rune weapons. They also will begin with a suit of M.D.C. body armor and 2D6x1,000 credits in additional weapons and equipment.

Bionics & Cybernetics: Dwarves are a mixed lot on bionics and cybernetics. While they appreciate the mechanics of them, they dislike their interference with magic and nature. As a result, any Anvil Dwarf involved with the magical creation of anything will never get bionics or cybernetics. More than a few Dwarven soldiers, who never had an interest in magic in the first place, are much more likely to get plenty of bionics and cybernetics, especially as they get wounded and need mechanical replacements for the body parts they have lost.

Money: Start with 1D6x1,000 credits or tradeable goods.

Space Minotaurs

As impossible and unlikely as it may seem, these are massive, hulking, red to bronze-skinned humanoids with the head and horns of a bull. In other words, the classic looking "Minotaur" of Greek mythology. No one knows whether they are a so-called "natural life form" evolving on their own, or whether they are the end result of genetic engineering by the Gene-Tech or some other "outside" force. There are actually a surprising number of naturally evolving bovine races, so natural evolution is not as remote as it may seem, however, the Space Minotaur's Mega-Damage physique and Super Strength suggests otherwise.

These muscle-bound giants are the front-line super-soldiers of the UWW. A far cry from the Minotaurs of other worlds and dimensions, the creatures are true powerhouses, able to absorb substantial amounts of Mega-Damage before going down for the count. More importantly, they know no fear and live to serve a greater good, something more important than just themselves. As such, the average Minotaur has no problem laying down his life for his family or friends. Those who fight on behalf of the UWW do so fanatically, and are very formidable opponents, indeed. Perhaps because they dwell alongside the prestigious Dwarven Guildmasters, the Minotaurs of the Three Galaxies show little to no interest in building things, only in combat, sports and roughhousing. They tend to be very aggressive and thrive on military and physical challenges.

Alignments: Any, but tend to be evil or selfish; 40% Anarchist, 25% Aberrant, 25% Miscreant and 10% other.

Attributes: I.Q. 2D6+1, M.E. 3D6, M.A. 2D6, P.S. 4D6+6 (supernatural), P.P. 4D6, P.E. 5D6, P.B. 3D6, Spd 4D6

Size: Seven and a half to nine feet tall (2.3 to 2.7 m).

Weight: 500 to 800 pounds (225 to 360 kg).

Mega-Damage Creature: 2D6x10 +P.E. attribute number, and an additional 2D6 M.D.C. per level of experience.

Horror Factor: 11

P.P.E.: 4D6

Average Life Span: 400 years.

Natural Abilities: Nightvision 100 feet (30.5 m; can see in total darkness), good color vision, superior sense of smell, fire and cold resistant (does half damage), fatigues at half the normal rate of humans.

Psionics: Standard.

Magic: None.

Combat: As per Hand to Hand Combat skills (all Space Minotaurs have a Hand to Hand skill, even females will have at least Basic or Expert Hand to Hand Combat, and most also know Boxing and/or Wrestling) *plus TWO* (the two extra attacks are part of the creature's natural abilities, an R.C.C. bonus).

Bonuses (in addition to possible attribute and skill bonuses): +1 on initiative, +2 to strike and parry, +3 to dodge, +2 to disarm, +3 to pull punch, and +3 to save vs Horror Factor.

Damage: Punching, stomping and kick attacks do Supernatural P.S. damage. A charging head butt with the Minotaur's horns acts as a *power punch* (counts as two attacks), plus it has a 60% chance of knocking the victim of the charge down. The victim loses two melee attacks/actions and initiative, in addition to damage.

O.C.C.: Any Phase World Men of Arms, or any Scholar/Adventurer, except Cyber-Doc. Space Minotaurs strongly lean toward warrior, criminal and adventurer type occupations.

Weapons & Equipment: Start with one melee weapon of choice and three other weapons of choice (high-tech or not), plus 1D4+1 ammo clips for each. They also begin with 2D6x1,000 credits in additional gear.

Bionics & Cybernetics: Space Minotaurs don't mind bionics and cybernetics and often will seek them later in life if they need them. However, since no cybernetics or bionics are likely to match their Supernatural Strength, Minotaurs will not accept bionic limbs lightly for their arms or legs, but when they do, they will be maxed out and contain two or more weapon systems. Implants on the other hand, especially for the head and other parts of the body, might be more readily sought.

Money: Start with 2D6x1,000 credits.

Notes: Space Minotaurs seem to have a liking for large swords and axes. Those familiar with modern weapons like Vibro-Blades and heavy weapons, including rail guns. They will wear body armor, although they usually must have it customized to fit their massive frame and hoofed feet, and love force fields.

Ratanoids

Ratanoids are a race of humanoid rodents who evolved from some sort of nocturnal, rat-like mammal. They tend to dwell in the shadows and corners of larger societies. Natural scroungers, thieves and vagabonds, Ratanoids can be found on every UWW world, whether they are welcome there or not. In the context of the Forge War, Ratanoids have proven their worth as spies, saboteurs and scouts as well as ace scroungers and smugglers who have a knack for finding proverbial needles in haystacks.

Magic is a major fascination for the Ratanoids, so there are Wizards, Warlocks, and Shamans among their numbers. That having been said, most Ratanoids lack the personal discipline to pursue the mystic arts, choosing rather to be vagabonds/drifters, spies, thieves, smugglers, and City Rat (no pun intended) type characters. Those who do learn the secrets of magic often attempt to control powers far beyond their ability to control. This is one of the things that has lured the *free* Ratanoids to Phase World and other places where an independent group or individual can find opportunities for adventure and wealth.

The only thing that keeps these sly schemers from open conquest of any world is their cowardice and lack of self-confidence. Though many a Ratanoid swaggers around exuding false bravado, and shooting off his mouth, as a rule, most Ratanoids lack a strong sense of self-worth and value. Most see themselves as second-class citizens who are not as smart or as good as humans, Star Elves and most other races. This deep rooted perception has prevailed for generations upon generations and is not likely change any time in the foreseeable future. Ironically, this low self-esteem causes the Ratanoids to dramatically underestimate themselves and keeps them from trying to better themselves. Ratanoids rarely attack unless they have overwhelming odds in their favor, though their guile is without measure.

Ratanoids tend to be quiet and shrewd observers, staying hidden in the shadows, ever vigilant and patient for the right moment to seize an opportunity. They are clever, cunning, sneaky and resourceful, although they sometimes play the fool and let their insecurities get the better of them. However, beneath even the most seemingly self-effacing or timid Ratanoid is an opportunist ready strike when the time is right. And even a Ratanoid has his limits and will fight to protect what is his, or to protect a loved one, and even what he believes in.

Ratanoid R.C.C.

Alignment: Any, but most NPCs are selfish or evil.
Attributes: I.Q. 4D6, M.E. 2D6, M.A. 3D6, P.S. 2D6, P.P. 3D6, P.E. 3D6, P.B. 2D6, Spd 3D6
Size: Four to five and a half feet tall (1.2 to 1.65 m).
Weight: 45 to 90 pounds (20 to 40.5 kg).
Hit Points: Standard: P.E. + 1D6 per level of experience.
S.D.C.: 30
Natural Armor Rating: None.
M.D.C.: By armor only.
Horror Factor: 8
P.P.E.: 1D6
Average Life Span: 55 years.
Natural Abilities: Keen color vision, nightvision 60 feet (18.3 m; can see in total darkness), excellent nightvision (can see in one tenth the light that humans need), poor day vision 200 feet (61 m), sensitive whiskers help them maneuver in the dark or when blind (usual penalties are half), keen hearing, climb 70% (instinctive), swim 70% (instinctive), and imitate voices 60% (instinctive). Also see bonuses.
Magic: By O.C.C.; uncommon.
Psionics: Standard; uncommon.
Combat: Two attacks per melee round or by O.C.C. Combat training and skills (such as Boxing).
R.C.C. Bonuses: +3 to parry and dodge, +2 to roll with punch, fall or impact.
O.C.C.s: Any, but lean toward City Rat, general repairmen, operators, spies, scouts, professional thieves, bandits, smugglers, safe crackers, private detectives, snoops, con artists and drifters/vagabonds (often with a focus on rogue, communication, and/or piloting skills).
Weapons & Equipment: Ratanoids begin with two weapons of choice, a suit of light or medium M.D.C. body armor, simple wardrobe, and 2D6x1,000 credits in extra gear.
Bionics & Cybernetics: Cybernetic implants and weapons are very appealing to the tricky Ratanoids, especially if the cybernetic implant is completely concealed. Ratanoid characters may start with 1D4 implants, if the player so desires.
Money: Ratanoids begin with 1D6x1,000 credits, but they usually supplement this through various acts of larceny.
Note: Pretty much everybody distrust Ratanoids, considering them to be thieves, liars and low-lives. Some outright hate them. They are tolerated within the UWW, but just barely. They do prove useful as spies and commandos, and so the UWW military has a purpose for them, but outside of that, they are intensely disliked. Elsewhere in the galaxy, they can expect nothing short of appalling treatment, even in the CCW.

Notes: Ratanoids will use any weapons or armor they can get their hands on. They love high-tech gizmos, especially small, easy to conceal items.

Naruni Enterprises

True Naruni are at the head of the Board of Directors, and the Uteni are the rank and file of the organization. Though members from every other race in the Three Galaxies can be found working for Naruni Enterprises, there are just two races – the *True Naruni* and the *Uteni,* who are the real foundation of the company and run the show. True Naruni stats are reprinted from **Phase World®** for your convenience, and the Uteni are the ones out in front, leading the organization into every major sales venture, acting as the company's public face.

True Naruni R.C.C.
Created by C.J. Carella

Most people think that the Uteni race of bald-headed aliens are the Naruni, but the truth is that the Uteni are simply the front-men and elite salesmen for the mysterious Naruni, a species whose origins remain unknown and goals remain uncertain. The Naruni people don't make public appearances, and always remain behind the scenes. There is no question that they are the driving force behind the trans-dimensional manufacturer and technologies dealer, but they shun the limelight.

The reason why the Naruni prefer to avoid the public eye is simple: their shape is hideous and reminiscent of miniature alien intelligences. Naruni are heavy-set bipeds with hippo-like skins and builds. Three long tentacles run down from where a human's nose would be (which are used for eating, breathing and combat). The tentacles end up in tiny fanged mouths reminiscent of the Splugorth (some people occasionally suggest that the Naruni may be some sub-species of the Splugorth or other alien intelligence, although their differences are much greater than any similarities). The Naruni's eyes are narrow slits with red, iris-less eyes peeking through. They usually wear cloaks to partially cover their disgusting features. Also, they are supernatural creatures whose presence disturbs and scares psychics and other sensitives.

The fact that the Naruni are supernatural beings has led many people to question their motives and goals. Although they seem content in their role as weapon and technology dealers, they are known to sell to all sides in a conflict, and care little about who wins, provided Naruni Enterprises gets paid. This has led some to suggest they are agents of "chaos" and may very possibly have even more sinister plans in store for the Three Galaxies, and other parts of the universe.

Alignment: Any, but most are Aberrant or Miscreant evil.
Attributes: I.Q. 2D6+13, M.E. 3D6, M.A. 3D6, P.S. 3D6 (supernatural), P.P. 3D6, P.E. 3D6+6, P.B. 1D6, Spd 3D6
Size: 6 to 8 feet (1.8 to 2.4 m) tall.
Weight: 300-500 lbs (135 to 225 kg).
Mega-Damage Creature: 2D4x10 M.D.C. +P.E. attribute number and 2D6 M.D.C. per level of experience, but may also use/wear force field generators for additional protection (200-300 M.D.C.).

Magic: None.

Psionics: True Naruni have all Sensitive powers plus Automatic Mind Block, Bio-Manipulation and Empathic Transmission. Considered to be Master Psionics.

Combat: Three attacks per melee round or by Hand to Hand Combat +1 (from the prehensile noses). Almost all True Naruni never train beyond Hand to Hand: Basic. They prefer to let others do their fighting for them.

R.C.C. Bonuses: +1 to entangle, +6 to save vs Horror Factor, and +3 to save vs disease.

R.C.C. Vulnerabilities/Penalties: Suffer double damage from rune and holy weapons.

True Naruni R.C.C.: Rather than select an O.C.C., most True Naruni follow a tried-and-true skill set that is as much a part of their culture as their involvement with Naruni Enterprises, their knack for ruthless business practices, and their penchant for shady dealings.

R.C.C. Skills:
Basic and Advanced Math (+20%)
Languages: Six of choice (+15%).
Lore: Demons and Monsters (+10%)
Basic Electronics (+15%)
Mechanical Engineering (+15%)
Weapons Engineer (+20%)
Intelligence (+10%)
Concealment (+10%)
W.P.: Any two.
Hand to Hand: Basic (never better than this).

R.C.C. Related Skills: Select 12 other skills, but at least two must be from Electrical and two from Mechanical. Plus select two skills at levels 3, 7, 10 and 13. New skills start at first level proficiency.
Communications: Any (+10%).
Domestic: Any.
Electrical: Any (+15%).
Espionage: Any (+5%).
Mechanical: Any (+15%).
Medical: Any.
Military: Any (+10%).
Physical: None!
Pilot: Any (+10%).
Pilot Related: Any (+5%).
Rogue: Any.
Science: Any (+10%).
Technical: Any (+20%).
W.P.: Any.
Wilderness: None.

Secondary Skills: The character also gets to select four skills from the previous list and one additional skill at levels 4, 8, and 12. These are additional areas of knowledge that do not get the advantage of the bonus listed in parentheses. All Secondary Skills start at the base skill level.

Available O.C.C.s (Optional): Instead of selecting the True Naruni R.C.C., above, the character can elect to be any Scholar/Adventurer O.C.C. With the G.M.'s permission, the character can also choose a Psychic O.C.C. True Naruni are ineligible for all other O.C.C. types, especially Men at Arms. These evil slugs just do not find personal combat of any sort appealing enough to follow it as a profession. That is what mercenaries and Repo-Bots are for.

Horror Factor: 11 (12 if over six feet/1.8 m tall).

P.P.E.: 1D4x10 +P.E. attribute number.

I.S.P.: 1D4x10 +10 per experience level.

Average Life Span: 1000+ years.

Experience Level (NPC): Average 1D6+4.

Natural Abilities: Supernatural strength and endurance, very long lived, and heal 1D6x10 M.D.C. per every eight hour period. Three prehensile, tentacle- or trunk-like noses with biting mouths at the end that do 1D4 M.D. per attack and have a 4-6 foot (1.2 to 1.8 m) reach depending on the size of the Naruni. The trunk-like noses can be used like a tentacle to pick up and use weapons and tools but without benefit of any bonuses and -15% skill penalty. A nose/trunk can completely regenerate, but takes 1D4+6 months.

Weapons & Equipment: True Naruni start with a single weapon (mostly for personal defense, usually something small), a force field generator for personal defense and 4D6x10,000 credits in additional weapons and gear. This is a huge amount of stuff to start with, but that is what being a True Naruni is all about, in part. These guys are all connected, and there is no way a True Naruni going out on his own will ever begin with less support from his friends and family.

Bionics & Cybernetics: True Naruni see these things as viable medical replacements, but that is it. They do not get bionics or cybernetics unless they really have a need for them.

Money: True Naruni begin with 2D6x100,000 credits. What can we say? These scum bags are all loaded, even those run by players. Of course, True Naruni all are plotters and planners, so chances are they will keep most or all of this money hidden away so they might have it to take advantage of a big business opportunity when one comes up.

Note: These fellows are just plain repulsive in every way. They might have a veneer of morals or manners, but in reality, they lack both. These characters are best suited as NPCs and villains, and any player wishing to play a True Naruni should get his G.M.'s approval first, and is likely to be an outcast starting out with half the gear and money noted above.

Uteni R.C.C.

Created by C.J. Carella

These aliens are the real backbone of any Naruni commercial venture. Consummate salesmen, traders, deal makers and hucksters, the Uteni are synonymous with Naruni Enterprises, and with double-dealing in general. These intelligent and persuasive beings, for all of their charisma and subtle charm, are not trusted by most folk, even if they have never dealt with Naruni before. Though the Uteni could be successful adventurers, they choose to remain on the back stage of the Three Galaxies, helping their Naruni masters pull the strings of the universe, all the while taking little or no credit for themselves. In fact, because they are the public "the face" of Naruni Enterprises, many people mistake the Uteni for Naruni.

Uteni are lithe, smooth-skinned humanoids with large heads, huge, black, almond-shaped eyes, and no mouth. They are striking because of these distinctions further set off by their light blue skin. Despite their alien appearance, their unusually high Mental Affinity makes it easy for them to win people over anyway. Most Uteni can be seen wearing official Naruni Enterprises dress uniforms at all times. "Rogue" Uteni can be easily identified by their wearing of non-company attire.

Alignment: Any, but tend towards the selfish and evil alignments. The truly good Uteni is an oddity, and they almost never work for Naruni Enterprises.

Attributes: I.Q. 3D6+4, M.E. 4D6+2, M.A. 3D6+2, P.S. 3D6, P.P. 3D6+2, P.E. 3D6+4, P.B. 3D6, Spd. 3D6

Size: Six to eight feet (1.8 to 2.4 m) tall.

Weight: 180 to 240 lbs (81 to 108 kg).

Hit Points: P.E. attribute number +1D6 per level of experience.

S.D.C.: 1D4x100 +20, in addition to O.C.C. and skill bonuses, giving them the rough equivalent of 1-4 M.D.C.

Natural Armor Rating: None; see M.D.C.

M.D.C.: Uteni's high S.D.C. effectively makes them *minor* Mega-Damage creatures (1-4 M.D.C.). They often use Naruni force fields (100-200 M.D.C.; self-regenerating) for additional protection and may also use/wear M.D.C. body and power armor.

Horror Factor: 8, but this has more to do with their reputation from Naruni Enterprises than their physical appearance or presence. See page 44 of **Phase World®** for info on the business.

P.P.E.: 1D6x10

I.S.P.: 1D6x10 plus an additional 1D6 per level of experience.

Average Life Span: 500 years.

Experience Level: 1D4+1 for NPCs. Player Characters start at level one.

Natural Abilities: Limited shape-changing. The Uteni's natural appearance is that of a hairless, light-blue biped, about eight feet (2.4 m) tall, with thin and spindly limbs, huge eyes and no mouth or nose (they breathe through their skin). They can, however, alter their size and features to those of any biped from four to nine feet tall (1.2 to 2.7 m; their weight remains the same). They cannot simulate body hair, and their skin color always remains the same, blue.

Magic: None. The Uteni know about magic and Bio-Wizardry but tend to avoid magic and magic items, relying instead on equally powerful *technology*. Uteni love advanced technology.

Psionics: All Uteni are Minor psionics and can select three powers from one of the psionic categories of Healing, Sensitive or Physical.

Combat: Two attacks per melee round or by Hand to Hand Combat training.

R.C.C. Bonuses: +4 to save vs Horror Factor. Being natural salesmen, Uteni have an additional +20% to their charm/impress percentage on top of whatever their M.A. attribute affords them.

R.C.C. Vulnerabilities/Penalties: Approximately 20% of all Uteni are compulsive gamblers, unable to turn down a wager even if their life depended on it.

Uteni R.C.C.: Most Uteni forfeit an O.C.C. in favor of their "natural" skill set, below, which is nearly identical to that of the True Naruni. The reason for this duplication of skills is the Uteni have practically been bred by the True Naruni to form the "second tier" of Naruni Enterprises, and as such, they bear the same skills that their masters bear.

R.C.C. Skills:

Basic and Advanced Math (+20%)

Languages: Six of choice (+15%).

Lore: Demons and Monsters (+10%)

Basic Electronics (+15%)

Mechanical Engineering (+15%)

Weapons Engineer (+20%)

Intelligence (+10%)

Concealment (+10%)

W.P.: Any two.

Hand to Hand: Exert (can be upgraded to Martial Arts or Assassin (if evil) at the cost of one R.C.C. Related Skill).

R.C.C. Related Skills: Select 12 other skills, but at least two must be from Electrical and two from Mechanical. Plus select two skills at level three, two at level seven, and one at levels ten and thirteen. New skills start at first level proficiency.

Communications: Any (+10%).

Domestic: Any.

Electrical: Any (+15%).

Espionage: Any (+5%).

Mechanical: Any (+15%).

Medical: Any.

Military: Any (+10%).

Physical: None.

Pilot: Any (+10%).

Pilot Related: Any (+5%).

Rogue: Any (+5%).

Science: Any (+5%).

Technical: Any (+20%).

W.P.: Any.

Wilderness: None.

Secondary Skills: The character also gets to select six skills from the previous list at level one and one additional skill at levels four, eight and twelve. These are additional areas of knowledge that do not get the advantage of the bonus listed in parentheses. All Secondary Skills start at the base skill level.

Available O.C.C.s (Optional): Approximately 66% of all Uteni simply go with their R.C.C. Skills instead of pursuing a formal O.C.C. Of those who do go for more specialized training, the following O.C.C.s are available: Bounty Hunter, Forger, Freelance Spy, Master Assassin, Safecracker, Smuggler, Professional Thief, Special Forces/Military Specialist, Headhunter, or any Scholar and Adventurer class. Note that Uteni who pursue an O.C.C. forfeit the R.C.C. Skills listed above.

Weapons & Equipment: Uteni begin with a single weapon of choice, typically something high-tech and easy to conceal (love Phase Technology) and 3D4x1,000 credits worth of extra gear.

Bionics & Cybernetics: They tend to avoid magic, chemical or mental augmentation, and full bionic conversion, but love cybernetic implants and partial reconstruction. Uteni characters may start with one bionic limb and up to 1D4+2 various implants, attachments and cyber-weapons.

Money: Uteni begin with 1D4x10,000 credits.

Note: The average Uteni's allies and enemies are identical to those of Naruni Enterprises. They are used to being hated and feared by most beings in the Three Galaxies, a condition that does not bother them. Uteni working for NE are too busy counting their fat payrolls or basking in the power of their employer to care what the rest of the galaxy thinks of them.

The rare, independent Uteni adventurer often is troubled by the reputation of his people for being Naruni lackeys and ruthless con artists and money grubbers. Such Uteni often reject money and materialism altogether (for a brief while, at least) before coming to terms with the unsavory deeds their people continue to do in the name of Naruni Enterprises.

Player characters start off with half the money noted above.

Gene-Tech R.C.C.

By Kevin Siembieda

The Gene-Tech, also known as Gene-Demons, may be "demonic" by nature, but are not supernatural creatures. Rather, they are wicked aliens of unknown origin and purpose. Many consider them harbingers of chaos, discord and suffering. Gene-Tech regard themselves to be a higher (the highest?) life form in the Megaverse and show a total disregard (sometimes complete disdain) for life in general and completely ignore the laws of even interstellar powers. They are cold-hearted, cruel and evil beings who are always dispassionate, aloof and menacing.

Talking to a Gene-Tech is like talking to a rock or computer program with an icy and edged personality. They seldom answer

Some believe the Gene-Tech *may* be related to the fabled Gene-Splicers found on Rifts Earth and occasionally in the Three Galaxies and elsewhere in the Megaverse. However, there is no evidence that this is the case, other than circumstantial behavioral similarities. Like Gene-Splicers, Gene-Tech are known to kidnap and experiment on innocent people. The most unfortunate "test subjects" will suffer through tests for pain tolerance, mental endurance, the effects of various diseases and other horrible, crippling and agonizing experiments before being killed. The, arguably, lucky ones see their genetic structure manipulated in ways that seem impossible. Transformations that are as easy for the Gene-Tech as a child stacking building blocks to be transformed into something new and different – often something superhuman, but almost always monstrous in appearance and with one or more physical or mental flaws/weaknesses. Gene-Tech may also add advanced bionics to their test subjects, especially when creating a "one of a kind work of art." At least, that's how the Gene-Tech see their creations – as works of art as much as *experiments* in genetic engineering. These "one-of-a-kinds" may be unwilling subjects captured and transformed against their will, or volunteers willing to take a wild chance. (Actually there may be as many as a dozen or so "one-of-a-kinds" who are *similar* creations, although each will look different and will have some sort of personality, physical, mental or mechanical nuance to set him apart from the others). *Unwilling captives* may be enslaved and forced to serve the Gene-Tech, but more often than not (90% of the time), they are released when the genetic wizards are done with them. Thrown away with the other useless garbage or deliberately unleashed into the universe for further research and study (i.e. so the Gene-Tech can see how their "creation" works in the real world or to enjoy the havoc their "creation" may bring about).

Gene-Tech are a bit more social than the legendary and completely enigmatic Gene-Splicers who shun social interaction of any kind and work in complete secrecy toward some unknown agenda. Consequently, a lone Gene-Tech or a small team of 3-7 *may* appear in a massive, alien spaceship or set up "shop" on a space station or (typically advanced) planet (Phase World has one such team of five) where they engage in their own machinations, but have a standing offer to hear "requests" from individuals looking to be transformed into something different and new. Everybody knows this about the Gene-Tech, so if one appears someplace, people know the mad scientist(s) will hear requests. If the request is rejected, as most are, the stoic creature will simply say, "no," or walk away without saying a word (beneath his acknowledgment). If the Gene-Tech are intrigued by the request they will grant it at no charge. However, one must understand that Gene-Tech are by their very nature, cold, clinical and wicked beings, so they may be "intrigued" by almost anything from a scientific challenge to the social, political, psychological, or other ramifications the transformation may have on the individual or more likely, those around him. Of course, a Gene-Tech may just as well grant a request on a cruel whim, i.e. the Gene-Tech knows the individual will suffer mentally or physically or in any number or combination of ways and finds it amusing to themselves. Thus, the fool who undergoes a Gene-Tech transformation is likely to find his new body and powers to be as much (and usually much more of) a "curse" as a blessing. **Note:** "A subject" *always* suffers from disfigurement (P.B. at least half what it was to start with), is often transformed

questions, ignore insults, and brush away or destroy those who intrude upon them with the casualness that a human might brush away an annoying insect. A Gene-Tech doesn't care about a person's problems (or a planet of people for that matter), whether it be a toothache or a life and death struggle against disease, insanity, the law or evil aliens. Empires can rise and fall around them and the Gene-Tech does not care. They are concerned only with their work, whatever that may be, and are always lost to their own secret agenda, presumably something beyond human comprehension.

into something monstrous, suffers from 1D4 insanities and 1D4 weaknesses/vulnerabilities, and is often something to be feared or loathed by others. The transformation is never exactly what the "subject" expects, although he or she *will* get the key powers/abilities requested – the cost, however, is seldom worth it.

One must also understand that these "unexpected and unwanted" side effects and outcomes are not necessary and are deliberately created/instilled by the Gene-Tech either as part of their own scientific or sociological experimentation (want to see how something works, or affects that race, the individual's psyche, etc.), or for fun – their idea of *a joke.* This is why they are known as "Gene-Demons," for they are heartless and cruel without any apparent rhyme or reason. When the Gene-Tech is done, the "subject" is tossed into the world to fend for himself. Protests and complaints over the results, or pleas to be changed back, fall on deaf ears, as do threats of retribution. If the victim attacks his makers, they either strike him down, dead like a mad dog, or incapacitate him and toss him back out into the world. Though sometimes a Gene-Demon will experiment and transform an entire group of people, they usually restrict their handiwork to *individuals,* and seldom accept more than one request in a million. On the other hand, for their own twisted science, psychological, anthropological and sociological experiments, Gene-Tech may transform a population anywhere from a quarter to an entire planet, although such extreme experiments are very rare indeed.

Gene-Tech appear as tall, thin humanoids with sculpted musculature, and long, slender fingers. The eyes and hair are dark, and their complexion is a pasty yellow-white or pale greenish-yellow. Most are over 1000 years old and look to be the equivalent of a 40 or 50 year old human. Those who look to be old are presumed to be many thousands of years old. Those who have a youthful appearance are only around 500 years old. Where they come from or exactly what purpose they serve is a mystery. Gene-Tech seem to serve no master nor world, and even their dedication to mad science often seems bizarre and self-indulgent. At least three-quarters have some form of bionic augmentation in the way of optics, sensors and implants, and half possess a bionic hand or entire hand and arm as a complete bionic surgical and medical appendage that can be removed and interchanged with other arms that fit the situation (see the cover painting).

Gene-Tech R.C.C.

Note: The Gene-Tech is NOT intended for use as a player character. They are maniacal *NPC villains* best left for the Game Master to use as a foil for the player characters and as a dramatic device.

Alignment: 50% Miscreant, 25% Diabolic, 10% Aberrant, 13% Anarchist and 2% other (typically Unprincipled).

Average Attributes: I.Q. 2D6+15, M.E. 2D6+15, M.A. 1D6+7, P.S. 2D6+15, P.P. 2D6+15, P.E. 2D6+15, P.B. 1D6+7, Spd. 2D6+15. They themselves have been genetically re-engineered, with only a small degree of desired randomness.

Size: 7 feet to 7 feet, 6 inches tall (2.1 to 2.3 m).

Weight: 260 to 300 pounds (117 to 135 kg).

Average Life Span: 1000 years plus another 2D6x100 years.

Hit Points: 4D4x10 plus P.E. attribute number and 2D6 points per level of experience.

S.D.C.: 1D6x100. This and their Hit Points effectively makes

them minor Mega-Creatures with about 3-8 M.D.C. Consequently, they also use force field generators to protect them (200-400 M.D.C. that regenerates at a rate of 1D4x10 per every 15 minutes) or M.D.C. body armor.

Natural A.R.: None.

M.D.C.: 75 from light body armor robe, plus force field from sphere.

Horror Factor: 10, but 15 if one faces them strapped down to an operating table!

P.P.E.: 6D6+15, but possess no natural magic powers.

I.S.P.: M.E. attribute number A10 plus 12 points per level of experience.

Average Level of Experience for NPCs: 1D6+9; use the Dragon's experience table for determining higher levels of experience.

Insanity: Obsessed with genetic, psychological and anthropological experimentation, study and torture. At least 70% are extremely sadistic and indifferent toward all other life forms (pathological). The lives of others have little meaning to these cold-hearted fiends. Some have suggested that Gene-Tech have an ongoing rivalry with the Gene-Splicers which also borders on obsession. Perhaps, but the Gene-Tech would never admit such a thing even if it were true.

Natural Abilities: Perfect 20/20 color vision, nightvision 200 feet (61 m), see the invisible, see in the infrared and ultraviolet spectrums of light, ambidextrous, great dexterity and agility, resistant to fatigue (half normal), impervious to disease, and resistant to cold (does half damage).

Magic: None.

Psionics: All *Sensitive* and *Healing* psionic abilities plus the following *Super-Psionic powers:* Bio-Manipulation, Bio-Regeneration, Empathic Transmission, Psychosomatic Disease, Telemechanics (all types), Telekinesis (super), Electrokinesis, Mind Bolt, Hypnotic Suggestion, Group Mind Block, Mind Block Auto-Defense, Psychic Body Field and Psychic Omni-Sight. Considered a Master Psionic.

Combat: Five attacks/actions per melee, plus one additional attack/melee action at levels 5, 10, 15, 20, and 25. Gene-Tech do not ever undergo formal Hand to Hand Combat training and claim to abhor violence. Actually, they love violence, conflict and anarchy as long as they are not personally caught up in it. They personally dislike having to fight themselves, preferring their Monster-X henchmen (described next) or some foolish pawn to do it for them. If attacked they tend to rely on their cunning and natural combat and formidable psionic abilities.

R.C.C. Bonuses (in addition to likely attribute and skill bonuses): +2 on initiative, +2 to strike, +1 to parry, +5 to pull punch, +8 to save vs Horror Factor, +8 to save vs symbiotic union and control, +8 to save vs possession of any kind, +10 to save vs poison and disease, +2 to save vs all forms of magic.

Gene-Tech R.C.C.: All have a high intellect, superior total recall, centuries of education and studies, and an analytical and inquisitive mind. They know entire skill categories: All Communication skills at 80%, all Electrical at 80%, all Mechanical at 85%, all Medical at 98%, all Science at 95%, all Computer skills at 98%, Pilot Related skills at 90% and Pilot: Spaceship and Hover Vehicles at 90%, W.P. Energy Pistol, W.P. Energy Rifle, W.P. Knife, W.P. Blunt and one W.P. of choice.

Secondary Skills: The character can also know 1D6+3 Secondary Skills at level one. No bonuses other than I.Q. are applicable. Selections can be made from: Domestic, Espionage, Military, Physical, Pilot, Rogue, Technical, Weapon Proficiencies or Wilderness.

Standard Equipment:

1. Flying Med-Assistant: A powerful and highly skilled robot artificial intelligence that appears either as a small hover device reminiscent of a toy flying saucer (see cover painting) or a glowing sphere about the size of a bowling ball. When held in the hand, the Gene-Tech and the Auto-Assistant can transmit massive amounts of data to one another in three seconds via the psionic Telemechanics power. Otherwise, the tiny robot can communicate via radio transmission or actually speak in a robotic voice.

M.D.C.: The Main Body has 70 M.D.C. as well as a defensive force field with 120 M.D.C. Flies via anti-gravity with a maximum speed of 80 mph (128 km); space/vacuum capable and moves in complete silence (equal to a *Prowl* of 70%).

Full Communications System: Includes language translator and radio/video receiver and transmitter. Transmission range is a maximum of 100 miles (160 km; double in space).

Full Bio-Med Scan Capabilities: Can monitor up to eight different patients/subjects.

Retractable Arm with Laser Scalpel: Can inflict a range of 1D6 to 6D6 S.D.C./Hit Point damage in 1D6 increments, or 1D6 or 2D6 M.D. as is needed. Used to assist in surgical procedures. The arm also has two tiny fiber optic light appendages and the robot can radiate light like a lantern.

Retractable Arm with Laser: This laser is used for cutting, burning away and other surgical procedures. It can also be used for self-defense or to protect the Gene-Tech. Damage is one S.D.C. point to 6D6 S.D.C. or one M.D. to 3D6 M.D. Maximum range is 100 feet (30.5 m).

Computer Program: Has the following equivalent skills: All Radio, Computer, Pilot Related and Medical skills at 94%, plus Basic Electronics, Basic Mechanics, Biology, Botany, Chemistry, Chemistry, Analytical, and Math (basic and advanced), each at 98%. Has an I.Q. 18.

Bonuses: +1 on initiative, +2 to strike, +4 to dodge, +1 to roll with impact, punch or fall.

2. Protective Robe: 75 M.D.C.; lightweight: 10 pounds (4.5 kg).

3. Multi-System Harness. Provides an additional 50 M.D.C. protection to the upper (main) body, can create a force field with 240 M.D.C. (regenerates lost M.D.C. at a rate of 30 every hour), has a bigger capacity computer, language translator, a bio-med scan that can monitor up to 10 patients/subjects within a 100 foot (30.5 m) radius, self-bio monitor (indicates the Gene-Tech's physical condition with data directly transmitted to implants for second to second information), long-range radio, loudspeaker/voice amplification system, and retractable laser scalpel (inflicts anywhere from 1D4 to 1D6x10 S.D.C. to 2D6 M.D.C. points of damage, maximum range is 10 feet/3 m).

4. Multi-System Optics & Communications Helmet: Includes a multi-optic system, a long- and short-range radio (can monitor and play 10 channels simultaneously) with scrambling capabilities, mini-computer and cryptography program, radar and radiation detection, bio-comp self-monitoring system and language translator. May be linked to Multi-System Harness and communicate with the Flying Med-Assistant as well as numerous monitors, computers and medical equipment.

5. Science/Laboratory Spaceship: Most of the older, more experienced Gene-Tech and virtually all pairs and groups have one medium to large spaceship that is basically a flying genetics and bionics laboratory. These ships are heavily automated and crewed by the loyal Monster-X. Groups and even wealthy individuals may also have one or more laboratories on 1D4 space stations of planets.

6. Nano-Biorestorers. An army of microscopic machines inside the Gene-Tech's body that immediately respond to injury. In game terms, internal organs are repaired in a matter of minutes (one H.P. or S.D.C. per minute), and the Biorestorers leap to action the moment the Gene-Tech gets injured. Also have one or two nano-healing chambers that can restore them to complete health (all Hit Points and S.D.C.) in a matter of 2D6 minutes. Such healing chambers are found on every Gene-Tech spaceship or base of operation (lab).

7. Other items: Just about every piece of medical, computer, sensor and laboratory equipment common to the Three Galaxies is available to the Gene-Tech. They also have a fair arsenal to equip their Monster-X protectors and to use themselves should that become necessary. Ultimately these mysterious beings could be equipped with just about anything other than magic.

Cybernetics & Bionics: One multi-optic eye and 1D4+2 other implants. Half also have an interchangeable bionic hand or arm: one for surgery and medical applications, one for mechanical repairs and one for combat (if necessary), etc.

Money: Most Gene-Tech have untold millions of credits (sometimes billions or trillions) at their disposal, which they use to maintain their nefarious genetic engineering experiments and other science operations.

Note: Most Gene-Tech secretly keep 1D4 clones in storage. These clones have blank minds and are created exclusively to serve as replacement parts and bodies for their creator should they ever be needed.

Gene-Tech Monster-X

By Kevin Siembieda

What this creature may have started out as is anyone's guess, but today the winged four-armed behemoth is known only as Monster-X – the Gene-Tech's personal bodyguard, servant and assistant. While the Monster-X may assist the Gene-Tech in surgery and laboratory work, these dull-witted misanthropes are best equipped as guards, enforcers, and spies. They are skilled trackers, excellent at surveillance and tailing, despite their size, and deadly in combat. For every one Gene-Tech, there are typically four (never less than two) Monster-X within earshot if not at their side. In addition, there are probably another 4-16 Monster-X per Gene-Tech out performing some diabolical mission or task for their master. Monster-X are used exclusively by the Gene-Tech and never sold into slavery or hired out to others. However, if it serves the Gene-Tech's purposes, he may "lend" one or two out, usually to observe test subjects in the field, or to accompany a group of hired guns/adventurers/mercs to make sure its master's best interests are served. The quad-armed gi-

torture and kill other beings, from cute little animals to humans, Kreeghor and Cosmo-Knights. They especially love the hunt, suggesting that they have predatory instincts. As if their physical acumen were not enough, the Gene-Tech have imbued them with special (super) abilities and limited psionics. One of which is telepathy, so that henchman and master may communicate freely without speaking aloud. This comes in handy when plotting what to do to somebody when they are standing right in front of them or strapped to an operating table.

Monster-X R.C.C., a Gene-Tech NPC Henchman

Note: This character can be an NPC villain or optional player character, but only if the G.M. allows it. If a player character, the creature will be a rare runaway who will be severely punished if ever found out by any Gene-Tech (they demand fierce loyalty and obedience from their minions and any known to have rebelled and run off are tortured and either forced back into "service" or, more likely, killed as an example to others). Runaways are also much more likely to be of a good or selfish alignment than usual, but most people will probably see the runaway as an untrustworthy monster and probably a spy working for a Gene-Tech regardless of what he says or does. That's just the way it is. The Monster-X's reputation precedes him and haunts him forever.

Alignment: Any, but typically selfish or evil: 40% Miscreant, 30% Aberrant, 20% Diabolic, 10% Anarchist (or other).
Attributes: I.Q. 1D6+6, M.E. 2D6+4, M.A. 2D6+4, P.S. 3D6+18 (supernatural), P.P. 2D6+13, P.E. 3D6+13 (supernatural), P.B. 2D4, Spd. 4D6+13 running and 2D6+13 x10 flying (150 to 270 or roughly 105 to 190 mph/168 to 304 km).
Size: Approximately 8-10 feet (2.4 to 3 meters) tall.
Weight: 500 to 800 pounds (225 to 360 kg).
Mega-Damage Creature: Main Body: 2D6x10 +180 M.D.C., wings (2) have 65 M.D.C. each, arms (4) have 65 M.D.C. each, legs (2) have 100 M.D.C. each, and the head 120.
Horror Factor: 12
P.P.E.: 6D6x2
I.S.P.: M.E. attribute number x5.
Average Life Span: 230+ years.
Natural Abilities: A pair of large bat-like wings with climbing claws at the joints (see attributes for flying speed). Can hover and glide without making a sound (basically Prowl 85% in the air) and even when flapping their wings they are surprisingly quiet. Not surprisingly then, the Monster-X has keen hawk-like vision and can see a rabbit at two miles (3.2 km) away. The extra pair of arms provides additional bonuses (see bonuses, below) and the creature can bio-regenerate 2D6 M.D.C. per hour. If a hand or arm is lost, it will grow back in 1D6+3 months. Impervious to normal heat and cold, and fire and extreme cold do half damage.

Special: Power of Adhesion: The character can attach himself to any solid surface by his fingers, hands, toes and feet. This means that he can walk on walls or ceilings, and climb any surface effortlessly.

The only limit to this power is the Monster-X cannot carry a heavy load greater than his/her own weight x3, which is still considerable for these supernaturally strong beings. Carrying a greater weight will cause the character to immediately fall off. Speed climbing and crawling along walls and ceilings is equal to half the running speed (see Spd. attribute).

ants are regularly dispatched to run errands for their Gene-Tech masters as well as to spy on rivals and enemies and to "collect" (i.e., kidnap) new test subjects.

Most Monster-X are surprisingly loyal and diligent in protecting their creators and guarding the Gene-Tech's laboratories, spacecraft and possessions. Individually, Monster-X are vicious, cunning and have an endless appetite for fighting and evil. They love to mix it up and enjoy the opportunity to bully, intimidate,

Restrictions: Loose rocks, crumbling plaster, ice, oil or other slippery substances will prevent the character from adhering to a surface (polished metal, chrome, and glass are not considered slippery substances and are easily scaled).

Other Adhesion related abilities and bonuses:

- Automatic Climbing skill equal to 90% proficiency (does not include rappelling); -15% when the character is wearing shoes and/or gloves.
- Add +10% to the Prowl skill but only when climbing on the ceiling, wall or other high place.
- +15% to Palming, Pick Pockets, and Concealment skills.
- +5% to Acrobatics and/or Gymnastics skills.

Special: Supernatural P.S.: This means the typical Monster-X does the following damage: 2D6 M.D. on a full strength punch or kick, 4D6 M.D. on a power punch or kick. The 2D6 M.D. punch damage is added to the damage of a hand-held Mega-Damage weapon such as a sword, axe, etc. Does 1D6 additional M.D. if P.S. is 25-30. Also has Supernatural Endurance.

Magic Powers: None.

Psionics: Deaden Senses, Death Trance, Impervious to Fire, Impervious to Poison, Levitate, Telepathy, See the Invisible, Sense Magic, Mind Block and Intuitive Combat! Considered a Major Psychic.

Combat: Eight attacks per melee round. Selecting a Hand to Hand style of combat provides one additional attack at levels 3, 6, 9 and 12 as well as the usual bonuses!

R.C.C. Bonuses (in addition to possible attribute and skill bonuses): +3 on initiative, +2 to strike, +5 to parry, +1 to dodge (+3 when flying), +2 to entangle, +1 to disarm, +3 to pull punch, +3 to roll with impact or fall, +1 to save vs psionic attack, +4 to save vs possession, +4 to save vs poison and disease, and +5 to save vs Horror Factor.

R.C.C. Skills: In most cases, as much instinct as training.
Basic Math (+10%)
Languages: Three of choice (+10%).
Radio: Basic (+10%)
Basic Electronics (+10%)
Surveillance Systems (+25%)
Intelligence (+18%)
Tracking (people; +25%)
Track Animals (+15%)
Prowl (+20%)
Find Contraband (+14%)
Streetwise (+10%)
W.P., any three of choice.
Hand to Hand: Expert (can be upgraded to Martial Arts or Assassin at the cost of one R.C.C. Related Skill.)

R.C.C. Related Skills: Select eight other skills at level one only.
Communications: Any.
Domestic: Any.
Electrical: None.
Espionage: Any (+10%).
Mechanical: Basic Mechanics, Automobile and Aircraft Mechanics only.
Medical: First Aid only.
Military: Any (+5%), except Trap skills and Field Armorer.
Physical: Any, (often take Boxing and Acrobatics).

Pilot: Any but tends to avoid military vehicles and boats.
Pilot Related: Any.
Rogue: Any (+5%).
Science: Biology and Math only (+5%).
Technical: Any.
W.P.: Any.
Wilderness: Any (+5%).

Secondary Skills: The character also gets to select four skills from the previous list (often Piloting and W.P.s or Physical) at level one and one additional skill at levels 4, 8, 12, and 15. These are additional areas of knowledge that do not get the advantage of the bonus listed in parentheses. All Secondary Skills start at the base skill level.

Available O.C.C.s (Optional): None. They are literally built and designed for the Gene-Tech's specific purpose as protector, enforcer, hunter/tracker and spy.

Weapons & Equipment: Monster-X start with one weapon for each W.P. and will have access to whatever their master allows them to have, which can be considerable or very little depending on the Gene-Tech.

A Monster-X player character will have three weapons of choice, some very basic adventuring gear, plus 2D6x1,000 credits worth of additional gear and hardware such as binoculars and optical/spy gear. Favorite weapons include energy rifles, rail guns, Vibro-Blades, and magic weapons.

Bionics & Cybernetics: None to start and tend to avoid them.

Money: NPCs who serve a Gene-Tech will have whatever his master allows him to keep. Many are allowed to keep items and a third of the cash from victims who fall to them. A player character who is a runaway starts with only 2D6x100 credits.

Golgan Republik

The Golgan Republik contains a wild array of alien races, but most of them are in the process of abandoning the Republik for a better life on their own. The Golgans themselves are still the dominant race, and a number of other races can be expected to stand with the them for the time being. However, it will only be a matter of time and circumstance before those minions go off on their own, leaving the Golgans to fend for themselves once more. For the moment, aside from the Golgans, the most prominent alien races in the Republik include the *Lurgess*, *Ultrovians* and *Zebuloids*.

Golgan

Golgans are tall, thin, pink amphibian humanoids whose distinguishing feature is their large eyes mounted on the side, not the front, of their head. Golgans also do not appear to have a mouth, though they actually do. It is just small and recessed when not in use, but to the casual observer, it might seem a wonder that these creatures can actually talk and eat. Golgans are an ancient race whose survival has rested more on their ability to organize and administrate than on their inherent natural abilities. Golgans are not particularly hardy creatures, but they know how to build an empire, and by getting other beings to do their fighting for them, these frail folk have lived long in the Anvil Galaxy, at times ruling huge portions of it.

The Golgans of today are a far cry from what they once were. Originally a happy and outgoing people, the Golgans have gradually turned cold, cynical and paranoid. Their once great accomplishments have been lost to greed and war. Their current situation is the direct result of their being invaded and attacked by their neighbors so many times. As a result, the modern Golgans trust nobody except themselves, and no government that does not have entirely Golgan leadership at the head of it. They still maintain a veneer of civility and warmth to non-Golgans and to foreigners to their society, but make no mistake: Behind every Golgan smile or handshake is a nervous alien waiting for the moment to pull his sidearm and start firing.

Alignment: Any, but the majority tend toward Anarchist or Unprincipled.

Attributes: I.Q. 3D6+5, M.E. 3D6+5, M.A. 3D6, P.S. 2D6+3, P.P. 2D6+1, P.E. 2D6+2, P.B. 2D4, Spd. 2D6

Size: Six to eight feet (1.8 to 2.4 m) tall.

Weight: 160-260 lbs (72 to 117 kg).

Hit Points: P.E. attribute number plus 1D6 per level of experience.

S.D.C.: 3D6 plus extra points from physical skills.

Natural A.R.: None.

M.D.C.: By armor or force field only.

Horror Factor: None.

P.P.E.: 3D6

Average Life Span: 200-300 years; females typically live up to a century longer than males.

Natural Abilities: Golgans are renowned for their advanced senses, which include *Heightened Sense of Smell*, *Heightened Sense of Taste*, *Heightened Sense of Touch*, and *Heightened Sense of Sight*. Generally, each Golgan individual will have *one* of the following enhanced senses, but some have more than one. Roll on the following table to determine: **01-75%:** One advanced sense. **76-90%:** Two advanced senses. **91-98%:** Three advanced senses. **99-00%:** Four advanced senses. Golgans with all four advanced senses often rise to very high positions in the Republik on the merits of their genetics alone, which gives them special governmental dispensation.

Heightened Sense of Smell: The Golgan has an exceptional olfactory sense with a range of about 100 feet (30.5 m). He can recognize/identify specific odors (70%+4% per level of experience), recognize toxins/poisons or chemicals by scent (50%+4% per level of experience), recognize a person by scent (50%+3% per level of experience), track by scent (50%+3% per level of experience), is difficult to surprise (especially if the Golgan is being approached by enemies upwind of his position), and he is +1 to dodge and +1 on initiative.

Heightened Sense of Taste: The Golgan can identify precisely the components of anything tasted. He can recognize common ingredients such as salt, sugar, spices, etc. (70%+4% per level experience) as well as exotic or foreign ingredients such as poisons, toxins, chemicals, etc. (30%+5% per level of experience). Furthermore, the Golgan will be picky about what he eats. He will almost always select the Cooking skill, and because of his advanced sense, receives a +10% bonus to it.

Heightened Sense of Touch: The Golgan has an uncanny and superior tactile sense. He has a soft, delicate touch and a rock-steady hand. He can recognize and locate very slight differences (scratches, dings, cracks, imperfections, etc.) in textures by touch (70%+2% per level of experience). He can identify fabric and material by touch (60%+2% per level of experience). He can notice minute changes in temperature by touch or close proximity (60%+2% per level of experience). The Golgan gets a +10% bonus to skills that require a light, delicate touch, including Forgery, Demolitions, Pick Pockets, Pick Locks, Palming, Card Sharp, etc. His penalties to strike, parry and dodge for being blind are only -5 instead of the

usual -10 and he is at +1 to strike on an aimed or "called" shot with a thrown item or weapon.

Heightened Sense of Sight: The Golgan can see a small sign or recognize a person's face up to one mile (1.6 km) away. He can also see in both the infrared and ultraviolet spectrums, granting him nightvision of 300 feet (91.4 m), and he has *X-Ray vision* that enables him to see through fabric or paper instantly, through up to one foot (0.3 m) of light material (wood, plaster, fabric, vegetation) per each melee round/15 seconds of concentration, and through up to six inches of heavy material (brick, stone, concrete, metal, M.D.C. materials) for every two melee rounds/30 seconds of concentration. Heightened Sight is the most commonly held Golgan super-sense.

Magic: None.

Psionics: None.

Combat: Two attacks per melee or through Hand to Hand Combat training.

R.C.C. Bonuses: None.

Golgan Administrator R.C.C.: Golgans are natural leaders, organizers and administrators. Though the recent failures of the Golgan Republik are not a good example of this, the truth is Golgans generally have an easy time getting others to work together toward a common goal and getting large organizations to work efficiently. Fully 80% of all Golgans are Golgan Administrators.

R.C.C. Skills:

Basic and Advanced Math (+20%)

Languages: Six of choice (+15%).

Lore: Galactic/Aliens (+10%)

Law (General; +15%)

History (+10%)

Research (+20%)

Cryptography (+10%; for writing secret memos and communiques)

W.P.: Any two of choice.

Hand to Hand: Basic (never better than Basic).

R.C.C. Related Skills: Select 12 other skills, plus select two more skills at levels three, six, nine, twelve and fifteen. New skills start at first level proficiency.

Communications: Any (+10%).

Domestic: Any (+10%).

Electrical: Basic Electronics only.

Espionage: Any (+10%).

Mechanical: Basic Mechanics only.

Medical: First Aid and Paramedic only.

Military: None (that's what soldiers are for).

Physical: Any except Acrobatics, Wrestling and Boxing.

Pilot: Any.

Pilot Related: Any.

Rogue: Computer Hacking, Concealment, Find Contraband, Gambling (Standard & Dirty Tricks), and Streetwise only.

Science: Any (+10%).

Technical: Any (+15%).

W.P.: Any.

Wilderness: None.

Secondary Skills: The character gets six Secondary Skills at level one, and two additional skills at levels four, eight and twelve. There are additional areas of knowledge that do not get the advantage of the bonus listed in the parentheses. All Secondary Skills start at the base skill level. Also, skills are limited (any, only, none) as previously indicated in the list.

Available O.C.C.s (Optional): Instead of selecting the Golgan Administrator R.C.C., the player can elect to make his character any kind of Scholar/Adventurer. Golgans are ineligible for any true Men at Arms, Magic or Psychic O.C.C.

Weapons & Equipment: Golgan Administrators start with one energy weapon of choice, a light suit of M.D. body armor, and 2D6x1,000 credits worth of extra weapons and equipment.

Bionics & Cybernetics: Golgans are neutral concerning bionics and cybernetics. They do not automatically start with any, but may acquire some later in life if they lose a body part or if for some reason they feel they need some kind of augmentation. Many Golgans get data jacks and internal computers for convenience's sake.

Money: Golgan Administrators start with 3D4x10,000 credits.

Note: All Golgans are intellectual elitists, looking down on those not of their station. They also are racist, looking down on any non-Golgan, all of which is exacerbated by their knowledge of the once glorious Golgan history. Golgans of today are the descendants of a once great interstellar power that has lost its station and greatness to be cast down to near the bottom of the heap in the hierarchy of the Three Galaxies. Most Golgans cannot come to grips with their reduced station even though it has been this way for centuries. A few open-minded individuals have broken free of this ancient and calcified mind set, and tend to be the mavericks of Golgan Society, the adventurers, the rebels, and the agitators.

Lurgess

The Lurgess (LURE-jess) are mysterious space-faring nomads, scouts, traders, miners, smugglers, pirates, and mercenaries who have long been a part of the amalgamated society that is the Golgan Republik. Because of their unusual biology, they are infamous plague carriers, often hosting up to a dozen different pathogens deadly to other races and which could infect huge areas if left uncontained. Although the Lurgess are immune to the diseases they carry, they are hyper-sensitive to nearly all other pathogens common to the Anvil Galaxy. Thus, for any Lurgess to mingle safely among "off-worlders," either the Lurgess must remain in a fully contained environmental suit or the aliens they are meeting with must wear similar protection. As a courtesy, and for their own protection, Lurgess routinely wear super-heavy environmental armor wherever they go, taking it off only when they are in their own private, specially pressurized personal chambers (home). Even when Lurgess are meeting with other Lurgess, they wear their armor until they can be sure their visitors have not picked up any foreign bugs that might prove harmful.

Predictably the Lurgess are disliked and shunned by nearly all sentients out of an inherent fear of infection. The vast majority of Lurgess are hard-working, honest, inventive, courageous and noble, but they are a walking bio-hazard not just to a single person, but to entire planetary populations. As a result, Lurgess are often *prohibited* from landing on *any* planet that is not colonized by the Lurgess themselves. For their part, the Lurgess often do the same to foreigners visiting their worlds. The risk of infection is just too great.

Unfortunately, the fear of this race is promoted by a very small minority of Lurgess terrorists, pirates and mercenaries who use their infectious nature as a terror weapon. After all, who won't give in to the demands of a terrorist whose threat is to pop his armor and contaminate an entire ship, station, city or planet? Who will fire on a Lurgess soldier when doing so risks breaching his armor and causing an infectious outbreak? For individuals such as these, the hatred of the Lurgess continues, despite the overwhelming efforts of the rest of the race to contribute positively not only to the Golgan Republik but to the Anvil Galaxy at large.

Alignment: A full 90% of Lurgess are good: 40% Principled, 50% Scrupulous with another 5% Unprincipled, 3% Anarchist and the remaining 2% are evil (any).

Attributes: I.Q. 3D6+1, M.E. 3D6, M.A. 3D6, P.S. 2D6, P.P. 3D6, P.E. 2D6, P.B. 2D6, Spd. 3D6

Size: Six feet (1.8 m) tall.

Weight: 150-200 lbs (67.5 to 90 kg).

Hit Points: P.E. attribute number plus 1D6 per level of experience.

S.D.C.: 3D6.

Natural A.R.: None.

M.D.C.: By armor only. Lurgess wear super-heavy suits of environmental power armor, described below, over a light environmental contamination suit (5 M.D.C.).

Horror Factor: 14 ("Cripes! You didn't *talk* to him, did you? He's a Lurgess! Quick, into the disinfecting chamber before you contaminate the whole ship!")

P.P.E.: 1D4x10

Average Life Span: 160-200 years.

Natural Abilities:

Contagion: At any given time, any Lurgess carries 3D4 super-lethal pathogens that will spell certain doom for any non-Lurgess exposed to them. An alien exposed to a Lurgess pathogen must immediately save versus disease by rolling 15 or better on a D20 for every melee round (15 seconds) he is exposed to the pathogen! If the character saves, it means he has not contracted a Lurgess disease. If he fails, he has contracted a disease and is quickly on the way to becoming a statistic.

For most people, exposure to Lurgess pathogens happens when a Lurgess' suit is breached somehow (by combat, an accident, or the rare case of a Lurgess intentionally opening his suit to infect those around him). In game terms, the radius of infection is 10 feet (3 m) for the first melee round (15 seconds), 30 feet (9.1 m) for the next melee round, 60 feet (18.3 m) for the next melee round, and 120 feet (36.6 m) for the next melee round. Thus, in just one minute a Lurgess can contaminate a 120 foot (36.6 m) radius. For every minute thereafter, the Lurgess will infect a radius of 120 feet (36.6 m) wherever he goes. After that, the infection will spread on its own, but at a rate determined by the G.M. Some Lurgess contagions spread through the air like wildfire, covering an entire city within a day or so, but thankfully, most Lurgess diseases require actual close proximity contact, and consequently, are reasonably easy to contain if caught quickly. Others are slower, requiring physical contact with contaminated surfaces. In all cases, the only way to avoid contamination is to not enter an area hit by a Lurgess plague, quickly seal it off and begin sterilization/decontamination of the environment and those contaminated – or to wear full environmental protection when you do. **Note:** There are cures for the majority of even the most virulent Lurgess plagues, but victims must be treated within 3-12 hours in most cases to survive, and these diseases spread so fast that hundreds, thousands and even hundreds of thousands can become infected (spreading the contagion) in a matter of 48 to 72 hours unless immediately contained.

The exact effects of a Lurgess contagion are also left to the G.M., since they are so varied in effect and intensity. Here are a few ground rules. Within 1D4 hours of exposure, characters will begin to weaken, generally at a rate of one P.E. per hour. Unless the character receives intense medical treatment (i.e., in a hospital, immobilized, and in a full environmental sort of treatment cell), his P.E. will eventually dwindle to zero and he will enter into a coma. When his P.E. dwindles to minus his original P.E. score (e.g.: when a character with a P.E. 15 reaches -15), he dies. Only intense, high-tech medical treatment will halt the progress of the disease, eradicate it, and begin bringing the character back to full health. While infected, characters will spread the contagion just as a Lurgess might to anyone who comes within a 120 (36.6 m) radius of them, everywhere they go. Again, only by receiving full environmental treatment can this effect be halted. If a crowd of people get infected, one can easily see how they might infect a much larger area once they disperse and start infecting other people.

G.M. Note: The Lurgess contagion is a cocktail of different super-virulent, super-lethal diseases. The Lurgess contagion should not be used as a weapon by player characters or NPCs, mostly because it is so debilitating and potentially threatening to game balance. It is really meant more as a dramatic device and adventure hook. What happens to the heroes when their Lurgess buddy's armor gets breached? How does one stop a Lurgess doomsday terrorist cell from infecting an entire planet? How does one retrieve their stolen property off a ship of Lurgess pirates or do they write it off as lost? What if the Cosmic Forge is contaminated or falls into the possession of the Lurgess? These are the sorts of things the Lurgess contagion is meant for, not to kill player characters or NPCs without any chance for survival. Use your head when implementing this character into your game for the best results. Let it get out of control, and it will hurt your game. Here endeth the lecture.

Magic: None. Lurgess are unable to practice magic.

Psionics: Standard, same as humans.

Combat: Four attacks per melee or by Hand to Hand Combat skill. The Lurgess *exoskeleton* is what adds an additional two attacks per melee (this is why untrained Lurgess have four attacks instead of just two).

R.C.C. Bonuses: Ironically, Lurgess are 100% immune to poisons of any kind. Note that diseases and poisons are *not* the same thing.

R.C.C. Penalties/Vulnerabilities: The Lurgess are extremely sensitive to any non-Lurgess pathogens. That means the very effects they can inflict on others they themselves will suffer if they come into contact with alien germ bugs. This means if a Lurgess is infecting a place, chances are, the Lurgess himself will become infected by some common germ too. The only time this is not the case is on lifeless worlds or hermetically sealed and filtered closed environments (like spaceships or space stations or even certain environmental habitats on worlds with hostile environments). In addition, all Lurgess are -6 to save against them and -10% to save vs coma/death. Also -1 to save vs magic.

Lurgess Nomad R.C.C.: Most Lurgess are space travelers, wanderers, merchants and explorers. Their diseased nature condemns most of them to lonely lives out in space, where they can do the least harm to the least number of people.

R.C.C. Skills:
  Basic and Advanced Math (+20%)
  Languages: Three of choice (+15%).
  Basic Electronics (+15%)
  Robot Electronics (+15%)
  Mechanical Engineering (+15%)
  Robot Mechanics (+15%)
  Nuclear, Biological & Chemical Warfare (+20%)
  Pilot Spacecraft: Small (+10%)
  Pilot Spacecraft: General (+10%)
  Salvage (+10%)
  Space Contacts (+15%)
  W.P.: Any two of choice.
  Hand to Hand: Basic, but a Lurgess Nomad can upgrade to Expert at a cost of one "other" skill and to Martial Arts (or Assassin if Anarchist or evil) at a cost of two "other" skills.

R.C.C. Related Skills: Select eight other skills, but at least two must be from Mechanical and two from Technical. Plus select two skills at levels three, six, nine and twelve. New skills start at first level proficiency.
  Communications: Any (+5%).
  Domestic: None.
  Electrical: Any (+5%).
  Espionage: None.
  Mechanical: Any (+5%).
  Medical: Any (+10%).
  Military: Any.
  Physical: Climbing, Swimming, Aerobics, Space Combat: Zero Gravity (basic or advanced), Space Depressurization Training, Space Movement, and Space Oxygen Conservation only.
  Pilot: Any (+5%).
  Pilot Related: Any (+5%).
  Rogue: Palming, Concealment, Prowl, Pick Pockets, Computer Hacking and Safe-Cracking only.
  Science: Any.
  Technical: Any.
  W.P.: Any.
  Wilderness: None.

Secondary Skills: The character gets four Secondary Skills at level one, and one additional skill at levels four, eight and twelve. There are additional areas of knowledge that do not get the advantage of the bonus listed in the parentheses. All Secondary Skills start at the base skill level. Also, skills are limited (any, only, none) as previously indicated in the list.

Available O.C.C.s (Optional): Instead of selecting the Lurgess Nomad R.C.C., the player can elect to make his character any type of basic Soldier/Grunt, Spy, Smuggler, Scholar/Adventurer or Psychic O.C.C.

Weapons & Equipment: Lurgess Nomads start with two weapons of choice plus another 2D6x1,000 credits in additional weapons and equipment. All Lurgess also start off with either the standard Lurgess Environmental Armor (described below), or a suit of power armor of their choice. Most Lurgess go with their standard Lurgess armor because it is a symbol of their culture and because it is non-threatening as well as able to take a hit without breaching.

Bionics & Cybernetics: Lurgess are fond of bionics and cybernetics because they offer a way out of their pathogenic nature. A *full conversion* Lurgess cyborg is no longer a walking plague factory. They can travel freely among other people and do not even let others know they are even a Lurgess, so they can live without the stigma that follows the Lurgess people. If a Lurgess cyborg's head or brains or other internal organs gets destroyed, then there is a 01-15% a contagion will infect the area of his death or the site where he is buried unless decontamination and containment procedures are taken – a Lurgess' remains are an active bio-hazard.

Still, most Lurgess prefer to live in their armored suit because undergoing a full conversion is as much an abandonment of their culture and heritage as it is an abandonment of their bodies. The average Lurgess just can't bring himself to do it.

Money: Lurgess Nomads begin with 2D6x1,000 credits.

Lurgess Environmental Armor with Exoskeleton

M.D.C. by Location:
- Main Body – 400
- Arms (2) – 150
- Legs (2) – 200
- Head – 250 (A difficult target to strike. Requires a called shot at a -3 penalty.)

Physical Strength: 50 (robotic).

Speed: <u>Running</u>: 150 mph (240 km). <u>Leaping</u>: 25 feet (7.6 m) high or across. Jet assist to 100 feet (30.5 m) high or 200 feet (61 m) across.

Bonuses: +2 attacks/actions per melee round, +2 to initiative, +1 to strike and parry, +2 to dodge.

Environmental Protection: This suit of armor is an entirely self-contained environment for the wearer. A Lurgess can spend the rest of his life in one of these suits because it is an environmental cell which contains raw material for food, a means of getting additional food and water, and waste processing. It is typically changed once a year.

While wearing this suit, a Lurgess is 100% safe from outside pathogens, as well as spreading his own contamination to the outside. There is little fear of a "leak" until the original M.D.C. of the suit is reduced by 80%. Whenever 20% or less of the armor is left, the character and those around him begin to fear for their lives and the suit will rupture when all M.D.C. is gone.

Weapons & Equipment: Lurgess armor comes unarmed. Characters can pay to have weaponry installed (as well as other features, such as tools, jet packs, etc.), but at twice the normal cost because of the peculiar nature of this armor's design and the general unwillingness of most weapon smiths to handle Lurgess armor.

Ultrovian

Ultrovians (ul-TROVE-ee-ens) are large, squat amphibian creatures with striped or spotted skin, fish-like mouths, and eyes on the sides of their head. They have broad torsos and thick limbs, casting an imposing image. As the resident spell casters of the Golgan Republik, Ultrovians fancy themselves experts in all matters arcane, even though their own abilities typically pale before the magical might of the UWW's top mages. Ultrovians are considered to have a great deal of raw talent when it comes to magic, but they do not have the long history of skill and technique needed to have truly mastered the mystic arts. As long as that remains the case, Ultrovians are overly concerned with *proving* their legitimacy as practitioners of magic. This means they might take foolish risks, try dangerous magical experiments, and make deals with supernatural powers they do not

fully comprehend. In this regard, Ultrovians are a bit like a kid who just discovered his dad's gun – powerful, but perhaps more dangerous than useful.

Be that as it may, the Golgan Republik considers having the Ultrovians in their ranks as a coup for the Forge War, as these aliens can easily travel to the galactic Core, bypassing the dangerous *Threshold*.

Alignment: Any.

Attributes: I.Q. 2D6+6, M.E. 2D6+6, M.A. 2D6+6, P.S. 3D6+6, P.P. 2D6+6, P.E. 3D6+6, P.B. 1D6+3, Spd. 3D6+6

Size: Seven to eight feet (2.1-2.4 m) tall.

Weight: 350-600 lbs (157.5 to 270 kg).

Hit Points: P.E. attribute number +50, plus 2D6 per experience level.

S.D.C.: 3D6x10 making them minor Mega-Damage creatures with the equivalent of 1 or 2 M.D.C. points.

Natural A.R.: 12

M.D.C.: By armor, force field or spell only.

Horror Factor: None.

P.P.E.: 1D6x10 plus whatever additional P.P.E. is afforded by one's Magic O.C.C.

Average Life Span: 300 years.

Natural Abilities: Ultrovians have a natural aptitude for spell casting, and automatically receive a bonus of +1 to their spell strength. They also recover P.P.E. at twice the usual rate.

Magic: By O.C.C., most are spell casters of some kind.

Psionics: None. Ultrovians have no psychic potential.

Combat: Two attacks per melee round or by Hand to Hand Combat training.

R.C.C. Bonuses: +2 to save vs magic, +3 to save vs Horror Factor. +1 to save vs insanity.

R.C.C. Penalties: For all of their magic abilities, Ultrovians are unable to regenerate their P.P.E. at an accelerated rate when on a ley line or a ley line nexus. In fact, when at these locations, they recover P.P.E. at half their usual rate. Likewise, an Ultrovian sorcerer (even a Line Walker) can only draw upon half the usual amount of available ley line P.P.E. Nobody has a clue as to why this is.

Available O.C.C.s (Optional): Approximately 80% of all Ultrovians take up some kind of Magic O.C.C. (any, except those that require psionics, like the Mystic). Another 10% become scientists or engineers, 7% some sort of scholar/teacher/explorer and the remaining 3% typically become an adventurer, man at arms or criminal, but that 3% are shunned by the rest of Ultrovian society.

Weapons & Equipment: Ultrovians begin with a common, low-power, magic weapon and a force field generating suit or a light to medium suit of magical M.D.C. body armor. Ultrovians also have a language translator, portable computer, notebooks, three writing utensils, and another 1D4x1,000 credits worth of additional gear.

Bionics & Cybernetics: NONE for practitioners of magic for the ill effect they have on spell casting, but non-magic O.C.C.s may get implants and bionics as they please. Start with none.

Money: Ultrovians begin with 2D4x1,000 credits.

Zebuloid R.C.C.

By Bill Coffin & Kevin Siembieda

The bizarre Zebuloids look as if they have evolved from some kind of armored jellyfish. Their heads are huge, circular domes covered in plating from which sprout two short, armored eye stalks from the sides along the bottom. Also from the bottom is a mass of writhing, sucker-less tentacles on which the Zebuloids stand and move, and which they use as arms and hands. They are in constant motion, either riding on their undulating tentacles or sitting still but with their tentacles reaching out to touch three or four things at once or just kind of twitching and undulating at all times.

Despite their weird looks, Zebuloids are extremely intelligent and compassionate. They love to pilot vehicles, starships and robots, and can perform multiple tasks simultaneously thanks to their mass of tentacles and the way their minds work. Their quick reflexes, advanced brains, and multitude of tentacles make it easier for them to process the many demands of piloting than it might be for most "standard" humanoids. Thus, a single Zebuloid can function as pilot, navigator, communications officer and gunner without missing a beat.

Considered monsters by so many other alien races, the Zebuloids voluntarily joined the Golgan Republik because the Golgans were one of the few groups of people who actually treated them with decency and respect. As such, Zebuloids are incredibly loyal to their Golgan patrons and will never abandon them, even when it becomes obvious that the Republik's final dissolution is imminent.

Alignment: Any, but 20% are Principled, 30% Scrupulous, 30% Unprincipled, 15% Anarchist and 5% other.

Attributes: I.Q. 4D6+4, M.E. 3D6+12, M.A. 3D6+3, P.S. 3D6+2, P.P. 3D6+12, P.E. 3D6, P.B. 1D6+1, Spd. 1D4x10+9

Size: Tentacle mass is 1D4+5 feet (1.8 to 2.7 m) tall/long but are usually curled at the bottom. The Zebuloid's giant, bony skull section is another 3-4 feet (0.9 to 1.2 m) tall for a total height of 7-9 feet (2.1 to 2.7 m). However, even tall Zebuloids can position their tentacles to make themselves roughly the same height as their companions. Besides, the low eye stalks make it easy for them to look at others eye to eye.

Weight: 220-250 lbs (99-112.5 kg).

Mega-Damage Creature: The main body of the armored head has 1D4x100 M.D.C. +3D6 additional M.D.C. per level of experience. The eye stalks (2) have 100 M.D.C. each and the 1D4x10+18 tentacles have 35 M.D.C. each.

Horror Factor: 13 from their frightful appearance to those who are not familiar with these gentle beings. Only H.F. 8 for those who come to know the Zebuloids, but that changes back to 13 if one faces an angry or evil Zebuloid.

P.P.E.: 2D6

Average Life Span: 90-120 years.

Natural Abilities: Keen, 20/20 vision with polarizing eyelids that automatically engage when needed, excellent hearing (though god only knows where the ears are hidden), high sense of touch, climbs at 98/98% and swims at 88% (maximum depth is 600 feet/183 m), plus the following special abilities.

Special: Pilot Savant: Zebuloids can jump into any kind of vehicle and have a 40% chance of accurately piloting it. Any specific piloting skill a Zebuloid takes gets an additional +20% bonus. It is not uncommon for Zebuloids to have a 98% ranking on several piloting skills.

Special: Tentacles: The Zebuloid tentacle mass automatically gives them W.P. Paired Weapons, in addition to the various bonuses listed below. A Zebuloid can stretch its tentacles to almost 20 feet (6.1 m), or they can shrink them in so much they fit underneath the alien's bony skull plate. When fully withdrawn, the Zebuloid sort of looks like a big turtle shell on the floor. They have 1D4x10+18 tentacles. All are extremely dexterous and have a high sense of touch. When 3-6 are used in concert as a separate bundle of tentacles, they can work like hands, or the super-long fingers of a hand, to manipulate one particular device without skill penalty. Even a single tentacle can use weapons, tools and objects with only a -1 penalty to their normal bonuses and -5% to the performance of a skill.

Special: Multi-Tasking, Compartmental Brain: Can perform as many as four separate and distinct tasks simultaneously, such as fly a vehicle, parry and attack, strike back and radio for help all at the same time.

Magic: None. The Zebuloids have never shown any interest in arcane matters.

Psionics: Standard.

Combat: 14 melee actions or attacks per melee round!

R.C.C. Bonuses (in addition to likely attribute and skill bonuses): +4 on initiative, +5 to parry, +4 to dodge, +4 to disarm, +6 to entangle, +5 to pull punch, and +4 roll with impact.

R.C.C. Penalties: None, aside from their inability to wear any kind of body armor. This makes Zebuloids a bit skittish when not in some kind of protective vehicle.

Zebuloid Space Nomad or Pilot R.C.C.

R.C.C. Skills: Zebuloids are just gifted in certain areas that make them ideal as navigators and pilots.

Languages: Three of choice (+15%).
Basic and Advanced Math (+25%)
Astronomy (+20%)
Navigation (+20%)
Land Navigation (+15%)
Pilot Spacecraft: Small (+20%)
Pilot Spacecraft: General (+20%)
Read (& Operate) Sensory Equipment (+20%)
Computer Operation (+15%)
Space Contacts (+10%)
W.P.: Any two of choice.
Hand to Hand: None. Can not take a Hand to Hand skill.

R.C.C. Related Skills: Select 14 other skills, but at least two must be from Communications, Piloting, and Pilot Related. Plus select two other skills at level three, six, nine and twelve. New skills start at first level proficiency.

Communications: Any (+5%).
Domestic: None.
Electrical: None.
Espionage: None.
Mechanical: Any.
Medical: None.
Military: Ship to Ship Combat (+15%) only.
Physical: Only space related skills.
Pilot: Any (+Savant Piloting bonus of +20%).
Pilot Related: Any (+Savant Piloting bonus of +20%).
Rogue: Computer Hacking (+10%), Concealment (+20%), Palming (+20%), Pick Pockets (+5%), Pick Locks, Prowl, and Streetwise only.
Science: Any.
Technical: Any (+5%).
W.P.: Any.
Wilderness: None.

Secondary Skills: The character gets four Secondary Skills at level one, and one additional skill at levels four, eight and twelve. These are additional areas of knowledge that do not get the advantage of the bonus listed in the parentheses. All Secondary Skills start at the base skill level. Also, skills are limited (any, only, none) as previously indicated in the list.

Available O.C.C.s (Optional): Instead of selecting the Zebuloid Space Nomad R.C.C. the creature can select any of the following: Spacer, Galactic Tracer, Space Pirate, Runner, Colonist, and virtually any type of space jockey/pilot, navigator, computer guru or systems operator type O.C.C.

Weapons & Equipment: By O.C.C. A Space Nomad will have a portable computer, language translator, backpack, and other basic gear.

Bionics & Cybernetics: Zebuloids do not like bionics and cybernetics and will avoid getting them, even if they are common among their chosen O.C.C.

Money: Zebuloid Space Nomads can earn a pile o' money as an exceptional navigator or pilot, but start with 2D6x1,000 credits or by O.C.C.

Altess R.C.C.s

The Altess Dynasty has, through genetic engineering and breeding techniques, refined its people into a slightly more evolved version of the human race. These are the Altess, and they are, according to the Dynasty, the new face of humanity itself. On the surface, there is nothing unusual about them except they are especially good looking and physically fit. However, they possess attributes and abilities far beyond the range of ordinary humans, as anybody who has tangled with one can attest.

The Altess

Attributes: I.Q. 2D6+12, M.E. 2D6+10, M.A. 4D6, P.S. 2D6+10 (supernatural), P.P. 2D6+12, P.E. 2D6+10, P.B. 3D6+9, Spd. 2D6+12

Size: Six feet, six inches (1.95 m) tall.

Weight: 140-180 lbs (63 to 81 kg).

Mega-Damage Creature: 1D4x10 +P.E. attribute number and 1D6 M.D.C. per level of experience.

Awe Factor: 10

P.P.E.: 4D6

Average Life Span: 250 years.

Natural Abilities: Same as normal humans but all are at the top level, i.e. perfect 20/20 vision, keen hearing, etc. They also bio-regenerate 1D4 M.D.C. per hour.

Magic: By O.C.C. only. However, the vast majority of Altess never pursue the mystic arts.

Psionics: Standard, though each Altess gets a bonus of +10% when rolling to determine psychic ability.

Combat: Three attacks per melee or by Hand to Hand Combat skill.

R.C.C. Bonuses (in addition to likely attribute and skill bonuses): +1 attack per melee, +2 on initiative, +2 to strike, parry and dodge, +3 to pull punch, +1 to disarm and entangle, +1 to roll with punch, fall or impact, +2 to all saving throws, and +20% to save vs coma/death.

R.C.C. Penalties: None per se, except that most Altess possess a jaded, superior attitude that makes Star Elves look humble in comparison. To their way of thinking, the Altess are the supermen destined to one day control the universe. Only they are so smug and secure, and so insulated by vast wealth and power, that they generally do nothing to advance their race's station in the Anvil Galaxy. As a result, the average Altess is lazy and non-productive, and far more likely to pay somebody to do something for him than to do something for himself. That is why, despite their potential as soldiers and champions, so few ever do anything with their lives aside from sip wine, hold dinner parties, engage in petty contests and challenges to prove their superiority in mind and body, and check up on their investment portfolios.

Altess Noble R.C.C.: This is what the Altess really seem to think they are cut out for – a life of living in luxury, enjoying the finer things, and generally distancing one's self from adversity and hardship as much as possible. For the Altess, that distance can be quite large, leading these haughty nobles to become a bit detached from reality. As a result, they tend to believe that they have a right to absolutely whatever they want, that everybody is beneath them, and that the sooner the Altess control everything, the better off the universe (or at least the Anvil Galaxy) will be.

R.C.C. Skills:

Basic and Advanced Math (+20%)

Languages: Three of choice (+20%).

Lore: Galactic/Alien (+15%)

Law: Space (+10%)

Art (+15%)

Breed Dogs (+15%)

Falconry (+10%)

History (+15%)

Research (+15%)

Seduction (+20%)

Hand to Hand: Basic, but may upgrade to Expert at the cost of one "other" skill or Martial Arts or Assassin (if Anarchist or evil) at the cost of two "other" skills.

R.C.C. Related Skills: Select 14 other skills, but at least two must be from Electrical and two from Technical. Plus select two skills at levels three, seven, ten and thirteen. New skills start at first level proficiency.

Communications: Any.

Domestic: Any (+10%).

Electrical: Any.

Espionage: Any (+5%; Altess love intrigue and backstabbing).

Mechanical: Any.

Medical: Any.

Military: Military Etiquette and Recognize Weapon Quality only.

Physical: Any (+5% where applicable).

Pilot: Any (+5%).

Pilot Related: Any (+10%).

Rogue: Any (+5% to most, but +13% to Seduction).

Science: Any (+10%).

Technical: Any (+10%).

W.P.: Any.

Wilderness: Any.

Secondary Skills: The character gets six Secondary Skills at level one, and one additional skill at levels 3, 6, 9, 12, and 15. There are additional areas of knowledge that do not get the advantage of the bonus listed in the parentheses. All Sec-

ondary Skills start at the base skill level. Also, skills are limited (any, only, none) as previously indicated in the list.

Available O.C.C.s (Optional): Well over 85% of all Altess opt for the Altess Noble R.C.C., which stresses leisure pursuits more than anything. The remainder either become some kind of skilled expert or "specialist," typically a know-it-all scholar/adventurer. Occasionally an Altess may take up espionage or become a man at arms. If the latter case, they usually join the *Armoria* – the Altess Dynasty's armed forces. However, less than one percent take a military career, though 3% enjoy spy work and espionage.

Weapons & Equipment: If they are on their home world, it is a safe bet an Altess Noble can get his hands on whatever weapons or equipment he needs. Adventuresome player characters can tap their formidable wealth to buy any necessary weapons, armor, gear or vehicles.

Bionics & Cybernetics: Altess Nobles find these things to be the height of kitsch. No matter how much one conceals the nature of an artificial body part or implant, the truth remains that one is partly mechanical, and that simply is *not* up to style. Injured Altess generally opt for expensive medical regeneration to replace lost body parts rather than rely on bionics or cybernetics. Of course, soldiers in the Armoria have no such compunction, and readily mod themselves out. Armoria characters may start with up to 2D6 different implants, features and cyber-weapons.

Money: Altess Noble Non-Player Characters (NPCs) have at their disposal between three and eighteen *million* credits (3D6x1,000,000)! By adventurers standards, this is a huge amount of money, but for the average Altess, it is just a day's petty cash. For Altess Nobles out on their own, their money is their power. They do not like to fight, they like to buy their way out of things. As a result, this money might very well dwindle rapidly as an Altess gets in and out of scrapes. Or, the Altess Noble could use this cash to fund adventurers, explorers or henchmen (i.e. the player characters) for his further gain, personal enjoyment or machinations, or secret intrigues or petty vengeance. Obviously, this kind of crazy money can upset game balance which is why only NPCs and villains should have these kinds of resources (Altess pulling the strings behind the scenes make excellent villains). Even then, the NPC should not be the player group's private backer with an endless pocket, and the Altess is likely to turn on them or place them in a position where they must defy or act against their benefactor/employer at some point – after all, they are *expendable inferiors*. **Note:** A player character is either an Altess who is undercover, slumming or a (at least temporary) social outcast for some despicable reason, with "only" 1D4x100,000 credits to his or her name and about 60,000 credits worth of equipment from weapons and armor to vehicles and wardrobe already purchased.

·FREDDIE·E·WILLIAMS·II·

The Halo

The outermost portion of the Anvil Galaxy, and the area most accommodating to carbon-based life forms such as humans and the other main races of the **Phase World®** setting, the Halo, is where much of the *action is*. The many different power blocs here vie for supremacy against each other just as much as they try to outwit and outpace each other in the race to discover and obtain the Cosmic Forge. Not only that, but Cosmo-Knights and their various allies and rivals have begun gathering forces within the Halo, ostensibly for a massed exploration or assault of the *Threshold*. Until they do, they are in the Halo, and all of the potential for conflict and catastrophe that comes with them is, for the moment, also the problem of the Halo's denizens. Add to this already unstable mix a healthy dose of deadly galactic phenomena, the ever-present threat of attack by unknown aliens, the presence of magic and inter-dimensional anomalies, as well as a hundred other hazards not yet encountered or catalogued, and the Halo is indeed a very exciting, amazing and dangerous place in which to live. For many of the heroes and hardcases who call the Halo their home, that very danger is what they like most about the place.

The Powers That Be

There are literally thousands of different governments, alliances, civilizations and societies extant within the Halo alone. Most of these control only a single planet or at best, a single solar system. The Halo contains millions and millions of stars – solar systems with or without planets – thus it stands to reason that there are more "small political powers" here than could reasonably be counted. These **Independent Systems**, as they are called, only make up a small portion of the Halo. The rest of it is controlled by *nine superpowers* referred to as **Power Blocs**. These are the real movers and shakers of the Halo and much of the Anvil Galaxy. When they go to war, the entire galaxy shudders. When power blocs like these experiences great prosperity, then so does the rest of the galaxy. For many Minor Powers, dwelling in the shadow of such impressive power blocs can be intimidating and perhaps even a little frustrating, since these mighty nine groups do so much to dictate politics, economics, and the overall mood of the Anvil Galaxy. In the long run, Minor Powers deal with the major Power Blocs the way one might when living at the foot of a great mountain chain. One gets used to living amongst forces far greater than he, and must be content with what *they* can do themselves.

The nine power blocs of the Halo include:

The Consortium of Civilized Worlds (CCW). The premier civilization of the Anvil Galaxies, and indeed of the Three Galaxies. A loose federation of worlds, the CCW is a major force of freedom, justice, equality and opposition to tyranny in this and the other of the Three Galaxies.

The Trans-Galactic Empire (TGE). A huge and oppressive government that rivals the CCW in its scope and power, the TGE is dominated by the evil Kreeghor, aliens bent on conquering all of the Three Galaxies and setting themselves as absolute rulers of everything.

The United Worlds of Warlock (UWW). The third largest power in the galaxy, the UWW is the top civilization in which magic plays an important role. Thanks to their ongoing magical experimentation, the UWW has become unusually powerful and prosperous, considering how young and relatively small their civilization is (for a top-flight Power Bloc, anyway).

The Cosmo-Knights. While not a power bloc or a political entity per se, the Cosmo-Knights have, for reasons they do not discuss outside of their order, converged on the Anvil Galaxy in greater numbers than ever before. For those who would hatch a crazy plot of galactic domination, or some other crime, the chances are good that if such deeds would affect an entire world or solar system, at least one Cosmo-Knight would arrive to get involved. The exception to this is entering magic-rich worlds, which might be peaceful, but whose eldritch energies still pose a threat to the mighty Cosmo-Knights.

Naruni Enterprises. Easily the Three Galaxies' largest single manufacturer of military technology, Naruni Enterprises holds a virtual monopoly on arms dealing in the Anvil Galaxy. They are challenged only by the Hartigal Combine, an organization that Naruni created itself and now faces rebellion from.

The Hartigal Combine. Formed as a subsidiary of Naruni Enterprises's Research & Development Division, the Hartigal Combine has broken away from Naruni and has established their own base of factories and sales channels. All they really do is knock off Naruni technology and sell it at a much lower price, and for that, Naruni has sworn to destroy them.

The Golgan Republik. Once an enormous civilization of peace-loving aliens, the Golgans were beset by enemies and marauders from all sides and very nearly destroyed. Now they are an aggressive, suspicious lot bent on absorbing as many other worlds around them as possible, so they might have a buffer zone against further incursions. Only the Golgans themselves are dying, and what remains of their civilization is rapidly unraveling.

The Altess Dynasty. The longest-lived human civilization in the Anvil Galaxy, the Altess Dynasty is ruled by a race of advanced humans who have unlocked the key to longevity and lazy power. They claim to be direct descendants from The First, but then again, so do a lot of other civilizations. The thing is, the Altess might actually have the means to *prove* their claim, and to many alien civilizations, this makes the Altess very dangerous.

The Central Alliance. A motley assortment of balkanized and warlike worlds brought together only by the sole military exploits of the gladiator-despot *Ogor Noldek*, who has personally conquered the worlds he controls, and has made cybernetic enhancement a virtual requirement for citizenship. The Alliance makes a small splash on the galactic politics stage, but the killer cyborgs this society produces are among some of the most eagerly sought after mercenaries and killers in the Anvil Galaxy.

The Consortium of Civilized Worlds

Population: 7 trillion sentient beings total, 2.1 trillion in the Anvil Galaxy.

Demographics: 21% Human, 20% Noro, 14% Wulfen, 11% Catyr, 10% Seljuk, 24% Other (over 200 races, each of which comprises less than 1% of the total population); in the Anvil Galaxy, three of the most prominent of these races include the *Durosk, Faustians* and *Iborians*, which are fully described in the Aliens section of this sourcebook.

Overview

The CCW is the largest and most influential civilization of the Three Galaxies, matched only by the Trans-Galactic Empire (TGE). Founded several centuries ago through the union of the human and Noro civilizations, the CCW received an early baptism of fire in its conflicts with the TGE. In the aftermath of that largely inconclusive conflict, the Consortium has opened its arms to any worthy civilization that wishes to join its ranks.

The CCW's main goals are self-defense and peacekeeping. It rules through the principles of "enlightened self-interest," and minimizes its intrusions in the affairs of individual governments. Member planets are free to conduct their own governments, laws and societies as they see fit, as long as certain rights are preserved for all citizens. For example: *Slavery* is forbidden throughout the Consortium's planets and citizens cannot be imprisoned or executed without a trial. In theory, all Consortium members are models of freedom and harmony. In practice, some worlds are ruled by exploitative dictatorships or other oppres-

sive governments who use loopholes in the loose laws of the CCW to oppress their people.

The Consortium comprises 231 **member races** and about 100 associated races spread over 5,000 inhabitable planets, thousands of space stations, bases and terra-forming colonies on hostile worlds. "Member races" include any space-faring species who control a planet belonging to the CCW. Many of these species control only one planet and may have just learned to build simple spacecraft. Member races are given full citizenship rights and can conduct their own affairs as they see fit, as long as they respect the bylaws of the Consortium.

Associated races are alien species whose civilizations are technologically underdeveloped. A strict policy of noninterference is enforced on those worlds, limiting contact to a few small trading and scientific outposts. Such restrictions in trade and communication with other worlds are monitored and enforced by the *Consortium Authority*. Associated races are protected by the CCW's armed forces. When they reach the appropriate level of technology, they are invited to join the Consortium as full members, but are free to declare independence if they wish to do so.

The CCW in the Anvil Galaxy is on more of a military standing than in the Corkscrew or Thundercloud Galaxies because of the **Forge War**. Local CCW commanders have devoted a fair amount of military and other government resources to search for the Cosmic Forge as well as to keep tabs on the TGE's activities, and to encourage many of the smaller independent civilizations of the galaxy to ally with the CCW rather than with the TGE or some other force. In this regard, the Consortium tends to play a little more hardball than it ordinarily would. The **GSA (Galactic Security Agency)**, the CCW's equivalent of the CIA, NSA and FBI rolled up into one, has been extremely busy and can be found in strength pretty much anywhere the CCW has a hold. Since they don't want to provoke a war with the Kreeghor/TGE, the CCW thought that to get things done it would expand its espionage base and flood their domain with covert GSA operatives who, with their skill and special abilities, can do much to thwart the TGE and speed the Consortium's pursuit of the Cosmic Forge without letting the TGE know that the heat is on.

In many CCW sectors, GSA offices are authorized to hire *independent contractors* on a temporary basis. Such freelancers are used most often for missions where "plausible deniability" is required, and where the operative probably doesn't stand a good chance of surviving (though they don't tell the hired mercenaries and adventurers that last part). In some sectors, the GSA office relies on freelancers so heavily that they practically *are* the GSA. Sometimes this works well, but mostly it is a recipe for disaster. Efficiency goes down, corruption goes up, and TGE infiltration becomes an epidemic.

Ironically, the search for the Cosmic Forge has stunted scientific development in the CCW, largely because funding is going into the military and the GSA. For most scientists to continue their work, they must find alternate funding somehow. In many cases, promising new technologies remain half finished while the CCW continues its high-stakes and expensive game against the TGE. The scientific community can only hope that when the Forge War cools off, they will receive their funding once more and the CCW can continue its otherwise steady march towards better technology in all fields — transportation, communications, medicine, weapons and armor, field generation, cybernetics, holographics, and so on.

CCW Government

The Consortium of Civilized Worlds is not as organized or controlled as a typical nation from 20th Century Earth. In some ways, it is similar to the American Confederacy during the Civil War; a loose alliance of "states" that has limited authority over the internal affairs of its members. All members of the Consortium must become signatories of the Civilization Compact. The Compact is a pledge to follow a number of basic guidelines. If those guidelines are ignored, the signatory planet can be expelled from the Consortium, or its government may be removed by force.

The rules of the Civilization Compact are fairly simple and not very detailed, since they are meant to cover many different races, cultures and civilizations. Like all laws, the Civilization Compact is often ignored, sidestepped, or broken. Several dozen worlds ruled by dictatorships or other exploitative and repressive governments are members of the Consortium. While slavery is illegal, in many places people become wage slaves, making barely enough to survive, or are eternally in debt to their employers. Some unscrupulous entrepreneurs quietly engage in limited slave trade outside of CCW space. Overall, however, most planets follow both the letter and the spirit of the Civilization Compact. There are four prime tenets to the Compact, otherwise known as the *Four Freedoms*. They are:

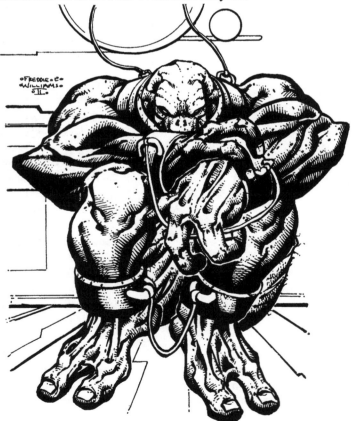

1) Freedom From Slavery. Slavery is outlawed in all Consortium planets and territories. Slaves may not be owned, sold or transported in Consortium space and any slaves who are found there are considered to be free people and are automatically granted asylum by CCW authorities.

2) Freedom From Conquest. No Consortium member may engage in the conquest or colonization of other worlds without the consent of the Consortium at large. Violent conquest of other planets is expressively forbidden by the Compact and it cannot be carried out under any circumstances. Permission to colonize uninhabited worlds is usually granted, but such activities are monitored to ensure that the planet does not have intelligent races or even the potential to evolve intelligent species who may be compromised by the colonization process.

3) Freedom From Anarchy. All signatory worlds must be represented by a planetary government. In special cases, only an area of a planet is granted membership to the Consortium and the rest of the world is left out of its jurisdiction. Ordinarily though, balkanized worlds are refused membership to the CCW. Likewise, member worlds that enter into civil war have a five year grace period to cease hostilities and reunite their civilization or they will face expulsion. This threat of exile is often enough to get warring nations to broker peace for the greater good of the world.

4) Freedom From Tyranny. All signatories must pledge to respect a number of certain rights, including the right to property, the right to a fair trial, and the right to elect government representatives. In the Anvil Galaxy, this Tenet has been expanded to include the right to personal expression, the right to worship freely, and the right to bear arms.

In addition to the Compact, each member world has its own form of government. Several hundred planets are also organized in sub-confederations of their own. The three biggest ones are the Human Alliance, the Noro Federation and the Wulfen Republic, each of which represents over a hundred planets and trillions of inhabitants.

There are three government branches in the Consortium of Civilized Worlds: The *Consortium Congress*, the *Ministries*, and the *Galactic Courts*. **The CCW Congress** proposes and approves laws and has representatives from all member planets. The number of Members of Congress (MCs) per planet is determined by the total population, economical, political and military contributions to the CCW and a number of other factors. The congress then elects a smaller number of Congressional Speakers who cannot exceed two hundred. It is they who do most of the debating on important issues. Laws are voted upon by the entire congress, with a two-thirds majority being needed to pass a law or proposal. Predictably, this system often makes it impossible to reach important decisions quickly.

The CCW Ministries are a number of political offices elected by representatives in a galactic-wide general election held every six Standard years. The Prime Minister is somewhat similar to a president, with the power to issue executive orders, pass decrees and declare war. There are also about a dozen other Ministers, including Defense, Interplanetary Affairs, and Discovery and Development, but their decisions can be overruled by the Prime Minister. However, overruling the edicts of a Ministry is not done lightly and can be taken to the Congress for arbitration.

Finally, the **CCW Galactic Courts** enforce the laws of the Consortium. A large corps of judges and public attorneys is established through the Consortium planets. There are two courts of appeals and a supreme court in each sector. A judicial sector comprises 2-40 planets, depending on their size and population. These two courts can overturn laws they find unconstitutional.

Alphabet Soup:
the CAF, GSA and TVIA

There are also three government organizations that have influence and jurisdiction on all member planets and the associated worlds. They are the *Consortium Armed Forces* (CAF), the *Galactic Security Agency* (GSA) and the *Treaty Violation Investigation Agency* (TVIA). Many citizens and government officials refer to these entities as part of the Consortium's "alphabet soup" – all of the agencies referred to by acronym rather by name. By that logic, the CCW itself might be lumped in with the alphabet soup, as well as the Consortium's many *Independent Defense Forces (IDFs)*, described in the next section.

The CAF (Consortium Armed Forces) protect the space ways and act as the equivalent of the Coast Guard. In addition to the space fleet, it has garrisons at every member planet to assist in matters of defense and security. Ordinarily, the CAF cannot intervene in the domestic affairs of member worlds, unless ordered to do so by the Consortium. However, things being how they are in the Anvil Galaxy, the Consortium Congress recently passed an emergency resolution authorizing CAF generals to conduct temporary "interdictions" on member worlds if there is reason to believe that a threat to the Consortium at large is present there. Examples include the presence of a terrorist network with the ability to destroy a planet, a large group of Kreeghor infiltrators, or the presence of some new alien staging an invasion route into CCW space. Naturally, locals don't like these interdictions and claim they are just the first step in a long slide towards tyranny on the Congress' part. Time will tell on that one.

Aside from emergency interdiction, intervention on a member planet can only be authorized by a two-thirds majority of the Consortium Congress. More common reasons for interventions might include crises that seem to threaten only that planet, such as political instability, economic meltdown, a rampant disease, natural disaster, pirate or mercenary attack, etc. The CAF is also involved in the further exploration of the rest of the Three Galaxies and beyond.

The CAF is not all guns and glory, however. Fully half of its strength is devoted to its exploration arm, known as the **Discovery Corps**. Members of the Discovery Corps are among the best trained and famous members of the CAF. The majority are trained officers with years of experience in space travel and exploration. The Corps are the brave souls who are spearheading the hands-on search for the Cosmic Forge. This includes traveling to worlds to dig up leads, scouting out possible worlds that may bear evidence of the Cosmic Forge's location, and crossing the Threshold to conduct explorations of the Core. The Discovery Corps has also been saddled with the occasional reconnaissance mission into TGE space to keep tabs on what the Kreeghor are up to. Discovery Corps scouts loathe such duty, claiming they are explorers, not spies. To the other half of the CAF and to the GSA, there is little difference between the two in this atmosphere of impending conflict.

Besides the CAF, the Consortium has the **GSA (Galactic Security Agency)** that serves a number of special functions. The agency acts as a *planetary police force* that is roughly the equivalent of the FBI. This police force investigates violations of the Civilization Compact, acts of espionage and terrorism, smuggling (especially the smuggling, sale and possession of harmful drugs, weapons and slaves), and other criminal activity that affects or involves more than one planet or people. The GSA also has a covert operations arm that conducts its own intelligence-gathering (spy) operations on other worlds. It is roughly equivalent to the CIA. As mentioned before, in the Anvil Galaxy, the GSA has received *enormous* funding in light of the Forge War, and they are perhaps the single largest government agency in the CCW in terms of personnel. Most of what the GSA does is top secret, however, so most citizens do not know that the GSA is as big as it is, nor do they know what they are up to. However, the GSA has been a little *too* good at covering its tracks, for there is just about no information on these guys whatsoever, which is a red flag to investigative journalists that clearly, the GSA are hiding plenty. For those few in the know, this has led to the joke that "GSA" really stands for "Got Secrets, Anyone?" (**G.M. Note:** GSA agents typically receive intensive training and whatever equipment or cybernetics they require. They are the best of the best in the galactic intelligence business, and they are very tough customers. They make for great Non-Player Characters as well as player characters, so don't discount the prospect of a GSA-intensive campaign, especially if you enjoy spy adventures and covert ops in space.)

TVIA (Treaty Violation Investigation Agency): The Consortium enforces the Civilization Compact through the Treaty Violation Investigation Agency. The TVIA is charged with discovering any violations of the Civilization Compact and other treaties and agreements, both within the CCW and between the Consortium and other planetary governments. Their chief mission is to ensure that primitive peoples are *not* exploited, enslaved or defrauded by the citizens, businesses and governments of the CCW. Inspectors make periodic visits to associated planets and often place agents undercover among possible treaty violators. The TVIA has often been charged with being corrupt and subject to bribery and petty internal politics. As a result, the Agency is now spending almost as much time policing itself as it is watching treaty violators. However, TVIA Internal Affairs is almost as corrupt as the very offenders it is policing, making a bad situation worse. With impending war against the TGE, however, cleaning up the TVIA, or enforcing the Compact is actually a fairly low priority for the CCW's top officials. They are too busy focusing on the Cosmic Forge and the Forge War and all those things they entail. Depending on how the future plays out, the CCW's overt neglect of upholding its own Compact might return to haunt them and threaten the stability of the entire Consortium.

Independent Defense Forces (IDFs)

Although the Consortium Armed Forces (CAF) keep garrisons on or near most member planets of the CCW, the organization simply does not have the manpower and funds to fully protect every planet. In the Anvil Galaxy, those systems bordering TGE territories have rather large forces in place, leaving the more "interior" systems to fend for themselves. That is okay by these member worlds, since they generally prefer to have a relatively small CAF detachment that can deal with major threats but which aren't large or powerful enough to become a law unto themselves. (Again, the systems bordering the TGE feel a little differently since they live on what will become a front line, so they want all the CAF units around them that they can get.)

For local protection, most member planets and planetary collectives have Independent Defense Forces, the Consortium's equivalent of a militia or National Guard. The IDFs are accountable to the government that funds them, and not to the CAF, although in an emergency, the CCW Congress can "draft" any and all IDFs into the regular armed forces. The mission of the IDF is to defend planets from outside threats. They do not have police or patrol powers and cannot operate beyond a planet's star system, except when "deputized" by a CAF officer. IDF deputization is typically reserved for recruiting additional forces to chase pirates, mercenaries or other belligerents who have hit a member planet and fled the system, requiring a chase/hunt and out-of-system confrontation. Rather than try to coordinate with the IDFs of any system the fugitives might flee to, the CAF simply deputizes the IDF of the victimized planet to go after the bad guys, with strict CAF supervision, of course. So far, this method works well, since IDFs do not like to ride roughshod over other worlds, and when they do track their quarry to a specific planet, then they work jointly with the local IDF to finish the job.

IDFs have their own uniforms, weapons and equipment. Some imitate CAF designs, often purchasing surplus uniforms and vehicles and then altering them slightly to distinguish them. Others prefer to make their troops stand out, and have completely different gear. At the "core worlds" of the CCW, where raids and other threats are almost unheard of, the IDFs are little more than a paramilitary club in which storekeepers, students and young professionals get to play soldier a few times a year in return for tax credits or scholarship opportunities. On frontier planets where the danger of violence is very real, the IDFs are as well-trained and equipped as the planet can afford. Naruni Enterprises often supplies IDFs within the Consortium. However, most CCW members distrust the trans-dimensional weapon dealers, so many of them make do with obsolete CAF ships and weapons purchased at very low prices and with generous credit terms granted by the government. A few have established weapons contracts with Hartigal Manufacturing for cut-rate Naruni tech, but the CAF frowns on this as it gets the Naruni bent out of shape. And, since the CAF and Naruni are major trading partners, the CAF is willing to step on a few IDFs' toes to keep their Naruni counterparts happy.

A few planets use the IDF as a private army with which to twist or avoid the Four Freedoms of the Compact. On a few occasions, rivalries or disputes between two worlds have ended violently when the IDFs of one or both planets involved decided to take matters into their own hands. There have even been some incidents when an IDF fired upon CAF ships or personnel! These have been isolated cases, however, since the largest IDF in the Consortium is only a fraction of the size of the CAF, and no planetary defense force could hope to successfully defy the CAF in the field of battle for long. Eventually the vast numerical superiority of the CAF would win, but the CCW does not like fighting its own worlds. It would rather blockade offending planets and starve them into submission, if at all possible.

Veterans of an IDF often move on to service in the CAF and vice versa. There is some degree of animosity between the two military forces, however. Many CAF officers distrust IDFs, seeing them as armies that are loyal to their *local interests* first and to the Consortium as a whole, second. Several IDFs view the CAF as an impersonal war machine that does not care about the fate of one planet as long as the greater whole is preserved.

Former IDF forces and personnel who dislike the CAF have a strong tendency to form their own private security companies, providing military solutions for large multi-planetary clients (governments without an army or big companies or super-rich individuals). While these organizations like to think of themselves as legitimate security experts, the CAF views them as mercenaries and borderline criminals to be monitored very closely. It is a good bet that every such security company has an extensive GSA file on them and their chief personnel.

Foreign Affairs

Trans-Galactic Empire: The TGE is the CCW's main rival, and the two have been locked in an intractable state of cold war for as long as anyone cares to remember. The state of hostilities between these two superpowers of the Three Galaxies is seen by many to be a barometer of the overall political stability of the region. At the heart of this conflict is a single unalterable truth: the Kreeghor-dominated TGE will not rest until it conquers the Three Galaxies. To expect anything else from the Kreeghor is like expecting a sun not to burn or water not to flow. The Kreeghor are creatures of war, and every molecule of their being cries out to fight and conquer, and as long as they continue to control the TGE, that civilization will remain on a permanent war footing. Unless equally powerful groups like the CCW oppose them, the CCW believes, the TGE would ride roughshod over the whole Three Galaxies (true), and so it is the CCW's duty both as a beacon of justice and out of self-preservation to counter the TGE's every move, especially in the Anvil Galaxy where the goal for this struggle is ultimate power itself: the acquisition of the Cosmic Forge.

In the news and entertainment of the Consortium, the Empire is presented as an evil, monster-ruled civilization where massacres and other atrocities are commonplace (an exaggeration, but with more than a grain of truth). The GSA covert operations branch spends most of its efforts secretly aiding the Free World Council and its freedom fighters, as well as spies on the Empire regularly. By the same token, a number of TGE Imperial spies also operate in the CCW, causing terrorism and unrest. Of course, both sides claim they are helping "freedom fighters" while their enemies support terrorists. Tensions remain high between these two collectives and many analysts believe that war is inevitable.

United Worlds of Warlock: The CCW and the United Worlds of Warlock have several treaties of mutual assistance, trade and even defense in the event of a major galactic threat. However, the Forge War has made relations between the UWW and the CCW a little strained, because both blocs want to find the Cosmic Forge before the other does, and both have their own particular edges to the race. The UWW can cross the Threshold more easily, while the CCW can scour the Halo for clues more efficiently due to its greater resources. Both power blocs distrust the TGE, and on that regard, the two will gladly ally to contain the Kreeghor and keep them from obtaining the Cosmic Forge.

Naruni Enterprises: The CAF is a major Naruni client, especially in the Anvil Galaxy, where the CCW's military budget has been cranked into overdrive to keep the TGE in line. Thanks to the CCW's high wealth, they can afford to buy in great quantity from the Naruni, and piece by piece, they are replacing home-developed CCW weapons and technology with off-the-shelf Naruni tech. While the Naruni are gleefully rubbing their hands at how much money they are making off the CCW, what they do not know is the CCW is reverse-engineering everything they buy from Naruni and are building entire factory worlds to produce this technology themselves. The Naruni's money train is about to derail, and the CCW (the GSA, specifically) is prepared to take the Naruni down a few pegs if the trans-dimensional company decides to get nasty about it. Lest the Naruni forget, they are a powerful commercial concern, but the CCW is a galactic government. They could squash Naruni like the bugs they are if they so desired. And if pushed to it, they will.

Hartigal Combine: This renegade offshoot of Naruni Enterprises is, in the short run, a thorn in the side for the CCW, since numerous IDFs are buying a great number of weapons from Hartigal in order to get more mileage out of their modest military budgets. Naruni Enterprises does not like this, and routinely requests the CCW to stop this sort of "manufacturing piracy" wherever it is detected. In response, the CCW seizes Hartigal facilities and inventories under the pretense of freezing the company's assets until it can decide what to do. Invariably, the CCW ends up confiscating the items and distributing them amongst the IDF that bought them in the first place, or giving them to GSA covert units. Since the CCW is about to freeze the Naruni out of their lucrative weapons deals anyway, they have little sympathy for the arms merchants' claims that Hartigal is ripping them off.

Golgan Republik: The CCW feels that the Golgans' expansionist tendencies make them a little too much like the TGE for their taste, and so they keep their distance from this mildly repressive and paranoid state. The CCW does keep tabs on the Golgan situation, however, and they realize the Republik might fracture at any moment. If and when it does, the GSA will be on the scene to entreat the remnant states to consider Consortium membership, if only to deny the same opportunity to the TGE.

Altess Dynasty: The Altess are intermittent members of the CCW, coming and going as they please. The frustrating thing about it for the Consortium is they can never figure out why the Altess join and then resign their CCW status. They make no treaty or Compact violations, they just seem to decide to join or quit on a whim.

Central Alliance: The CCW sees the Central Alliance for what it really is: a collection of gladiator worlds populated by attack cyborgs too fascinated with their own onboard weaponry to govern themselves properly or make a really beneficial impact on the Anvil Galaxy. The Central Alliance is probably the only major power bloc *not* actively seeking the Cosmic Forge. They are content to fight amongst themselves, and so the CCW leaves them to their own devices. GSA agents routinely infiltrate the Central Alliance to steal the secrets of their unusual cybernetic technology, and to keep tabs on the government and CA society.

Cosmo-Knights: The Cosmo-Knights are recognized by the CCW as a law enforcement agency, as long as any and all Cosmo-Knights operating in CCW space are "Bonded Deputies." A bonded deputy is an authorized agent who knows and implements the laws of the Consortium. In general, Cosmo-Knights cannot intervene in domestic affairs unless they can prove that those accused of a crime, be it the government, business or individual, were involved in violations of the Consortium's rules. The Cosmo-Knights seem particularly adept at ferreting out such treachery. Should the CCW and TGE ever go to war, the Cosmo-Knights are certain to side with the CCW.

Kingdom of Rynncryyl: Besides the Trans-Galactic Empire, Splugorth-occupied worlds are another source of trouble. The CCW has no formal relations with about half of the Splugorth domains and is effectively in a state of war with two or three of them at any one time. The Splugorth Kingdom of Rynncryyl, in the Anvil Galaxy, is one of the Splugorth entities the CCW is in open war with, even though it would much rather devote its energy and resources in containing the TGE. The Rynncryyl Splugorth are relentless slavers who can't stop themselves from raiding Consortium space for new "inventory." These raids are a constant source of casualties and violence, and after extended efforts to open diplomatic channels with the mad Splugorth King, the CCW threw it all out the window, declared war, and has set itself to destroying the kingdom utterly. In a rare show of mercilessness, the Consortium generals in charge of the Rynncryyl campaign will not rest until the Splugorth Kingdom is utterly destroyed, thinking that any fragments left will ultimately reform and regrow into yet another threat to the CCW.

Even Splugorth worlds that have established diplomatic ties with the CCW are not to be trusted and are constantly sending spies and saboteurs to harm CCW interests. As operations have begun against the Rynncryyl Kingdom, the strained relations with other Splugorth worlds and systems in the Three Galaxies have become even more so. The Splugorth are generally happy to see the renegade Rynncryyl taken down a peg, but the CCW's success in destroying the kingdom would be disconcerting to the other Splugorth Kings, who do not want to see "lesser beings" come to believe they can challenge the power of the Splugorth. For now, the alien intelligences are holding their position where Rynncryyl is concerned, but if the CCW gets too aggressive towards them, they will certainly band together to put the Consortium in its place, and possibly ally with the TGE for mutual defense or revenge.

Gene-Techs: Considered the vilest of villains, all Gene-Tech (and Gene-Splicers) are to be destroyed or apprehended immediately upon their detection within CCW space. The GSA secretly wants to capture a Gene-Tech (or a Gene-Splicer) ship intact so they can study their technology.

Omegan Order: This rogue order of Fallen Cosmo-Knights is considered an enemy of the CCW, and of the Anvil Galaxies at large. The CCW will destroy any representative of the Omegan Order it finds, no negotiations possible. The CCW takes such a hard line against the Omegans in part because of the CCW's alliance with the true Cosmo-Knights, and in part because Omegans are responsible for the destruction of numerous CCW exploration ships sent to the Core.

Xodian Collective: The CCW knows virtually nothing about this strange alien civilization, though it would very much like to. If only the Omegan Order would stop destroying CCW diplomatic envoys, the Consortium is convinced they could establish a meaningful relationship with the Xodians.

K!ozn: The K!ozn (Kot sin) are a race of extraordinarily advanced but incredibly secretive beings – so secretive that few people have any idea what they even look like. They have little use or patience for anybody from the Halo, and so they consider the CCW a pesky flea to be discarded whenever they come buzzing around. The Consortium of Civilized Worlds appreciates this philosophy although it does not agree with it. The K!ozn's apparently superior tech level is what keeps the CCW from making any threats against these super-intelligent, super-aloof aliens. They know any sabre-rattling to the K!ozn Continuum will be ignored, so CCW operatives must content themselves to deal with the various K!ozn minions sent into the galaxy to see why the Halo is suddenly interested in the Core, and why they can't just stay on their side of the Threshold.

Independent Worlds: Often, independent worlds call in the CCW to arbitrate disputes, or to help them deal with disasters or invasions. The Consortium can be trusted not to take advantage of the situation and to be extremely fair. Many worlds fear that this reputation is undeserved, however, and that the CCW uses its trustworthy facade to slowly gain more influence and power over independent planets to get them to join the Consortium. Despite some problems with corruption and illegal operations of unscrupulous corporations, the CCW is completely above board and always makes an effort to be fair and equitable to all parties.

CCW Society

With hundreds of races and thousands of worlds, it is hard to generalize about the society of the CCW. There is one social distinction that cuts across all the differences in race, money and class: the difference between people who make their home "in space," and those who don't. There are *Spacers*, often called "nomads," "vacuum addicts" and less complimentary things, and the *Groundsiders*, also referred to as "dirtsiders," "mud people" and other contemptuous nicknames. **Spacers** are typically ship crew members, explorers, soldiers and adventurers. They are not afraid of the vast universe they travel in, but they know and respect its deadliness. Groundsiders are people who are content with staying on one world and who only travel beyond its confines when they absolutely have to, and usually to set foot on another planet.

Spacers make up less than 10% of the Consortium's total population. Their importance is disproportionate to their size, however, because they help to keep commerce alive between the planets, defend them from invaders, and find new worlds to colonize. Their lives are so romanticized in movies and computer games that many children dream of becoming Spacers when they grow up. At the same time, they are held in contempt by many adult Groundsiders, who consider them to be shiftless vagabonds and glory hounds of an unscrupulous nature. The fact that they can be on one planet one day and one hundred light years away on the next has contributed to those sentiments. Many have a long history of leaving behind friends and lovers, unpaid debts, and causing trouble and running away rather than facing the consequences. By the same token, Spacers have a rough code of honor, especially among themselves. These honorable characters usually share the same disdain for rogue Spacers who give them a bad name as the Groundsiders. Meanwhile, most Spacers look upon Groundsiders as narrow-minded conservatives too frightened to leave the ground, or as wealthy snobs (land owners) or cowardly intellectuals who have a long history of unfairly blaming Spacers for all their troubles and local crime. Most Spacers feel the wealthy Groundsiders are more likely to lie, cheat or steal from them.

Another common aspect of Consortium society is a general dislike for war. The *Noro* culture has spared no effort to share with other races the consequences of mindless violence. Even the Wulfen and Seljuk races have come to recognize that war is only honorable if no other means of resolving a conflict are viable. This attitude has led to a general distrust of mercenaries and warriors. Many people feel that warriors (and even soldiers) cannot make important rational decisions, because they are naturally inclined to be aggressive and start a war. What they don't realize is that most soldiers who have experienced the horrors of war firsthand are often the strongest supporters of peaceful solutions. Still, on several planets, soldiers and warriors are treated as coldly and belligerently as Spacers.

This pacifistic tendency has frequently harmed the CCW, both on the battlefield and at the negotiating table. Fortunately, enough people recognize the need for a strong defensive force to keep the peace and maintain the law.

Daily Life in the CCW

Technology dominates the lives of the denizens of the Consortium. Without it, survival would be impossible for the teeming billions who work, party and dwell in the enormous cities, space stations and new colonies scattered across the galaxies. Technology and the benign government of the Consortium have brought about the highest standard of living in the Three Galaxies; the average citizen of the Consortium enjoys luxuries and comforts undreamed of on Rifts Earth.

More than 80% of the CCW's population lives in cities or suburbs. The average city has a population in excess of one million people, and several of them have as many as 100 million people! The remaining 20% of the population is divided between Spacers, farmers and colonists of new or inhospitable worlds. Most city dwellers work in the service sector, anything from restaurants and entertainment services to communication networks, stores and professions in law or medicine. Factories are largely automated and require very few workers. The Consortium has a large middle class, about 70% of the total population. The wealthy comprise about 10% of the total; the rest have incomes below the poverty line, and live in the slums that exist in almost every city. Even the poor have better lives than many citizens of other worlds, thanks to extensive social services provided by most CCW planets.

Information networks are everywhere. All but the poorest households have a "terminal," a combination computer, telephone, TV and answering machine that is plugged into a huge information network. Through the "terminal," the household members can order movies, holograms and virtual reality shows, communicate via video and audio anywhere on the planet and stations in orbit, plus they can access video libraries and databases, all without leaving the house. Magazines and movies can be purchased and printed out or stored on CDs for easy access.

A sizable percentage of the population (30%) works out of their homes, using their "terminals" to send their work to their employers, saving companies the expense of office space. This has led to a number of problems, including the "shut-in" phenomenon: people who rarely leave their house and who often develop mild agoraphobia (a fear of open spaces). These shut-ins prefer to live in their holographic or virtual reality world, where they can be in complete control. Shut-ins are common on densely populated worlds where as many as 15% of the population may suffer, to varying degrees, from the malady. However, it is almost unheard of on fringe, or recently colonized planets (less than 0.5%).

Law and Citizenship

The Consortium's laws are very complex, due to the fact that it is a loose federation of worlds rather than a monolithic entity like the Trans-Galactic Empire. Since there are hundreds of "sub-governments" in the CCW with often contradictory laws, the Consortium has to separate local and galactic laws, and decide which laws apply in each case. To deal with this, all sentient beings in the CCW are granted dual citizenship, which makes them citizens of both the Consortium and one planet or planetary collective. Some people (including almost all Spacers) have single citizenship, making them members of the Consortium but not of any other worlds or nations within its vast territory.

Taxes are always more favorable for local citizens than for Consortium citizens, so most people who reside and work on one planet will usually become citizens of that planet. Foreigners (those without CCW citizenship) are still subject to Consortium laws within CCW space. CAF personnel (Consortium Armed Forces), regardless of their original citizenship, are bound by CCW laws only.

Dual citizens are subject to the laws of both their "home planet" and the Consortium. While on the citizen's home world, local laws have precedence; everywhere else, the person is subject to Consortium laws. For example, the planet Motherhome (see Rifts® Phase World®, page 56) has very harsh environmental laws. Starting a campfire without a license has a stiff fine (5,000 credits) and up to one year of community service as a penalty. This law applies only to Motherhome citizens. A CCW citizen would pay the lower fines dictated by Consortium law.

Local laws change a great deal from world to world. The only constants are those defined by the Civilization Compact with edicts that insist slavery is outlawed and trial by jury is required for all criminal matters; beyond that, pretty much anything goes. Most planets have laws that are close copies of the Consortium's codices. Others keep the laws of their original culture and civilization. About 70% of all Consortium planets, for instance, prescribe the death penalty for a number of crimes, from first-degree murder (80%) to grand larceny (5%)! Consortium law has the death penalty for only the most severe crimes, like engaging in genocide, large-scale slavery, and mass murder.

Crime

"Crime is the price a free society must pay," is one common saying in the Consortium. Since the government is not constantly watching its citizens, opportunities for crime exist, and are exploited by the greedy, selfish, desperate, power hungry, and insane. Most criminal activity occurs in the poorest sections of cities and planets. Furthermore, the poorest 10% of the Consortium's society is 50 times more likely to be the victims of violent crime than the wealthiest 10%. The large majority of planets in the Consortium (70%) have criminal rates as low as those of Japan's during the late 20th Century. Piracy, smuggling and slavery tend to occur in frontier and isolated planets.

Despite the best efforts of both local and galactic authorities, however, criminal networks have developed on several worlds, sometimes with links that stretch between planets or even galaxies. Some of these crime rings are suspected of being fronts for the Trans-Galactic Empire, the Splugorth and Naruni Enterprises. In the Anvil Galaxy, the largest of these criminal organizations are the *Korgian Legion*, the *Uganza*, and the *Galton Ring*.

The Korgian Legion is more of a terrorist ring and mercenary crew than straight-up outlaws, but they are a significant contributor to crime within the CCW anyway. Exactly what the Legion's political motivations are is a bit of a mystery since the group is extremely factionalized and it has carried out militant actions against sites in the CCW, TGE, UWW, and every other major power bloc in the Anvil Galaxy. They show no undue dedication one way or the other regarding the Cosmic Forge, and they have issued no public statements, manifestos, or other indications of what makes this group tick. However, they are very active, carrying out guerilla actions and flat-out terrorism all over the galaxy. To fund their actions, the Korgian Legion has a "domestic crime" branch that commits acts of theft and piracy as a means of funding the group's larger war effort. To this end, the CCW provides the most target-rich environment, especially the Consortium's enviable Utopia Worlds (six of which reside in the Anvil Galaxy). Thus, while the Legion affects everybody in the Anvil Galaxy, it is the CCW who has taken the lead in cracking down on this nefarious group. So far, most of the Consortium's efforts have floundered, as the Legion is made up of some very smart and slippery people who hold to an absolute vow of secrecy. The few Korgian operatives taken into custody killed themselves within hours of their capture, using nothing more than mental conditioning to get the job done! Apparently, Korgian soldiers are trained to simply shut down their heart and brains if caught, using a mysterious form of mental conditioning known to authorities as the *Korgian Protocol*. Little else is known about it except that it does a fine job of denying CCW intelligence officers of useful information about the Korgian Legion. The Legion apparently is made up of all sorts of races and it uses whatever technology it can get its hands on. It does not appear to be a major user of magic.

The Uganza is a huge and tightly networked crime syndicate that has taken control of the CCW member planet *Uganze*. Crime had always been epidemic on the planet, and it almost forbade it entry into the CCW, but since the TGE was on the verge of conquering that planet, the CCW made an exception and took Uganze under its wing to deny their rivals. It is a move the CCW has regretted ever since, as the planet is not only ungovernable due to its anarchy and crime (kidnaping and drug dealing are the two leading industries there), but crooks have begun leaving the world and traveling to other CCW planets, bringing their criminal intentions with them. Fed up, the CCW government issued an ultimatum to the planet: straighten up and fly right within five years or face expulsion from the CCW. Sensing an opportunity, the leading crime families on the planet went on the offensive and waged war on their competitors. Only when they defeated each one, instead of destroying them, they simply folded them into their *own* organization, creating an ever-stronger amalgamated crime empire that is rapidly taking over the whole world. Within two years, the syndicate (known as the *Uganza*) has conquered the planet. To control crime, they simply levied taxes on it and laid down rules for how certain activities had to be carried out. Contract murder, for example, could no longer include women or children. Prostitutes had to undergo monthly health and psych checkups, extortion could not exceed a certain percentage of a victim's income, and of course, 33% of *all* criminal profit is kicked back directly to the Uganza, who soon found themselves making crazy amounts of money. Now the Uganza is petitioning the CCW to be recognized as the formal government, which provides the Consortium with a new dilemma. The Uganza is obeying the Consortium compact to the letter, and there is no legal grounds for expelling them from the confederation. But the CCW finds the Uganza to be utterly distasteful and wishes they could be cut loose. There is one year left until the CCW deadline, when it will be forced to make a difficult decision. Until then, the GSA is sending undercover agents to infiltrate the world and destabilize things so the CCW might have a plausible reason for ejecting the planet from its ranks. It is an ugly way of handling the problem, but the CCW people in charge of it feel, in this case, the ends justify the means, even if it might mean throwing the entire planet into the cold of the Anvil Galaxy, where it will have a considerably harder time surviving without the aegis of the CCW to protect it from outside interference from pirate nations, the TGE, and other interstellar predators.

The Galton Ring is a small but highly organized gang of pirates, consisting of maybe one or two hundred people. Despite its size, the Galton Ring's exploits have made them legendary (some would say "infamous") throughout the Anvil Galaxy. They are a blight on interstellar travel and a black eye for the CCW's law enforcement community. The Galton Ring got its start some 50 years ago when the human pirate *Gora Galton* assaulted a CCW courier ship containing, among other things, the Crown Jewels of Thoridia, a diplomatic present from the government of that planet to the CCW government. Thoridia was under consideration for inclusion to the CCW, and it made this offering as a gesture of its good will and firm intent. When Galton pinched the jewels, it caused quite a disturbance, to say the least. Thoridia withdrew its application and was subsequently courted by the TGE, which Thoridia then joined. The TGE, upon reviewing the case, approached Galton and offered her a position as a "black-level" privateer for the TGE. That means they would never take responsibility for her actions – she was 100% deniable, but, every time she hit a CCW ship, they would match the value of her theft 100%. For Galton, this was a dream ticket. If she handled it right, she'd make more money than she could ever spend. So, she recruited every other pirate she could trust and cut them in on the action. She turned her singular efforts into a network affair, and before long, the CCW was seeing an unacceptable number of high-value cargo ships disappearing en route.

In the years since Galton has begun working for the TGE, she has made untold *billions* of credits in stolen cash, merchandise, spaceships, and Kreeghor bonus payments. She is so successful, in fact, that she and her cronies (who also are now fabulously wealthy) are having a tough time finding places to hide their money. An idea floating among the group is they pool their resources and simply buy an independent world and set up a permanent base there. Meanwhile, the group's TGE money train is about to derail – their exploits are so successful that they are breaking the TGE's black ops budget for that part of the galaxy, and pretty soon the TGE will have to cease paying out its bonuses. This would be no big deal monetarily for Galton and her friends, since they have more cash than they know what to do with, but getting cut off would be a grave insult to Galton, who might very well turn her sights on TGE ships out of revenge. The TGE has already predicted this, so they are considering assassinating her instead and blaming it on the Consortium. That way, their Galton problem goes away and the CCW catches the blame for it. Meanwhile, all of these developments are unknown to CCW intelligence. The Consortium knows who Galton is and that her ring is nabbing CCW ships, but they know nothing about how much money she has, her plans to buy a planet, or the extent of her connection with the TGE. Considering how much time and money the CCW has spent investigating and trying to bring Galton to justice, that level of non-progress is just embarrassing, and suggests maybe Galton has paid off some very powerful people in the CCW government to look the other way. In the meanwhile, Galton is always willing to recruit new pirates into her organization, provided she feels she can trust them.

Major Worlds of the CCW

Below are just a handful of some of the more prominent worlds in the Anvil Galaxy region of the Consortium of Civilized Worlds. They are meant to give the reader ideas for adventures, campaigns, or designing worlds of your own. Have fun with them!

Koga Junction: If the CCW were to have a capital world in the Anvil Galaxy (it doesn't), then Koga Junction would definitely be it. Covered with enormous factories, shipyards and other facilities serving the Consortium Armed Forces, Koga Junction is the single largest maker of CAF starships in the galaxy. It also is the regional administrative headquarters for *CAF Fleet Command* and the *GSA*.

Security on the planet is just incredible, since there is so much here to protect. No ship can even enter the star system without first receiving a CAF intercept which scans incoming ships for weapons. Suspicious spacecraft are turned back, boarded or destroyed, depending on their nature and conduct. More than a few friendly ships have been destroyed by the security teams here, so most folks should just stay away or play it real safe when making an approach. Because it is a purely military and intelligence world, Koga Junction is outside the political spheres of the Consortium Congress, the traditional news media, entertainment networks, and so on. The top administrators of the planet see things only in terms of the Forge War and containing the TGE, and while that keeps the CCW on its toes, the personnel here tend to feel a bit isolated from the rest of CCW society. Some factions of the CAF and GSA stationed here wonder if maybe things would run better if they simply took power, dissolved the Congress and ran things more directly. Clearly, this is treasonous thought, and it is more the exception than the rule, but it shows that there is a seed of sedition growing on Koga Junction, and nobody may be willing to accept it exists to uproot it.

Thrant: The civilian counterpart to Koga Junction, the massive world of Thrant is dotted with huge arcology cities that are home to the *Consortium Congress* and over 60% of the government's central administrations. Still, the planet is not considered the regional capital, but it does have more than its share of power. Security for the world is tight, but most of it is up in orbit, screening whoever comes and goes from the world. Entrance and exit protocols take about 72 hours on average while every traveler's record, ID, and passage manifests are thoroughly scanned, checked and cross-referenced. Ever since Kreeghor assassins set a homemade fusion bomb in the Consortium Congress chamber (it failed to go off due to a malfunction in the timer), the representatives here are willing to live under a security microscope to keep things safe. Groundside security is handled by the GSA, which has a massive presence on Thrant. Not only are their main offices and training facilities on the world, but they have set up perhaps the largest communications monitoring system on any single planet in the Anvil Galaxy. GSA comm techs filter all communications on and around the world, running them through megacomputers and AI screens for any language or codes that would reveal possible terrorist or enemy intent. So far, this network has been instrumental in thwarting over five separate terrorist plots to the planet, but the civilians who know of the net (and of GSA intent to place more such nets on other CCW worlds) are afraid that it is a sign the CCW is losing its way. They fear that in striving to contain the tyranny of the TGE, the CCW might become tyrannical itself.

Dalgond: Once a beautiful Earth-like planet, Dalgond had huge deposits of various ultra-valuable minerals and as such, attracted the attentions of the largest mining companies in the CCW. Over the span of a century, these companies managed to

strip mine the entire world, exhausting its mineral wealth and leaving the world a barren, scarred and pitted rock in space. Technically, the Compact frowns on such foul exploitation, but all of the metal was being bought by the CCW to upgrade its battle fleets, so the government was willing to overlook this particular case of environmental catastrophe. Unfortunately for the Dalgond locals, their world had been reduced to ruin with no hope in sight. Or was there? The deepest mine shafts had revealed that a million years ago, a subterranean civilization lived on Dalgond and chronicled their society's history on the walls of their warrens and under cities. These strange hieroglyphics have been of intense interest to archaeologists who are convinced this ancient people (who must have died out because there is no evidence they existed to the present day) had some kind of contact with the *Cosmic Forge*. When news of that got out, GSA agents descended on the world and have maintained a presence there. Despite their best efforts, though, TGE spies as well as operatives from various other power blocs have all made trips to Dalgond to see the hieroglyphics themselves. This has turned the capital city of Dalgor into a hotbed of espionage, as spies and black ops folks from a dozen different power blocs mix it up and try to outwit each other. At least three people disappear each week in Dalgor, a silent testimony to the ongoing spy war being fought there with no collateral damage to speak of, and no end in sight. For GSA spooks, a tour of duty in Dalgor is a coveted assignment, especially for those looking for combat experience.

Voria: Positioned on a vital space lane where five trade routes intersect, Voria is a major economic power that makes all of its money in the sale and resale of goods and services. There is little primary industry (i.e., agriculture, manufacturing) on the planet, but it does okay because so much is sold here that the locals have no need to import anything – they just buy everything they need as it passes through. Trade guilds run the planet like one big marketplace, and instead of political factions, there are competing sub-guilds that control matters of government and economy as if they were the same. This kind of arrangement has been tried on other worlds to no effect, but it works out remarkably well here, probably because of the huge intersection of trade lanes. With so much merchant traffic coming through Voria, it would be impossible for it to *not* make a bundle of money off that. Voria is also notable because it is the nexus of three ley lines in space. This would ordinarily make the planet a mecca for spell casters, but the guilds who own the planet refuse to admit any sorcerers to the planet, something that rankles visitors from the UWW, who could use the planet's unique position to their advantage. Oddly, the world has never had any trouble with dimensional portals opening up there or other dimensional phenomena, although mystic scholars suggest that Voria is long overdue for the ley line equivalent of an earthquake, where a nexus will virtually explode, tearing open portals to multiple different places in the Megaverse at once. What happens after that is anybody's guess. It could destroy the world if monsters flood through, but if these gateways are to friendly worlds, and if the Vorians handle it correctly, they might turn their mercantile crossroads into something even more lucrative than it already is.

Gaelerash: This world is the Anvil Galaxy headquarters for the *CCW Scouting Corps*, making it one of the most important worlds in the ongoing search for the Cosmic Forge. Like Koga Junction and Thrant, Gaelerash has insanely tight security, largely because the CAF and GSA fear what might happen if enemy operatives were to infiltrate this world and access the CCW's data archives detailing their leads and progress regarding the Forge quest. While the Scouting Corps itself appreciates the security concern, they are explorers at heart, not spies or soldiers. They are unhappy enough with being forced to run reconnaissance missions against the TGE and other governments, but they accept that as part of the current political situation. What they really can't stand, though, is having a bunch of GSA goons telling them how to behave on what the Scouting Corps considers "its" world. As a result, some Scouting teams have stopped sharing their findings with GSA liaisons, preferring to hang on to that information should they ever need it as a bargaining tool against the GSA. So far, the GSA doesn't know about this, but it is a sure bet that they will find out, and when they do, they will do everything they can to gut the Scouting Corps, replacing its ranks with much more GSA-friendly personnel who don't mind serving their government's security interests first and satisfying their sense of wanderlust and galactic exploration second.

Lareinnon: The CCW captured this planet from the TGE when the two fought their first war, so many years ago. The planet is a breadbasket world capable of producing huge quantities of pretty much any kind of agriculture known in the Three Galaxies. The soil here has a special combination of minerals, enzymes and microorganisms that make it the most perfect growing medium in the Three Galaxies. The Kreeghor had never used the world for farming but instead harvested the soil itself and sent it to other planets to "seed" them and hopefully transform those worlds into additional breadbasket planets. The project never worked, but the TGE is convinced its principle is sound and have always wanted to resume their experiment. The CCW has a deadlock on Lareinnon, having turned it into a major farming world and exporter of agro-produce. So it was with a heavy heart that Kreeghor generals decided three years ago that if they could not have this world, then the CCW wouldn't either. Using treacherous locals as their agents, the TGE has introduced over 2,500 different forms of viral agents to the world in the hopes of destroying the delicate balance in the soil. The aim is to transform this cornucopia into a barren wasteland. So far, there have been no results, but the TGE scientists who engineered the virii insist it will take at least another two years to start seeing crop failures. In the meantime, the GSA has gotten wind of the plot and is trying to find out who among the local populace might have helped the Kreeghor. The problem is this remains an intensively rural world where the locals trust each other far more than some slick-looking GSA operative. As a result, if there are Kreeghor agents Groundside, chances are their friends and families will harbor them, even if their misdeeds might spell catastrophe for the planet.

Niathh: A small outpost world right on the border separating the CCW from the TGE, Niathh is a bit of a strategic way point for both superpowers. Despite this, Niathh has remained largely uninhabited and pristine. It has never been a major battleground for any of the hot and cold wars that the CCW and TGE have fought against each other, though the CCW did use Niathh as a major listening post, because the planet has unusual harmonic frequencies that enable long-range scanners to intercept TGE communications traffic deep within TGE territory. This makes Niathh very important to the CCW intelligence effort, and as such, the Congress invoked a special clause in the Compact denying the Niathhi the right to secede. For the moment, keeping them on as "executive members," a euphemism for "people forced against their will to be CCW citizens."

Having enjoyed a great deal of independence, the Niathhi were not about to take the Congress' actions lying down, and they announced their secession from the CCW anyway. Since the world had no major military presence on it (it was withheld so the TGE thought this was an unimportant world, rather than a central intelligence gathering spot), the Niathhi were able to take control relatively quickly, converting the listening post into a broadcasting station. Now, the Niathhi use this stolen CCW technology to route criminal transmissions of information and money from anywhere to anywhere in the Anvil Galaxy. The space ports here have become havens for pirates, smugglers, data thieves, and rebels, and if the CAF does not do something soon, the planet will become a veritable criminal fortress, impossible to reclaim without having to fight a major guerilla war against the insurgent Niathhi.

Liremos Prime: For years, Liremos Prime has made its mark as a data processing giant. A place where backup copies of data arcologies could be safely stored and replicated without fear of corruption or security breach. The CCW government, in particular, made heavy use of Liremos Prime's data banks to store the official governmental archives. Furthermore, hundreds of worlds maintain backup copies of their entire economies' actions on Liremos Prime. The artificial intelligences used to manage all of this information are a marvel of technology themselves, possessing organic structures and capable of developing genuine emotions. Thought a bit freakish at first, these "organic AIs" were found to be a lot more reliable than a standard Artificial Intelligence, since they had feelings of loyalty and pride in their work.

For a century, this worked just fine, but about four years ago, a corruption arose in AI7521, the intelligence in charge of maintaining tertiary security protocols on all data influx channels. Feeling a bit "off," AI7521 sought the counsel of its friend, AI1933, as was their custom. Moments after that meeting, AI1933 began suffering the same "off" feeling that its friend had felt, and in turn sought another friend for counsel. It turns out these AIs had developed the equivalent of a virulent form of *insanity*, and they were spreading it among themselves at a very rapid pace. By the time technicians discovered this problem, over 80% of the AI population was corrupted and growing more and more off-kilter each day. To keep things cool, most of the data network has simply been shut down, freezing the corrupt AIs in stasis, but sooner or later, clients will need to access to their information, and to do that, the data network will have to come back online and these corrupt AIs will have to be dealt with. What the managers fear most is one of these AIs somehow uploading themselves out of the network, perhaps to a starship's central computer, or to the brain of a Naruni Repo-Bot or some other dangerous and highly mobile form where they could travel freely, spreading corruption as they go to any computer that might be susceptible to it.

Y'kn: With increasing intensity, this developed planet, home to nearly eight billion people, suffers from storms of "skipper meteors," a little-understood scientific anomaly that phase in and out of reality on their path through the Megaverse. Right now, the meteor swarm is skipping right into the path of this world, so they show up with little to no warning before they blast the planet. The biggest shower yet is on its way, and the frightened populace is trying to get off the planet before the "big one" hits. The wild thing is, this situation is far more than it seems. The reason why these skipper meteors are so poorly understood is because they are not just meteors. They are the equivalent of alien kamikaze vessels launched millions of years ago by a race of hostile aliens who imparted a fragment of their consciousness into each skipper meteor so they might steer them to their target. The skipper meteors hurtling toward Y'kn were caught in a strong chronol distortion that chucked them forward in time by a few million years, throwing them off course (the galaxy is in a different place than it was a million years ago), putting this innocent world in the line of fire. Were a team of psychics employed to establish contact, they could probably get the skipper meteors to hold off from impacting on Y'kn. Should that work, the CCW might wish to research these things further, seeing if maybe more of these meteors could be fabricated somehow and used as a secret weapon against the TGE.

Acalel: This sub-zero world is a rich mosaic of super-deep slush oceans, icebergs the size of starships and icecaps the size of continents, etched with deep canyons where the locals have built their hardy, technologically advanced cities. There are also huge floating cities as well as undersea settlements that filter the slush water for nutrients, trace minerals, and exotic micro-organisms for use in biological research. This work is a lot more hazardous than it sounds because workers must routinely don pressure suits and go out into the water to service/repair the filtration machinery. Robots never seem to work for reasons unknown (the microorganisms screw up their circuitry channels, actually), so live workers are the ticket. Problem is, these workers are represented by a coalition of ultra-militant labor unions that have no problem kidnaping government officials and the executives of the various companies that operate the filtration network.

A recent spate of accidents and pay cuts threaten to shut down the entire planetary economy, as well as introduce some nasty insurrection in every major city on this world. The only way things will get better is if conditions improve for the workers, and the only way that is going to happen is if the union leaders and the company's government leaders see eye to eye. But there are too many egos involved, and too much bad blood, and for both sides, the only way to settle things is by force. As a result, the unions and the companies have been hiring mercenaries and assassins in preparation for a dirty street war that will make Acalel the scene of a planetary-scale St. Valentine's Day massacre. The local government has done a great job of covering all of this up, for fear of the CAF intervening and taking over the filtration network (which would rid the corrupt government officials here of the substantial profit sharing they have received at the expense of the working population). The local government is also powerless to do anything about this situation, and is basically sitting things out and hoping for the best. In the meantime, all sorts of criminal elements have come to Acalel sensing an opportunity to get in on the impending action and either snatching a piece of the filtration industry for themselves or putting down strong criminal roots during this time of virtual non-government. What this planet really needs are some heroes to come in and clean things up, but so far, there have been no takers.

Trans-Galactic Empire

Population: 6 trillion total; 1.5 trillion in the Anvil Galaxy.

Demographics: Kreeghor (25%), Humans (15%), Machine People (10%), Wulfen (9%), Silhouette (6%), Monros (5%), Noro (5%), Others (25%; prominent races in the Anvil Galaxy include the *Kelesh*, *Qidians* and *Sinestrians*).

Overview: The Trans-Galactic Empire is an autocratic civilization ruled by the Kreeghor, a warlike race of inhuman creatures. The Kreeghor are the dominant race of the Trans-Galactic Empire, but not the only one with power or influence. Unlike the CCW, the Trans-Galactic Empire has a policy of expansion, armed conquest and slavery. As a result, many of its subjects are in open rebellion against it or wish they could be free of the tyrannical regime. Only the overwhelming military might of the Kreeghor keeps their subjects in line.

The Kreeghor were the result of Splugorth bio-engineering, a former slave race that rose against its tormentors and was able to overthrow them, but only by becoming as savage and bloodthirsty as their one-time masters. The Kreeghor have spread through the Three Galaxies like a plague, conquering and colonizing planets at a frenzied pace. Those who dare to oppose them are destroyed or defeated and enslaved. At first, the Kreeghor constantly engaged in the routine enslavement or genocide of other races, but as they matured as an intergalactic force, they realized that those policies would eventually lead to their destruction. The Kreeghor then decided to accept worthy conquered races as "near equals" who could play a role in their Empire. A brutal war with the *Wulfen Empire* proved them worthy of this new policy. Instead of destroying the Wulfen, they conquered them. The Kreeghor praised their enemies' martial spirit and offered good terms to any planet that surrendered to them. Many Wulfen warriors decided to join forces with the Kreeghor and turned against their own kind. This was especially true of clans or tribes that had grievances against the Wulfen royal family, and who decided revenge was worth the price of betrayal. To this day, millions of Wulfen warriors are the Kreeghor's allies. The same tactic was applied against several human-inhabited worlds and now humans are an important part of the TGE as well.

The Trans-Galactic Empire's golden age came to an end with the formation of the Consortium of Civilized Worlds (CCW) several hundred years ago. Shortly after the CCW's founding, it fell under TGE attack, and in the brief but fierce bloodletting that followed, both civilizations fought each other to a standstill. At last, the Kreeghor's found an enemy who could not be easily beaten. An enemy that would plague the Kreeghor dreams of galactic conquest forever more. Realizing that all-out war would destroy both civilizations, the TGE sued for peace with the CCW, but they vowed that one day they would have final victory over the Consortium. An uneasy peace treaty was signed, but centuries of resentment remains strong, especially in the Anvil Galaxy, where the TGE and CCW *compete* directly with each other for winning new worlds to their cause and acquiring the Cosmic Forge.

For the TGE, the *Forge War* is almost a welcome diversion from its problems in the other two galaxies, where a raging civil war has led to the loss of a substantial amount of Imperial Territory. Breaking away as the *Free World Council*, a number of renegade systems, led by fierce and clever freedom fighters, have defeated the TGE on more than a few occasions. The FWC now has open support from the CCW as well as other independent systems that fear TGE expansion and throw their lot in with those who have so successfully resisted the Kreeghor's dreaded Empire. This particular rebellion began on the planet of *Good Hope* (page 73, **Phase World®**) and soon spread to several conquered worlds and became an organized, well-armed rebellion. Instead of conquering new worlds in the Corkscrew and Thundercloud galaxies, the Kreeghor and their minions now have to recapture dozens of rebellious planets, with success far from guaranteed.

So far, no rebellion in the Anvil Galaxy has come close to the success of the Free World Council, but Kreeghor overlords fear it is only a matter of time. After all, the CCW is strong here and getting stronger. It is allied with the United Worlds of Warlock, making the TGE definitely outgunned in the Anvil Galaxy. With so much trouble in the other two galaxies, and the ability to expand pretty much halted in the Anvil Galaxy, the TGE have special need for the Cosmic Forge. Many in the upper echelons of leadership feel that only the Cosmic Forge can save the TGE in what may be its darkest hour. Without ultimate power in their clutches, the Kreeghor fear that it may be only a matter of time before their Empire gradually falls into tatters. For them, the Cosmic Forge is really their only certain avenue to victory, or so they have convinced themselves. This makes its recovery a make or break issue. Either the Kreeghor shall capture it, and with it rule the whole universe (or at least the Three Galaxies), or they will lose it to their hated enemies, and will surely face ruination.

Already many Kreeghor generals see the impending Forge War as the first sign of the coming doom. Many Kreeghor want to attack the CCW now instead of waiting for the Cosmic Forge to turn up. Perhaps, just perhaps, the CCW is not as strong as it appears, and if the Kreeghor were to score a quick victory over their adversary, it might scare other parties off the search for the Cosmic Forge! Of course, this is a fairly hair-brained idea, but the generals of the TGE are looking at their Empire in a state of decline for the first time. The decline is not something they are even remotely prepared for, and it is freaking them all out in a huge way. As a result, the leaders of the TGE, especially in the Anvil Galaxy, are beginning to make rash decisions and poor snap judgements, succumbing to a gnawing panic. This makes the Empire very dangerous and very unpredictable. Chances are, the TGE will not find the Cosmic Forge on their own. If they do get it, it will probably be because they lucked on to it or stole information from the UWW or CCW and acted upon it.

Government

The Trans-Galactic Empire is a monarchy, ruled by the Kreeghor Emperor and the Royal Family. The Royal "Family" is made up of members of the Royal Kreeghor sub-species, a super-powerful variant of the Kreeghor race (**Phase World®**, page 74). A few heroic or famous subjects of the Empire, both Kreeghor and non-Kreeghor, are sometimes "adopted" into the Royal Family but this is an occasion most rare and not seen more than once every ten or twenty years, tops. Royal Family members command the military and disdain all other forms of public service as "button pushers" unworthy of true warriors. They are granted large estates and farms worked by slave labor and live off the rents produced by them. The Emperor has a Privy Council made up of the most powerful members of the Royal Family. The Privy Council has 6 to 12 members and each of them is second to the Emperor in authority.

Below the Royal Family are a number of Ministries, usually filled by non-Kreeghor public servants (mostly humans and Wulfen). The Ministers take care of the bureaucracy and administrative duties, such as tax collecting, funding, and other tasks. Their proposals have to be approved by the Emperor, or one of the members of the Privy Council. Corruption is rife among the Ministers. The Kreeghor don't pay as much attention to business affairs as they should, so most Ministers skim money off the top and hide it beneath layers of bureaucracy. As long as the imperial machinery is kept running, the Kreeghor do not mind some petty theft. However, should these bureaucrats cross their masters, the Ministers can be removed and killed at the whim of the Emperor.

Planetary holdings are controlled by military governors answerable only to the Royal Family. These governors can be of any race, but all are chosen for their loyalty to the Empire, and are fanatical pro-imperialists with little tolerance for dissent. The rest of the government is run by the military which fulfills the role of policing, tax collecting and other government tasks.

The Imperial Legions

The true symbol of the Trans-Galactic Empire is the marching legionnaire in full combat armor. Kreeghor, Wulfen, human or alien, the Imperial soldiers are well-trained, armed to the teeth and for the most part, ready to kill in the name of the Empire. Although the Army also acts as the police, most of the soldiers' training is military, with little to no expertise in formal criminology. As a result, working a crime consists of rounding up the usual suspects and beating a confession out of somebody, followed by a fair trial and a speedy execution (broadcast on live holovision, of course). When responding to crimes in progress, the *Imperial Guard* simply show up and begin firing, usually resulting in plenty of collateral damage and injured or killed innocent bystanders. With any luck, the Guard will have nailed the perpetrator too, making it all worthwhile in their eyes. "Better to lose some civvies and bag the perp than to miss the mark and lose the jerk," as they say.

Although the TGE civilian populace hates and fears the Imperial Army, many people join it because of the privileges and power enjoyed by soldiers. Military personnel are exempt from civilian laws and answer only to military courts. Disputes between legionnaires and civilians are usually decided in favor of the soldiers, and enlisted men can often get away with murder, as long as the victims are not wealthy or powerful. Imperial propaganda portrays soldiers as heroes and role models, a line nobody really believes but they live by it anyway. The legionnaires' great deeds are often immortalized in movies and songs (usually of terrible quality – the Kreeghor are just not cut out for making art and song), and they are not only well paid, but enjoy generous retirement and injury pensions. The Empire

knows its welfare depends on its armed forces and does its best to keep them happy.

A special branch of the Imperial Army, the **Invincible Guard,** is even more vicious, pampered and glorified. Through intense bio-engineering, Invincible Guardsmen are transformed into genuine super-beings with incredible powers that put them on par with the legendary Cosmo-Knights (who, incidentally, are hated by the TGE for their constant opposition to it and alliance with the CCW). The Invincible Guard are living symbols of the Empire's power, and they are at liberty to roam freely, dispensing imperial "justice" as they see fit, and supporting imperial military operations. All Invincible Guardsmen are given a minimum rank of lieutenant in the army and many of them rise to higher ranks, all the way up to general. Many, if not most Invincible Guardsmen are arrogant and fanatically dedicated to upholding the Empire. To them, the Empire does not make mistakes. It is never in question. Its righteousness can not be doubted, and their ultimate victory over the Three Galaxies is assured. These are the original super-patriots, and their conviction to the Empire's cause reveals them for what they really are, dangerous fanatics with too much power and absolutely no sense of how to use it responsibly.

The Invincible Guard takes its orders directly from the Kreeghor Emperor and nobody else. Their orders supersede all others, and even when not acting under direct command from the Emperor, it should be assumed that whatever they do has the Emperor's tacit approval. This gives the Invincible Guard total freedom to do whatever they want to whomever they want in the Empire, even to members of the Royal Family! This has helped keep the Empire stable even during its recent troubles – to depose the Emperor, one would have to get rid of the Invincible Guard somehow, and without the help of somebody like the Cosmo-Knights, the Invincible Guard are not going anywhere. (For more information on the Invincible Guard, check out the **Phase World® Sourcebook**, page 32.)

Foreign Affairs

In the eyes of the Trans-Galactic Empire, there are two kinds of foreign powers, enemies who are to be defeated by force of arms and enemies who are to be deceived by diplomacy. The Splugorth-controlled worlds are among the former, and the Consortium of Civilized Worlds and the United Worlds of Warlock are among the latter. In any dealings with other worlds, the Trans-Galactic Empire will try to strengthen itself by undermining everybody else. At first, they had no skilled diplomats, since the Kreeghor are a warrior race with little use for peaceful arts and trades. In more recent times however, a well-trained diplomatic corps (made up mostly of non-Kreeghor representatives) has been developed. Now, Imperial Ambassadors are received by all major civilizations in the Three Galaxies. However, their goals for conquest and intergalactic domination remain unchanged, and most power blocs know that, making the Kreeghor's diplomatic missions difficult ones.

The Free World Council: About a hundred years ago, a popular revolt exploded on the planet of *Good Hope*. The planet, populated mostly by humans and Wulfen, had been suffering under a tyrannical human governor. Among other things, the governor seized the offices of a local news service and had every employee executed by torture for the crime of reporting rumors of corruption in the local government. This last crime sparked a riot. The governor ordered the army to take a tank company and, in his words, "Drown those rioters in their own blood." Rather than slaughter thousands of innocent people, a number of human and Wulfen soldiers led by Army lieutenant *Michael Klass* rebelled against their officers. Supported by an angry mob, the soldiers attacked the Governor's Palace with tanks and artillery pieces, reducing it to burning rubble. When the smoke cleared, Klass realized he was now leading a revolution. Already a popular officer who had also proven himself to be a compassionate and fair man, he had little difficulty rallying others to his cause and in no time at all his ranks swelled with fresh volunteers. Klass also proved to be a gifted military leader and he was able to defeat the loyalist forces with surprising ease. In a daring stroke, Klass led a commando team to capture the powerful war satellites orbiting the planet. This successful surprise attack gave them control over the orbital death dealers and also provided the rebels with a 24 vessel fleet that was captured along with the satellites. Once the entire planet was under the rebels' control, Klass publicly denounced the Emperor as a ruthless tyrant and asked all members of the Trans-Galactic Empire to rise against their oppressors.

News of this successful uprising spread throughout the Empire despite efforts to suppress all reports coming from Good Hope. For the first time in centuries, a world had successfully fought and defeated the Imperial Army! A military expedition dispatched to recapture the planet was delayed by strikes, sabotage and riots on several other worlds. The governors of those planets reacted to these rebellious outbreaks with brutality, slaughtering thousands of people. These measures backfired by stirring more discontent. Then the unthinkable happened again. Instead of being content with their winning back of Good Hope, the rebel fleet, consisting both of the captured ships and additional merchant ships outfitted with weapons and armor, swooped down on planets locked in conflict and helped the local rebels overthrow the governments there as well. Two other planets were freed from the grip of the Trans-Galactic Empire.

Finally, a large fleet was sent against the three rebel planets. To the surprise of the Kreeghor, the fleet was met by a huge armada of ships, including pirates and smugglers who had been convinced by Klass to join the rebellion. Other ships had been provided by Splugorth-controlled worlds, always happy to cause chaos among their former slaves. Among the rebels also stood a dozen Cosmo-Knights, each equivalent in power to a small starship by themselves! A massive space battle was fought with inconclusive results. The rebels suffered enormous losses, but so did the Imperial fleet and it had to withdraw without finishing its mission. The planets and the rebels were battered but remained free.

Since then, the rebels have managed to capture and hold on to over two dozen planets, and there is open rebellion and warfare on dozens of other worlds. Several space routes are war zones and any ship flying through risks being raided or destroyed by one side or the other. Klass was assassinated thirty years after the revolution, but his granddaughter *Rachel Klass* has carried on the struggle. The freedom fighters call themselves the **Free World Council**. Their goal is to defend liberated worlds, carry the revolution to other oppressed planets, and establish democratic governments. The Free World Council has attracted many different people to its banner. Most of them are dedicated revolutionaries, people who have suffered under the TGE, and now want revenge. Others are men and women who will not stand for Kreeghor domination. Some have joined out of greed and ambition, hoping to use the revolution to gain power, fame and wealth. Many criminals facing the wrath of the TGE joined the rebellion out of sheer self-preservation.

So far, the rebellion has not managed to make a serious dent in the Kreeghor's holdings; only a couple dozen worlds compared with the Trans-Galactic Empire's thousands of planets. However, the fact that the Empire has not been able to crush the freedom fighters is an insufferable offense to the Kreeghor and the rebels are a constant thorn in their side.

Consortium of Civilized Worlds: The TGE and CCW butt heads throughout the Three Galaxies, but especially in the Anvil Galaxy where the two compete directly for the Cosmic Forge. The only reason why the TGE does not wage all-out war on the CCW is because their adversary is just as strong (if not stronger) as they are, and total war is likely to bring liberated and independent worlds to assist the CCW and spell ruin for the TGE. Among more fanatical generals and Imperial Guardsmen, however, waging war against the CCW is the only prudent course anyway, regardless of what ill effects it brings down on the Empire. Such militants often find (or make up) reasons to confront and skirmish with CCW forces on their own initiative, small battles that could easily blow up into something major if they are not halted quickly. When this happens, usually other TGE units have the unpleasant task of restraining their out of control comrades and bringing them back home. With Invincible Guardsmen who are on the warpath, pulling them away from the field of battle is very difficult, and half the time they must be destroyed rather than restrained – or left to go wild, branded as madmen or malcontents condemned and disavowed by the TGE, but who does nothing to stop them, claiming these lone rebels are beyond the reach of TGE authorities.

United Worlds of Warlock: The UWW has staunchly allied with the CCW against the TGE, so they are considered only marginally less of an enemy than the CCW. Seeking to drive a wedge between those powers, the TGE routinely tries to find something, anything, that might pull the CCW and UWW apart, but so far, they have failed.

Naruni Enterprises: The Naruni sell a great deal of weaponry to the CCW, and therefore are also on the TGE's lengthy list of enemies. In the Anvil Galaxy, Naruni Enterprises has the good sense to stay away from TGE territory and operatives, so the Empire rarely gets the chance to directly slam the arms-dealing enterprise the way they would like. However, Invincible Guardsmen will sometimes seek out Naruni production facilities and supply ships to destroy them just to spite the arms dealers and to teach them a lesson, "Sell to the enemy, be treated like the enemy."

Hartigal Combine: The TGE treats this renegade manufacturer as a subsidiary of Naruni and/or the CCW. When the day comes for the Kreeghor to rule the galaxy, Hartigal shall lie in ruins like so much else of the CCW civilization.

Golgan Republik: The Kreeghor appreciate the Golgans' imperial tendencies, and they certainly appreciate their efforts to build a buffer zone around their home world. They also respect their military history and self-reliance, but the time has come for the Republik to go. It is weakening and fragmenting, and the TGE would like nothing more than to grab whatever is left of the Republik before the CCW or some other power gets their grubby little fingers on it.

Altess Dynasty: The Kreeghor disregard the Altess' claims to special lineage. Frankly, many Kreeghor feel the Legend of the First is something of a farce. After all, they were engineered into existence by the Splugorth and so could any of the other races in the galaxy. Claiming to be built by some mythic and all-powerful progenitor just sounds stupid to the Kreeghor, and so the TGE has no interest in taking seriously a civilization like the Altess Dynasty, to which the myth of the First plays such an important role.

Central Alliance: The Kreeghor admire the sheer viciousness of these people, their love for combat, and their lack of the more delicate emotions so often showed by the citizens of the CCW and UWW. The TGE would like to incorporate the Central Alliance into their Empire, but there is no telling if these people would come willingly, and the TGE has enough problems without bringing a bunch of cybernetic thrill killers into the fold. For the moment, the Central Alliance forms a buffer between a segment of the TGE and the CCW, which means on the other side of it, CCW border forces are lesser than elsewhere. Thus, the TGE considers the Central Alliance as a good spot for mounting a quick invasion, should the Emperor ever decide to take such a route. It would be fortunate if the people of the Alliance took part in a Kreeghor march to glory, but if they do not, then so be it. The Kreeghor will just march over them instead.

Cosmo-Knights: Bah! Cosmo-Knights! The TGE considers them to be the utmost of enemies, and they are to be destroyed on sight. Unfortunately, TGE weaponry does little to harm the Cosmo-Knights, and so the Kreeghor feel particularly vulnerable to them. Though the Invincible Guardsmen were formed in part to foil the Cosmo-Knights, they never quite match up. Still, what the Guardsmen lack in power they make up for in conviction, and there have been plenty of times when several Guardsmen have attacked Cosmo-Knights despite the odds and came out victorious. To the Kreeghor, that is proof of the true power of Imperial courage.

Kingdom of Rynncryyl: Only the Splugorth, the race that created the Kreeghor, and the race from which the Kreeghor won its freedom, are more hated than the CCW. The Kreeghor actually will deal and negotiate with the CCW, and if they can avoid war, they will do it. (They won't like it, but they know that avoiding war with the CCW better suits their interests for the time being.) The Splugorth, however, get no such treatment. Any and all Splugorth presence in the Three Galaxies is to be destroyed at once, under direct order from the Emperor. Having said that, the TGE knows where the various Splugorth Kingdoms are in the Three Galaxies, but they have not sought them out for destruction yet because they have greater fish to fry just now. Should things quiet down with the rebellion and the Forge War, the Splugorth had better expect a TGE invasion force right away. In the Anvil Galaxy, the only major Splugorth presence is the Kingdom of Rynncryyl, the most diabolic and most insane Splugorth in the Three Galaxies! Since he keeps his Kingdom in the Threshold, the TGE find it easy to ignore him, but should any of his ships or minions be found anywhere near TGE space,

then the Imperials will move to engage, shooting to kill. The Splugorth know this and keep a respectful distance.

Gene-Tech: The enigmatic Gene-Tech are viewed as dangerous beings who refused Kreeghor invitations to join the Empire and who serve their own dark purpose or some secret, higher power, making them an unknown quantity that drives the Kreeghor crazy. The fact that the Gene-Tech go around mutating and creating new races, and stirring up trouble, reminds the Kreeghor of the hated Splugorth and earns the Gene-Tech similar treatment from the TGE as the Splugorth. The Empire would not mind plundering the Gene-Tech to get their hands on their revolutionary and extensive genetic engineering knowledge, because with that expertise in their arsenal, the Invincible Guardsmen could be made much more powerful than they already are, and Kreeghor shock troops could also be made to wield special powers and modifications. Of course, the Gene-Tech ignore or decline TGE requests for their help or to sell them even a scrap of their knowledge, which is a slap in the face that only makes the Kreeghor hate these mad scientists all the more.

Omegan Order: The TGE likes these guys because they are enemies of the Cosmo-Knights, and an enemy of their enemy is by default a friend. Only the Omegan Order wants nobody's company, so the TGE is content to leave them be, taking heart in the trouble they inflict on the CCW. Should, however, the Omegan Order get in the TGE's way while they look for the Cosmic Forge in the Core, the TGE will not hesitate to smash them into pieces. Nothing must stand in the way of finding the Forge.

Xodian Collective: The TGE has had limited contact with the Xodians, largely because their territory in the Core is nowhere near where the TGE has been focusing its search attempts in the center of the galaxy. What little they know about the Xodians points to a race that might serve well as an addition to the Imperial Guardsmen, if they learn the proper respect for Kreeghor superiority, that is.

K!ozn: The TGE is frustrated by the K!ozn's superior attitude and refusal to deal with Halo power blocs as if they were equals. Still, the TGE respects the K!ozn's apparently superior technology, and the various soldier races the K!ozn have sent out on errands have performed most admirably. Truly a race not to be trifled with.

Independent Worlds: The Empire has tried to gobble up as many of these as possible, especially in the Anvil Galaxy where they need all the allies and subordinates they can get to tip the scale against the CCW/UWW alliance. The problem is, most of the Independent Worlds in the Anvil Galaxy are either beyond the Empire's reach, safely within the shadow of the CCW, or are powerful enough to make any kind of Kreeghor takeover a long and bloody affair. The long and short of it is that the TGE has no more worlds to conquer in the Anvil Galaxy. Not like they used to, anyway, and so they must focus their energies on defeating the enemies at hand — the CCW, the UWW, and whatever secondary power blocs dare oppose them.

TGE Society

The Empire runs on a very simple system: citizens can do what they want as long as they don't interfere with the Empire, break the law, or willingly or accidentally get in the way of somebody more important than they. On the surface, life in the

Trans-Galactic Empire is not too different from that of other worlds. People go to their jobs, start their own businesses, and lead seemingly normal lives. Closer examination reveals that things are not as normal as they seem.

TGE Daily Life

First of all, there is always a visible military presence in the lives of the Imperial subjects. Armed patrols can be seen on all major streets. Propaganda posters proclaiming war victories can be seen on every street corner, and movies and television have clearly militaristic undertones and zealous, patriotic programming. A sizable percentage of the population is directly involved in the military. Every town, city and village has an armed garrison. Every child born in the Empire has seen tanks rolling down the streets or military jets flying overhead.

Also, there is always an atmosphere of fear. If a person says the wrong thing in public, he might get a visit from an armed squad. Most of the time, the person is just intimidated and threatened by the soldiers, but sometimes the victim just disappears, never to be seen again. Any criticism of the Empire is met with censorship, repression and violence. The Royal Family has the right of life and death over all subjects (there are no citizens in the TGE, only "subjects" without legal rights). If a Royal likes your home, he can evict you and move in himself. These privileges are not enforced often, but each injustice reminds people that they have no rights or defenses against their powerful masters. Imperial propaganda tries to counter all of this with claims that the Empire has brought peace and prosperity to all member planets. Many people believe in this and are actually dedicated to the betterment of the TGE. Those who disagree are afraid of speaking their minds.

Slavery is legal in the Trans-Galactic Empire. Convicted criminals, captives of war and the descendants of slaves make up most of the slave population. Parents can sell their children into slavery if they want to. "I'll sell you off if you don't behave," is a threat commonly heard in many poor households. People can even sell themselves off to pay debts. A slave can buy his freedom if he manages to save enough money. However, this is exceedingly difficult because they don't get wages, but slaves can save up tips and gratuities. Slaves have very few rights. Owners can kill or abuse them with relative impunity. Escaped slaves that are guilty of treason are tortured or executed when captured. Most wealthy households have one or more slaves – some have dozens. Entire factories, mining operations, farms and plantations are often run on slave labor.

Racism is rampant in most parts of the Trans-Galactic Empire. The Kreeghor and a few "worthy" races, such as the *Machine People*, the *Silhouette* and the *Wulfen*, enjoy more privileges than others. These people are rarely mistreated by the authorities, are always given the benefit of the doubt, and usually win any legal trouble they have with members of other species. A slave's word against one of the these races is dismissed entirely. Humans, the second largest race after the Kreeghor, are treated as second-class citizens unless they are members of the armed forces.

Law and Order

The laws of the Trans-Galactic Empire are simple and brutal. Suspects are assumed to be guilty until proven innocent. The au-

thorities can search any premises without need for warrants, and arrest suspects on the flimsiest of evidence. Those convicted of minor offenses (petty theft, littering, etc.) are fined heavily, often the equivalent of several years' worth of pay. If the person cannot pay, they have to work it off in labor, performing such duties as garbage collecting and street sweeping. Thieves, con men and political dissenters are condemned to hard labor, erecting buildings or working in mines, or sold into slavery. Murderers, rapists, and convicted traitors are either executed (often by torture) or condemned to one of the Hellworlds, brutal prisons deliberately designed to be worse than death (described elsewhere).

Unlike the Consortium, the Trans-Galactic Empire has only one legal system in force throughout its territories. Kreeghor law is "efficient" as the Kreeghor refer to it. The accused are assumed guilty until proven innocent, and money and power talks. Most punishments range from lengthy prison sentences to slavery and death. Prison is spent on the **Hellworlds**, those planets specifically intended for use as prison environments. Typically Hellworlds are the worst real estate in the Empire's dominions, and spending any appreciable amount of time on one is considered to be a worse punishment than death. Imperial propaganda makes a big deal out of the fact that the law is never "easy" on criminals, and criticizes the CCW for "coddling murderers and hooligans" because they lack the intestinal fortitude to be properly harsh on lawbreakers.

Despite the harshness of the laws, crime is at least as common in the TGE as it is in the Consortium. Since most people are afraid of the cops, very few step forward and press charges or act as witnesses against criminals. As a result, a lot of petty thieves, murderers, and racketeers often get away with a lot, as long as they are careful not to step on the toes of the Royal Family and their lackeys. Criminal gangs dominate the slums and poor neighborhoods of most cities in the Empire. The Kreeghor only sweep them up when they are suspected of collaborating with either the Splugorth or the Free World Council. The Gun Brothers have a few teams operating in the TGE, but they are being constantly hunted down by the authorities, who execute them without mercy (usually on the spot).

Smuggling is a common offense. Imperial tariffs are extremely high, in an attempt to try to protect the Kreeghor monopoly on most manufactured goods. As a result, spacers willing to take risks can make an enormous profit running the Imperial blockades and selling products from other civilizations. Weapon smuggling, especially to the Free World Council, is also extremely profitable. The freedom fighters will pay any price for good quality military equipment, and they have the funds (typically loot from the Imperial treasure houses) to pay for it. They are especially eager to purchase Naruni weapons.

There is no police force in the Empire. Instead, the Imperial Legions act both as the military and law-enforcement agency.

Worlds of Interest

Serti Gandle, Prime Dominion. This is considered the throne world of the TGE's section of the Anvil Galaxy. Controlled by *Gura'g Kuorg*, High Prince of the Kreeghor Royal Family, Serti Gandle is where all Imperial authority radiates from in this part of the universe. When the Emperor has something important to say, he sends it along to Serti Gandle and trusts that world to disseminate it properly.

This planet is the home of the *Kreeghor Armadas* and the *Imperial Army* in the Anvil Galaxy, as well as the *Invincible Guardsmen*. The world is an impenetrable fortress, filled with shipyards, factories, barracks, and other kinds of typically military architecture. The whole world looks like one big military base, which is pretty much what it is. Serti Gandle bristles with defensive screens, scanners, automated weaponry, starship patrols, and various other security measures. At any given time, there are at least 1,000 assorted warships either in orbit or on the ground ready to deploy, and a standing army of 2-3 million troops remains on constant alert should they be needed. There also remains at least a dozen Invincible Guardsmen on the world at all times, even though those super-warriors would probably prefer to be out and about, stirring up trouble for the CCW and its allies. While it is typical Imperial practice to go overboard securing its important worlds, they really must do so here, since Serti Gandle is, tactically speaking, like putting all of their eggs in one basket. Were the CCW or UWW to destroy this planet, they would decapitate the TGE forces in the Anvil Galaxy, dealing it a blow from which it would probably never recover.

To call Serti Gandle a police state is to drastically undervalue the meaning of the words "police state." TGE citizens have no business being on the world – only military and Royal Family and specially appointed visitors may even enter this star system, let alone land on the planet below. Oddly, this is also where the

Empire receives all of its ambassadors from other power blocs. The Kreeghor think that by making envoys meet here, under the presence of such an awesome array of the Empire's might, visitors will be intimidated and more acquiescent to the Empire. Actually, it has just the opposite effect – ambassadors tend to be offended by having to kowtow amid such a display of force, and they leave resolved to work with the Empire all the less. Serti Gandle is a dark, wet, miserable world where the sun never shines, it never stops raining, and the air smells mildly of sulfur and smoke. It is a Kreeghor paradise, and they consider it to be the most beautiful planet in the Anvil Galaxy. Figures.

Keblinka. Long ago, this world used to be part of the *Golgan Republik*, but as that power bloc has crumbled, the TGE has snapped up what it can along the way. Keblinka is a world that tried setting up its own coalition government with five other planets shortly after breaking away from the Republik. This coalition primarily served Lurgess aliens, a race best known as the carriers of ultra-virulent plagues that will destroy virtually any other carbon life form that comes into contact with it. When traveling among other people, the Lurgess wear environmentally sealed exoskeletons, but they long for a place where they can live without these things, and so this system of worlds was meant to be such a place. The TGE invaded shortly thereafter, unfortunately destroying all life on four of the five planets and capturing the fifth so they might exploit the rich gold, silver and diamond deposits there. The Kreeghor quickly learned of the virulent Lurgess and their contaminated world, but not after they had bombed the planet back into the Stone Age, destroying all Lurgess containment suits. The TGE has scoured the planet of the Lurgess contagion, but they kept the Lurgess population to work the various mines being dug. So, they built enormous and horrific concentration camps in which the poor Lurgess are forced to live and work (the camps are right on top of the mine entrances). The Empire also built a large space station orbiting the planet, and soldiers working guard duty on the planet's surface do so for three-day shifts, wearing environmental armor the entire time. When they return to the space station, the armor must be scoured and purified or the soldiers are not let through the station's bio-hazard zones. As for the camps, they have become hideous examples of Kreeghor cruelty, and the Imperials inflict every kind of cruelty and torture upon their Lurgess prisoners while working them to death. Even the Coalition States of Rifts Earth might balk at the kind of harsh treatment the Kreeghor inflict upon the Lurgess daily, but that is the Kreeghor to a tee – vicious, cruel, and happiest when inflicting pain on the helpless. Rumor has it a team of Cosmo-Knights and/or mortal adventurers is planning a raid on this world, with the intent of destroying the mine facilities and rescuing the Lurgess. Secondary objective is to destroy the TGE space station.

Thiradon III. The Thiradon system used to be a heavily populated corner of the TGE until harmonic disruptions caused the two worlds closest to the sun to explode without warning. The Kreeghor overlord commanding the third planet was warped by this catastrophe, and ever since has become obsessed with random chaos. He exhibits it with an unnatural love for gambling and games of chance, and he runs enormous festivals every quarter-year which turn Thiradon III into a huge carnival and casino during that time. The local government foots the bill for the festivals, largely by jacking up taxes on the locals to 70%

or 80%. Locals are not welcome to the festivals, only military personnel, Royal Family and specially invited off-world guests. The array of games to play is mind-boggling, but all of them permit gambling in some form. These festivals typically last for 21 days, after which the 32 players who have accumulated the most prize money will play off against each other in a single-elimination tournament. The winner of that tournament gets the right to play the overlord himself in a thee-day series of games. If the challenger wins, he gains control of the planet forever or until the next games festival unseats him. If the challenger loses, he gets beheaded on the spot. Surprisingly, many of the Empire's best game players yearn to get into the "Elimination Tournament," because it is considered a great honor to do so and the prize is an entire planet. Other than gaming halls, shady financial institutions and various entertainment centers, there is little honest industry on this world at all. Apart from its shiny, flashy cities, the planet is dull, dreary and inhospitable.

Zeihan 12, Prison World. Zeihan 12 is, predictably, the twelfth moon of the gas giant Zeihan Major. Each of the twelve moons is like a miniature planet on its own, many of which are verdant worlds with Earth-like atmospheres and support impressive populations. "Z12," as it is nicknamed, is the outermost planetoid moon, and meteorite impacts have, over time, reduced it to a cratered ruin with a trace atmosphere consisting mostly of noxious, corrosive vapors. The gravity is several times that of the Earth, and it is bitterly cold all of the time. What's more, the lack of atmosphere makes anybody on the surface *not* in an environmental suit susceptible to dangerously high radiation exposure. A mild case of overexposure resembles severe sunburn. A major case results in scarring, disfigurement, mutation or death. All of these things together made Z12 the perfect candidate to become one of the TGE's infamous Hellworld prisons. The warden, a particularly sadistic Kreeghor who goes only by the name of *Mr. Z*, runs an open facility – that is, there are no walls, no contained environments of any kind. Inmates are free to come and go as they please. The catch is, they are never, ever allowed inside a protected environment. They must spend their entire time outside, in an environmental suit. The harsh conditions are rough on these suits, so they need constant repairs and replacement. There is only one repair facility on the planetoid, under Mr. Z's personal care. Prisoners with damaged suits may walk in an airlock and remove the suit and wait for it to be repaired again – this is a grueling experience since the airlocks are not well insulated and some prisoners freeze to death before they get their suits back. More importantly, though, Mr. Z charges for all repair work, and there is only one industry on Z12: rock mining. Using only hand-held tools, the prisoners must bust rock down to small enough pieces to carry (Remember, under high gravity conditions) and cash them in to Mr. Z. The warden gives a pittance for every load of rock, all part of a carefully figured formula that makes it so prisoners must work at 100% all the time if they hope to get enough money saved up by the time their suit needs overhauling. Prisoners who somehow damage their suit or suffer a malfunction usually either die or buddy up with a friend for as long as they can, sharing life support between the suits, etc.

The average life expectancy on Z12 is one year. The longest lived inmate on the world is General Diego Galveh, a CCW military hero who was taken prisoner by the TGE during a clandestine raid on one of their factory worlds three years ago. Since it was a black op, General Galveh was disavowed and left to his own fate, as he knew he would be. He has survived for thee years, and not a day goes by when he does not think of some way to escape or organize a rebellion that might save his and every other inmate's life. Taking out Mr. Z won't be easy. He lives in an armored bunker with a command staff of 30 armored Kreeghor troopers, all of whom are combat veterans who are just aching for some action.

Thelag Vohann, Weapons Research World. Knowing that the CCW has effectively hired Naruni Enterprises to conduct weapons research and development for them, the TGE is facing a long-term deficit in weapons technology. The embattled evil empire can hardly sustain another drawback in its race for supremacy over the CCW, and so it has established a network of R&D planets across the Three Galaxies. These worlds enjoy curiously free rein to conduct whatever experiments they like, so long as they ultimately benefit weapons and armor development. So far, the project is showing promising results, but nothing definite has come out of it yet. Within a few more years, however, the Emperor expects a quantum leap in his armies' destructive capability, or every scientist recruited for this project will face execution. (Talk about your killer deadline!) Despite the incredibly tight security at Thelag Vohann, the premier TGE research world in the Anvil Galaxy, the science teams there want out. They do not believe they can give the Emperor what he wants in time, and they sure aren't going to work hard the next few years just so they can be executed. So, they are trying to find a way off their world. Agents from the CCW have contacted them, but have been unable to send operatives to actually make contact with the scientists and get them out. For that, a GSA covert strike team or some really talented mercenaries will be required. A likely candidate might be *Col. Wolf Harker*, commander of the *Tharsis Division*, a mercenary company that has done black ops for the GSA in the past. Only thing is, Harker is missing in action, having not reported in from the last time the GSA sent him out on a secret mission...

Qidia. Home to the Qidian race, an alien people recently absorbed into the TGE and none too happy about it, Qidia is turning out to be a risky proposition for the Empire. The Qidians, despite their other talents, have a deeply developed warrior culture, and they are renowned for their skill at unarmed combat. Most Qidians know one of a number of native martial arts, and with these skills alone, rebel Qidians have been able to defeat Kreeghor soldiers with relative ease. The Imperial Army first tried to destroy every school, village and monastery where Qidian warriors might train, but that has only generated more rebels. Now, the Empire is offering lucrative positions to any Qidian who teaches his skills to the Imperial Army. So far, there are few takers. The Qidians, a reserved and inward folk, are simply biding their time for when the opportunity comes to body slam the Imperials on their world and show them that Qidia is free and always will be.

Troma Nydae. One of the largest terrestrial planets in the Anvil Galaxy (it is easily more than ten times the diameter of Earth), Troma Nydae is largely covered with dense and vibrant jungles. Some civilizations might look at this place as a natural treasure and leave well enough alone, but not the Trans-Galactic Empire. To them, this world is good for lumber and coming up with hot, new biotechnology. Kreeghor scientists believe that the extreme bio-diversity in the planet's jungles makes Troma Nydae a gold mine for developing all sorts of pharmaceuticals. In fact, the planet is so incredibly rich in plant and animal life that the TGE scientists stationed here hardly have to do any work to produce new wonder products. They need only understand the natural processes before them and figure out a means of industrializing them for export. It is like the deepest Amazon on a planetary scale. The only civilization present is the loose network of TGE outpost cities – heavily armed, supplied and fortified, but cut off nonetheless. Aside from the scientists and workers living here, these cities are also a haven for freelance merchants who can make a killing selling exotic merchandise to the isolated laborers of Troma Nydae.

Dirakath. Situated very close to its sun (not unlike Mercury to our Sun), this planet is subjected to scorching heat and intense radiation. In a brilliant move, the scientists of this planet established a system of orbital lenses and mirrors that would soak up all of this energy and beam it in tight pulses to the other worlds of the system. There, energy collectors in orbit over those other worlds would catch the energy and use it to charge energy cells. Some of it would be beamed down to the planet's surface, where it would feed into the planetary power grid. This method loses a lot of energy from the original pulses sent out from Dirakath, but it still delivers lots of clean, free and limitless energy to the other worlds of the system. One hundred years ago, the TGE overran the system and captured this unique energy transferral system. The TGE being the TGE, they immediately wanted to make a weapon out of this. They succeeded only in dismantling the energy transfer network and adding a few more lenses and projectors to those already in orbit over Dirakath. The result is that Dirakath is basically a huge gunnery station, forever collecting solar energy, storing it up, and able to fire off intensely powerful energy bolts to anywhere in the galaxy. The Kreeghor have not yet tested this weapon system fully, but they are convinced that an energy blast from this system could vaporize the largest battleships at close range. Once (or if) the Kreeghor get this system to work right, they intend to install them on all of their conquered systems as a cheap and simple means of providing each system with a powerful super-weapon to fight off enemy invasion. Consequently, operations on Dirakath have been targeted for sabotage by enemy forces.

Sirab Ona. The TGE invaded this world over 250 years ago, receiving little initial resistance from the locals. After a brief campaign, the TGE assumed control of the cities and assumed that any resistance on this world's immense and inhospitable wilderness would be sporadic at best. Well, they were wrong. Dead wrong. As it turned out, this world had a huge, rural indigenous population. The standing armies of the cities the TGE defeated were probably the weakest of all factions of local warriors, all of whom had honed their art by fighting each other all their lives in never-ending factional conflicts. With a foreign invader to turn their sights to, the locals unified, scrounged up what M.D.C. weapons they could, and began resisting. A quarter of a millennia later, the same insurgent kind of war is still going on with no end in sight. The thing is, the TGE is really doing a lot of good for the locals, who, until TGE dominion, were under the heel of monsters, interstellar bandits, and the like. Are the TGE tyrants? Yes. Are the oppressed benefitting from it? Yes. Does this put the rebels into a very ambiguous gray zone? Yes, but before the TGE took over, the world was plunged into bitter and severe factional wars. Despite their tyrannical culture, the TGE made this world a better place in which to live, and that is causing some of the locals to wonder which is more important: freedom from slavery (as under the TGE) or freedom to vote, to speak freely, etc.

Pomadon, World of Demons. Pomadon has long been a part of the TGE's Anvil Galaxy territory, but it never figured prominently as a military outpost or manufacturing center. It was just one of hundreds of worlds filled with Imperial subjects who lived their lives, paid their taxes, and volunteered for military service. Several decades ago, a massive explosion at the planet's main fusion reactor caused a chain reaction that ultimately destroyed 80% of the world's energy-making industry. The chain of fusion reactions was similar to the nuclear war that sparked the Coming of the Rifts on Earth, and as anybody from *that* embattled world can attest, what would come next was not pretty. Indeed, the fusion explosions killed billions of people, and the P.P.E. surge from that opened up numerous Rifts along the planet's modest ley lines. Since then, Pomadon has become a world infested with extra-dimensional monsters and demons of every kind. The TGE has little experience in fighting such things, and though they have responded bravely and with extreme firepower (orbital bombardments are routine), they still are no closer to closing the dimensional portals and preventing more demons and monsters from coming through and replacing the ones already slain by Imperial legionnaires. Unless the TGE finds a permanent solution to the problem of Pomadon, they will end up having to deploy battle groups here forever just to keep the demon menace contained. TGE scientists, however, are intrigued by the monsters coming through here and would like to capture a few so they might be studied for future bio-engineering projects. (**G.M. Note:** Space restrictions prevent us from detailing any of the monsters plaguing Pomadon, so we encourage you to use either of the random monster generators in the **Rifts® RPG,** use existing creatures in other Palladium RPG books or make up your own. Note that Pomadon has only one tenth the amount of magic or number of dimensional Rifts of Rifts Earth.)

The United Worlds of Warlock

Population: 500 billion, 400 billion of which are in the Anvil Galaxy.

Demographics: Star Elves (20%), Humans (15%), Wulfen (15%), Dwarven Guildmasters (15%), Space Minotaurs (6%), Ratanoids (7%), Others (22%; includes supernatural beings like demons and Elementals, as well as dozens of other races).

Overview: Long before the Consortium of Civilized Worlds (CCW) was even a concept, the magic users of the Anvil Galaxy banded together for mutual defense against evil powers such as the Kreeghor, the Gene-Tech and the Splugorth. Pooling their talents to create incredible technological and magical means of traveling through space, this civilization soon established a wide-ranging society in which magic surpassed non-magical technologies to become the dominant form of industry and power. Here, magic is commonplace and the standard, not machinery, and here all people through whom magic flows like blood in their veins are welcome. Thus was born the *United Worlds of Warlock*, and they continue to be a strong force in the Three Galaxies, especially the Anvil Galaxy, to this day. In terms of size and raw power, the UWW ranks behind the Consortium of Civilized Worlds and the Trans-Galactic Empire, making it the third most influential power bloc in the Anvil Galaxy. For a society not bent on expanding its territory or subjugating others, this degree of prominence is neither expected nor unwelcome. To the vast majority of decision makers in the UWW, their vast domain and power amount to nice perks and a degree of authority and independence they never thought they would enjoy.

The first civilization to use magic instead of technology to travel throughout the Anvil Galaxy was controlled by the Elves – soon thereafter to be known as "Star Elves." These so-called "Star Elves" never learned how to build true spaceships; instead, they opened dimensional portals from one planet to the next, never leaving the atmosphere. Soon their jeweled towers rose in several dozen worlds. Under *High King Silverlight* (who continues to rule, thousands of years later), the *Star Kingdom* became a powerful space-faring culture.

Before long, the Star Kingdom made contact with a coalition of practitioners of magic of diverse alien races. This coalition eponymously called itself the *Warlocks*, in reference to their traditional leaders, those Warlocks whose magical abilities granted them mastery over the elements themselves. Unlike the Star Kingdom, the Warlocks also tried to combine high technology and magic to travel between worlds. When Warlock ships first visited the Star Kingdom, they were amazed at the Elves' lack of conventional spacecraft of any kind. Likewise, the Elves found the Warlock ships to be fascinating, and soon the two parties both saw in each other unique strengths. Both societies realized they had much to gain by joining forces, and so they did. The Star Elves quickly realized the advantages an enemy who could control space would enjoy over them and resolved to build their own space fleet. Fortunately, the Warlocks were not interested in conquest. They had occupied a handful of uninhabited worlds, but their main interest was *exploration*. The Warlock Council and the Elven High King met shortly after the first contact and a treaty of cooperation and mutual assistance was signed. The Star Elves exchanged their dimension spanning magicks for alien secrets of magic and technology. Elven explorers discovered that ley lines existed in space and that their Rift Jump Drives (described in **Phase World®**, page 152) were even more effective if they followed those ley lines. Within a decade, all the cosmic ley line systems were mapped and used as space-lanes.

The alliance slowly grew, and as they expanded they met other civilizations. To their misfortune, their first neighbor turned out to be a Splugorth dominion. The Splugorth and their minions did not waste any time, attacking an Elven planet by surprise, slaughtering half the population and enslaving the rest. The Warlocks and the Elven Star Kingdom rallied their forces for a counterattack, but they found themselves outnumbered and outgunned by the Splugorth's space fleet. Although the Splugorth warships were not experienced in fighting magic-wielders, their numbers were much greater and their technology roughly equal in power and capabilities. In desperation, the magicians sent pleas for help through the ley lines, hoping somebody out there would come to their rescue. Indeed, what a rescue there would be!

In the middle of a major space battle, a planet-sized dimensional Rift opened above the combatants. Through the space distortion came a horde of crude starships made of riveted iron and steel, enchanted to resist the hardships of space. The newcomers poured magic fire and lightning on the surprised Kittani starships, destroying several of them and scattering the rest of the fleet into a panicked rout. Some of the strange ships' weapons projected mini-Rifts among the enemy, tearing ships apart or transporting them to other dimensions. The Star Elves and Warlocks took the opportunity to regroup their own forces and tear into their enemy's ranks. In the ensuing bloodbath, the Splugorth minions lost nine-tenths of their ships. This day would later be known as the *Battle of Newcomers*, to commemorate the most dramatic entrance of the Elves and Warlocks' newest ally, the Dwarven Guildmasters.

The Dwarven Guildmasters (a.k.a. Anvil Dwarves) were from the other side of the Anvil Galaxy. Due to natural phenomena the Dwarves were powerless to stop (they were most likely harmonic disruptions), their worlds were literally falling apart into shattered belts of planetoid-sized chunks of lifeless rock. Their territory no longer habitable, the Dwarven Guildmasters were a people without a home. But, hearing the distress call from the Star Elves and Warlocks, they sent their advance fleet to the scene where it helped deliver one of the most reeling blows any Splugorth civilization had suffered in a single battle. A hurried meeting and treaty between the Star Elves, Warlocks and Dwarven Guildmasters soon followed, with the Star Elves and Warlocks promising to share their technology and their territory in return for a military alliance with the Dwarven Guildmasters. The Anvil Dwarves agreed, and the **United Worlds of Warlock** were born.

Immediately thereafter, this combined force followed up on its victory at the Battle of Newcomers and assaulted a major Splugorth slave world, liberating the slaves and running the Splugorth intelligence *Ythcryss* out of this dimension! (Yythcryss died shortly thereafter at the hands . . . . er, tentacles of his fellow Splugorth.) In the process, they captured a great deal of new knowledge, including pyramid technology and stone magic (see **Rifts® World Book One: Atlantis**), making their magic expertise even more supreme among the Three Galaxies. Since then, a few other Splugorth worlds have joined the UWW, giving them a small population of Splugorth minions to use for spying and covert operations against their most hated enemy.

Government

The UWW is a very loose federation, with more diverse laws and cultures than even the Consortium. The lack of centralization means that member planets are able to have any type of government, from enlightened democracies to savage dictatorships. More than anything, what is important is that the member worlds all use magic, and that they all stick together in times of crisis. The UWW was forged from the fires of war against the Splugorth. Now, it finds itself in a similar crisis as they race against the Splugorth, the Trans-Galactic Empire, and even their old friends, the CCW, to find the *Cosmic Forge*. Now more than ever, member worlds are able to overlook each other's governmental indiscretions. So long as they remain united toward finding the Forge, all is forgiven.

The government of the United Worlds of Warlock is the fusion of three very different government systems. The Elven Star Kingdom was a monarchy, controlled by the Star Elf High King and his *Star Chamber*, a group of advisors and ministers. The Warlocks were ruled by a *Sorcerers' College* that was elected by a vote among all magicians in the coalition. The Dwarven

Guilds were a loose coalition of craftsmen's guilds, each of which elected a representative at the *Guildmasters' Council*.

To accommodate all these governments, the **Parliament of Worlds** was formed. This ruling body included the full membership of the Star Chamber, the Sorcerers' College and the Guildmasters' Council. The Parliament also added two representatives from each member world. A *Consul*, roughly equivalent to a president, is elected by a majority vote in the Parliament. So far, the only Consul has been the Elven High King, Silverlight, who has been elected for the past one hundred elections! Silverlight's fairness, charisma and intelligence have made him stand head and shoulders above all other candidates.

Each member world has to select two representatives. How this is done is left to the individual planet. Some worlds are run by monarchies, dictatorships or oligarchies who simply select the representatives. Others hold democratic elections.

The Warlock Navy

The Warlock Navy is the military arm of the United Worlds. This is a wholly volunteer force recruited from all member worlds. Every planet pays dues to keep the Navy armed and supplied. The largest contribution comes from the Star Kingdom and the Dwarven Guildmasters, who provide most of the Navy's ships and their crews. The Navy's role is basically defensive, fighting both outside threats and the Dark Covens. The best known Navy members are the elite *Warlock Marines*, highly trained soldiers equipped with fearsome power armor.

Since its creation, the Navy has fought in over a hundred minor conflicts, from large-scale Splugorth raids to skirmishes with the Trans-Galactic Empire, pirate fleets, Star Hives (a common threat in some UWW areas) and the occasional Dominator and supernatural intelligence. It has been successful most of the time.

Interestingly, it has *not* played a major role in the *Forge War* yet. While the CCW and TGE are pouring much of their military resources in the quest to find the Cosmic Forge, the UWW would much rather hold its Navy in reserve and send out individual operatives to seek clues to the Cosmic Forge and make discreet scouting trips to the Core of the galaxy. Part of the reason for this is that the Navy ships used by the UWW are largely hand-crafted and difficult to mass-produce. These ships are more time-intensive than they are resource-intensive, so every time one is lost in battle, it presents a big hole in the UWW's forces that cannot be filled right away. Thus, the Navy is used only for serious interventions. Navy ships do not patrol often, again because that exposes them to unnecessary danger. They spend most of their time in hangars, awaiting the call for deployment. Then they come like a dagger from the shadows, appearing seemingly out of nowhere, in force, to slam the enemy before they know what hit them.

Some of the less refined elements of the UWW, such as its Space Minotaurs, Ratanoids and some other races, serve as the Navy's Marines – highly trained mobile infantry ready to charge into action at a moment's notice. Over the years, though, the Warlock Marines, as these forces are called, have grown frustrated that they must rely on the Navy to get them into battle, a Navy that is perhaps a little too reluctant to fight! Elements within the Warlock Marines have clamored for getting alternate spacecraft, perhaps Naruni ships or CCW surplus – more expendable vessels that can be used without undue concern. That way, the Warlock Marines can be more visible to the UWW's enemies, and present a strong front to anyone who would oppose the UWW. So far, such requests have been denied time and again, and the Marines are growing impatient and disgruntled. Though there is no real talk of mutiny, the Admirals of the Navy realize that unless these soldiers are given a major war to fight – and soon – they might self-destruct. Of course, with the Forge War upon the entire Anvil Galaxy, these warriors might have the fight they have been spoiling for sooner than they expected.

The Dark Covens

Not all the organizations and governments of the United Worlds of Warlock are benevolent. Chief among the would-be despoilers of Warlock are the evil cults collectively known as the *Dark Covens*. Many members of the covens are Witches, evil Shifters, Space Warlocks, Demon Magi and the priests of evil gods. Others include vampires, supernatural creatures, and minor demons masquerading as humans or Elves. These groups are the common scourge of magic-using societies, and they are all too common in the United Worlds.

Despite their name, however, the Dark Covens are not a unified group. In fact, many compete and fight against each other, because they serve different (and antagonistic) entities. Vampires in particular are often at odds with demon worshipers and other practitioners of magic. Still, each separate group is often a formidable force in its own right. Many covens have infiltrated entire planetary governments, influencing whole worlds through a number of converted or mind-controlled puppets.

Historically, the Dark Covens have never posed a threat to the stability of the UWW at large, or even to an entire planet. They are the UWW's equivalent of a criminal underworld, only they are a purer, more sinister form of evil that merits utter eradication in the name of all that is good and pure in the universe. What is making the Dark Covens really feared now, however, is that they too are hot on the trail of the Cosmic Forge. Many times, the Covens infiltrate UWW sorcerers' colleges and pilfer secret information on the UWW's leads on the Forge's location, bringing them that much closer to finding this source of ultimate power and using it to abominable purposes. The Parliament of Worlds is determined to destroy the Dark Covens, every last one of them, before this happens, and to do that, they have authorized select groups of the Warlock Marines to search out Coven hiding spots and eradicate them. These small strike fleets hope to make up in surprise what they sacrifice in firepower. The Covens are really terrorist-type groups that are not a big army, but a network of guerilla fighters, assassins, agents and villains adept at spreading fear, suspicion and turmoil. Should any one Coven be attacked suddenly by a Warlock Marine strike team, the Marines will almost certainly carry the day, especially since they will have at least a few mid to high-level spell casters among them in addition to their Space Minotaur and Ratanoid troops.

Despite the early successes of the Warlock Marines, the most prominent leader of the Dark Covens, a Witch named *Azriel Darkling,* remains elusive. She routinely sends threatening communications to the Parliament of Worlds, and vows that soon she shall unleash a destructive force upon the UWW that will strike fear into the hearts of all the people living in the Three Galaxies.

Foreign Affairs

Enemies include the Splugorth worlds, pirates, Dark Covens and the Star Hives (described elsewhere). Splugorth ships are attacked on sight when they encroach on UWW space. Members of their minion races are immediately detained and questioned whenever they are spotted. Travelers and criminals who are likely to be Splugorthian spies are interrogated extensively, their activities watched closely and, in many instances, they are escorted out of UWW space and asked not to return.

Consortium of Civilized Worlds: The UWW and the CCW are on more or less friendly terms. They conduct quite a bit of trading with each other, and even though they do not always see eye to eye on a lot of things, both civilizations are content to let the other operate as they see fit. In the Anvil Galaxy, these two civilizations are both allies and rivals regarding the Cosmic Forge. They have sworn to help each other prevent the TGE from getting its clutches on the Forge, but at the same time, neither one wants to lose the race to get the Forge themselves. Unlike so many other power blocs in the Anvil Galaxy, rival CCW and UWW forces will probably *not* come to blows when trying to get the Cosmic Forge. They will deceive and outwit one another, but war between these two major powers, even over something as monumental as the Cosmic Forge, is not going to happen.

Trans-Galactic Empire: The UWW has long mistrusted the TGE and is unlikely to trade with them for any reason. Border skirmishes between TGE and UWW forces are more common than the UWW is comfortable with, and the UWW was only too happy to join with the CCW to help contain the TGE's search for the Cosmic Forge. That said, however, both the UWW and the TGE have a unique common enemy in the Splugorth, and it is not inconceivable for the UWW and TGE to one day team up to eradicate the Splugorth Kingdom of Rynncryyl in the Anvil Galaxy. That remains a very hypothetical situation, though, and for the present, the UWW sees the TGE much more as an enemy than as even a circumstantial ally.

Naruni Enterprises: Being masters of magic, the UWW has little use for Naruni weaponry or ruthless Naruni business practices. In general, these arms merchants are not welcome in UWW space, but at the same time, possession of Naruni technology is not prohibited either. Some elements of the Warlock Marines have secretly contacted Naruni to make weapons purchases for them so they might act more freely against the UWW's enemies. The Naruni, masters of discretion that they are, have kept such communications quiet, until such time as it might benefit them to use it for extortion or blackmail purposes.

Hartigal Combine: Just as the UWW has no use for Naruni Enterprises, it certainly has no use for this renegade subsidiary of it, either. Most folks in the UWW do not even know this organization exists, much less are inclined to do business with them.

Golgan Republik: The UWW has formal relations with the Republik, but the two powers are hardly bosom buddies. Certain member worlds of the UWW agree wholeheartedly with the Golgans' approach to repressive government and empire-building, while others feel the Golgans are just a bunch of despots and imperialists who try to gloss it over with polite manners and the veneer of civility. Either way, the Golgan Republik is falling apart, and as it does so, numerous worlds rich with P.P.E. and strong ley lines are becoming available for the UWW to make allies or to offer membership status.

Altess Dynasty: The haughty Altess, having alienated most other power blocs in the Anvil Galaxy, are used to going it alone, especially on the search for the Cosmic Forge. The UWW maintains formal relations with the government, but it does so for formality's sake and nothing more. The UWW is interested, however, in reports that the Altess have made *huge* leaps and bounds toward finding the Cosmic Forge, and that of all the power blocs on the hunt, they are said to be the closest to the prize. The UWW had long thought they, themselves, were the closest, since they can travel to the Core region and search it easily. The Altess lead troubles the UWW, and so they have begun making subtle overtures to the Dynasty that perhaps they should join forces and search for the Forge together.

Central Alliance: These barbaric cyber-gladiators are everything the UWW is not: purely focused on warfare and technology, with no appreciation for the mystic aspects of the universe. Since the UWW have little trade with the Central Alliance, and since they do not border them or share similar military concerns, the Alliance is effectively a non-entity to the UWW.

Cosmo-Knights: Seen as champions of truth and justice, the UWW hails the Cosmo-Knights as heroes and protectors, and gives them free passage anywhere within UWW territory. The UWW respects the Cosmo-Knight's neutrality in the search for the Cosmic Forge, though they suspect that the Knights know more about the Forge than they are letting on. Some members of the UWW Parliament of Worlds suspect the Cosmo-Knights somehow know the Cosmic Forge can never be found, which is why they are not bothering to look for it.

Kingdom of Rynncryyl: These hated Splugorth slavers are to be destroyed upon sight. The UWW is not interested in any negotiations with them at all. And neither are the Splugorth, not after the UWW captured some of their worlds, colonized their cities, and have successfully turned Splugorth technology back against the very people who invented it.

Gene-Tech: Considered to be a criminal element with the power of an independent solar system, the Gene-Tech rank somewhere between the Splugorth and the TGE as far as the UWW is concerned. It would take an atrocity on the Gene-Tech's part against the UWW to spur the Warlock confederation against them, however, and honestly, the Gene-Tech are far too smart for that. Should the Gene-Tech manage to find the Cosmic Forge, however, the UWW will spare no effort to destroy them and capture the Forge for themselves. The thought of what the Gene-Tech might do with the Cosmic Forge is just too mind-boggling to consider.

Omegan Order: These renegade Cosmo-Knights are a blight upon all of civilization, according to the UWW. Given the UWW's friendly relations with the Cosmo-Knights, the Omegan Order is considered an enemy of their state. Should the Cosmo-Knights ever request UWW aid in destroying the Omegan Order (an unlikely scenario, but one the UWW considers possible), the UWW would be only too happy to oblige. Especially since they know that the Omegan Order is nowhere nearly as powerful as the Cosmo-Knights are, and a united effort to destroy them would surely succeed. The problem is the Omegans are safely across the Threshold, which makes them difficult to assault for anybody who can not magically transport themselves there. Individual UWW mages can, but their Navy can not.

Xodian Collective: The Xodians are of interest to the UWW because they seem to be at least mystically attuned, if not outright users of magic energy. Either way, any race that eschews technology as much as the Xodians seem to can't be all bad. UWW envoys to the Core have met with the Xodians on a few occasions, and although these aliens are difficult to understand, a possible alliance in the future is not out of the question.

K!ozn: Though the UWW respects this ancient and advanced race's seniority, it does not appreciate its holier-than-thou attitude to the rest of the Anvil Galaxy. It also does not like that the K!ozn seemingly have appointed themselves protectors of the Cosmic Forge. K!ozn intervention has already cost the lives of plenty of UWW scouts and mystics, and the UWW wants to see that stopped. However, the UWW is alone in this sentiment for now, only because it spends far more time in the Core than the other Halo power blocs, and has more opportunities to establish a bad rapport with the K!ozn. Everybody else is too busy competing against or fighting each other for clues to the Cosmic Forge or trying to cross the Threshold to appreciate just how intractable the K!ozn are going to be to anyone searching in the Core for the Forge. The UWW does not think the K!ozn have it, but do believe the K!ozn know where it is. And for that, the UWW is willing to keep trying to deal with the K!ozn, showing them how worthy they are as trading partners, and so on.

Independent Worlds: The UWW has never been particularly aggressive in its expansion. It eagerly seeks new worlds with which to do business and if those worlds look like they might be good members, then the UWW extends an invitation to join their federation. Ultimately, the decision is up to the invited world or system or power bloc to join. The UWW is not really into coercing others to join them. They firmly believe that their member states should be 100% volunteers; loyalty born of free will is the foundation of a strong alliance. Even among worlds the UWW has not extended membership invitations to, the UWW has a reputation as fair dealers and a power bloc that is as good as its word. As the Forge War heats up, the UWW has been calling in its many favors to various independent worlds as they shake down the Anvil Galaxy for clues as to the Cosmic Forge's whereabouts. Most of these independent worlds are glad to help out their benefactors, since they generally think the UWW might use the Forge more responsibly than the CCW or any other power bloc.

Society

The society of the UWW is even more diverse and heterogeneous than the one of the Consortium. Almost every single planet has its own culture, customs and social classes. The main distinction in the United Worlds is that of magic-users and "mundanes." About 70% of the member worlds use some sort of magic or combinations of mystic disciplines as their primary form of technology. The rest are those "mundanes" who rely mostly on science and conventional technology. There is some friction between the two groups, but for the most part it is reduced to the occasional snide remark or rude joke about the disadvantages of relying on magic versus technology, or vice versa. Of special interest recently, has been the effort from the mundane side of the UWW to acquire conventional warships and military technology as a more easily replaced component of the UWW Navy. The Dwarven Guildmasters and Star Elves who command the mystical spacecraft of the Warlock Navy see this gesture as a little insulting. After all, the mystic armada has served the UWW well so far, who cares if it does not deploy so often? The UWW's power lies not in a visible show of force, but in the minds of its enemies who all know that beneath the surface of this quiet civilization are untapped powers of unthinkable destruction.

Daily Life

It is hard to refer to an "average" day or citizen of the UWW because it is so incredibly diverse from world to world, system to system. Mundane worlds are very similar to the CCW in terms of personal technology, quality of life, and so on. Worlds where magic has replaced technology are largely the same kind of setup except there is a magic equivalent for every piece of ubiquitous technology in CCW life. For the vast majority of UWW citizens, life is good, filled with peace and prosperity. The low population of the UWW means that most worlds have low population densities. Nowhere will one see the super-crowded arcologies found in the CCW, TGE and elsewhere. The most concentrated things get are certain planetary capitals which might be as densely developed and populated as a large city of 20th Century Earth, only magic is everywhere one looks, not pure technology.

Law and Order

There is no galactic body of law in the United Worlds. Each planet or planetary collective formulates its own laws. The Parliament of Worlds (see Rifts Phase World, page 85) only has jurisdiction in interplanetary affairs, and even then only when a planet requests aid. This means that the only time the United Worlds' government and armed forces will intervene is in case of a major emergency or disaster. Two member planets can even declare war on each other, and unless one of them asks for help, the Warlock Navy will only stand by!

There are only two main guidelines that all members agree to obey: 1) No member planet or collective can declare war or attack an outsider planet or collective; doing so might drag the entire United Worlds into a war. If a planet does this anyway, it forsakes its membership and the UWW will not help it in the conflict. 2) The other rule enforced throughout the United Worlds is against the worship or service of "supernatural intelligences" and so-called "demons." To the eyes of the UWW, this category refers to any entity that feeds on the life energies of sentient beings or seeks to torment or subjugate mortals. This includes vampires and vampire intelligences, demon and devil lords, and most supernatural monsters. "Gods" who desire worship but do not demand human sacrifices are exempt from this law. Despite the law, many cults (collectively known as the *Dark Covens*) operate secretly in the UWW.

The largest groups in the UWW, the Elven Star Kingdom and the Dwarven Guildmasters, have similar bodies of law. Most laws are very similar to the Consortium's, but with more emphasis on imprisonment than rehabilitation testing periods.

Worlds of Interest

Alfheim: The home world of the Elven Star Kingdom, Alfheim is a major center for magic, perhaps the greatest such place in the Anvil Galaxy. Not only is the planet itself crisscrossed with ley lines, but the world is "boxed in" by three ley line nexi in space above the planet. Each of these nexus points are created by the intersection of three different ley lines, making Alfheim easily the most ley-line intensive world in the galaxy. In terms of raw P.P.E. available, the extensive magic and technology on the surface runs nonstop, feeding exclusively off the world's groundside ley lines and even receiving ambient P.P.E. energy from each nexus in the sky.

The world is mostly a pastoral wonderland with the occasional metropolis looking like it was pulled from the pages of a fairy tale. Tall towers, graceful arches, slender yet strong walls, cobblestone pathways, all of these things define the look of these beautiful places, especially in Star City, the capital of the world. Here does *High King Silverlight* rule from his breath taking Palace of Diamonds, widely considered to be the most marvelous piece of architecture in the Three Galaxies. How could it not be? It stands 1000 feet (305 m) high and is made of pure crystal, decorated with colored jewels. The palace serves as the center of government for the United Worlds of Warlock and King Silverlight's home. He rarely leaves here, though being the master of magic that he is (15th level Wizard who knows *all* Wizard/Line Walker spells) he can make his presence felt a world away if he so desires.

Tempest: This world is full of Elemental beings of all types – Earth, Air, Water, and Fire. From time to time, rumors surface that new Elementals arrive on Tempest – Mud, Smoke, Dust, Mist, Lightning, Wind, Light, Darkness, Star, Time, Life, Death – but the existence of any of these beings has never been confirmed. Of course, the Parliament of Worlds never deny them, either, leading some to believe that perhaps there is on Tempest a secret project to establish contact with new and undiscovered Elemental Planes (if indeed there are any) and create entire new schools of elemental magic from them. In the meantime, however, life continues on Tempest in ways that make the planet inhospitable for anything besides an Elemental or a proper Warlock. All over the planet's surface, Elementals play their games. Their "games" cause constant storms, earthquakes, hurricanes and volcanic activity that make it almost impossible for normal humanoid life to survive. This also makes it impossible to invade this world, as Splugorth raiding parties learn the hard way each and every time they try to snatch a few Elementals off Tempest to be sold in the Phase World slave auctions. To date, no Elemental has ever been successfully captured, a statistic that Rynncryyl the mad would dearly love to change.

The Smithy: This planet is the ruling world of the Dwarven Guildsmasters. It is filled with factories and forges that create rune weapons and other magical devices and items as well as technological items. Spaceships, vehicles, weapons and other pieces of equipment are manufactured here, most of which are exported to other worlds within the UWW. If magic could be industrialized, it would be here. The magic weapons and enchanted items are still handmade, but there are millions upon millions of Dwarven craftsmen who blend magic with the material world and even with technology, always hard at work hammering out the latest magic items for UWW consumption. What is really amazing about this world is that the endless factories and metalworks covering the surface were actually contained within a massive pocket dimension at one point. When the Dwarven Guildsmasters abandoned their old empire, they lost all but one of their manufacturing planets. Determined not to lose their last and greatest magical production facility, they managed to lift the entire industrial infrastructure off the planet and transport it into a special pocket dimension of the Guildsmasters' creation. After that, all they had to do is find a suitable world on which to replace their massive factories. Apparently, the Guildsmasters could do this again, but precious few of them know the secrets behind such an enormous feat of magic. Rumor has it that over 100,000 Dwarves willingly gave up their lives to generate the P.P.E. needed for such an operation. Still, the thought of the UWW transporting entire planetary infrastructures to other worlds has interesting colonization possibilities, and more than a few UWW mages have suggested transporting the surface development of a few UWW worlds to a beachhead in the Core so future scouting missions have friendly territory to retreat to.

New Midgard: Technically speaking, this planet is ruled by the gods of the Norse Pantheon – Odin, Thor, Magni, Heimdall, Loki, Balder, Hel, Njord, Freyr and Freya (See **Rifts® Conversion Book Two: Pantheons of the Megaverse®** for details). Indeed, these gods routinely visit the world, but more so as a retreat or place to vacation for a while to take their troubled minds off whatever is bothering them back in Asgard. This was the way of life on this planet for eons before the UWW ever came to be. That the federation stumbled across a retreat for Norse Gods is a bit of a shocking coincidence for both sides,

and very quickly, the UWW agreed that they would cordon off the world and prevent outsiders from troubling the Norse deities. Odin, for his part, thanked the UWW leadership for their wisdom, and that is about all he or any of the other gods have ever said to anybody from the UWW. Perhaps as a sign of this appreciation, the Asgardian Dwarves on New Midgard man a number of magic factories, producing *Rift Ships* decorated with sea-serpent motifs and well stocked with all sorts of personal magic weapons and items. Upon completion, these ships and their contents are piloted to UWW docks and donated to the Warlock Navy. Periodically, somebody in the Parliament of Worlds suggests that maybe the gods should be recruited for a military drive against the Splugorth, but other members shoot down the ideas as pure lunacy. Recruit the GODS? Yeah, right.

As the Forge War gets underway, though, some UWW loyalists are afraid the Norse Gods will learn about the Cosmic Forge and will begin looking for it themselves. Indeed, there are those who insist that Asgardian minions of all kinds can be encountered throughout the UWW, and they can only be looking for one thing: the Forge of Forges, as they like to call it. **Note:** There seems to be little difference between Asgardian Dwarves and the Anvil Dwarves, leading some scholars to believe that, since the Asgardian Gods had set up shop in the Anvil Galaxy so long ago, the Dwarven Guildsmasters might very well be the descendants of Asgardian Dwarves, who for some reason established their own realm. Such a theory may not be far off the mark, as Asgardian Dwarves *have* been living on the planet for a very long time, as well as Asgardian Elves, Valkyries and numerous other mythical creatures. These folk generally do not leave the world, preferring to stay on this, a satellite territory of Asgard itself.

Alexandria, True Atlantean Colony: Alexandria is an important member planet of the UWW, having one of the largest concentrations of *True Atlanteans* in the Megaverse — over 50,000 members of this ancient and wise species (for more information on the True Atlanteans and their place in the Megaverse, refer to **Rifts® World Book Two: Atlantis**).

The Atlantean colony in Alexandria is dominated by *Clan Acherean* (pronounced Ah-keh-reh-ann), an influential group whose members have largely abandoned the practice of wandering the Megaverse to provide a safe haven for their nomadic brethren. Alexandria is a frequent site for the periodic gatherings of the various other Atlantean Clans. It is also a dimensional port of no small importance (although it pales to insignificance when compared to Phase World's Center).

The planet was a Rift-torn wasteland when the first Atlantean nomads arrived thousands of years ago. The inhabitants were all alien refugees brought to that world by freak dimensional anomalies and disturbances. Their lives were fraught with danger from both the Rifts themselves and demonic or monstrous creatures that often arrived through them. The True Atlanteans realized that the planet was a super-rich P.P.E. battery and that the only way to control its chaotic energies was to build a network of pyramids at major ley line nexus points.

The leader of the trans-dimensional band, an Elder Atlantean from Clan Acherean, called for help and thousands of members responded. Hundreds of Stone Masters (see **Rifts® Atlantis**, page 99) combined their powers to raise pyramids and tap into the powerful ley lines of Alexandria. Monitoring the flux of mystical energies was a full-time job, so the Atlanteans found themselves forced to stay on the planet. Cities soon grew around each major pyramid, and trans-dimensional trade flourished. When the ships of the United Worlds of Warlock arrived to Alexandria, the planet was already a prosperous and advanced world.

Clan Acherean was glad to relinquish power and allowed UWW administrators and officials to set up shop in their cities. The Atlanteans concentrated on managing the pyramids and then on venturing into the rest of the Three Galaxies to right wrongs and protect the innocent. Many Atlantean Undead Slayers, sorcerers and champions have come from Alexandria.

Thyrgord, Realm of Anarchy. This planet was settled by humans and Star Elves many centuries ago, and for all of that time, it has been the model of civility, productivity, and political stability. Except, every 25 years, the locals ritually abandon all government and dissolve all laws for exactly one year. During this time, there is pure anarchy. No social order of any kind, leaving the citizens to survive on their own however they would like. Often there is some looting and civil war, as well as those who flee the planet for the next 12 months. However, the majority of the people actually make anarchy look like a workable situation. Since everyone has magical knowledge or special abilities, everyone can pretty much defend themselves adequately, so there is little outright savagery being practiced upon one another. Make no mistake, this place is dangerous during its "anarchy world" period because pirates, bandits and would-be despots descend upon the planet to make their bids to take it over. They never do, because the populace bands together to fight them off. From the locals' point of view, anarchy year does them a service by flushing out all of the bad guys and would-be conquerors from their immediate area and forces the Thyrgordian society to take care of them all at once. The next anarchy year is due to begin in three months and this time, things are a little different. The mad Shifter *Furog Huld* is rumored to have come to Thyrgord, and during the Great Anarchy, he shall surely summon some kind of unspeakable horror to the world so it might visit terrible destruction upon the populace. That is why, from now until the Anarchy begins, Thyrgordian authorities are conducting a relentless search for this villain, offering a one million credit reward to whoever bags him first.

Rhilith, Home of the Gear. Rhilith is one of the very few United Worlds that has no ley lines or strong source of magic energy, so it has no significant magic-using population, and has no schools of magic anywhere. It is a technological power, consisting largely of high-tech science R&D facilities as well as the occasional civilian arcology and manufacturing complex. FTL propulsion is the specialty here as well as interstellar communications.

Rhilith was offered membership in the UWW 35 years ago as a way of showing the UWW's gratitude for the role the Rhilithians played in the *Yorian Genocide*. During that bleak time, the neighboring planet of Yoria was in the grip of a savage civil war in which numerous factions were busy conducting various form of mass murder upon each other. Yoria had a substantial magic-user population, but it was perhaps the one group of people on the planet universally hated by all. Historically, magic users were always wealthier than other Yorians and generations of frustration about that came to a boiling point during the civil

war. Unless somebody got involved, the magic-using population of Yoria would be exterminated. The Rhilithian High Command decided they could not stand by and watch this atrocity unfold, so they sent a huge strike force of their best ships carrying their best troops to Yoria. In a tough three-week campaign, Rhilith rescued the remaining 10 million magic-users from Yoria and gave them the choice of settling on Rhilith or on the UWW world of their choice. Forever grateful for their heroism, the rescued Yorians never forgot their Rhilithian saviors. A few years later, Yoria and nine other worlds prepared to make an allied assault upon Rhilith, this time jealous of that planet's high standard of living, and for their rescue of Yoria's hated magic users. This time, the Rhilithian High Command knew they could not survive this battle, but they bravely prepared for the worst. As the battle began, Dwarven Guildmaster ships from the UWW swooped in and scattered the attacking forces, saving Rhilith from certain doom. To cap it all off, the Dwarven ships came with an offer of membership to the UWW, an offer Rhilith readily accepted. Today, life is still good on this tech world, and its loyalty to the UWW is unquestioning. Whatever the UWW needs, the people of Rhilith will gladly supply.

Kron Omega. This tortured world is home to a cult of insane Warlocks who call themselves the *Agony and Ecstasy*, or "A/E" for short. The A/E have been a thorn in the side of UWW politics for years. They are the de facto rulers of Kron Omega, and though they aspire to one day *destroy* the planet, they conduct no overt criminal activity, nor do they abuse the planet's population (90% of the populace belongs to A/E, so everyone is pretty much on the same page, philosophically speaking). The A/E's driving motivation is that their magic powers are *really* meant for destruction, and nothing else. They believe that the true powers of the universe are released when things are destroyed, and so they believe their magic should only be used for destructive ends. And what more destructive end could there be than to destroy their very own planet? The rest of the UWW simply shakes their head at this insane reasoning, but to the A/E, this is the only honest way of approaching life. Those who spend their time creating things, they believe, are chasing a fool's dream. Since everything falls to dust, trying to fight that process is not only an exercise in futility but it disrespects the simple beauty of the destructive process.

For years, the Parliament of Worlds simply disregarded anything this world had to say, because it invariably came back to them wanting the Warlock Navy's help to destroy the planet. Aside from it being a gross misapplication of military power, the Parliament was not going to help *anybody* destroy a planet for any reason unless it was to save the UWW itself from grave danger. That being the case, the A/E have been left to their own devices. Little does anybody know that the TGE have surreptitiously provided 1,000 nuclear warheads to the A/E, who are busily digging deep shafts in which to place the bombs and then detonate them. T-minus one year and counting . . . .

Ikarus. This world is home to just ten beings, the ancient Great Horned Dragon *Ikarus*, and his crew of adventuring allies: *Solbriad*, an ancient Fire Dragon who recently took part in the war in Tolkeen, on Rifts Earth (and is fairly depressed over the outcome); *Mikao*, an ancient Ice Dragon who is sick and tired of Solbriad's bellyaching about the damn Tolkeen thing; *Obsidius*, an ancient Night Stalker dragon who wishes she could relive her

Hatchling Days and longs for adventure still; *Karadoun the Penitent*, a reformed Temporal Raider who gave up his life of evil so he might crusade for justice at Solbriad's side; *Yewen the Misunderstood*, an ancient and powerful Sphinx who developed quite a taste for fine liquors in his later age; *Elerad*, a venerable reptilian sorcerer whose works of scholarship and mystic symbols are among the finest in the Megaverse; *Indigar Shallow*, a disgraced Godling who was expelled from a Pantheon he would rather not mention because the whole thing is still too painful for him; *Brusephus the Forgotten*, an Elven arch-mage who once was famous throughout the Megaverse but has retreated into obscurity; and *Galak*, a reformed Dominator who has spent his last years hunting down and killing his very own people. These ancient heroes have retired to Ikarus so they might live out a long and peaceful retirement where they do nothing but take in slow days recounting old war stories. The UWW considers these living legends to be honored guests, and all have honorary seats on the Parliament of Worlds. There has been talk of trying to get these fellows to help with the search for the Cosmic Forge, but the consensus is that if Ikarus and his friends want to help, they will do so of their own accord. Until then, best to leave them in peace.

Skaltin: These are not real planets, but huge artificial planetoids that orbit near asteroid fields. Each Asteroid Eater is a self-contained mining and manufacturing colony. Asteroids, planetoids, moons and even small planets are stripped of all useful minerals, which are then processed to build ships, weapons, computers and other materials. Most of the crews/inhabitants of the Asteroid Eaters are Dwarves. Many are born, live out their lives, and die in their huge habitats, never having set foot on a real planet. The largest Asteroid Eaters can hold a population of five million; the smallest are little more than oversized ships that hold 5,000+ inhabitants.

Most Asteroid Eaters are considered to be installations belonging to a planet or corporation. A few of the largest ones, however, have declared their independence and are treated as full members of the UWW, with their own representatives and laws. One of these artificial planets, *Ironring*, is ruled by the demonic Inglix the Mad.

Naruni Enterprises

Population: 200 million sentients (estimated) working full time, plus 1-3 billion "temps." **Note:** This number only deals with Naruni personnel located in the Three Galaxies; nobody knows how many people work for the corporation throughout the Megaverse. Also, this does not include slaves or indentured servants. True Naruni (0.1%; fewer than 200,000)

Demographics: Uteni Shifters (30%), Molock Enforcers (20%), Pleasurers (5%), Humans (10%), Shapechangers (of one kind or another, 5%), and Others (30%).

Overview: Naruni Enterprises is a trans-dimensional weapons, vehicles and technology manufacturer known throughout the Megaverse as much for the quality of its goods as for its ruthless business practices. Like the Splugorth, they sell and trade throughout of the Megaverse. Presently, they are about half as well known, powerful, and hated as the Splugorth.

Naruni Enterprises has regional headquarters throughout the Three Galaxies in CCW, TGE, and independent space. They also have a massive trade and finance complex in the city of Center, on Phase World itself.

No one race runs the trans-dimensional corporation. Rather, its employees are chosen from all over the Megaverse, with a preference toward those from high-tech worlds. However, most of Naruni Enterprises' top management and owners are *True Naruni*, and the bulk of the company's second echelon consist more of *Uteni* than of any other humanoid race. Naruni factories are located in other dimensions, where hundreds of thousands of vehicles, weapons and munitions are produced every day for sale on hundreds of worlds.

Naruni Enterprises and the Splugorth are ruthless competitors so the Naruni try to avoid dealing with them or Splugorth controlled worlds. The Splugorth have no liking for the corporation, whom they see as a group of meddlers and an increasingly annoying rival in trans-dimensional commerce currently dominated by the Splugorth. The fact that Naruni Enterprises seems to frequently arm the enemies of the Splugorth hasn't helped relations between the two either. The weapons and vehicles sold by Naruni Enterprises are among the best in the Megaverse. Only the Kittani and similar high-tech civilizations can match them. However, Naruni items are very expensive.

To make a sale, the salespeople at NE allow governments and large businesses to buy on credit. The weapon merchants are friendly, cheerful and helpful in consummating the sale, but when it is time to collect the debt, the corporation is ruthless! If the purchaser cannot pay in cash, the corporation will consider trading goods or services, but is more inclined to acquire (seize) mining and land rights as payment. On several worlds, this credit and collection policy has enabled Naruni Enterprises to seize entire planets! Naruni Enterprises will get its money any way it can. At first, it will pester delinquent clients, then it will sic its crack legal teams on them. If that does not work (which is about half of the time), Naruni gets really nasty.

In some instances they have taken the entire population of an indebted kingdom or planet to sell into *slavery*. In other cases, they have forced the population to build and operate high-tech factories and into a life of hard labor. Beautiful lands, sometimes entire planets, are transformed into giant, smoke-belching factory worlds. Few dare to fight Naruni Enterprises because they have resources across the Megaverse and access to troops, allies and weapons that dwarf any one planet or even most collectives of planets. These military assets are all part of the dreaded **Naruni Debt Collection (NDC)** division. ("Oh, 'Debt Collector' has such an ugly ring to it. Please think of us as the military wing of the *Accounts Receivable department*.") The NDC has been known to raze entire cities in order to impress upon delinquent clients just how important it is to stay on top of one's bills. The NDC rarely destroys a client outright, because one cannot get paid by the dead, usually, but it *will* wreak utter havoc on a planetary scale until it gets what it came for. In almost all cases, when the NDC arrives on the scene, the debtors somehow find a way to cough up what they owe even if it means making painful, even terrible, choices. It is just not worthwhile to resist.

The NDC works best on Independent worlds. The CCW does not care for Naruni Enterprises in general (though it buys and uses a great deal of Naruni equipment) and it despises the NDC. Any NDC forces operating within CCW territory are considered invaders to be destroyed on sight. Of course, not all CCW military forces are equipped to handle the NDC, so sometimes this order goes unheeded. For the Naruni, causing trouble with the CCW is something to avoid because they are a major business partner. Thus, it goes the more discreet route when collecting debts, which usually means sending Repo-Bot assassin/enforcers directly to a debtor's home or place of business and shaking him down that way. Either way, Naruni always gets paid what it is owed. *Always.*

Naruni's heartless pursuit of its profits have marked it a renegade organization by the Cosmo-Knights, many of whom have no qualms about attacking or harassing Naruni operatives on sight. Indeed, Naruni starship convoys have begun disappearing all over the Anvil Galaxy. The average shipment now has only a 50% chance of reaching its destination. The Naruni Board of Directors is convinced that Cosmo-Knights are behind this, but are at a loss as to how to address the problem.

Having said all of this, it should be pointed out that Naruni is not an entirely evil organization. Its chief rivals, the Splugorth, have the "sinister behavior" market cornered, lock stock and barrel. No, the Naruni might be loan sharks and vicious debt collectors, but they do not practice overt slavery nor do they develop, manufacture or distribute street drugs or Bio-Wizard devices of any sort.

In the Anvil Galaxy, Naruni regional offices are having a field day as the bulk of the civilizations here have begun their frantic search for the Cosmic Forge. Suspecting that many of the parties searching for the Forge will come to blows when they cross paths, the Naruni are busy positioning themselves to make a killing by selling ALL parties weapons, spacecraft and equipment. Naruni manufacturing worlds have been producing excess inventory for a full five years now, and sales representatives have been working hard to worm their way into the halls of government and the trading nexi of the galaxy. That way, when the inevitable "Forge Wars" do erupt, Naruni Enterprises will be ready, willing and able to capitalize on it, selling their latest arms to all interested parties. This, more than anything, shows the true nature of Naruni Enterprises. They are not one of the truly evil forces at work in the Anvil Galaxy. They are simply heartless opportunists who strive to make a profit however they can, even if it means taking advantage of other people's greed, hate and stupidity. To Naruni Enterprises, fomenting war and chaos, dealing with known evildoers, and standing by without lifting a finger while innocent people are trampled is just the price of doing business. Naruni is a callous, uncaring organization who would not lift a finger to stop the destruction of the entire Megaverse if they could figure out how to make a quick credit off it. Their desire for money is not the source of their evil; the means by which they get that money, is their evil complicity.

The Naruni Board of Directors

The Naruni Board of Directors has 20 to 24 members, depending on the current situation regarding internal politics and intrigue. More than one member has been forced to resign, or has been "retired" permanently by a plasma cartridge round. Two-thirds of the board seats are held by True Naruni and Uteni traders (each of them rich beyond reason), and who collectively hold 60% of all Naruni Enterprises stock. Another important member is the godling *Thraxus* (described in detail on page 20 of **Phase World®**). He holds 50% of all stock and is worth trillions of credits. The rest of the board are from all over the Megaverse, including a demon lord and an alien intelligence!

The express goals of the company are simple: Expand their holdings and assets, stay on the leading edge of technology, and "maintain a climate favorable for the marketing and distribution of Naruni products." This last phrase can mean a number of things – including the need to maintain a climate of war in the Megaverse to guarantee a market for advanced weaponry.

Naruni Enterprises, unlike other trans-dimensional forces, is not in the business of forcible conquest. They see war as a wasteful activity that rarely pays for itself. It is far more profitable to sell weapons to those involved in war! The few large-scale conflicts in which Naruni Enterprises was directly involved were launched against the weakened survivors of a previous war, who were unable to put up much resistance and who were enslaved and sold to pay their debts.

Naruni Enterprises will not turn down cash transactions, and makes a healthy profit from perfectly legal sales to those who can afford the prices. However, not all of Naruni's dealings are above-board. The Board of Directors has an elite unit of secret employees, the **Social Studies Branch**. On the outside, this branch is funded to examine social conditions in the Three Galaxies and the rest of the Megaverse, supposedly as harmless market research. In reality, funds go to mercenaries, secret agents and other freelancers, most of whom do not realize they are even working for NE. These agents then help instigate wars and skirmishes in selected areas. The Social Studies Branch is not used to make trouble, because there are enough wars and conflicts around to satisfy the Board of Directors. Should things slacken off, however, the SSB will conduct a little "social engineering" of their own.

Another important branch of the company is the **Research and Development Department**. This group reports directly to the Board of Directors, many of whom are renowned weapon designers themselves. However, few new or innovative weapon systems have been developed over the last few decades. It seems that technological development has become stagnant for some reason. The Board of Directors is particularly frustrated by Naruni's inability to learn the secrets of Phase Technology and its lack of success in competing in the magic market.

Naruni Products & Services

Straight up, there is no commercial interest that produces better quality, or more sophisticated weapons and military technology on the scale maintained by Naruni Enterprises. There might be some R&D firms with slightly more advanced technology, but they do not and probably will never have the market share that Naruni does. These guys are synonymous with heavy hardware, especially in the Anvil Galaxy where so many power blocs are arming themselves for any number of confrontations, the preparations for the impending Forge War being among the most current and sweeping. Naruni weapons are, in large part, the standard design for military technology in the Three Galaxies, and there are far more worlds that use them than those who do not. The TGE is a notable exception, as is the UWW,

but Naruni technology is very common in the CCW, among the independent worlds, and with those who live between worlds, like spacers, pirates, mercenaries and adventurers. To some it is incomprehensible that a single manufacturer could so completely dominate a marketplace as huge as the Anvil Galaxy, but Naruni Enterprises has certainly done that. There are other effective monopolies in the Anvil Galaxy, such as **MacroCode** (makers of civilian and military software solutions; 96% of all computers in the Anvil Galaxy run MacroCode systems, even though they really aren't all that great and MacroCode's few competitors routinely put out better product), **Nuke** (a super-popular sugary beverage sold in vacc-sacs or aluminum blisters), **ICP** (a private entertainment and news broadcasting service watched by well over 66% of the galactic population, including TGE subjects; the TGE censors it, though), and **Ganymede GoSystems** (the leading producer of personal transportation technology, specializing in jet packs, exoskeletons, and even a personal space travel suit that enables single fliers to travel to 25 light years on their own). **Naruni** is just one more monopoly in a galactic economy full of them. One of the things about a monopoly is that it stunts competition. In Naruni's case, this means there have been no substantial upgrades or redesigns to its products in over 50 years. However, even if Naruni were out of the picture, the fact remains that technological innovation in all things stagnated across the Three Galaxies hundreds and hundreds of years ago. Despite the turbulence and occasional war, there is no incredible crisis threatening all life in the galaxies, so, as a result, people in the Three Galaxies are using the same technology designs they have had around for up to a thousand years. They are familiar, comfortable, reliable and get the job done. While the Anvil Galaxy does not mind this, it is the reason why certain low-tech worlds are beginning to close the technological gap with Naruni and even introduce new technologies.

G.M. Note: Space restrictions prevent us from reprinting the basic stats for Naruni weapons, but they can be found in **Phase World®, Phase World® Sourcebook**, and **Rifts® Mercenaries** titles. Also, *all* Naruni tech is collected in one handy location in the monstrous **Rifts® G.M.'s Guide**. Check it out! For new and improved Naruni tech designs as well as a host of other new hardware for the **Phase World®** setting, keep an eye out for the upcoming **Phase World® Technical Manual** sourcebook.

Foreign Affairs

Consortium of Civilized Worlds: Easily Naruni Enterprises' biggest customer in the Anvil Galaxy. The CCW has been undergoing a weapons upgrade initiative for the last decade or so, and is gradually replacing its outdated HI-series energy weapons with Naruni hardware. In some cases, local CAF commanders, fond of the look and feel of their old weapons, are simply having the guts of them replaced with Naruni interiors so the weapons seem just like their old selves, but they behave like a comparable Naruni weapon. Rumor has it GSA operatives just *love* using retooled CAF weapons refitted to Naruni spec. The Naruni have no idea, however, that the CCW is double-crossing them by reverse engineering the Naruni weapon designs and building knock-offs of their own. This is going to really hurt Naruni sales when the CCW cancels or significantly (by 60-70%) reduces its orders, since the Naruni have grown so reliant on CCW sales.

Trans-Galactic Empire: The Naruni have little use for these belligerent fellows because they do little arms sales to them. Plus, the TGE's generally grumpy attitude towards them lets the Naruni know they are not welcome.

United Worlds of Warlock: Those worlds that do not rely on magic tend to be pretty good customers. However, a growing number of these worlds are beginning to fall behind on their payments, and Naruni would very much like to collect. How they go about this is tricky, since the company can't hope to send a whole bunch of Repo-Bots and battleships into UWW space and begin pushing around member planet governments. Sending undercover operatives to harass and murder government officials on these worlds might do the trick. So might sabotaging the tech Naruni Enterprises has already sold to these clients with the promise that the sabotage will be repaired or undone somehow upon receipt of payment. NE has done this before. For example, they have been known to install a time lock on the CPU of energy weapons with a 90 or 120 day timer. When the guns are paid off, the Naruni sales rep sends the buyer the unlock code for the guns. The Naruni don't like doing this often because the whole thing works by not telling the client that the guns are timed out in the first place. That way when the guns stop working, the client comes to the sales rep looking for a refund. And *that* is when the deadbeat gets the news about the time delay lock. If the Naruni did this to all of their clients, the method would lose its shock value. Worse, clients would buy huge amounts of guns and just throw them away after 89 days without paying at all, or they might try to deactivate the timers.

Hartigal Combine: Traitors! Pirates! Thieves! This subsidiary was once a loyal element of Naruni Enterprises, but now it has gone off on its own to sell direct copies of NE hardware at dramatically reduced prices! They even offer zero percent financing and 30 day money-back guarantees! There is not a single Naruni sales rep or field operative who wouldn't like to nuke the Hartigal home office. In the long run, Naruni Enterprises might do just that. The companies are, in effect, fighting a civil war now, with strike teams routinely conducting industrial espionage and sabotage on each other's facilities. Execs for both sides are not safe in this high-stakes war of corporate takeover vs unpopular profit sharing. It is a no holds barred rivalry that can only end badly for one side or the other (and that "other" is most likely to be the Hartigal Combine).

Golgan Republik: As this great power bloc disintegrates, more and more of its component societies will need to arm themselves, and Naruni sales reps are only too happy to oblige. NE saw that the Republik was in trouble a long while ago, and has quietly established a dense sales and marketing network on the Golgans' planets so when their Republik did fall apart, Naruni would be there to sell to the pieces.

Altess Dynasty: Being the fabulously wealthy power bloc that they are, the Altess are, among other things, enormous Naruni Enterprises clients. Their entire military is outfitted with the latest Naruni hardware, and nothing but Naruni ships fly over the Altess home world. The Altess have even managed to buy a dozen Repo-Bots for use in the Dynastic Bodyguard, but only after paying ungodly sums of money to get NE to part with them. Rumor has it the Naruni sales reps hid a latent program in the 'Bots' heads so they would transmit everything they see and hear back to NE headquarters, thus giving the Naruni a great means of spying on their Altess customers.

Central Alliance: If this bloc did not have the annoying tendency to design and build its own technology, it would have been another great Naruni client. Instead, it handles all of its hardware needs itself. On the few cases when these guys do buy from NE, they pay up front in cash so the Naruni debt collectors can never have an excuse to come knocking on the Alliance's doors.

Cosmo-Knights: The Naruni stopped trying to sell these Boy Scouts anything a looooong time ago. They do not appreciate the occasional Cosmo-Knight raid on NE factories and cargo ships. Sure, NE makes a profit selling to monsters, rebels, pirates and raiders, but does that *really* make them so bad? Apparently certain Cosmo-Knights think so. Go figure.

Kingdom of Rynncryyl: Sadly, NE and the Splugorth are rivals and even enemies, which the Naruni would much rather see changed. After all, the Splugorth are fond of their own weapons and of Bio-Wizardry, but certainly they could use some Naruni blasters, too, right? Naruni Enterprises sees the Splugorth as disgusting, vile and worthy of scorn, but that still does not mean they wouldn't be a decent trading partner, if only they could get the Splugorth to trade. The Splugorth idea of a fair trade is they take everything and then enslave the salesman.

Gene-Tech: The Naruni don't really know much about these strange aliens except that they are distrusted and often reviled throughout the Anvil Galaxy, and that they drive around in spaceships of their own design and manufacture, and that they have never ever placed an order with Naruni Enterprises. Sales reps are forbidden from abandoning sales prospects, but for the Gene-Tech, the upper management will make an exception. Still, there are more than a few ambitious mid-level execs who wouldn't mind taking a secret team of Repo-Bots and commandeering a Gene-Tech ship or laboratory to see what secrets it might hold...

Omegan Order: While these renegade Cosmo-Knights might be persuaded to use Naruni or any other standard energy weapons, there are two major problems with selling to these people. One, they are utterly untrustworthy, and are likely to simply steal whatever arms are brought to them. Two, they are across the Threshold, a barrier that Naruni Enterprises has made no effort to cross. To them, there is no reason to risk the hazards of the Threshold when there is so much business to be done.

Xodian Collective: The Naruni hardly even know about these aliens, much less have a plan for selling them weapons. Besides, from what they can tell, the Xodians don't really need any weapons.

K!ozn: Selling directly to the K!ozn is out because of the Threshold problem and because there is every indication the super-advanced K!ozn have weapon designs that are equal (or even superior!) to whatever the Naruni have to offer. Still, the Naruni are very interested in finding a lone K!ozn operative and dealing with him. That way, there is the chance the sales reps might somehow gain access to K!ozn technology and reverse engineer it for themselves.

Independent Worlds: This is the last great frontier for Naruni Enterprises. At any given time, there are dozens – no, hundreds – of great business opportunities to be had with the small fries of the Anvil Galaxy. To such customers, Naruni Enterprises really comes off like an invincible juggernaut; indeed NE is larger and more powerful than many independent civilizations, so those who deal with them had better be on their toes. They had also better keep up on their payments, because NE really can push around these smaller powers, repossessing their entire world if they fail to make payments. For young sales reps, debt collectors and executives, working the independent territories is where one cuts his teeth before moving on to bigger things like serving the CCW account.

Society & Daily Life

Naruni Enterprises is as ruthless a bunch of cutthroats as any band of pirates or mercenaries in the Three Galaxies. One does not simply work for this company, it becomes their life, their nation, their everything. The successful Naruni worker eats, breathes, sleeps and dreams "the job." It is omnipresent. To those who maintain the illusion that they might have a personal life outside of their work, serious mental therapy is prescribed, along with heavy-duty personality alteration drugs and the occasional electro-shock treatment. Nothing revives one's company loyalty better than a couple of blasts to the old frontal lobes, eh?

Any other company could not get away with this kind of fanatical work environment. However, NE is so large that it has an entire population of captive workers who spend their entire lives in the care of the Naruni. Employees live on NE property, wear NE clothes, eat NE food, get NE medical care, everything! Even if they wanted to, most employees really could not escape. Maybe some of the higher execs could, but they make so much money doing what they do, that they rarely consider leaving. Their mental conditioning is so strong by the time they get to that level of power, having a sudden attack of individuality or developing a taste for personal freedom is virtually unheard of.

Nobody gets fired from NE, they just keep getting demoted. No matter how lowly one's position is, NE supervisors can always find something worse for those unable to do their job properly. Quarterly evaluation reports are all anybody really lives for, and most often, people get a "satisfactory" rating or less, no matter how hard they have been working. To advance, pure hard work and good attitude is not enough. One must know the right people, get a little lucky, and have no fear about sabotaging their superiors and their competition. Backstabbing is a hallowed cultural tradition within NE, and nobody ever gets to the top without having become a master at it. As a result, there can be no real friendships within NE. Even husbands and wives have cause to distrust each other and their children. Everybody is fair game. Everything is an opportunity for the person with the guts to go for it. Everybody is expendable. *Everybody.*

Daily Life

Get up. Go to work. Stay at work. Stay late at work. Receive payment. Return to domicile. Eat. Sleep. Repeat.

Law and Punishment

There are no set rules within Naruni Enterprises. The only rule is, your superiors set your rules. That's it. There is no going over your supervisor's head. There is no alternate committee to take grievances to. Everybody ultimately answers to just one person, so it is in everyone's best interest to make sure that one person likes them a *lot*. This means not only giving 1,000% to the job, but blatant brown-nosing, sycophantery and groveling are expected. There is no escape from this, but those with the company know no other way of life. They credit this kind of harsh conditioning as the reason why Naruni Enterprises is at the top of its game in the weapons field and everybody else is scrounging for whatever scraps Naruni leaves behind.

What makes this savage ladder of authority work is that no matter how bad somebody has it, they have somebody else to take out their frustrations on. And, life does not necessarily get better or worse depending on one's rank. There are employees at the bottom of the pile who get along great with their supervisor and are happy as can be, and there are top-level executives whose superiors hate them and therefore make their lives living hell.

Another constant is that no matter how well one does their job, some level of hazing or mistreatment should be expected. In fact, since so many superiors get backstabbed by their subordinates (and end up serving *them*), doing a really good job usually shows dangerous levels of ambition. As a result, the eager beavers get harassed and pressured (and sabotaged) extra by their superiors to teach them the cardinal rule of Naruni Enterprises: one is expected to do a good job, but don't do it so well that you expect to advance to mine.

Crime and Order

As mentioned before, since the only rules are those laid down by one's superior. On the surface, it might look like anybody can indulge in criminal conduct if their superior has not specifically forbidden it. But it does not work that way. Assume that *Sulg* the sales rep answers to *Durg* the low-level exec. Durg lays down the rules that Sulg lives by. Sulg is ultimately answerable to Durg in all things. Thus, if Sulg gets drunk one night, starts a fight and steals a hovercycle, investigators will report Sulg to his superior, Durg. Sulg's shortcomings are Durg's shortcomings, and so *both* get into hot water. Sulg obviously is in trouble with Durg because his misconduct made his superior look bad.

Durg is in trouble with *his* superior because he could not keep his subordinate in line. Durg has also made his superior look bad, though not as much. This ripples upward the chain of authority until finally somebody near the top does not even notice that something happened. Meanwhile, poor Sulg is going to get it from Durg. Durg might demote the hell out of him, dock his pay, assign Sulg to the worst duties in his job description, etc. Until Durg has sufficiently vented his anger.

Pretty harsh, huh? But there is a mechanism to keep superiors from going overboard themselves. Simply put, a subordinate remembers when his boss was tough on him, and there always comes a time when an employee has the opportunity to stab his boss in the back or not. This is where loyalty comes in. It is a rarely felt sensation among NE employees, but it does happen, and every supervisor hopes that they don't entirely drive it out of their subordinates, for if they do, they are only assuring that they will definitely get it in the back one day.

This whole system is a delicate balance of fear; fear from one's superiors, fear from one's subordinates. Fear is a great motivator, and it does wonders to keep the galaxy's largest and most sinister colony of evil workaholics running smoothly.

Worlds of Interest

As a rule, the Naruni are not interested in planetary conquest or colonization. From time to time, they will buy entire solar systems much like how a smaller company might buy land on which to build an office or absorb a smaller company. In such systems, the Naruni set up extensive manufacturing, storage, distribution and administrative facilities, sometimes employing the entire native population of those worlds. It makes better business sense to hire and train the locals than to kick them off.

In addition to these worlds, the Naruni also possess a mixed bag of planets and entire systems that came to them from clients who defaulted on their debts. In some cases, the clients just signed over their territory while in other cases the NDC moved in and took the place over. Either way, NE is now the undisputed lord of such domains, and they usually turn them into sales centers and local distribution stations. Though such worlds are put to a relatively mundane purpose, that does not mean they don't see their share of adventure. Those looking to steal from the Naruni, those who have a grudge against the company, and those living on the planet and looking to stir up trouble all have a reason to make NE's life difficult, and on company planets, harsh trouble can and does occur.

NE 192-2393. The Naruni bought this planet from its previous owners to use as a massive waste dump. Not that NE can't molecularize its trash – it can and does – but it knows that not all civilizations have such capabilities. Indeed, on many independent worlds, vast garbage piles dot the landscape, providing terrible environments for disease, wild predators, unsavory scavengers, and so on. NE created NE 192-2393 as a vast experiment. They have imported garbage from all over the Anvil Galaxy and created a planetary junkyard which they now monitor. The Social Studies department have deposited small populations of prisoners from other worlds' penal systems here to see what kind of civilization they will build. R&D have deposited numerous hostile organisms here too to see how they might survive in a post-urban environment, and malfunctioning robots have been deposited here as well, to see how they might repair and maintain themselves with only refuse to sustain them. Besides yielding lots of market-worthy information, monitoring NE 192-2393 is like a live-action soap opera for much of the company. Betting pools on what will happen next in a given sector are rampant, and NE has thought about broadcasting the monitors to other worlds and charging syndication rights for them.

NE 654-0081. This world once was home to an ancient and honorable civilization that made the mistake of buying products from NE that it really could not afford. Unwilling to live under the Naruni's harsh repayment conditions, these people rebelled, and ultimately the NDC came in and blitzed the whole place to smithereens. Since then, the shell-shocked locals of this world are desperately trying to survive in the Naruni-generated wreckage of their home world. Into this situation comes master sales rep *Tillin Kadmire*, an Uteni salesman who is reportedly able to sell water to a fish, he is *that* good. His mission is to mingle among this hostile and impoverished population in order to sell them basic survival goods. This is the hardest sell the Sales Rep Executive Committee can come up with, but Tillin handles it expertly. He has had cyber-cameras implanted in his skull, so his sales trips to this world are broadcast live to the many different ongoing educational programs the company runs to keep its sales force in good shape. Tillin's sales techniques are copied by almost everyone in the Company, and he is their equivalent of a war hero.

NE 000-0001. This is the world of origin for Naruni Enterprises, or so it claims. Here, the company built an enormous museum chronicling the great and glorious history of the company, with endless exhibits, displays and holovision shows to explain and glorify every aspect of the company, its mission and its history. Tourists outside the company almost never come here. It is part of the basic training package all new sales personnel must undergo. Really it is a form of mental endurance test, for the recruits are forced to go through three full days of museum touring, with each exhibit just a little more boring and minutely detailed than the last. At the end of the third day, with the visitors near exhaustion, a pop exam is sprung and the visitors must answer correctly 100 questions about the exhibits they just saw. These are fill in the blank questions, and a visitor may not leave, rest or eat until he has successfully completed 100 questions. Alternately, if the visitor gets 1,000 wrong answers, he is immediately demoted and sent back to whatever world he is domiciled on, where his superior can determine his fate.

NE 207-1839. Failure to make good on weapons payments has turned this once-thriving world into a total battle zone. The NDC was called in to extract payment and lay a little smack down on the locals to remind them of the importance of timely payment of one's debts. However, the resistance here is stiff, as the locals are expert guerilla fighters and hey, they're armed to the teeth with Naruni hardware so they are definitely well equipped. The NDC Field Commander loves war and personally wishes the fighting here drags on forever, even though he knows that if this goes on for too much longer, the home office will simply order the planet nuked and closed for business.

NE 234-9753. Several years ago, the Social Studies Department predicted a massive war and political meltdown in a stretch of independent space along the southern edge of the galaxy. That war scenario never panned out. In fact, the worlds in question were overtaken by a wildly popular pacifism cult that would make sure these worlds would never go to war again. Good for the locals, bad for Naruni Enterprises, which had ramped up all sorts of weapons production to meet their predicted demand here. Now, the company had a whole lot of extra guns, equipment, ships and robots and nobody to sell them to. Rather than redeploy them elsewhere, the Naruni simply bought a small planetoid orbiting a lonely gas giant, and they turned this little world into a giant warehouse. Containing millions upon millions of bits of Naruni merchandise, NE 234-9753 is the company's biggest single inventory depot in the Three Galaxies. The whole place is automated, and an army of Repo-Bots is on hand to handle security break-ins (thieves just can't resist trying to sneak into this place and steal a few cargo loads of valuable merchandise).

NE 111-2987. This world came into Naruni possession when Accounts Receivable foreclosed on it after the locals could no longer make their payments. Rather than face the wrath of the NDC, the locals just fled the planet, leaving behind entire cities, roads, and a civilization with no people in it! R&D took it over and turned it into a research colony, where scientists could live in a fairly pleasant environment while they work on new and intriguing products. The trick for these scientists is to improve products just enough to make the client want to upgrade from what they already own, but not so much of an improvement that old merchandise loses its value. This is the sort of research most of the world does. Elsewhere, though, are secret R&D enclaves dedicated to ultra-advanced research. Probability engines. Meson weaponry. Anti-Matter generators. That sort of thing. Whether or not the company will ever bring such stuff to market if and when working prototypes are finished remains to be seen. Most think the company just wants this stuff to be worked on in case they find a need for it.

NE 101-1010: This world was an exemplary administrative center that handled all kinds of financial information transfer. Bank accounts, interest computations, investment returns, that sort of thing. Life turned upside down, however, when a cadre of particularly vicious supervisors apparently entered into a sick contest with each other to see who could drive the most subordinates to suicide. At that, the supervisors waged an all-out psychological war on everyone below them, and productivity came to a standstill. Some clusters of subordinates actually rebelled against their superiors, slaying them and assuming their authority. Civil war was on the verge of breaking out when somebody with a cool head activated the Social Contingency – a platoon of Repo-Bots programmed to crack heads and get everybody back to work. Only the lead Repo-Bot had some kind of corruption of programming problem, because it interpreted its orders to mean that the entire world needed to be taken into its control. So, the Repo-Bot led its troops to the highest rungs of power on the planet and had all of the top execs killed on the spot. The Repo-Bots assumed the top exec positions on the planet, something that had never happened before! Five years later, this situation is working out nicely, so the higher-ups do not want to change anything. Still, the lead Repo-Bot's behavior was interesting, and a few folks in R&D would like to see if that 'bot simply glitched up on them or is the beginning of a new kind of independence to be expected among all Repo-Bots.

NE 357-5748. This world is under the impression that it is an independent planet, but it really is owned and controlled by Naruni Enterprises, who spend a great deal of time and energy making sure that a) the locals do not discover the truth about their world, and b) travel to and from the planet remains very restricted. The company does this so they can have a totally unbiased audience for testing Naruni products. The society of this world has experienced a terrible civil war, a war which the Naruni generated so it would have an ongoing situation in which it could test weapons and it would not really raise too many eyebrows. So far, this world has proven to be extremely useful, but recently a few citizens escaped and intend to break the truth wide open on this chamber of horrors. Naruni top execs have ordered these escapees slain immediately, but they might already be too late for that.

NE 252-4861. This world has recently seen all of its life snuffed out within the span of a week. The cause of the catastrophe is not yet known, but the company is keeping as tight a lid on this as possible. Spin Doctors are already filtering cover stories back to the families of the slain, and R&D is examining the world for any traces of a pathogen or molecular death agent that might have been used to kill the population. (Whatever R&D finds will probably find its way into a weapons research project of some kind.)

NE 145-2929. This is another large office world for Naruni Enterprises, only its major distinction is that a single True Naruni runs it, and recently he has received a shocking dressing down from his superior over declining productivity, lost profits, and various personal matters of the exec's that his superior finds offensive. The end result is the exec stands to be demoted severely very shortly. The question is, will he order all of his subordinates – pretty much the whole planet – to commit suicide along with him? That way, the exec thinks, the world may be spared the disgrace by association that awaits them all once he is gone. Plus, it would really stick it to his superiors, which is always a bonus.

The Hartigal Combine

a.k.a. Hartigal Manufacturies Amalgamated, LDC

Population: One billion employees; Anvil Galaxy only. No presence in other galaxies.

Demographics: Humans (77%), Uteni (13%), and Other (10%).

Overview: The Hartigal Combine was a subsidiary of *Naruni Enterprises* created 25 years ago. When it was started, NE top executives felt they were suffering from a culture gap between their largely Uteni sales force and the largely human markets they were trying (with little success) to penetrate in the independent territories. To bridge this gap, NE formed a subsidiary of itself that would basically be a smaller version of the company, only it would have a human face and human relationships with the clients. The merchandise and pricing would be the same, but the feel would be human.

The plan worked well for a few years, but then R&D got involved with it. Feeling that the company was not moving ahead fast enough in terms of weapons development, they saw Hartigal as the perfect testing ground for new technology. Even before Hartigal got off the ground, company R&D folks were all over the project, trying to turn this thing into their own private laboratory. In the end, the top executives gave the scientists what they wanted, and Hartigal began focusing strongly on new weapons development. In just a few short years, they had come out with some interesting variants on already existing weapons, but the customers weren't biting. They liked the standard Naruni designs, and saw no reason to switch! Moreover, the research project had cost a lot of time and money, and it would never pay for itself. Heads certainly rolled over the debacle, and true to Naruni fashion of passing the buck, the trouble eventually shook its way down to the Hartigal staff, who were told to shoulder the blame for everything. The Hartigal people, unused to catching hell for things that were not their fault, resented this treatment, and after about a year of it, they seceded the company from Naruni Enterprises. Hartigal took with them all the money they had made for NE and they took their clients with them, too. They set up base on a desolate planet in the independent territory near the CCW border, and from there they opened shop. Hartigal Manufacturies Amalgamated, LDC was born.

Naruni executives were shocked. You can't just *leave* the company like that! You have to get permission from your superiors, and fill out forms in triplicate, and get permission, and go through channels and form committees, and . . . . and . . . . you surely can't take clients *with* you!

Hartigal employees were having none of it. If the Naruni wanted to treat themselves like slaves, they were welcome to do so, but Hartigal Manufacturies would work differently. Oh, it would sell the *exact* same merchandise, alright, but at a lower cost (Naruni tech carries a nearly 85% profit margin on every sale; even cutting that in half, the seller still makes a killing). Hartigal also knocks off CCW HI-series weaponry, but the CCW considers that "open-source" technology and does not care if anyone copies it.

In the short time Hartigal has been on its own, it has made great inroads with new clients, and it is fast becoming the premier weapons dealer among the independent worlds of the Anvil Galaxy. In the grand scheme of things, this is a small market in a small galaxy, and there is simply no way Hartigal could ever come close to matching Naruni Enterprises' god-like stature in the whole market. But it rankles the company nonetheless. They still can't believe that Hartigal dared break away, and that Hartigal is selling Naruni designs as their own is flat-out offensive. Naruni's top executives have decided that Hartigal must pay dearly for their indiscretions. That means a state of informal war is now on between the two companies. On one side, a huge and powerful manufacturer with enough money and resources to

field an army larger than most government forces. On the other side, a small, nimble target, difficult to hit and adept at fighting dirty. Actually, this is a pretty good match up, and whoever wins or loses will inherit the ever-growing gold mine that is the Anvil Galaxy weapons marketplace.

Government

Unlike Naruni Enterprises, Hartigal is a fairly open society. Its employees are both citizens and shareholders, with the option of buying into the company as much as they like. Hartigal holds shareholder meetings every half year, allowing the employees to air their grievances in an orderly fashion, and to vote on important issues to the company. The workers can also vote members on the Board of Directors in and out, including the CEO of the company. This is an important thing for the workers, many of whom once toiled thanklessly for Naruni Enterprises since the day they were born. Having anything approaching a voice in how the company is run is like a dream come true to the Hartigal populace. Having other things like vacations, fair pay, respect and a cordial atmosphere makes their newfound situation seem all the more unreal.

Employees are reviewed by their superiors, but those superiors must get clearance from *their* superiors before promoting, demoting, hiring or firing anyone. This double-check system keeps executives from abusing their power, but it is not so cumbersome as to prevent things from getting done.

Military

Hartigal Security Solutions, LDC is the company's internal security specialist as well as the primary provider for external security at company installations, factories, buildings, etc. HSS also provides bodyguard cover for Hartigal VIPs, performs rescue operations for kidnaped Hartigal personnel, works to prevent industrial espionage and sabotage, and all manner of other such services. Hartigal is hardly big and wealthy enough to field a substantial military, but it does have quite the security force. In military terms, these fellows would rank as elite Special Ops troops excellent for discretionary warfare, but not the sort of training to fight a stand-up war. Ordinarily, Hartigal would not fret over that, but it is becoming clear that Naruni Enterprises has no intention of letting Hartigal chart its own course, and so is preparing to lay siege to all known Hartigal worlds – an unusual move for the Naruni, who usually avoid all-out military campaigns. So far, Hartigal's appeals for military aid to the CCW and UWW have gone unanswered, so it must seek alternate means of protecting itself: hiring mercenaries.

In the last twelve months alone, Hartigal has assembled a huge fighting force out of freelance warriors from across the galaxy. These hard-bitten veterans are all crack fighters and spoiling for some action. Although a bit unruly and not used to following orders, they have proven reliable so far, and in the few skirmishes with the NDC, these soldiers have proven they are worth their generous salaries. Money is an issue with them, though, and the majority of the mercs are accepting initial cash payments plus a cut out of future weapons sales earnings for five years. Should Hartigal survive their Naruni onslaught, they will be paying quite a lot for their victory, but survival sometimes carries a heavy price.

Be they mercenaries or internal security, everyone fighting for Hartigal is equipped with the latest Naruni-style weapons, armor, force field defenses, and equipment. This really bugs the Naruni, who are used to having an edge in firepower, but now are fighting their own technology.

Other Agencies

Hartigal Technical Solutions (HTS) is the Research & Development wing of the company. Really, they are not interested in finding out how to manufacture anything new. They are interested in finding existing technology, reverse engineering it, and producing cheap knock-offs of it. So far, they have focused on putting out Hartigal versions of all common personal weapons in the Three Galaxies. Their second big achievement was a knock-off of the Naruni Repo-Bot, which could be programmed for anything ranging from simple combat missions to complicated covert work. Hartigal has even figured out a way to slot in cybernetic brain chips so full conversion cyborgs can use a Hartigal Repo-Bot as a chassis, giving them noteworthy firepower, endurance and versatility. These knock-off Repo-Bots are a smash hit for the department, even though they are *not* as formidable as the genuine article (30% less M.D.C., 20% lower attributes and speed, and 10% shorter-range for weapons) and sales of them have gone through the roof. Everybody who can afford them has placed orders, ranging from governments in need of automated commandos to wealthy individuals looking to have some heavy-duty personal protection when they are out and about.

Naruni Enterprises is furious over the Repo-Bot knock-off, since they designed those machines for use as a shock device for themselves. They were held in reserve and then brought out against delinquent clients in a terrifying show of force. This gave the Repo-Bots a mystique that got more results than any of their onboard weaponry. Hartigal's flooding the market with cheap Repo-Bot knock-offs is threatening to destroy that mystique altogether, especially since Hartigal's knock-offs are of lower quality and easier to destroy. The least Hartigal could do was rename them, think the Naruni.

Foreign Affairs

Consortium of Civilized Worlds: Hartigal has no beef with the CCW, even if they do buy all of their weapons from the Naruni. Hartigal likes to stick close to Consortium territory, though, in the hopes that when NE makes its next assault, maybe Hartigal can persuade the CCW to intervene.

Trans-Galactic Empire: Hartigal does not knock off only CCW and Naruni weapons. They have also produced their own versions of the energy pulse weapons used so often by the TGE. Energy pulse guns are sort of the "second string" weapon of the Anvil Galaxy. Though well designed and great in combat, their use by the TGE has stigmatized them, and they are not as popular in the rest of the galaxy as Naruni weapons or old-style HI-series weapons. Still, they are far cheaper to make than either Naruni or HI hardware, and for that reason, Hartigal really wants to make a business plan for EP weapons to get off the ground. One idea is to manufacture them faster, better and cheaper than the TGE does, and sell them to the Empire. Of course, this would create diplomatic problems with the CCW, but Hartigal is in the business of profit, not conscience, and if it must deal with the Devil, then so be it. Heck, the TGE might go for such an arrangement just to counter the CCW's arrangement with the Naruni.

United Worlds of Warlock: There has been very little market opportunity for Hartigal in the UWW, so they no longer maintain any permanent sales positions there. Hartigal would not mind trying to mass produce magic items, but to do that they would have to learn magic and study the Dwarven Guildmasters' methods extensively. Consequently, Hartigal doesn't know if it would be worth the trouble, but they have dispatched about 100 spies to research the matter for future consideration.

Naruni Enterprises: The Naruni have sworn to destroy Hartigal for its treachery, and Hartigal is more than ready for the fight. So far, the conflict between these two companies has been limited to increased competition, dirty tricks, skirmishes out in space, the occasional theft of each other's cargo, attacks to cripple and maroon cargo ships, and a few acts of factory sabotage. However, things are heating up. Hartigal recently lost three executives to a Naruni assassin, and "pirate" raids on their cargo vessels have jumped up 40% in the last two months, so they are now preparing for all-out war on the Naruni upper levels of management. Hartigal is currently going through its ranks of security experts and mercenaries to put together a big hit and sabotage squad to decapitate Naruni Enterprises and leave it leaderless. Even a foiled attempt (which is likely) will only serve to escalate the level of violence and aggression of the Naruni.

Golgan Republik: Hartigal has had some success selling cheap weapons to the breakaway factions of the Republik, as well as to the Republik itself. Though it finds working both sides of a civil war distasteful, there can be no denying it is very good for business. On a few occasions, Hartigal has provided a few of its best mercenaries to fight in the Republik Conflict, basically as living advertising for the power and reliability of Hartigal weaponry.

Altess Dynasty: The Altess' main power comes from their incredible wealth generated by the licensing of their very sophisticated home-grown technology. The Altess are not weapons builders, though, so they buy a lot of Naruni weapons. The Altess never have problems paying their arms dealers and their sense of superiority precludes them from buying "cheap imitations," it's just too gauche. However, if the Naruni ever lost the favor of the Altess, these arrogant superhumans *might* take a more serious look at Hartigal. Perhaps needless to say, Hartigal likes that idea and is busy trying to develop a plan to trick Naruni Enterprise into disrespecting their Altess clients and taking NE's place. Consequently, Hartigal maintains diplomatic relations with the Altess and kisses up to them like they have never before. Always one to appreciate the adoration of "lesser beings," the Altess allow the Hartigal agents to stay and have recently given them their own embassy, a turn of events that makes the Naruni's blood boil. For now, Naruni Enterprises has nothing to worry about, but who knows what may unfold in the future?

Central Alliance: The Central Alliance makes heavy use of old, secondhand weaponry originally manufactured by Naruni Enterprises, the CCW, and other companies years ago. They have also been known to buy from a number of knock-off manufacturers throughout the galaxy. However, the Alliance finds itself swimming in old, cheap, deteriorating weapons that no longer work reliably. Now that the bloc's civil wars are finally coming to a close, the powers that be are looking to upgrade weapons across the board. With their history of buying knock-offs in the past, they really like the idea of buying from Hartigal because it produces some of the finest and most reliable knock-offs on the market. Best of all, Hartigal has the ready inventory, the sales force, and tantalizing product that is right in the Alliance's price range. Unless something goes terribly wrong, Hartigal stands to make a *ton* of money off the Central Alliance over the next decade or so.

Cosmo-Knights: Hartigal really has no contact with these defenders of justice, but they unanimously agree with and support their actions. Were the opportunity to arise for Hartigal to help the Cosmo-Knights in any way, they would surely do it. Of course, the company's potential dealings with the TGE might very well prevent such an opportunity from ever arising.

Kingdom of Rynncryyl: Hartigal despises the Splugorth and considers them to be vicious slavers, killers and space scum from the Threshold. Even if the "Sploogies" were to offer Hartigal the weapons contract of a lifetime, the company would probably turn it down. Of course, every company has its price, even Hartigal, and the Splugorth *do* hate Naruni Enterprises so intensely, who knows what they might consider to hurt NE? Maybe an unlikely alliance between Hartigal and the Splugorth is a possibility? It would require Hartigal receiving a sinful amount of money, though.

Gene-Tech: Hartigal does not recognize these guys as a legitimate power bloc. Moreover, the Gene-Tech don't buy weapons, so Hartigal has no reason to deal with them.

Omegan Order: Hartigal does absolutely no business across the Threshold, and as such, has no contact with the Omegan Order. A few Omegan operatives have come across Hartigal sales reps on this side of the Threshold, but each time, the company has found a convenient reason not to sell these fallen knights anything. Hartigal fears that dealing with them would forever tie the two organizations together somehow, plus the Omegans simply creep out most Hartigal workers.

Xodian Collective: Hartigal has no intelligence on the Xodians, other than knowing these aliens do not use weapons, and so Hartigal writes them off as a sales opportunity.

K!ozn: Though Hartigal has no contact with the K!ozn Continuum on the far side of the Threshold, K!ozn operatives and their minions can be found in the Anvil Galaxy exploring and stirring up trouble from time to time. For some reason, the K!ozn are very fond of Hartigal weaponry, and they have been buying a lot of it through third- and fourth-party vendors. Why such advanced aliens want Hartigal versions of already existent weapons is one mystery. Why the K!ozn want to conceal the purchases is another.

Independent Worlds: These are the bread and butter for the company. Indie worlds constitute 66% of all sales at present, with no letup in sight. Hartigal hopes that should their war with the Naruni get really ugly, maybe some of their indie clients will help defend the company from defeat or destruction.

Society

Hartigal culture is, in most respects, a direct response to the brutality of living and working for Naruni Enterprises. The company was formed to get away from the Naruni way of life and all it entails. As a result, Hartigal society stresses freedom, teamwork, trust, friendship, self-determination, and the rights of individuals to enter and exit the organization as they see fit. The Hartigal company is dedicated to forming *honest business partnerships* with its clients, not just exploiting them or bullying them, as Naruni so often does. Thus, honesty, forthrightness, and candor are all part of the Hartigal culture. This has already paid off – on many independent worlds where Hartigal does the bulk of its business, the company has a well-deserved reputation for fairness, openness, and flexibility. They are willing to work out payment plans with delinquent customers without sending in big armies or sinister collection robots. They are willing to give refunds or exchanges for less-than-happy customers. And they openly recruit from their client worlds, further strengthening the ties between the company and those it serves. In many ways, Hartigal is a model society that other power blocs of the Anvil Galaxy would do well to emulate.

Daily Life

Daily life in Hartigal mirrors that in the CCW, where employees/citizens generally lead comfortable, high-tech lives on residential planets filled with luxury and convenience. Those who do not live on such worlds typically stay in equally comfortable orbital stations or enormous freighters that make endless circuits through Hartigal territory, delivering inventory from factories to sales outlets and ferrying important personnel around Hartigal's network of worlds.

Hartigal's peace and quiet is disrupted by the ongoing troubles with Naruni Enterprises, though, and many citizens are a little apprehensive at what the Naruni might do to get even. Ru-

mors of terrorist activity swirl through Hartigal communities, and stories of assassinations and sneak attacks are ever-present. Despite this climate of fear, the resilient Hartigal folk soldier on, keeping their chins up and looking to the future with more hope than dread, which is a lot more than their counterparts at Naruni Enterprises can say.

Law and Order

Hartigal internal security enforces the law within the planetary network. Hartigal has adopted the CCW code of law, and has had no difficulty implementing it.

Crime and Punishment

There is little crime among Hartigal worlds, mostly because everybody is united against the Naruni and dedicated to making a better life for themselves. This makes them too busy or too patriotic to victimize each other. More importantly, though, Hartigal employees are universally well taken care of, so there is little cause for theft or jealousy. In the few instances when employees do commit a crime, internal security handles it, and doles out punishments exactly as the CCW would. Most of the crime on Hartigal worlds is committed by outsiders such as pirates, thieves, drifters, hostile aliens, and Naruni troublemakers.

Worlds of Interest

Harker's Enclave. A backwater world where Elden Harker, renegade scientist and theoretical genius, has established a hermitage of sorts where only like-minded eccentric geniuses are welcome. Nobody knows for sure where this world is, but both the CCW and the TGE want to find it and they want to find Harker, since he worked for both sides at one time and has a great deal of their classified scientific information. He is a major security risk to either side. Hartigal has taken an interest in the world because they accidentally stumbled onto its location and are now secretly monitoring it for any new technologies being developed there. In fact, they kinda hope to convince Harker to sell or license them some of his innovations.

Panhelion Prime. The Panhelion Council is a collective of people who work for Hartigal but live in space stations orbiting stars in systems without planets. This particular system is where this weird culture/religion got its start and is the strongest. The people's aversion to "hard earth" is part of their belief structure, and nobody from Hartigal is about to question that. This system is just part of an exotic trinary star system with no worlds. In the center point of the three stars, numerous galactic phenomena are known to occur, and the Panhelion scientists appear to be on the verge of unlocking the secrets of most of them. The question is, do they do this for their own protection, for the benefit of Hartigal, or do they wish to turn their knowledge into weapons technology in a bid to destroy the galaxy's planets one by one?

The Sargasso. This is no planet, but a set of four asteroid belts connected by dense clouds of dust. It is all part of a young solar system that is still accreting into planetary mass, but for the time being, it is the home to many smugglers, pirates and crooks of every kind to whom the numerous asteroids provide cheap homes and protection. Hartigal maintains control over the system because they are mining the asteroids. They have an agreement with the criminal types – we leave you alone, you leave us alone. It is working okay for the moment, but as soon as a Cosmo-Knight shows up to clean things out (and they always do), then the Hartigal mining interests will be abandoned in order to avoid undue attention from the Knight.

Theora. This world is a genuine pirate kingdom, like Madagascar of old. A fleet of seven different pirate clans have come together, selected a king, and taken over this sparsely populated world to make it their base. The thing is, it was a sparsely populated Hartigal outpost, and the company now has a major piracy problem on its hands. Lacking the overt military power necessary to rout them, Hartigal must appeal to larger powers (good luck) to get these lawbreakers off their world, or they must rely on adventurer types and their newly created mercenary army to sneak into the enemy's camp quietly and take care of the problem in a short, sharp stroke.

The Tengen Archipelago. In this solar system, all of the planets are in permanent alignment. It appears some advanced, ancient civilization did this. On the third and fourth worlds, there are a ton of artifacts to be uncovered that would support this theory, only the locals, for whatever reason, have shown no interest in unearthing these treasures. The artifacts are valuable to the scientific community as well as to the collectors' community since they are made of precious metals and minerals (gold, silver, teelium, etc.). Thus, there are one has a lot of scrupulous and unscrupulous Hartigal off-worlders trying to plunder the hidden riches of these worlds. The locals don't really care what happens to their heritage; they are (for the most part) willing to sell out their past for money and trade things that would propel this society into the interstellar arena. The Sellout has been good for the people materially, but some are worried they are doing irreparable damage to their history, so they are now seeing rebels and resistors dedicated to kicking out the foreigners and keeping the people's cultural treasures right here, where they belong. So far, this is not a revolution scenario, but it is causing quite a bit of unrest.

Hoddes. This high-gravity world has proven to be an outstanding environment for testing new exoskeletons, power armor and combat robots. Most of the world is dedicated to testing facilities and prototype manufacturing, and as such, has been nicknamed the "Toy Box." Naruni spies and saboteurs have had a terrible time infiltrating the place because for some odd reason, Hartigal employees stationed on Hoddes for more than a year develop a strange psionic link to one another – a sort of non-intrusive mental bond that tells them when there is an enemy or intruder in their midst. The power only works on this world and fades within 2D6 days after leaving the planet.

Tralan Antassif. This is a major gateway world for moving Hartigal inventory. As mentioned earlier, the company maintains a circuit of freighters within their own network of worlds to move finished goods from factory planets to outlet planets. Tralan Antassif is a nexus world between this circuit and the many external trade circuits Hartigal maintains with worlds outside of the company's territory. From this planet, freighters load up with inventory and deliver it to worlds that have already placed an order. They also stop off at other points of opportunity along their path to make on-the-spot sales to those who need weapons *now*. These freighters travel with heavy warship escort, especially since pirates and Naruni (masquerading as pirates) find these targets too tempting to resist.

Che'Vad. Hartigal was given this world as a gift from the *Mortu Consulate*, a tiny kingdom of humans and other races

who, with Hartigal weaponry, managed to break free of the disintegrating Golgan Republik. Though the Mortu made good on their payments to Hartigal, they also gave them one of their own worlds in an unprecedented show of generosity. Hartigal is mulling whether or not to give the world back. What might be the deciding factor is a set of interesting ruins discovered by archaeological teams at the bottom of the world's deepest ocean that indicates there used to be an alien civilization here. There is also evidence from these ruins that these aliens knew a *lot* about the Cosmic Forge and *may* have had something to do with deciding where it would be hidden.

Gandon Point. This world is on the end of a long, exposed "salient" of Hartigal territory that extends deep into the realms controlled by Naruni Enterprises. This makes the world effectively a siege state, as Naruni warships routinely blockade the world and subject it to bombardments of "accidental weapons drops" and "weapons malfunctions." Of course, nobody believes these lame Naruni excuses for firing on the planet, and Hartigal is busy massing a fleet to relieve the planet, to reinforce it, and to shatter the Naruni vessels orbiting there.

Hydekker. Hartigal treasures this world for its vast deposits of heavy metals, precious elements and other valuable mineral resources. The company is strip mining it as fast as possible because seismic surveys reveal serious harmonic instability throughout the planet. This means the world could explode at any time. At least the world is a lifeless crater field, so there will be no environmental loss if and when it goes kablooey. Hartigal employees must volunteer to work the planet, and they do so at triple hazard pay, making this one of the most lucrative, and dangerous gigs within the entire company. Some miners are trying to burrow channels deep into the earth to ease the onset of the planet's harmonic disturbances. The theory is they could coax the world into cracking in half rather than just exploding. This would be great for mining, since the deep deposits could be accessed with ease. However, it is just a theory, and one that could prove to be explosively wrong to those intent on proving it.

Golgan Republik

(Editor's Note: The misspellings of "Republik," "Politik," "Scientifik" and other such misspellings in the Golgan section are intentional. It's just an affectation to set this power bloc apart from other cultures.)

Population: 2 trillion sentient beings, though as the Republik breaks down, that number dwindles little by little.

Demographics: Golgan (50%), Lurgess (14%), Ultrovians (13%), Zebuloids (13%), Other (10%). Full descriptions of these races are found in the **Aliens** section of this book.

Overview: Founded by the Golgan race over a thousand years ago, the Golgan Republik is really a massive effort by the indigenous people to create as much of a buffer zone around their home worlds as possible. The Golgans used to be a peace-loving people, but after several wars with their neighbors (in which the Golgans suffered terribly), the Golgan culture became hard-edged, paranoid and cynical. Though the Golgans won their wars and annihilated their enemies, they live in constant fear that they will be attacked again. Rather than rebuild their shattered worlds into the glorious examples of architecture they once were, the Golgans threw their considerable resources and strength into militarizing their whole society. They built vast fleets of starships and trained enormous armies of billions of soldiers, all ready, willing and able to die for their beloved Republik.

The Golgans embarked on a 300-year quest to conquer or otherwise assimilate as much of their neighboring star systems as they could. At the end of the period, the Republik was at its height, with nearly 2,000 star systems and 5 trillion sentient people under its control. Since then, it has gradually lost power as more and more of its worlds rebel and break away. Today, the Golgan Republik is in a state of steady disintegration, and the government has little power to stop it. Essentially, the civilization expanded too far, too quickly, and became terribly over-extended. In many cases, the very military units stationed on conquered foreign worlds were the ones leading the revolts. By the time the rest of the Golgan military could respond, the rebellion was effectively over, and to bring the breakaway world back into the fold would require a full war effort that would cost a lot of time, resources, manpower and energy. And for what? By the time the Golgans retrieved their rebel world, the planet would have been reduced to ruin and no good to anybody. So, the Golgans simply let these worlds go in the hopes that maybe they could at least retain them as trading partners.

For the Republik, this approach, merciful though it may have been, sounded the death knell. Knowing that their government is not likely to destroy them for breaking away, any world disen-chanted with the Golgan way of life is now rebelling, flooding the government with too many secession crises to deal with. The end result is that the outermost edge of the Republik is crumbling rapidly, and within another century, all that will remain are the three or four core Golgan systems that created the Republik in the first place.

Government

The *Council Politik* is the ruling body within the Republik. It is like a big parliament in which every non-Golgan world gets a single representative and every Golgan world gets two representatives. The Council is a representative democracy, with a simple majority carrying all votes. The Council tries to be accommodating to everybody, but in the end, the Golgans control the majority of representatives in the Council, so more often than not, it is they who get what they want. At present, the disintegration of the Republik is slowly draining away non-Golgan representatives from the Council, making it increasingly difficult for non-Golgans to ever rally enough votes to overturn unpopular Golgan decrees or laws. The result is that entire non-Golgan populations are growing tired of their waning power in this society, and are more apt to rebel, speeding the Republik's collapse. If the Council wanted to halt the epidemic of rebellion, it would redistribute the voting power among the Council reps, making it so the Golgans did not have such an unfair share of power. However, being as paranoid as they are, the Golgans will never agree to this, and would rather cling to what power they have for now (and lose it in the long run) than give up a little now (and keep their authority well into the future).

It is this kind of shortsightedness that has hamstrung the Republikan government all along. Daily matters are carried out by a massive, redundant and impersonal bureaucracy that makes the old Soviet system on Earth look like a smooth-running social machine. Everything takes longer than it should, nothing gets done quickly, and by the time the government accomplishes anything, the result is inadequate or way overdue. Ironically, this paralytic form of governance came about because the Golgans wanted to include all of their conquered people in the process of getting things done. Thus, there are millions of permanent bureaus, committees, oversight boards and other such venues for citizens to get involved in the governmental process. Talk about too much of a good thing! As result of having so much over-input, the Golgan government is smothering under its own weight. Nothing gets done, the people are unhappy, and a bad situation is only getting worse. The Golgan system could work on a much smaller scale, but for a massive and multiracial empire, it is a recipe for disaster.

Military

The Republikan Guard is the primary military force, consisting of Army, Navy and Marine branches. It is exclusive to Golgans, however, and it is reserved mostly for dealing with external threats to the Republik. **The Auxiliary Guard** is the secondary military force, consisting exclusively of non-Golgans. Every non-Golgan planet has its own Auxiliary Guard force, and these are supposed to uphold the law and suppress any rebellion. However, with politics falling along racial lines, the Auxiliary Guards are often just as eager to rebel as the citizens, which makes the secession of worlds from the Republik a fairly simple process.

Breaux

The Republikan Guard is armed with the latest Naruni weaponry, armor, ships and equipment. They are also well trained and well motivated, and overall, present a fine fighting force. The problem is, they are not being used since the Council Politik is so convinced that invisible enemies lurk outside of the Republik's domain, waiting for the right moment to strike. Thus, the very force that could keep the Republik together is instead deployed along the outermost borders, their eyes and guns turned outward into space, where no real danger exists, instead of inward to the Republik, where a bloodless civil war is already underway.

Auxiliary Guards are often armed with secondhand or obsolete equipment. Most of them use HI-series knock-offs as their main weapons, and armor and equipment put together locally, or from some generic manufacturer off-world. These Guardsmen tend to be better motivated than trained, and most are adept at guerilla fighting, so if the Republikan Guard were ever to intervene on a rebel world, there would be one heck of a fight.

Foreign Affairs

Consortium of Civilized Worlds: Most of the worlds that leave the Golgan Republik end up allying with or joining the Consortium. As far as the CCW goes, since there is very little fighting in this wave of secessions, the Golgans must not mind that so many of their worlds are joining them. However, there *is* great resentment. That the CCW would so openly and readily invite Golgan Republik breakaway worlds to join them is an affront of the first order, and the Golgans will never forget it.

Trans-Galactic Empire: As a result of what they see as the CCW openly stealing their worlds (perhaps even secretly encouraging rebellion), the Golgans have secretly begun to consider the TGE a potential ally in the Forge War. The Golgans no longer have the resources to contribute meaningfully to the search for the Cosmic Forge because they are so busy trying to keep from self-destructing. But they do know that the Forge War is heating things up between the CCW and the TGE, and ultimately, the Republik will have to choose a side. The Golgans would like to show their support then for the TGE as a way of surprising the Consortium and getting back at them for gobbling up so many of their breakaway worlds. Conversely, no non-Golgan wants to join or partner with the TGE for fear that the Empire will take it as an invitation to just move in and take over. As bad as life can be under the Republik, with its excessive rules for everything and blatant preferential treatment to all Golgans, things would be far worse under the Kreeghor Imperials.

United Worlds of Warlock: Any Golgan world with a strong magical or spiritual culture that breaks away from the Republik automatically seeks recognition and perhaps membership from the UWW. For their part, the UWW is happy to comply, repeating the same kind of insulting conduct that the CCW has done so much of already. That, coupled with the Golgans' naive thoughts of hooking up with the TGE, makes the UWW an enemy state not to be trusted. The Golgans do not want to let on about this just yet, though, preferring that the UWW think that they are on good terms with the Republik when they actually are not.

Naruni Enterprises: The Republik is on the verge of defaulting on several very large weapons shipments it recently received from the Naruni, and they have absolutely no way to make payments. This is a disaster in the making, and the Council Politik would rather pretend the problem does not exist rather than try to work it out. Those few representatives who do see this problem for what it is insist that the Republikan Guard can repel any efforts by the Naruni to collect on their debts. This is why the Guard was formed, and armed with the very cream of Naruni weaponry, they will make sure that no part of the Republik falls into Naruni hands...right?

Hartigal Combine: Facing foreclosure from the Naruni, the Council Politik is considering establishing trade channels with Hartigal both to keep new weapons coming into the Republik, and as a gesture of defiance to Naruni Enterprises. Many Auxiliary worlds of the Republik have already been buying weapons under the table from Hartigal, so the Council Politik feels that perhaps now is the time the entire Republik opens a joint account with the rogue manufacturer. At least that way, maybe they could get a volume discount. Of course, if the Republik can not pay Naruni, it might not be able to pay Hartigal either, something that is making the Hartigal reps a little wary of jumping into bed with the Republik right away.

Altess Dynasty: The Altess are one of the few power blocs that successfully resisted conquest by the Republik. Though the Altess no longer hold a grudge from this old war (it happened over 200 years ago), the *Golgans* have not forgotten. They have sworn to make the Altess pay for their insolence, although how they might do that has always been a bit of a mystery. After all, the Republik had a chance to crush the Altess once before, and they failed to get the job done. Since then, the Altess have shown few signs of weakness that the Republik could capitalize on, and the chances that the Golgans will ever get their shot at vengeance dwindle further with each passing year. Conversely, the Altess have been indifferent to the Republik's collapse, showing no interest in grabbing up newly independent worlds for themselves. They are too busy counting their money and living in the lap of luxury to care what some half-baked superpower thinks or does.

Central Alliance: The Central Alliance consists of worlds that broke away from the Republik nearly 300 years ago. For this, they can never be forgiven, and the Golgans consider them all to be enemy states. That said, these Alliance worlds were themselves so fractious and riven with infighting that the Golgans smirked at their barbarity and wrote them off as perhaps something better left apart from the Republik anyway. Now that the Central Alliance is solidifying and turning into a new power bloc just as the Golgans' power is declining, many Golgan reps in the Council Politik fear that the Central Alliance might turn its eyes on the Republik and strike in its moment of weakness. Numerous Golgan generals insist that it is in the Republik's best interests to send a pre-emptive strike force of Republikan Guardsmen into Central Alliance territory to shake things up. So far, cooler heads have prevailed on this, but for how much longer can they hold out?

Cosmo-Knights: Cosmo-Knights interfered on numerous occasions during the Golgans' initial phase of conquest. On several campaigns, entire worlds were prevented from assimilation by timely Cosmo-Knight intervention, and the Golgans consider the knights to be *evil menaces* bent on spreading their warped brand of justice throughout the galaxy. That is not the case, of course, but that is how the Golgans see it. They are also powerless to do anything to the Cosmo-Knights, but they remain ever watchful for an opportunity that would allow them to strike down a Cosmo-Knight and get some payback.

Kingdom of Rynncryyl: Splugorth slavers have raided Golgan space on a number of occasions in the past, and their presence is one of the reasons why the Republik was formed in the first place. Now as the Republik is falling apart, many Golgans fear that Splugorth agents are waiting in the wings, ready to strike from the shadows and deal a death blow to the teetering Golgan civilization. The thing is, in this case, they may be right.

Gene-Tech: The Golgans appreciate the skill and technology the Gene-Tech command, but that is the extent of any good feelings they have for these vicious genetic engineers. Republikan Guardsmen destroyed a Gene-Tech ship skimming the border zone a few years ago, and ever since, the Republik has been on the lookout for some kind of retaliation. Reports that a clan of Gene-Tech have taken over a desolate planetoid not far from the Republik's southern border persists, as do additional rumors that the Gene-Tech have reactivated an army of billions of genetically modified warriors, all of whom want a piece of the Golgan Republik. The story is almost certainly absolute poppycock, but for the paranoid Golgan Republik it seems to be a very real danger.

Omegan Order: Though the Golgans distrust the Cosmo-Knights, they distrust the Omegan Order even more. The Cosmo-Knights are just warped, the Golgans think, whereas the Omegans are flat-out EVIL. They should be destroyed, of course, but by somebody besides the Republik, which has more pressing matters to attend to.

Xodian Collective: The Republik's official stance on the Xodians is that they do not exist, and that they are a figment of the Consortium's imagination. Nobody has ever given much reason to explain this odd stance. It just popped up somehow, and the Council Politik has gone along with it. Non-Golgans are quickly coming to the conclusion that the Xodians do exist, and that they would not mind contacting them sometime.

K!ozn: The Republik is convinced that K!ozn agents are afoot wherever there is rebellion within the Republik. The Golgans do not like the look of these strange aliens, nor of their even stranger minions. As far as the Golgans are concerned, the K!ozn cannot possibly be as smart and sophisticated as they pretend to be. They must be putting on some kind of front to impress or trick the power blocs of the Halo. Yeah, that's the ticket!

Independent Worlds: The Republik is surrounded by independent worlds, most of which were once part of the Republik and broke away. Those that are not old members of the Republik were once assaulted by the Republik but successfully resisted (there are only a few of these) or were at one time connected to an enemy of the Republik. All of this feeds into the typically paranoid culture of the Golgans, who see them all as envious upstarts or vengeful enemies. All of which makes the Golgans feel they are, and forever will be, a nation of people in a sea of enemies.

Society

The Golgans, as a race, have become dour, cynical and excessively wary of their surroundings. Since the Golgans control the reins of power in the Republik, their culture dominates the overall society, making it a gloomy, unhappy place where there is little hope or reason to look ahead for the future. However, the Golgan way is not present *everywhere* in the Republik, and the incredible diversity of races that make up this society all contribute a little bit of their own cultures into the mix. Especially on worlds that are not predominantly Golgan, things feel very different.

Daily Life

The worlds of the Golgan Republik range from rich to poor, agricultural to industrial, high-tech to low-tech. Throughout this wide disparity of lifestyles, one thing remains constant; all Golgans have it better than non-Golgans. They either get paid more for their job, have better land reserved for them, get tax breaks, are given exclusive access to certain technologies, etc. It is the foundation of daily life in the Republik. It is also a major reason behind the Republik's imminent collapse.

Law and Order

There is a law or regulation for *everything* in the Golgan Republik. No matter what one does, they must consider that the chances are good they have accidentally forgotten to cross a "T" or dot an "I" somewhere, and will be made to suffer for it. On most worlds, the Auxiliary Guard enforces the laws and regulations of the Council Politik, but in many cases, the Guard let a lot of infractions slide because they do not agree with them. The Republikan Guard is able to enforce the law anywhere in the Republik, but it rarely does so because it is deployed in deep space, and because most Republikan Guards feel civil law enforcement is beneath them.

Crime and Punishment

The Golgans are not necessarily cruel people or overly harsh lawmakers, but they do expect people to uphold even the tiniest details of the law. Those who do not face "revokation" of social privileges, such as reduction in pay, restriction of travel, prohibited access to the Golgan information network, and so on. Basically the entire society runs on a big demerit system, and people are allowed to transfer their demerits on to other willing recipients. This means that families and groups of friends often have large "demerit pools" that are used to keep any one member from going to jail. Jail is only for those who have excessive demerits, and since one loses demerits for time served without additional penalties, as long as one keeps his nose clean in between infractions, jail time is a remote possibility at best. Really, the whole system is made to harass the public and keep them always on their toes when around the government. Those with absolutely no demerits are always given some, just as those with tons of demerits will only get more if they truly deserve them. Like so much else in the Republik, this system does not work because so many people are part of enormous demerit pools. Given a large enough pool, a person can commit premeditated murder and get away with it, so long as he has enough pool mates who are willing to soak up a fraction of the demerits assigned. In fact, entire planets have seceded legally, stating that the whole population has formed a single demerit pool capable of absorbing the demerits awarded for treason. Faced with such an argument, the feckless Council Politik simply shrugs its shoulders and sends the newly liberated world on its way.

Worlds of Interest

Gologo Maxus. This is the world from which the Golgan people originated. It has never left their possession, and is the capital world for the Republik today. Despite its importance governmentally, it is a sparsely populated world, having only a few major cities. The rest of the land is left wild out of an age-old Golgan fear that if they over-exploit their home world's resources, their own society will crumble because of it. Every other world in the Republik has been worked over pretty severely in terms of resource extraction, leading, in most cases, to irreparable environmental damage. But Gologo Maxus remains a relatively untouched place. All Golgans are expected to return here at least three times in their life. The reasons behind this old custom have been forgotten, but the practice lives on and as a result, Gologo Maxus is probably the only capital world in the Anvil Galaxy that does more tourism business than government.

Kadobe, Mutant World. Strange radiation from the sun is mutating everybody in the Kadobe star system, arguably the single most populated set of planets in the Golgan Republik. Some Kadobans are getting sick or deformed, some are only marginally affected, and some are getting *special abilities* and *super-powers,* generating an entire generation of super-powered heroes, villains and freebooters. This is especially problematic for the Republik, as Kadobe is a hotbed of rebellion. If its people develop super-powers, they may not be content only to secede. They may want to help other worlds do the same.

Daradan. More than a century ago, the Council Scientifik appropriated this uninhabited world to conduct various biogenetic experiments on it. Through a typically Golgan snafu, the government failed to renew funding for the Council Scientifik, and Daradan was left to go wild. Now, years later, the Republik is in need of additional living space, as its prime worlds are all leaving and the overcrowding on some of the older, more Golgan-only worlds is reaching epidemic proportions. Daradan is seen as a potential colonization target, only it is now crawling with all sorts of monstrous plants and animals, courtesy of the unfinished biogen experiments that were left to evolve on their own. While the government wrings its hands trying to figure out how to clear the planet for settlement, it has in the meantime become a favored spot for big game hunters, pirates, smugglers, renegade scientists, explorers, mercenaries, exiled governments, religious refugees (some of whom find this world to be a holy place), ex-government types, and others.

Naanta. This super-tech utopia world is one of the few crown jewels remaining in the Golgan Republik. Covered with orderly, clean, efficient arcologies, powered by endless fields of top-line fusion reactors, home to over one hundred and fifty billion sentient beings, and absolutely no shred of rebellion on the entire world, Naanta is indeed what many Golgans wish their entire society was. However, this is just the public face to the world, a Potemkin village to make the Council Politik feel better. The truth is that while Naanta is a highly advanced world, it simmers with crime and revolution, and the Auxiliary Guard stationed here have evolved into one of the most ruthless and efficient anti-crime, anti-terrorism units in the Golgan Republik. On the streets of Naanta, there is war going on, a hid-

den war, safe from the eyes of the beautiful people living so high in the arcologies. This is a down and dirty fight for nothing less than the stability of one of the Golgan Republik's remaining bastions of stability.

Kaluda. This lonely planet is the home world of the *Zebuloids*, strange tentacled aliens who have long been a part of the Republik. Kaluda is also home to *Red Moon Squadron*, an elite force of starship pilots who, as part of that world's Auxiliary Guard, patrol the space lanes in search of intruders and pirates. In part because Kaluda has its own shipyard industry and builds very efficient craft and in part because Zebuloids are naturally excellent pilots, Red Moon Squadron has an astounding 250:1 kill ratio! That means for every ship Red Moon Squadron loses, 250 ships, on average, are destroyed. The Squadron is so good that piracy has stopped not only for this system but for the surrounding systems as well. The Republik is considering putting the Squadron on "tour" so it can go around the Republik on a free search for bad guys to destroy. Of course, Kaluda is on the verge of seceding, and when it does, it will deprive the Republik of a fine star force. With little other industry to rely on, the world will most likely hire out the Red Moon Squadron as mercenaries to operate for whatever parties wish to use them in the Forge War.

Skandau. A huge gas giant with nine planet-like moons, Skandau was once colonized by the Golgans as a strategic way point for traveling starships. The various moons hosted a number of friendly outposts to foreign and domestic traffic, and the taxes on fuel, food, and other commodities sold to travelers more than made the system pay for itself. For a long time, it stayed this way, isolated and underpopulated. However, as the *Forge War* began, refugees from the neighboring *Nefertidi* system fled to Skandau's moons to avoid marauding TGE forces who were tossing entire worlds in search for clues to the Cosmic Forge's location. The refugees never left, and the Republik is still trying to figure out what to do with them. These people are not welcome – though the Republik is falling apart, the Golgans are still picky over who they admit into their ranks – but to mass deport them means a trip back to the TGE and probable death. (The TGE doesn't look kindly on those who flee the Empire for any reason.) Moreover, Skandau's other moons are some of the few worlds still willing to stay with the Republik, and if the Golgans eject the refugees, rebellion will surely result. What to do? Whatever the Republik does, it had better do it fast because the refugees are quickly overwhelming the moons on which they live, and if the government does not get involved, starvation and environmental depletion will follow.

Mekanik. A Golgan experiment in independent machinery, Mekanik has been a fully automated world – no organics allowed – for 66 years. It is a production facility for various kinds of military and civilian technology, especially planetary engineering processors, a vital component in any terra-forming project. The intelligent machinery has been given its mission and left to its own devices (no pun intended) on how to complete said mission. Aside from routine supply drops and pickups of finished products, the world receives no contact from the outside. Automated defense satellites keep pirates and other interlopers at bay. Amazingly, it is all working well except for the fact that during the latest session of the Council Politik, two humanoid robots claiming to be from Mekanik showed up on the Council floor and announced that they were Mekanik's official representatives. The Republik does not know what to make of this. The prospect of Mekanik determining its own fate to any degree could be catastrophic, especially if it decided to secede and take all of that terra-forming machinery with it. On the other hand, if the Republik denies representation to this robot world, rebellion might also result. The Mekanik representatives have asked that the Republik give their answer to this within 100 days. 10 days are left, with no resolution in sight. However this ends up, it probably will not be good. (**G.M. Note:** For players wishing to play an intelligent robot from Mekanik, please check out the Robot R.C.C. Rules in the **Rifts® Sourcebook**. Or, for convenience's sake, simply play a Naruni Repo-Bot, but without all of the on-board weaponry. For other robot designs, check out **Rifts® Sourcebook Two: The Mechanoids®.**)

Ulmore. This is one of the few worlds where the Republikan Guard actually did respond militarily to a planetary secession. It was almost 300 years ago, and the Ulmorian Auxiliary Guard had decided they wanted to be in charge of their world, and that they no longer needed the accursed Golgans telling them what to do. Incensed, the Golgans sicced the dogs on the Ulmorians, and a fierce battle ensued. In the end, the Republikan Guard destroyed pretty much everything on the planet, and the Ulmorians were either killed or fled the world. (Many of them established a new world for themselves just beyond Republik territory, in a system renamed Ulmore II). Saddened by this wasteful episode, the Republik cordoned off the entire world as a memorial to the needless violence civil war causes. It was supposed to be a reminder to all subjects that secession can bring only ruin. It instead eroded the Golgan resolve to ever respond strongly to secession again, and in turn only encouraged more worlds to break away from the Republik.

Adraodus. A plague outbreak on this world forced its Golgan colonists to take refuge in deep subterranean cities where the environment could be purified more easily. Long after the surface plague subsided, the Golgans stayed underground, digging deeper to expand their cities, instead of reaching back to the surface. Now the world is an utterly massive honeycomb of underground passages, chambers and shafts. In fact, some of these passageways have gone all the way to the planetary core! The ingenious engineers here have figured out a way to harness the tapped core energies for fuel, heat, and as a rudimentary weapon in case the planet itself comes under attack. Though it is a theoretical measure, the engineers think they can vent a jet of molten core out of the planet at incoming enemies, melting them instantaneously! They also think a core vent can move the planet just a little bit off its orbit, which might be useful if a comet or asteroid threatens to hit the planet. Of course, doing any of these things threatens to exhaust the core, and cause the gradual and unstoppable cooling of the planet. It would take millions of years, but eventually all life on the planet would die, and it would become like a big asteroid or rocky moon.

Jaoril. Site of the *Battle of Endless Konquest*, Jaoril is considered by Golgan military historians to be the place where the Republik's golden age of expansion began. Here, Golgan armies defeated the *Order of Darkness*, a sinister cult that had control over the entire planet and was in the process of orchestrating a global suicide event. Whatever purpose all that death was supposed to serve never came to bear, but the Golgans who destroyed the Cult and most of its followers have been hailed as heroes. Though Jaoril has become a massively redeveloped world, there still exists a huge stone courtyard, some 100 miles (160 km) square, in which the shattered hulls of the ships that fought in the battle rest as a monument to Golgan glory. Not all of the cultists were destroyed, however. A few of them lived, and today, a secret underground version of the Order of Darkness exists and plots the destruction not only of this world, but of the entire Golgan Republik, and after that, the Anvil Galaxy itself. For the Order of Darkness knows exactly where the Cosmic Forge is, or so they claim, and when they finally figure out how to get to it, they shall have all the power they need to bring their dark vision for the universe into reality...

The Altess Dynasty

Population: 100 million sentient beings. The low population is a result of careful and deliberate efforts taken by the Altess to achieve ZPG – Zero Population Growth. This cause is the central theme to Altess culture and government.

Demographics: Human (88%), Other (12%). Humans definitely have preferred status. Any other race is considered second-class (at best). Most aliens here are as slaves. Less than 1% of the alien population within the Altess Dynasty is free, and those who are almost always are in the process of getting out.

Overview: The Altess Dynasty is an unusual blend of social engineering, genetic engineering, and political engineering. It is one of the most stridently human-supremacist power blocs in the Anvil Galaxy, but through adept diplomacy, artful dodging, and outright bribery, it has managed to ascend to the top circles of galactic power, somehow avoiding destruction along the way.

The Altess are a race of humans from the Altetch star system, deep in the heart of the western Halo. They claim to have descended directly from *The First*, that mythical race that once commanded the Cosmic Forge. According to Altess legend, when the Cosmic Forge went into hiding, it revealed to the Altess where it would go, but in a way that no single Altess could know. The Cosmic Forge is said to have imparted upon each Altess alive at the time a tiny fragment of its hiding place, like a single piece to a puzzle. Each Altess would have this fragment of knowledge in their head, a tiny shard of an ancient and amazing truth they could telepathically project to whoever wished to receive it. For the Altess to divine the location of the Cosmic Forge, they would *all* have to link their minds and thoughts at once, all simultaneously sharing their single piece of knowledge. Only then would the location of the Cosmic Forge unlock itself in their minds, and only then could they, "the chosen people," inherit the Cosmic Forge for themselves.

This might not seem like such a difficult thing to do. Only back then, the Altess were a savage and violent people, endlessly locked in warfare. For them all to share with each other their innermost secret would require a miracle – or several thousand generations of social evolution. The latter proved to be what happened, and now, so very many millennia after the Cosmic Forge went into hiding, the Altess are a much changed people. They no longer fight amongst themselves, they possess a

highly advanced culture and technology, and they have mastered the art of thought-sharing, making it all the more possible for them to share the knowledge of the Cosmic Forge's whereabouts.

So why haven't the Altess yet unlocked the Forge's location? That is perhaps the greatest unanswered question for this civilization to solve. The leading theory is that the race widely dispersed after the Cosmic Forge imparted its location to them all, and in the subsequent generations, the Altess have had to come back together, realigning their bloodlines so they more or less match up to what they once were. Basically, the Altess must engineer their genetic lineage in such a way that it comes full circle and is as close to what it once was as possible. The Altess have done this, but it still is not enough. There are just a few pieces of their collective memory missing, and nobody is quite sure of where to find them. For the Altess, this is like having an entire puzzle completed with just two or three pieces missing. Only this is no mere puzzle to be solved; this is the key to unlocking the doors to ultimate power.

As a race, the Altess have grown rather philosophical about all of this. To them, while the rest of the galaxy knocks itself out trying to find the Cosmic Forge, the Altess are already 97% of the way there. All they have to do is wait for those last few pieces of genetic information to come their way, and their quest is over. To keep their race from fragmenting again, the Altess have instituted a practice of Zero Population Growth. Basically, it is a method by which no new Altess are born until one of them dies. The number of Altess must remain constant at all times or else they risk losing more of their collective genetic memory.

In the past, Altess despots believed that if they killed as many Altess as possible, the race's collective genetic memory would keep redistributing itself among the survivors until only one person could have the entire knowledge of the Cosmic Forge's location. Nearly 9,000 years ago, a maniacal overlord named *Jurgo Kilter* believed in this method and set to exterminating all of his fellow Altess, hoping it would impart upon him more knowledge of the Forge's whereabouts. By the time Kilter was himself slain, fewer than 200 million Altess remained out of the seven billion there once were! Some scholars believe that this irrevocably ruined the Altess' chances of ever reuniting their genetic memory, and the best they can do is what they have now, an incomplete key that can never be made whole.

Most Altess accept this and are content to move on with their lives. It is not that hard, since the Altess live very good lives, indeed. After the Kilter Massacres, the Altess began working feverishly on ways to extend their life span, to reduce the death rate among them as much as possible. After a few centuries, they perfected genetic engineering techniques that extended their life span to well over 1,000 years. That, coupled with incredible medical and regenerative technologies, made it so that an Altess could pretty much live forever. With such long life spans, the average Altess has an enormously long period of time to amass wealth, which many of them do. All told, the Altess are the richest population per capita in the Anvil Galaxy. Each Altess citizen has more money than many independent governments. A large portion of this usually is in cash deposited in banks all across the galaxy, while the rest is tied up in an elaborate network of investments spanning the Anvil Galaxy. This makes Altess wealth very diversified and immune to catastrophe. It also gives them a vested interest in everything that goes on in the Anvil Galaxy, so they have learned to keep their ears to the ground. Historically, they have learned to be neutral in galactic politics, though they are not above pulling some strings in the background every now and again to make sure certain events or trends turn out their way.

Government

The Altess Dynasty is a tightly knit collection of noble families who have emerged from the barbaric state the Altess were once in. Through careful social engineering and the development of methods to make themselves immortal, the Altess Dynasty is part of a very stable ruling tradition that has remained unchanged for thousands of years. Politics moves at a glacial pace with these people, and to say that the current regime is long lived is to slight the term "long lived." The Altess measure the time of their regimes by *generations*, not years. And the configuration of years to generations to the number of the dynasty carries special significance, too. For example, the current regime is in the 11th year of the 11th generation of the 11th Dynasty. Not only have these ruling families governed for a very long time, but they have reached a critical juncture in their time – the three 11s signify that something very big is going to happen to these rulers, and it is going to happen soon. The Altess believe it will be something to do with the Cosmic Forge; either the Dynasty will be dragged into the forefront of the Forge War, or somehow they will gain the missing knowledge they need to unlock the Forge's secret location.

The Dynasty itself is a simple aristocracy. All ruling authority derives from the Dynasty's bloodline. Unless you are blood or married to it, you can not rule. Simple as that. The dozens of royal families all have equal footing, and they come together once a decade in the *Concession of the Bond*, an arcane ceremony in which matters of state are decided upon. In the interim, governmental matters are decided upon by the families themselves, who have total control over their territory within the Dynasty's sphere of influence.

Military

Each royal family maintains its own force of soldiers (usually volunteers but sometimes conscripts), and on top of that, each family is expected to maintain a certain percentage of the *Armoria*, the joint military that addresses security for the Dynasty as a whole. The Armoria is meant to repel attacks from pirates, despots, hostile aliens, and the like, but it has seen very little action in some years. As the Forge War threatens to push the Altess into the middle of rival galactic superpowers, the Armoria has gone into a heightened state of alert. It has also purchased additional arms and armor from the Naruni and even a few assorted third-party vendors who specialize in secondhand and knock-off weaponry. The Armoria can't possibly use all of this at once, but the Altess believe in maintaining a ridiculously large stockpile of spare military hardware just in case they should ever need it. At present, the Altess have enough extra weapons and equipment to completely refit the Armoria six times before supplies are exhausted. Considering that nearly all of this equipment is top-line Naruni product, that makes for one formidable cache of firepower.

Despite this incredible stockpile, the chances are that the Altess will never have to use it. Over time, they have done well with their first and most powerful weapon: money. The Altess are so incredible wealthy that they have usually been able to just buy off their enemies or hire mercenaries to take care of them. Or, the Altess will sometimes hire the enemies of their enemies to get involved on the Altess' behalf. This sort of thing has been the Altess' first line of defense for millennia, and it works. The best thing about it is that it has never even come close to depleting the Royal Treasuries. Hell, the interest off the interest off the interest from the Treasuries could fund a substantial army for ten years, so it is no wonder the Altess can bribe just about anyone to do just about anything. That being the case, the Altess are no pushovers, and they make it clear whenever buying off a foe that this is it, this is the end of all hostilities for at least a century or so. The Altess are not about to tolerate some greedy despot who intends on extorting another payment out of the Altess every few years. Against that sort of opposition, the Altess *will* go to war, and they will spare no expense, and bar no holds until their enemies are destroyed. When the Altess military goes after a target, it conducts what it euphemistically calls "hereditary victory." That means they will not only destroy their opponents, but they will destroy their immediate family, including children. The Altess have and will carry this out on a global scale, as evidenced by the horrific *Cipher War*, in which the Altess fell under attack by the *League of Blood*, a pretentious pirate armada that had taken over a few independent worlds and fancied themselves rulers of the galaxy. The Altess bought them off once, and the Legion immediately came back for more. In short order, the Armoria not only destroyed the Legion's fleet, but they made sure *every single* pirate was slain, as was his family and his friends. The relatively innocent civilians of the conquered worlds were spared, but they were given the message that the Altess expected them to root out any sympathizers of the Legion of Blood and execute them immediately. So scared of the Armoria were these people that they actually followed the order, hunting and killing pirate sympathizers for months thereafter.

Events like the Cipher War have given the Altess military a reputation as a sleeping dragon. Most of the time, it is quiet, even invisible. But when it awakens, the very cosmos shakes, and those foolish enough to stir the dragon shall know in short order what it feels like to be slain by one.

The Royal Treasuries

Each royal family keeps account of its own wealth, but they are all required to report their holdings to the jointly administrated *Royal Treasuries*. This organization is like a massive accounting firm and investment center for the entire Dynasty. Not only does it maintain exact figures on the net worth of the Dynasty, but it also manages all investment activity (apart from what the nobles themselves may want to dally in) and makes the numbers public knowledge to everyone in the Dynasty, noble and commoner alike.

This last part serves two purposes. One, it keeps the nobles honest with each other and helps reduce any feelings of competition or jealousy. Nearly all of the royal families are similarly wealthy, and even the "poorest" among them has wealth far beyond the imagination of most Halo governments. Wealth, as it were, is a relative concept to the Altess, who are used to having absolutely anything they want. They see wealth and poverty as

alien concepts borne of societies that still deal with things like population growth, economic cycles, and resource depletion. The Altess figured these things out (in a way that works for them, anyway) long ago, and as such, have freed themselves from thinking in terms of rich and poor. They are simply Altess, and part of that means having enough resource capability to satisfy one's wildest urges. Since the Altess are born into this kind of life, they end up not abusing it. Knowing in one's heart that he can have anything curiously has an opposite effect on the Altess, who are content to live modest personal lives. They build grand cities and palaces and use incredible amounts of high technology to lavish a comfortable life on themselves and their people (nobody wants for much among the Altess), but on a personal level, the Altess do not mark their lives by consumption and spending. Having no sense of poverty, they have no need to distance themselves psychologically from it by exercising their buying abilities over and over and over again by obtaining things they do not really need. Most of the Anvil Galaxy sees this outlook as something weird, but the Altess know it for what it is — the way everybody would look at life if only they had the means to.

The Royal Academies of Science

This well funded sector of the Altess is charged with developing new technological breakthroughs. They have all the time they want, and are under no pressure to produce. That is the Altess way. The absent need for urgent production today is the result of an interesting initiative the Altess took some thousands of years ago. Back then, they gathered some of the top minds in the galaxy and gave them a fully funded haven where they could dedicate their lives to pure research. In time, these scientists came up with hundreds of great inventions, technologies that would change the face of life in the Anvil Galaxy in every possible aspect. Weapons. Transportation. Food. Clothing. Environment. Education, Communications.

Once the Altess felt they had enough such items, they retired their science teams and stockpiled their work. From there, the Altess made a huge fortune licensing out their super-tech designs to those who wanted them. These licensing agreements and royalties continue to this day, and by now, nearly 50% of the galaxy is paying some kind of royalty or kickback to the Altess without their knowing it. Those societies that are aware of the royalties being paid to the Altess are usually angry about it at first, but then when they learn exactly what the Altess have done to deserve those royalties, the bellyaching stops for good.

Foreign Affairs

Consortium of Civilized Worlds: The Altess are one of the very few powers that are just not impressed by the Consortium. All they see in these worlds is a bunch of small powers huddling together out of fear of the rest of the galaxy. The Altess deal with the Consortium and even are a member of it from time to time, but only because it suits their purposes for the moment.

Trans-Galactic Empire: The TGE is, by Altess standards, the sad work of a degenerate and barbaric people so governmentally retarded that to even call them a proper "civilization" requires one to ingest massive amounts of painkillers first. The Altess would endeavor to destroy such an offensive society if they were not convinced that it would destroy itself first. The Altess have seen the TGE's like before, and they know full well it will one day go the way of the dodo bird.

United Worlds of Warlock: Though the Altess have no use for magic (they are a profoundly scientific people), they find the UWW's mastery of magic to be interesting, at the very least. With views as jaded as the Altess, any other body politic that is fresh and new should be appreciated. And the Altess appreciate the UWW quite a bit, even if they don't let on that fact to the UWW. The Altess also feel that after them, the UWW stands the best chance of finding the Cosmic Forge. They are light years ahead of the CCW and TGE, which are both like children in a dark room fumbling for a light switch they can't possibly reach.

Naruni Enterprises: The Altess buy copious amounts of weapons from these people, but only because it is convenient to do so. Were there no Naruni Enterprises, the Altess would simply build a company of similar stature to provide it with weaponry. Though the Naruni do not know it, the Altess collectively own 39% of Naruni stock, giving them quite a say in how that company operates. The Altess do not use this power, but instead are holding it in reserve for some special day. Like when Naruni tries bullying the Altess into doing something the Altess do not like, at that point, the ownership question will come up, and the Altess will flex their stockholding muscles to get the Naruni off their back. If that is not enough, the Altess have more than enough cash to simply buy Naruni Enterprises out from under its owners/rulers, if they so desired. Altess Industries, anyone? Of course, this is not the Altess' style, and they would be far more content to beat the Naruni up with the threat of such action than actually doing.

Hartigal Combine: Altess find these people to be very polite, accommodating and pleasant to have around, mainly because the Hartigal are trying to cozy up to them to get the Altess to buy their goods instead of the Naruni. The Altess are impressed by Hartigal's "go-getter" attitude and hard work, but have no intention of buying Naruni knock-offs from them. (For one thing it would hurt their secret partial ownership of Naruni Enterprises. However, favorably impressed with Hartigal, the Altess have secretly, through third parties, purchased 7% of the Hartigal Combine to cover their bets.)

Golgan Republik: The Golgans actually tried to invade Altess territory a while back (it was a few hundred years ago, but nearly all Altess nobles still remember it like it was yesterday). The Golgans lost the battle, of course, and even though the Golgans are still angry over it, the Altess could not care less. They knew the Golgans were crazy to try taking over the Dynasty, and they were glad to help educate them to this. The Altess hold no grudges against the Golgans for their aggression, but they do find the Golgan people generally distasteful, and the Altess find it very entertaining to watch the Golgan Republik come apart at the seams.

Central Alliance: The Cyber-warriors of the Central Alliance remind the Altess of how they once were, thousands of generations ago. Perhaps that is why the Altess have taken a kind of guardian angel status with these people. The Alliance does not know it, but the Armoria has standing orders to act on the Central Alliance's behalf if it is attacked. An assault upon the Cental Alliance is, therefore, an assault upon the Altess Dynasty.

Cosmo-Knights: The Altess find these do-gooders interesting, but living as long as the Altess do, they know that the Cosmo-Knights have not yet done anything to substantially change things for better or worse in the Three Galaxies. For every villain they defeat, another surfaces. Perhaps this will change with the Forge War and the knights' assault upon the Threshold, but few Altess are optimistic about it. They will simply sit and wait to hear about what happened, even if that takes ten, twenty, or a hundred years.

Gene-Tech: That goes the same for the Gene-Tech, in part because these genetic engineers remind the Altess a little about their own efforts to bioengineer themselves into superior beings and maintain their bloodlines. Gene-Tech are viewed as unknown quantities best to be driven out of Altess territory. Any Gene-Tech to fight back or to dare alter the genetic structure of an Altess is to be destroyed without mercy.

Kingdom of Rynncryyl: The Altess find these monsters despicable in every way, and they feel the Three Galaxies would be a better place if they were destroyed. There is no further discussion to be had. Be gone with them!

Omegan Order: The Omegans are filthy swine who do not even deserve the title of "knight" in any form. This hatred is purely cultural – as nobles, the Altess tend to value honor and dignity, things which the Omegans totally lack. Moreover, while the Altess have little use for the Cosmo-Knights, they at least respect their position in the galaxy and the valor of their deeds. The Omegan Order have no such deeds to worship, no outward signs that indeed, these warriors are worthy of one's praise and adoration. All the Omegans offer is a resounding aura of evil and the desire to be feared. The Altess can not accept that. They have been around the block too many times to be scared by the likes of this rabble. The sooner the proper Cosmo-Knights destroy the Omegans, the cleaner and brighter the entire galaxy will be.

Xodian Collective: The Altess remember that long ago, during the 2nd or 3rd Dynasty, a large force of Xodians crossed the Threshold and established a dominion in the Halo for about a century before they returned from whence they came. They left little to no evidence that they had ever been here, and to this day, the Altess are not exactly sure what they came here for or why they returned to the Core. The Altess enjoy not sharing this information with the rest of the galaxy, which is collectively beating its head against the wall trying to figure these strange aliens out.

K!ozn: The Altess' immortality makes them special among the Halo, and for that reason, K!ozn representatives have sought audiences with the Altess royal families on several different occasions. The Altess find the K!ozn a mysterious but pleasant and intriguing people, if a little hard to understand. The Altess know they are dealing with a superior intellect, and they make no pretension to intellectual equality, something the K!ozn appreciate. The K!ozn come to the Altess because they wish to recruit them in an effort to make sure *none* of the Halo powers ever learn where the Cosmic Forge is located. If the Altess agree to join the K!ozn, the K!ozn will share technology with them, as well as territory within the Core. The Altess are generally fascinated by this offer, but as mentioned before, they like to move on things very slowly, and the Forge War might be over before they even give a response to the K!ozn offer.

Independent Worlds: The Altess have, from time to time, built enormous Empires by Proxy, a term they like to use for when they dangle bribes of cash, technology and military help to neighboring (and relatively low tech) worlds in return for their help and cooperation. This has given the Altess a reputation as big spenders and fair employers. Should the Altess need to really get dirty in the Forge War and hire mercenaries, the populations of many surrounding independent worlds would be glad to offer their services.

Society

The Altess dominions are about as close to a Utopia as one is likely to find in the Anvil Galaxy. The civilization's incredible wealth makes it so that nobody is wanting for anything. There are no appreciable shortages of anything, and huge forces of robots carry out almost every aspect of daily work, so the citizens do not have to toil . . . . ever. No Altess worlds are overcrowded. They have no poverty. There is no material crime, only crimes of passion (people have no need to steal). If anything, the people's worst enemy is *boredom*, as their every need is met and their lives are seemingly endless. Those who crave some kind of excitement volunteer for combat duty in the Armoria and hope that they see some kind of action. Otherwise, Altess citizens are likely to spend some years adventuring out in the rest of the galaxy, just for fun. Given that the *entire* Altess bloodline must be assembled at once to unlock the key to the Cosmic Forge, runaways and kidnap victims are dealt with as if a national treasure has been stolen. No effort will be spared to bring such folk back to the fold, safe and sound. This means that Altess adventurers are almost always on the run from their home and have a large force of Armorian guards after them. Though the Armorian guards will only use non-lethal capture methods against Altess runaways and adventurers, they might not be so easy on whoever might be harboring them.

Daily Life

For the vast majority of Altess citizens, daily life is one of endless leisure. Robot servants handle all mundane work, manufacturing and processing basic goods and necessities, leaving their Altess human masters free to do whatever they like. Most Altess devote their time to sport, art, philosophy, travel, and other such diversions. Still others turn to meditation, martial arts, storytelling, and so on. Over the course of their lives, Altess end up trying about every hobby and diversion they can think of before they learn that their favorite pasttime is merely doing nothing but watching the universe go by. All Altess are strong students of history (largely because they can live through so much of it), and so they take great pleasure in viewing current events, putting them into some kind of historical context, and trying to extrapolate what will happen in the future. Altess (especially nobles) love to get together and talk about these sorts of things for *days*.

It should be noted that there is little noticeable difference in quality of life between nobles and non-nobles. Indeed, to most non-nobles, the only thing they lack is a voice in the government, but most of the time, these people realize that they do not particularly want one.

Most off-worlders visiting the Altess see their lifestyle as a kind of paradise, and for a few days, they revel in it. But after a while, strangers simply can not digest the slow pace of life, the abundance of everything, and the constant need to do nothing. Stir-crazy within a few weeks, off-worlders almost never ask to stay with the Altess, which makes it all the easier for them to keep their bloodlines pure.

Law and Order

Crime is almost unheard of among the Altess. With so much material abundance, crimes like theft become irrelevant. There is no need to steal when nobody has something that can not be gotten by somebody else. Violent crimes are still possible and happen occasionally, but the Altess are culturally bound together by their common desire to unlock the knowledge within them that will point the way to the Cosmic Forge. An act of murder jeopardizes that cause, hurting the murderer as much as the murdered. This helps prevent killings, as well as the fact that the Altess are generally a jaded, non-violent people who are not quick to fight with people. As a result, few crimes of passion end up hurting anybody, so the whole thing can be brushed under the carpet.

Crime and Punishment

In the few cases where somebody does something worthy of punishment, they are sent before whatever noble family governs over them. The accused is required to enter a plea, but since all legal proceedings take place behind closed doors, there is no telling what the client will get. Nobles adjudicating the case can assign whatever fate they see fit.

Exclusive Immortality

The Altess believe they have gained virtual immortality through thousands of generations of subtle genetic engineering, filtering out almost anything in their DNA that promotes aging or biologic decrepitude. As a result, they age at nearly 1/100th the rate of other humans. On top of that, however, is their highly advanced medical industry which can cure almost any illness, repair almost any damage, and even regress one's body to a younger, healthier state. As a result, Altess can pretty much live forever – or at least for several thousand years. Only self-termination or unforeseen death (accidents, combat, etc.) can take their life.

Sadly, what makes the Altess immortal does not translate to other races, not even to other humans. Only a true Altess (no half-breeds) gains the benefit of their unusually long life span. And only an Altess living within the Dynasty will find access to the unique medical technology of his home. The Altess do not export their rejuvenative technology anywhere, and even if they did, it would not help any other races, as it is finely tuned to work on Altess genetic patterns only. This special technology is also not portable, so individual Altess cannot take it with them, unless they somehow bring what amounts to a miniature hospital wherever they go. A few eccentric Altess have been known to do this, but it is frowned upon as being in bad taste and overly attractive to nosy off-worlders.

Other humans can breed with the Altess, but the resulting children will have entirely human, not Altess genes. That means the child will have none of the Altess parent's special abilities, genetic knowledge of the Cosmic Forge, or the incredible Altess life span. The Altess have engineered themselves to be like this so their knowledge of the Cosmic Forge does not scatter across all humans in the Three Galaxies.

Worlds of Interest

Kars Alta. Through an odd state of geology and erosion, the majority of the world looks like an endless array of stone towers, cliffs and other weird rocky protrusions. There is virtually no flat land anywhere. It is as if the entire world is a huge bed of nails, or the back of a giant stone hedgehog. The cities there have had to use some pretty wild architecture to graft onto these weird stone columns and cliffs, and as a result, the building-makers of Kars Alta have become really famous. This snowballed into the world becoming a major center for arts, education and engineering among the Altess as well as other peoples from across the Anvil Galaxy. As the Forge War has begun to ignite, places like Kars Alta, renowned gathering spots for people from across the Galaxy, are becoming hot spots for spies and assassins working for the various governments that are searching for the Cosmic Forge. These cat-and-mouse games go on with an emphasis on keeping things discreet, but sometimes, one of these "secret wars" spills out into the open, and the Altess must take care of it to maintain order. Otherwise, the Altess are content to let one of their worlds be a subtle battleground of the Forge War. To them, who are not participating in the conflict, seeing so many worlds running around after something they will probably never find is of great amusement to the Altess.

Ramis. A mysterious natural force on this planet virtually halts the aging process of any creature living on it. Off-worlders who know about this planet suspect that the Altess' own immortality must have incorporated some serious study of this place. As if to bolster that theory, Ramis is one of the very few worlds that the Altess refuse to let off-worlders set foot on. A large contingent of the Armoria blockades the world at all times, intercepting traffic before it gets within the planet's atmosphere. The Altess also have a few UWW mages on the payroll to detect the passage of magic-users to Ramis. Conventional wisdom states that the Altess fear their method for immortality might become common knowledge if visitors are allowed free access to their world. Of course, those who know the Altess insist that they might be putting this whole thing on as an elaborate joke, a huge prank to amuse an endlessly jaded people.

Alderensys. A typically Altess world, this planet has every high-tech feature one might expect on a luxurious Utopia. Apart from the extremely comfortable living arrangements, spacious cities, parks and rural areas, Alderensys has two items of special interest. The first is their artificial ring. Like a ring of Saturn, this ring circles the planet, way out on the outer edges of the planet's gravity well. Only instead of rocks and ice particles, this ring is a continuous space station. Though it is ribbon-thin compared to the bulk of the planet, this station is a huge habitat capable of housing billions of people. It is the gateway through which all visitors come and go, and it is practically a society unto itself. The second landmark is a planetary system of space elevators that connect the ring to Alderensys' surface by way of hundreds of thin, nearly indestructible cords. (Each 10 foot/3 m length has 850 M.D.C.) Huge gondola-type craft ride on these cables which winch up and down from the ring in a continuous circuit, giving the folks of this world a cheap and easy way to reach orbit. From far away, this world almost looks like the spherical hub of a bicycle wheel, with the ring as the rim and the space elevators as the spokes. Though these elevators are highly useful, the Altess built them just to see if they would work. Given how successful they have proven, the Royal Academy of Sciences has licensed out the Altess space elevator to numerous third parties, none of whom have gotten their elevators on-line yet.

Minamede. This world sustained a massive crater impact just one hundred years ago, blasting the atmosphere into nothing, and turning what biosphere existed into a faint memory. The size of this planet and the size of the impact it took should have shattered the world into a million pieces. Why it did not shall probably continue to puzzle scientists for many years to come. Some think the Altess have developed a secret process that makes worlds invulnerable to things like black holes and harmonic disruptions, while others think that the Altess must be as much in the dark about this event as everybody else.

The most likely explanation is that this world contains a large amount of *stenthamine*, an exotic, impact-resistant metal that is sometimes used in anti-ballistic armor and spaceship hulls. If Minamede has stenthamine deposits beneath its crust, it not only will be a very impact-resistant planet (as it has already proven itself to be), but it is a huge cash cow just waiting to be exploited. Of course, just because the Altess *can* make a ton of money off this world does not mean they actually will go ahead and do it. They have enough money as it is. They will need a more compelling reason than wealth to justify tearing up a planet.

Nocturne, Endless Night. One of the longest-held Altess worlds, Nocturne is so named because its unusual rotation and orbit always place it behind the inner planets of the system. Thus eclipsed, Nocturne is always darkened, like night. Every thousand years or so there is a small window in the eclipse alignments, and there is daylight for a few hours, during which time a large part of the population goes a little crazy. Rioting, random violence and suicides all spike like mad during these "bright times," causing considerable disruption to the world in general. Some say the endless night of this world is to keep hidden the Cosmic Forge, which is secured deep in one of Nocturne's endless subterranean lava chutes and passages. Others say that Nocturne is a living test of the Altess people, to see if they can, despite their advanced society and genetic conditioning, resist the madness that comes from a momentary brightness that interrupts a lifetime of night.

Hewn. Considered by many Altess to be a sister world to Alderensys (described above), Hewn is a similarly Utopian, high-tech world with a technological distinction all of its own. Hewn is the sole planet of its solar system, and it is really far from its sun (about where Uranus would be in our solar system). While this makes life difficult on the planet (it is very cold and dark there), it makes it the perfect place for the **Rodulan Acclerator**, an inventive form of cheap FTL propulsion that only the Altess would have dreamed up, much less put into action. The Rodulan Accelerator is based off the concept that the farther away from a central point an orbiting object is, the faster it tends to go. Case in point: a musical record playing a song. A point right near the center of the record travels at one speed, but a point on the outer edge of the record travels a different, higher speed because it must cover more ground if it is to keep up with the point close to the center of the record. On Hewn, the Altess have extrapolated this concept into a *space elevator* that stretches all the way from the surface of Hewn almost to the system's sun. Essentially it works like a big slingshot or the children's game "Crack the Whip." A starship enters orbit and hooks up with the end of the FTL tether. The tether pays out as the planet below spins in orbit. Slowly, the ship begins to move as it is tugged along. Bit by bit, the space elevator keeps paying out, and the ship attached to the end accelerates more and more. By the time the cable pays out entirely, the ship is moving an 99% lightspeed. It lets go of the tether and rockets out of the system under no power. Of course, it will take some time for any ships traveling like this to reach the nearest star system, but the Altess built this for kicks, not for practicality. Numerous foreign spies have visited this world to take a look at the device, and to assess its military and economic value, if any.

Altess Prime. This is the Altess "origin world," where according to legend, their race initially descended from *The First*. In later ages, as Altess dynasties came and went, this world became the ceremonial place where each new eon of leadership would begin. As a result, Altess Prime holds an almost religious significance to this otherwise secular, rational people. A full division of the Armoria keeps watch on this world at all times, for even though there have been no attacks on the planet in over one thousand years, with the Forge War beginning and the Altess' neighbors getting jumpy over who might find the Cosmic Forge first, the Altess is not taking any chances. Though they can and will stay out of the conflict as best they can, some wild-eyed bomber pilot might go rogue and fire a spread of weapons at the Altess to provoke a reaction. With Altess Prime so far on the edge of Altess territory, the chances are better for that world, more than others, to accidentally get caught in the Forge War cross-fire. Were the planet seriously damaged or destroyed, the sanguine Altess would go on the warpath, seeking to annihilate whoever dared desecrate their most beloved of worlds.

Novus IX. Featuring high gravity and terrible environmental effects (toxic atmosphere, high magnetic fields), Novus IX has become the premier training world for the Altess Armoria. All Armoria soldiers must spend at least one tour of duty (four years) on this world. Here they toughen up, learn to maximize their natural abilities, and hone their impressive body of skills. By the time soldiers leave Novus IX, they are ready for anything, and are deployed across the Altess empire. Little does anybody know that the planet is building up a huge chronol displacement field in its core, and pretty soon the whole world will leap *elsewhere* in time. The Armoria's best and brightest are stationed here, as is a sizeable amount of top Armoria hardware. What should happen when this planet disappears could severely impact the rest of the Altess Dynasty. In the present, the Altess are out a major military resource when they need it most – during the beginning of the Forge War. In another time, the sudden presence of the Armoria and their equipment might seriously upset future history or the ancient past. Unless one were to travel with the displaced, there might be no way of knowing what effect on reality the travelers might have.

Galdon. This world contains many ancient temples devoted to the worship of the Cosmic Forge. They all predate Altess recorded history, and it is the Altess' belief that their ancient, barbarian ancestors once lived and worshiped here under the watchful eye of The First. In the subsequent eons, the local Altess have done well to develop this world with as much of a sense of the world's natural environment as of the huge techno-cities the Altess are so fond of building. The result is an incredibly lavish, beautiful world covered with sprawling eco-arcologies, buildings where the structures seam perfectly with the planet's natural rain forest-type environment. Most impressive, however, is the monumental **Vault of Memory**, a massive museum of sorts where the collective history of the Altess has been gathered and organized. One *could* pore over every detail of this exhibit, but Altess statisticians figured that if a visitor spent just three seconds on every exhibit housed in the Vault, it would take him over a century to get to the exit. For those willing to sift through this mountain of history, there are endless treasures to find – long-lost technology designs, the locations of ancient ruins and lost civilizations, secret trade routes to unknown parts of the Anvil Galaxy, and more. What it does *not* contain, however, is any overt reference to the Cosmic Forge. That, it seems, has been removed by Altess superiors who thought it better to keep such things secret. That still does not discourage off-world visitors, many of whom spend their lives combing the Vault for any snippet of information that might crack the search for the Cosmic Forge wide open.

Zyvult. This world is home to the Altess Financial Directory, the centralized database through which the records of all Altess financial transactions must pass. These databases do not hold any irreplaceable information. They are more like the means through which the galactic public may see how the Altess make and handle their money. By retrieving financial reports from the Directory (known as "X9s"), one might see exactly how much any one of the royal families of the Altess is worth. Most off-worlders don't bother with this because it just depresses them to see how filthy rich these Altess really are. However, those who study the Altess financials come to appreciate what many call the "Altess problem." The Altess' riches are widely dispersed in investments all over the Anvil Galaxy. If the Altess wanted to, they could shift their various holdings and buy out entire governments or sections of the galaxy before anybody could do something about it. Or, if the Altess decided to "cash out" all of their accounts at once, the resulting sell off would crash the entire Anvil Galaxy interstellar economy and cause a galactic depression the likes of which nobody has ever seen. This does not sit well with financiers outside of the Altess' sphere of influence. Even though the Altess have shown no inclinations to do such damaging things with their money, the truth remains that they *could* if they wanted to, and that makes them extremely dangerous.

Central Alliance

Population: One trillion sentient beings.

Demographics: Human (21%), Other (79%; no other race constitutes more than 2% or 3% of the Central Alliance. It is a remarkably diverse society).

Overview: The Central Alliance occupies a large stretch of space on the inside of the northeastern corner of the Halo. This part of the galaxy has long been considered an interstellar wasteland, filled with inhospitable systems or worlds with rough environments, barbaric peoples, and social orders too fractious and warlike to ever get anything done. Most of the worlds here no longer have FTL capability, and they end up becoming a sort of social black hole into which derelict spacers, traders and pirates fall into when they make planet-fall, never to be seen or heard from again. On one of these nameless worlds, a brilliant military leader named *General Ogor Noldek* grew tired of his world's endless faction warfare. Taking charge of his faction's military, he waged war on all other elements of his planet's power structure until, after a lengthy period of conquest, he conquered the whole world. Gaining command of a few FTL troop ships, he expanded his campaign to neighboring worlds, each of which were just as balkanized and riven with internecine conflict as his had once been. General Noldek knew if he could unite worlds such as these he would become one of the most powerful men in the galaxy. But how?

Campaigning on his home world was one thing. He knew the territory and his soldiers were willing fight long and hard to regain control of their homeland. Every single one of these warring worlds before General Noldek's army posed a similar challenge. There was no way Noldek's men could ever triumph over so many hostile planets. Over one or two, maybe, but not a hundred, a thousand.

Noldek realized that he would have to convince his future subjects to *willingly* subject themselves to his authority. To do that, he would become something these people could all respect: killing power.

Already a brilliant martial artist at the top of his form, General Noldek hired off-world mercenary cyber-docs to transform him into an inhuman killing machine. Noldek's nearly superhuman physical attributes enabled doctors to graft an unusually intense array of cybernetics to his body, making him bigger, better and badder than almost any other cyborg one was likely to find in the Anvil Galaxy, or anywhere else. Casting a most fearful

image, General Noldek ventured to the worlds before him, broadcasting a challenge to the entire population there that he would be holding a contest of arms against any and all tribal leaders willing to participate. This played on the egos of the local warlords who ruled these lawless worlds, and one by one, General Noldek met them all in widely televised single combat. With his skills and cybernetics, the General easily crushed his opponents (victims?) and within three years, he had assembled a vast empire of over one hundred systems, all swearing loyalty directly to General Noldek.

In the years that have followed, a huge cult of personality has surrounded the General, making his grip on these worlds all the stronger. Through his draconian but effective leadership, Noldek brought peace to worlds that had never known any, civilization where there was once barbarity, industry and commerce where there was once only poverty and thievery. This collection of worlds, which General Noldek renamed the *Central Alliance,* had risen from the dust of the galaxy and emerged as its most unlikely new superpower.

Government

The Central Alliance is a fairly straightforward military dictatorship. General Noldek has absolute authority. What he says, goes. Only his empire has grown so vast that he cannot possibly oversee the administration of dozens of worlds personally. Thus, he has created a sinister order of lieutenants simply known as **the Mechanism**. Made up exclusively of full-conversion cyborgs, the Mechanism is a motley assortment of warlords and cyber-gladiators who somehow have been found and taken in by General Noldek and given extraordinary power. Noldek assigns a single member of the Mechanism as a regional governor to every planet of the Central Alliance. These are *sub-dictators* who are free to run their worlds as they see fit, on three conditions.

First, the citizens of each world are not to be victimized without the express permission of General Noldek. Noldek might be a harsh warlord, but he understands good governance, and he believes that the only legitimate reasons to crack down on one's subjects are excessive lawlessness, rebellion, or other such unrest.

Second, each world must maintain a consistently positive gross planetary output. In short, each world must be a productive member of the Alliance. It must maintain industry, keep joblessness low, and produce enough global revenue that it can afford to pay an annual tithe to General Noldek. He in turn, uses that money for "federal" projects (like funding the military or handling a natural disaster) that affect the entire Alliance.

Third, each world must pass judgement on their governor every four years. This is a simple vote of no confidence. If the people do not like what their governor has been doing, they vote against him. A simple majority carries the vote. The military is ineligible to vote. This is a civilian matter only, and it is the means by which the people can keep their immediate leadership from abusing them. Governors who are voted out are stripped of all cybernetics and exiled from the Central Alliance forever.

These three laws have helped the Mechanism function as a fair but tough means of government. There are the occasional abuses of power and civilian crackdowns, but on the whole, life is much better in the Central Alliance than it had been before General Noldek took over, and for the Alliance's many citizens, that is good enough. Only two governors have ever been voted out of office, and both times, it was by a narrow vote. General Noldek keeps a close eye on his governors, in fact, it is what he spends much of his time on, to make sure they are also doing right by his personal standards.

General Noldek reserves the right to dismiss a governor at any time for any reason. If the governor objects, he may challenge Noldek to single combat, to the death. These death duels are broadcast throughout the entire Alliance, and they are considered top entertainment – like a national election and the latest professional wrestling or badman contest rolled into one. There have only been seven death duels since the Alliance was founded – two of which were really attempted coups by disloyal governors. In each duel, General Noldek won brilliant victories, shredding his opponents (literally!) with his incredible strength, speed, skill and ability to handle the many different cyber-weapons installed on his personal chassis. However, Noldek is not immortal, and his body, enhanced as it is, is slowly succumbing to the march of time. Sooner or later, a member of the Mechanism will challenge the General and will defeat him, gaining control of the entire Alliance as his prize. This shall be the true test of the government, and it is a day Noldek tries to put off as long as possible, but one he also knows must eventually arrive.

Military

Each governor of the Mechanism is also charged with assembling and maintaining a fighting force sufficient to keep the peace on his planet. These provincial armies are often called **Little Machines**, or if they belong to a particularly ruthless governor, **Mean Machines**. They consist largely of combat-ready cyborgs as well as the occasional heavy vehicle, aircraft and starship support. Little Machines are really military police forces meant to handle urban peacekeeping and the occasional infantry mission. They are not fully diversified armies able to wage total war on a planetary scale. That is what General Noldek's personal army, the **Cyberhawks**, is for. These soldiers *are* part of a fully diversified, fully integrated, fully lethal fighting force on par with anything the CCW or the TGE can field in battle. The big difference between the Central Alliance and those other superpowers is that the CCW and TGE have numerous army groups the size and strength of the Cyberhawks – the Central Alliance has just this one group. Thus, while the Central Alliance could win a major battle against either of those two ultra-powers, it could never win a sustained war without some kind of miracle or utter ineptitude on the part of the CCW/TGE.

All Central Alliance forces use generic weaponry and equipment. HI-series weapons and Energy Pulse weapons are standard throughout the Central Alliance. All of this tech tends to be old, generic, and beaten up, giving the Central Alliance forces a scruffy look, like they have been through Hell and back and they are in no mood for anybody's nonsense. While this is hardly the spit-and-polish appearance many armies strive for, it certainly works for the fighters of the Central Alliance, who take pride in looking like they practice what they preach: victory through superior soldiering.

Foreign Affairs

Consortium of Civilized Worlds: Just as the CCW has little interest in interacting with the Central Alliance, the Alliance feels the same way about the CCW. For one thing, the two civilizations are pretty far apart from each other, and the Central Alliance is not particularly into jaunting about the Halo. For another thing, the CCW is consumed with the search for the Cosmic Forge, something the Central Alliance has no interest in. The Forge Mythos has never factored prominently in any of the cultures of the Central Alliance worlds, and so most of its citizens do not believe the Cosmic Forge exists. For them the Cosmic Forge quest is a fool's crusade. If the rest of the galaxy is willing to destroy itself over this imaginary thing, they are welcome to it, but the people of the Central Alliance are smarter than that and intend to play no part in the coming storm.

Trans-Galactic Empire: The Alliance feels the same way regarding the TGE as it does about the CCW. It too is seen as a large, meddling super-society that is way too interested in the Cosmic Forge for its own good. Only the TGE is a lot more expansionist than the CCW, and General Noldek knows full well that if the TGE ever thought they could successfully invade the Alliance worlds, it would do so. Right now, only the TGE's other problems, coupled with the savage rebellion the Imperialists would face from rebellious Central Alliance cyborgs, are what keep the TGE from considering their conquest.

United Worlds of Warlock: The Central Alliance is far away from the UWW's sphere of influence, and so the two civilizations have almost no contact. Even if they were neighbors, they would have little interaction since they are so different culturally. The Central Alliance embraces the very things about technology that the UWW finds repellent. Likewise, the UWW is far too emotional and spiritual for the down-and-dirty mind set of the Central Alliance. Ships passing in the night, these two are.

Naruni Enterprises: Naruni representatives keep trying to sell lots of shiny new weaponry to the Central Alliance, but General Noldek's troops aren't having any of it. For one thing, the Alliance can not afford Naruni weaponry. Not in the quantities Naruni is trying to sell, anyway. For another, General Noldek has heard about this company's ruthless business practices, and he would just as soon steer well clear of them.

Hartigal Combine: Hartigal understands that the Central Alliance is tired of rebuffing over-eager Naruni sales reps, so they are looking into ways of infiltrating the Alliance and selling them weapons on the sly. That way, they don't feel like they have been played by a big-time arms dealer and Hartigal gets to unload some merchandise at the same time.

Golgan Republik: The Golgans represent exactly the kind of stuffy, overbearing, bureaucratic sort of government that General Noldek despises. His direct, dictatorial manner of ruling, and that of his lieutenants of the Machine, have drawn sharp criticism from Golgan representatives. The Central Alliance members threw the Golgan representative out when they first met, insulting him gravely, and earning the eternal scorn of the rapidly disintegrating Republik.

Altess Dynasty: The Central Alliance just does not get the Altess. For the cyborgs it is all about getting dirty, fighting hard, living short, violent lives. The Altess are none of those things, content to live a long, boring existence while amassing incredible wealth that nobody ever seems to spend! For these reasons and others, the Central Alliance tries to steer clear of the Altess, and vice versa.

Cosmo-Knights: The Cosmo-Knights have, on a few occasions, arrived on an Alliance world and destroyed their governor and his minions for perceived crimes against the people. General Noldek does not believe any such thing could be, since his citizens would have told him about it, right? *Right?!?* As a result, the Central Alliance considers Cosmo-Knights to be enemies, even though the average CA cyber-soldier knows he does not stand a bit of a chance against even one Cosmo-Knight rather than a legion of them.

Kingdom of Rynncryyl: Being so close to the Threshold themselves, the Central Alliance has more than its fair share of contact with the Splugorth Slavers and pirates who prowl the empty space of the Anvil Galaxy, looking for likely victims. So far, the CA has successfully defended itself against the half-hearted attempts of Rynncryyl's marauders, but it is only a matter of time before a massed Splugorth assault hits hard and fast, and when it does, there is no guarantee that the Central Alliance will survive the attack.

Gene-Tech: Likewise, the Central Alliance sees all too much of these foul and mysterious beings. Though General Noldek can appreciate the idea of genetic manipulation and augmentation, it is diametrically opposed to his and the Alliance's approach toward mechanical augmentation. Gene-Tech are seen as duplicitous, dishonorable and malevolent beings best to be avoided. If they cause trouble in the Alliance, those responsible are destroyed.

Omegan Order: These fallen Cosmo-Knights mean almost nothing to the Alliance, which has never even tried to cross the Threshold, much less mix it up with a small army of fallen Cosmo-Knights.

Xodian Collective: The Xodians are also a total mystery to the Alliance, mostly because they have never crossed the Threshold to make contact with the Xodians themselves.

K!ozn: The Central Alliance knows nothing of the K!ozn, both because their civilization is across the Threshold, and because the CA is a fairly lowbrow society based on little more than cheap thrills, unnecessary cybernetic modification, worshiping a cult of personality, and other unsavory characteristics. K!ozn operatives do not associate with civilizations that clearly have a long way to develop. And the Alliance has a long way to go, indeed.

Independent Worlds: The Alliance keeps tabs on all of its independent neighbors to make sure they are not up to any funny business. Otherwise, the Alliance does a great deal of trading and intelligence swapping with its many friendly neighbors.

Society

More than anything, the people of the Central Alliance are defined and united by a single thing: cybernetics. This civilization revolves around its beloved leader, General Noldek, who is a monstrous super-cyborg. His lieutenants are cyborgs, and most of his soldiers and the solders of his lieutenants are cyborgs (mostly because they have all received terrible injuries during their careers that necessitated cybernetic replacement). As such,

replacing one's body with machinery is seen as a badge of office and a mark of honor. For the people of the Central Alliance, having some kind of visible cybernetics is a show of loyalty, a sign that you are like General Noldek and the warriors of the Machine.

This has become such a tradition that many Alliance citizens, upon reaching young adulthood, undergo some kind of ritual cybernetic surgery, replacing a perfectly good body part with an obviously mechanical one. The body part to be replaced is up to the recipient, and usually personal wants have as much to do with the surgery as what one can afford. Those without much money might just get a simple cyber-eye installed, where those who are loaded will have a limb replaced, or maybe even undergo partial conversion. Full conversion is seen as the ultimate sign of loyalty and social station, but the majority of Central Alliance *citizens* cannot afford it, and so only those who are filthy rich or who are part of the noble military get full conversion.

Though most people in the Central Alliance have some measure of cybernetics, few of them carry weapons in their on-board machinery. Concealed cyber-weapons are usually outlawed by planetary governors unless the user gets a special permit to use them. Off-worlders wearing concealed cyber-weapons must often detach them or cut the power supply to them for the duration of their stay. Obvious, outwardly showing weapons, however, usually are *not* prohibited, even though they are more destructive than the hidden kinds! This is all part of the Alliance mentality, that it is okay to have weapons on you, it's just not okay to hide them. Hiding is sneaky and dishonorable.

The Central Alliance is made up of a wild variety of alien races. In fact, every major race of the Anvil Galaxy can be found living somewhere in the Central Alliance. In many societies (the CCW notwithstanding), this alien diversity might cause social friction, but not in the Alliance. Here, the people's excessive love for cybernetics equalizes everything, and regardless of one's alien race, the cybernetics they sport are a much more defining characteristic.

G.M. Note: Player characters hailing from the Central Alliance may be of any "standard" alien race/R.C.C. Regardless of what O.C.C. or R.C.C. the player selects, the character automatically gets either 1D4 bionic implants of choice, or they get an entire limb replaced and empowered with 1D4 special features (weapons are frowned upon but if the character wants to break the law and put them in, it's his risk to run). Often, as people get wealthier in the Central Alliance, they upgrade their cybernetics, adding more and more machinery to their bodies. This is how most folks who end up as partial cyborgs do it – they piecemeal themselves into the role. Player Characters who wish to play a partial cyborg can simply pretend that their character hails from a rich family or that he is an older person who has amassed a personal fortune and spent it becoming a cyborg. Full conversion cyborg characters will almost always be part of the Central Alliance military. Full conversion cyborgs are not outlawed in the CA, but their presence almost always speaks of somebody who fights for the Alliance. Those who have undergone full conversion but do not serve in the military draw suspicious stares from their fellow citizens. Why undergo such a great show of patriotism and then not use it?

If the G.M. approves, any of the cybernetic designs from the **Warlords of Russia™** sourcebook (Light Machine, Heavy Machine, Cyborg Shocktrooper, etc., or some variation of them) may be used in the Central Alliance. Clearly, these would not be the actual Russian cyborg designs, but their "alien" equivalent. G.M.s, if you have the **Warlords of Russia** sourcebook, we strongly urge you to consider converting over Russian' Borgs for use in the Central Alliance. They are bigger, badder, cooler, and fit the Central Alliance ethos of turning oneself into the nastiest looking machine possible.

Daily Life

The quality of life in the Central Alliance varies from world to world. There are no really wealthy, high-tech planets in the Alliance. The best one can do would be to live on a highly industrialized planet that might be considered "lower middle class" in the CCW. The majority of Central Alliance worlds feature poor shanty town-like settlements built around the base of large, imposing cybernetic factories. The ubiquitous cybernetics in this society is its only consistent show of high technology and development. But even the cybernetics people wear are run-down, beaten up and look second- or third-hand. After all, before General Noldek conquered these planets, they were the galactic equivalent of modern-day Afghanistan or Western Africa – states so riven with internal conflict that there could be no meaningful industry or enterprise. The people were living short and violent lives, often in terrible squalor. General Noldek has changed all of that and is bringing real economic strength and stability to these worlds. The standard of living remains low, but it is getting better every day, and slowly the people are learning how to live a better, calmer, more comfortable life than they and their ancestors led prior to the arrival of General Noldek.

Law and Order

Law enforcement and local legislation is left to each planetary governor, who can pretty much make whatever laws he likes and enforcement how he likes. The only controls are the four-year vote of confidence, and the basic ground rules General Noldek laid down. Outside of all that, the governors have free rein. Most of what these governors create is what amounts to a benevolent dictatorship, where they rule absolutely, sometimes harshly, but they at least try to be fair and generous. For the most part, the laws of any world in the Alliance are simple: do your job, leave other people alone, pay your taxes, show support for your local governor. Some worlds make cybernetic replacement a mandatory show of loyalty. Other worlds require all citizens to join the local military at some point. And still other worlds have unique cultures that the Alliance have not been able to supersede, and so they have an interesting blend of old tradition plus new order. A good example is the *Holy Order of Tuyrene*, a prominent religion among many Alliance worlds. One of the tenets of this order states it is ungodly for one to unnecessarily modify one's body with machinery (cybernetics) when one does not need them. However, on a few planets where this religion is strong, the governors have made it mandatory that all adult citizens get some kind of cybernetics to show their allegiance to General Noldek. The citizens and religious figures get around this by establishing traditions of ritual amputation prior to adulthood as away of ridding one's self of spiritual uncleanliness. For the next few years, these amputees are going through a period of "spiritual reflection" that ends with adult-

hood, and a cybernetic replacement for the body part that got taken off. It is a series of compromises that allows the governors to have their law and allows the locals to have their traditions. This is a good example of how law and order work in the Central Alliance – it is largely left to the leaders to make laws and to the citizens to figure out ways to fit their lives around them. Most people really do love their new government, and they want to work with it, not against it, even it means retooling their ancient culture and ways of living.

Crime and Punishment

Local governors are allowed to punish people as they see fit, but they must not get too rough on them, or they will face unpopularity and eventual votes of no confidence. Or worse, they will receive ill favor directly from General Noldek, who will 86 the unpopular governor without warning.

On most Alliance worlds, minor infractions of the law result in fines or temporary suspension of cybernetic privileges. That means the offender has his cybernetics detached for a certain period of time but is free to keep living his life as usual. However, loss of cybernetics is a great shame in the Alliance, roughly equivalent to being locked up in the stockades for a few days. Wherever one goes, everybody will see that they are a lawbreaker. More importantly, the convict's humiliation is made all the worse because he probably cannot function at 100% efficiency since he might be missing an arm, leg, eye, etc. This punishment works really well against more heavily tricked-out cyborgs and it keeps them from abusing their power. For a partial- or full-conversion cyborg to lose their cyber-privileges would reduce them to utter helplessness, something that most Alliance folk would never quite live down. Thus, fear of losing one's machinery is often enough to keep people in line. It is a beautiful system, because the governors do not have to do much to enforce the law. The law ends up enforcing itself, and by using this kind of shame tactic, there is no real need for large prisons or penal systems. There only needs to be enough of that to contain off-worlder offenders, or cyborgs who re-install cybernetics while such rights have been suspended. Such offenders remain locked down until their sentence is up, and afterwards, their revocation of cyber-privileges usually is permanent.

This system does nothing to address grievances between citizens, however. Rather than having a large and unwieldy civil court system, the Central Alliance routes all civilian disputes to gladiatorial arenas where the combatants simply duke it out to see who is right. This stems from long, rich dueling traditions present on nearly every Central Alliance world prior to General Noldek's conquest of them. These fights have a hundred different names – "duels of justice," "grudge matches," "bouts of honor," "slam festivals" – but they all boil down to a simple contest of arms between two hostile parties. While such duels are usually between two civilians, they also can be used by a civilian against a soldier, a governor, or even General Noldek himself! Soldiers are discouraged from dueling as it might make it seem that their ranks are fractious. In cases of military disputes, officers try to exhaust every possible means of resolution before a duel is approved.

In legal duels, the accused party has the right to determine what kind of weapons will be used – none, hand to hand, ranged, exotic, etc. Prior to the fight, each combatant has the appropriate hardware attached to whatever cybernetics will accommodate it. If either combatant does not have the cybernetics to accommodate the duel's weapon of choice, the parties can either undergo further cybernetic conversion so they *can* use the weapons of choice, or new weapons are picked.

Duels of this sort are usually arranged for a single day once a month. On these days, the duels are broadcast live throughout the Alliance. Viewership of these is always high, and lots of folks lay bets on who they think the winners shall be. The culture of the Alliance is such that people watching these duels will genuinely support whoever wins the match. Most matches are to the death, but if the defeated party asks for mercy, the victor is expected to be sporting and grant it. The point of these things is not to slaughter one another but to resolve their differences. There are a ton of cases where combatants in the arena emerged as friends and stayed that way for life thereafter.

A final note: The use of illegal weapons or devices in legal duels is not only forbidden, but it is a great source of shame. Any such cheating will result in the loss of the match as well as permanent revocation of all cyber-privileges. To cheat like this, especially in a broadcast duel, is fairly stupid, since there are so many folks watching, it will be easy to get caught.

Worlds of Interest

Noldek's World. The capital world of the Central Alliance, the home world of General Noldek, and the administrative capital for the entire civilization. Life here is akin to what the CCW might consider "upper middle class." The world is a small one, dominated by numerous shipyards and cyber-factories. Here, Noldek has built his own personal army. He also conducts cybernetic research here, working on new cybernetic chassis for him and his troops.

Shortly after the Central Alliance was formed, immigration to this world grew to a near-epidemic. General Noldek finally put a stop to it entirely, not because this planet could not absorb any more visitors, but because it was bleeding so many other worlds dry of people! As such, getting any kind of visitation rights to this planet are hard to come by, even for citizens who live there. Those who leave Noldek's World for any reason might not find a place for themselves when they try to come home. As a result, those who live here usually stay here forever. It has isolated the planet somewhat, and its populace is beginning to evolve on a different cultural track than the rest of the Central Alliance. Whereas most Alliance worlds are rural and bound by ancient traditions, the people of Noldek's World are increasingly urbane and favor new philosophies over old traditions. This cultural gap will only widen in time. If General Noldek does not do something about it, his own capital world might find itself culturally isolated from the rest of the interplanetary society.

Cybernary. The heart of cybernetic design and manufacture in the Alliance, Cybernary is a medium-sized world covered with factories and heavy industry of all kinds. Much of these facilities are in poor working order, but the overall industrial strength of the planet is formidable, and it provides the Central Alliance with the bulk of its cybernetic parts and chassis. The "gearheads" who design new cybernetic hardware do so in direct competition with General Noldek's personal cyber-designers. A less-than-friendly rivalry exists between

these two groups, who are routinely trying to outdo each other. For the moment, they are both neck and neck with their latest designs, but the Cybernary designers believe they are on the verge of developing a whole new line of cyber-weapons that will make current Central Alliance technology look positively Stone Age in comparison! If true, General Noldek's cyber-designers might not recover from this.

Draulik. The vast majority of people living on this sparsely populated world have undergone full cybernetic conversion because the environment here is so harsh. Full cyborgs can roam the world freely and not have to worry about its lack of breathable atmosphere, lethal amounts of UV radiation, presence of mutative pathogens, etc. Anything less than full conversion means one must live with maintaining a life support system of some kind, which on this world is a serious liability. One failure, and you could be looking at death in a matter of minutes. The problem with living under full conversion is that most of the people here are ordinary civilians, not soldiers. This does not sit well with the planetary governor, who would like to see more volunteers for the local military. It also does not sit well with neighboring Central Alliance worlds who do not know why Draulik inhabitants undergo full conversion but don't mind passing judgement on them anyway. These people tend to see Draulik as a world filled with shirkers who like having the power of full conversion, but who do not want to execute the duties that come with such power (like military service).

Shallow Hope. Though General Noldek officially took over this massive terrestrial world early in his campaign to forge the Central Alliance, there still exist huge mountain ranges in which live factions of locals who do not accept Noldek as their leader, who see cybernetics as an unholy plague upon all peoples, and who have vowed to fight a guerilla war until General Noldek and all of his cyber-minions leave. Most of these rebels have become adept in the magic arts, and are experts at hit and run warfare. They cannot infiltrate the cities of this world too well, since they have no cybernetics on them, but they are a terror in the wilderness and good at sneaking close to settlements, hitting them hard and vanishing before anybody ever knows what hit them. Moreover, the mountains and caves these rebels live in are very treacherous, and the governor's troops have had a really hard time finding rebels to kill them. With so many places to hide, the guerilla war is likely to go on here for decades to come. Such a depressing situation has prompted the locals to change this world's name from its traditional *T'ni* to *Shallow Hope*. If the governor does not resolve the situation here in one year, General Noldek will come back with his own armies and take the situation into hand personally. This is what most of the locals are hoping for, since they have lost confidence in their own governor, who is just botching the war against these insurgents in the worst way.

Grighton. The Central Alliance worlds do not carry out much trade with neighboring worlds, largely because there are so few spaceships within the Alliance, and almost all of them belong to General Noldek. A notable exception, however, is the world of Grighton, which has always been a trading nexus in this part of the Halo, and continues to be one today. This small, almost planetoid-sized world orbits a white dwarf on the innermost edge of the Central Alliance, right on the border with the Threshold. This has made the world a popular spot for pirates, smugglers, fugitives, adventurers and mercenaries over the years. Eventually, the world was colonized by merchants who wanted to trade with the shady, but cash-rich strangers who passed by so often. Most of these spacers had huge amounts of illegally gotten money and goods they needed to get rid of, and Grighton would be such a place. In time, the world became pretty rich (relative to other worlds in this part of the Halo) and even maintained a modest fleet of trading ships. When General Noldek came through looking to include this world into the Central Alliance, the Grightonese accepted without a fight. They knew General Noldek would treat them fairly, and the planet would always have more than enough money to live well after paying whatever taxes the General required. Besides, Grighton had been seeing a little too much of Splugorth and Gene-Tech ships in recent years for comfort's sake, and being part of Noldek's larger alliance would be a nice security screen to fall back on. For Noldek, Grighton is his empire's link to the larger interstellar community, and he aims to keep it that way.

Ungersoll. Even for the Central Alliance, this world is poor. It is the home of Ungersoll Motors, a failed cyber-design firm that went out of business just a year ago. Ungersoll had a boom in business right after the Central Alliance was formed and people everywhere were rushing to fit themselves with cybernetics and show their support for the new leader. Ungersoll was the only factory in place to fit the need, but these guys were really designers of industrial machinery, not cybernetics, and were unfit for the task. It didn't stop them from trying, however, and soon the entire planet was sporting Ungersoll implants. Too bad these implants were all poorly designed, poorly built, and prone to failure. Within a few years, the populace had broken down, with malfunctioning cybernetics and not enough money to afford repairs or replacements. The company went out of business trying to make good on all of its product defect claims, and ultimately, the board of directors ended the debacle by dissolving the company and then committing mass suicide out of shame. Since then, this place has been the home of misery as the people shuffle about on twitching, sparking cybernetics that work only half the time. It is as if the world itself has broken down, and nothing is rushing to fix it.

Hammerhead. This world has always made a business out of local dueling traditions, and with the advent of the Central Alliance and cyber-dueling, Hammerhead's gladiator arenas have become even more popular. Here, cyber-athletes routinely compete against each other in vicious battle matches featuring every kind of cyber-equipment presently available. The crowds go wild over this stuff, and gambling on the matches is a handsome secondary industry, generating a lot of revenue for those running the betting parlors. But if you are not a professional gambler, cyber-athlete, or if you don't run a fighting school, arena, or gambling den, there is little hope to make good on this world. Like so many other places that peg their hopes on dirty industries like gambling and professional combat, Hammerhead is in a quiet state of crisis. The majority of people live dirt-poor lives, full of despair that only goes away under the harsh lights of the gladiator arenas, under the loud cheers of the fans in the stands, under the flashing displays of the gambling machines, or under the momentary rush of a winning bet. These are the things that keep society going on this world. Were the gambling or gladiator industries to stop, Hammerhead would melt down, and only the intervention of an outside entrepreneur or a huge building project financed by Noldek himself could lift the planet from the quagmire.

Xleena. This world has long been considered the Anvil Galaxy's *junkyard*, a place where folks could dump hazardous or regulated waste (spent nuclear rods, bio-hazard material, etc.) without fear of retribution. People have always lived here, making their money as junk dealers and salvage experts, and somehow, they have evolved to deal with the disease, the radiation, and all of the other stuff in the air that might kill the ordinary alien or human. When the Central Alliance took over, the cyber-craze hit this place hard, and virtually everybody on the plant is a partial or full conversion cyborg. The thing is, most of the cyborgs here have jacked themselves up with cybernetics built right from the junk pile, giving the cyborgs here an even nastier, rustier, more rundown appearance. The funny thing is, people from other worlds think that Xleenan cyborgs look really cool, and the "corroded" look is becoming a huge fashion statement across the Central Alliance. For the Xleenans, it is merely the best way they can turn themselves into machines and keep running. **G.M. Note:** Xleenan cyborgs, no matter what their attachments or degree of conversion, will have 35% more M.D.C. because of the extremely tough parts used in construction. However, they will also be 50% heavier and 50% slower, so cut all combat bonuses in half.

R250-728. The Central Alliance is not known for space exploration, but General Noldek has sponsored the colonization of a single world that is right on the line between the Halo and the Threshold. Its galactic catalogue number is simply R250-728, and it appears to be an ancient outpost of some kind used by alien spacers. So far, a contingent of about 1,000 Central Alliance cyborgs live and work here, digging around to see what they might find. General Noldek himself is convinced that the aliens who used to run this world left behind valuable technology he and his soldiers can use. Already the colonists have found dozens of destroyed old alien spacecraft in unsalvageable condition. But there is every indication that there is more tech to find, and that at least a good chunk of it will be usable. The question is, what exactly will this tech be able to do? Some think this place was an ancient listening post from which alien astronomers could broadcast and scan across the Threshold, maintaining contact with people in the Core. Others think the place was a fortress to hold the line against marauders from the Threshold. And still others believe this was a science world that was destroyed by an experiment gone awry. Who knows? Maybe all three theories are wrong, or maybe they all are right! For the moment, anything is possible here as Alliance cyborgs struggle to piece together the history of this strange and isolated world.

New Triumph. Shortly after the Central Alliance formed, Splugorth slave ships from the Kingdom of Rynncryyl raided the world with the intent to take as many slaves as possible. Noldek and his army responded swiftly, taking heavy losses but ultimately destroying the raiders. The Central Alliance had sent a clear message to the Splugorth that if they wanted to take the Alliance's worlds, they had better be prepared to fight for them. Since then, there have been only very small isolated incursions that the Central Alliance turned away easily.

To commemorate the great battle, the world renamed itself New Triumph, and to those who live here, General Noldek is like a god. He is credited for saving them against the Splugorth menace, and they are convinced that whatever the Splugorth throw at this world when they return (and they *will* return), General Noldek and his brave cyborgs will be able to send it all back to where it came from. The local military is very strong, with huge numbers of volunteers who have undergone partial and full conversion. Only Noldek knows that Rynncryyl is planning a big invasion of this world and perhaps the Central Alliance at large, and only he knows that against a huge, organized Splugorth front, this planet, and indeed the Central Alliance, cannot withstand that sort of firepower. By defeating the Splugorth once, the Central Alliance may have sealed New Triumph's fate forever. Time will tell. Meanwhile, the General searches for strategies and tactics that might win the day, and/or a possible alliance with some outside power.

The Threshold

A large portion of the Anvil Galaxy is just empty space, an intimidating void that separates the densely populated Halo from the mysterious Core. This great gap to cross is the *Threshold*, and it is the bane of many Spacers and adventurers.

The vast majority (75%) of ships that try crossing the Threshold never make it. Most of them just *disappear* without a trace. It could be that these ships are instantly destroyed, or it could be that they suffer a prolonged attack but somehow are prevented from sending out a distress call. Or maybe they get caught in a huge chronol shift that rockets them into the incredibly distant past or future. Or maybe harmonic disruptions destroy everything within a certain radius of the Threshold borders. Or it could be one of a thousand other hypotheses ventured by scientists to whom the Threshold is as frustrating as it is fascinating. Clearly, something terrible is going in there. Only nobody has even come close to figuring out what it might be. Though most are never seen or heard from again, there are the lucky ones who claim to have made it through to the Core side, only to be mysteriously teleported back to the Halo, usually near where (and sometimes when) they started their trek.

There is no evidence one way or the other that suggests who or what might be responsible for either result. Some Spacers think that hostile aliens – of which there are probably many in the Core – are to blame for the destruction of space craft in the Core. Of course, the most anybody in the Halo ever glean from ships that vanish are frantic distress calls that don't make much sense before they get cut off, presumably destroyed at the source. To date, no ship has ever lasted longer than three weeks in the Core before destruction or, more commonly, it gets mysteriously whisked across space and time and instantaneously appears right back in the Halo. Some scientists think there might be some undetectable kind of wormhole abundant in the Core that causes this "return trip" phenomenon. Others go back to the "hostile aliens" theory to suggest that these unknown aliens take pity on some space ship and send back to where they came from rather than destroy them. After all, what few aliens known to inhabit the Core all seem to be radically advanced with technology equal to or well beyond *Phase World* standards. Perhaps one of these aliens simply put intruders from the Halo travelers back where they think they belong.

Beyond all this, however, lurks the nagging question: why? Why destroy those who visit the Core, or forcibly eject them? What is it that the denizen of the Core want to keep hidden from the rest of the universe? Of course, many (including supposedly reliable lore) point to the *Cosmic Forge*, thought by many to be hidden in the Core somewhere. Could it be that someone or something is protecting the Core and dispatching those who seek it out? Perhaps aggressive and hostile explorers into the Threshold or the Core are destroyed, where the honestly curious and peaceful are simply "put back" home! Perhaps there is no secret alien civilization or guardian organization trying to keep people away. Perhaps it is the Cosmic Forge itself taking direct action to keep its whereabouts secret. Whatever it is, so long as there is a Cosmic Forge to find, multitudes of people will search for it, and look to the Core as a likely hiding place. And by extension, so long as there is a Threshold, especially one that might be the last great obstacle to finding the Cosmic Forge, then there will always be people willing to cross it to claim the device.

G.M. Note: There are no set rules for exactly what will happen to ships that cross the Threshold, because we feel there should not be any. Crossing the Threshold is a dangerous and often fatal experience that rarely leaves those who attempt to do it, unscathed. Certainly there are those lucky few who manage to do succeed, if only for a few short weeks (naturally the player characters may try to be counted among that minority), but even if death and destruction are avoided, a fate unknown awaits those who explore the even more mysterious and unknown Core. Exactly how long the heroes may stay in the Core, what they find there, and what kind of damage they sustain going through the Threshold is left almost entirely to the Game Master. It is his or her call to say what happens to those who try crossing what is supposed to be the uncrossable. Maybe the characters' ship suffers major damage. Maybe the heroes themselves are hurt. Maybe the crew get caught in a nasty spatial phenomenon that carries them to a parallel dimension or different part of the Galaxy or universe for that matter. Or are captured and studied or enslaved by some sort of non-carbon based life form. Whatever the fate of the player characters, do not impose an outcome with no chance for survival or just to torture them. Impose a result that has some cool adventure hook to it. If the characters' great pirate ship gets mangled on the way through the Threshold, give them an opportunity to repair it. If the heroes go mad during the trip, give them a chance to cure themselves. If they get captured allow them to escape. Let the explore the unknown and triumph in the challenge of the experience, especially if there is no tangible reward/treasure (which there probably is not). Let them boldly go where no one has gone before and escape, even if they can never find that place again. Remember, the players are attached to their characters, and nobody likes it when a G.M. callously hurts or takes away their character. Instant death just plain stinks in a role-playing game. After all, this is supposed to be heroic adventure that challenges the player character's courage and ingenuity. Make it so.

The Powers That Be

The Threshold is believed to be mostly empty space . . . . or is it? Surely, there must be something behind all of the disappearances and strange encounters that Spacers run into every time they try crossing from the Halo to the Core. But what? Theories abound, but sooner or later, they all at least touch upon two major villains known to inhabit the space where the Halo meets the Threshold. They are **The Splugorth Kingdom of Rynncryyl,** one of the four great Splugorth Kingdoms of the Three Galaxies, and the **Gene-Tech,** feared if not reviled by all, these sinister genetic sculptors craft untold monstrosities for reasons unknown. Some believe they know the reason, and claim a band of Gene-Tech (or could it be the even rarer and more malevolent Gene-Splicers) are creating an entire mutant armies from innocent victims in the hopes of selling them to desperate warlords and would-be conquerors across the Anvil Galaxy.

The Splugorth Kingdom of Rynncryyl

Population: 20 billion (estimated). The Kingdom of Rynncryyl makes up about 25% of the total Splugorth population in the Three Galaxies.

Demographics: High Lords and Conservators (1%), Overlords (20%), Powerlords (2%), Slavers (1%), Blind Warrior Women (5%), Kittani (2%), Metzla (5%), Gargoyles (3%), Humans (10%, most are slaves), Wulfen (10%, most are slaves), Other Mortal Races (36%; this segment of the population comes from all over the Three Galaxies and even from across the Megaverse; about half of them are slaves and the rest are generally nervous free citizens), Supernatural Creatures (5%; includes but is not limited to Dragons, Elementals, Demons, Devils and other supernatural beings; about 30% of all of these creatures are slaves, even a few unfortunate Dragons and other creatures of magic). For details on most of these races, check out **Rifts® World Book Two: Atlantis** sourcebook.

Overview: The alien intelligences known as the Splugorth (see **Rifts® Atlantis** for more information) have long been a major presence in the Three Galaxies. At any given time, there has been at least one Splugorth Kingdom somewhere in the Three Galaxies either waging a war of conquest upon its neighbors, preparing to wage such a war, or is recovering from losing such a war. Living in peace is not the Splugorth way, and the various Kingdoms of the Three Galaxies prove that without a doubt.

The Splugorth have known much success in conquering, ruling and dominating scores of planets and even one or more solar systems, but whenever they have made a bid to take over a large section of a galaxy, or perhaps even an entire galaxy itself, those ambitions inevitably bring about utter destruction from the other power blocs present in the vicinity. In the case of the Anvil Galaxy, the last time the Splugorth made a serious bid to take over the entire galaxy, it was only 50 years ago, by the reigning Splugorth power in the galaxy today, the *Kingdom of Rynncryyl*.

Lord Rynncryyl is an utterly mad Splugorth intelligence that is obsessed not only with controlling the Anvil Galaxy, but with finding the Cosmic Forge. Some fifty years ago, Lord Rynncryyl deluded himself that he possessed the power to shatter both the CCW and the TGE at the same time. He thought if those powers would crumble, then certainly all of the other powers of the galaxy would either disintegrate or they would just swear allegiance to the Splugorth to avoid a shattering invasion. Then, with at least the Halo under his command, he could cross the Threshold, conquer the Core (how he would do this nobody knows) and then have the entire galaxy at his disposal, from the innermost Core to the outermost Halo. He could then scour the entire Anvil Galaxy for clues to finding the Cosmic Forge. As he saw things unfolding, he would find the Forge, and with the ultimate power it would give him, he would first take over the other Three Galaxies, and then he would set about to enslaving neighboring galaxies to his god-like authority.

Ooooooookay.

The trouble with Lord Rynncryyl is that he is a well known figure in the Anvil Galaxy. He and more importantly, his minions are forever getting caught in crazy schemes to manipulate galactic politics or cause wars between superpowers, that sort of thing. This plot of Rynncryyl to conquer both the TGE and the CCW gets points for ambition, but none for execution. Strong though Rynncryyl's armada might have been, his Kingdom controls only 25 *worlds* split between three star systems. His domain is a drop in the bucket compared to such giants as the CCW or the TGE, both of which maintain *intergalactic* civilizations that span thousands and thousands of worlds. Without some kind of miracle in his pocket or an alien doomsday weapon to even the score, Lord Rynncryyl had no chance. He would get slaughtered, and that is exactly what happened. Both the CCW and the TGE independently came down on Rynncryyl's forces like hammers, destroying most of them and leaving a few ships to limp home and tell of the defeat they suffered.

Ever since that ill-fated (and irrational) campaign, Lord Rynncryyl has been absent, even among the subjects of his own Kingdom! Frankly, he was lucky to still have a Kingdom. Surely the CCW or more likely, the TGE could have destroyed it entirely, if they had not started fighting amongst themselves. In the last days of the war, CCW and TGE ships were closing in on Splugorth territory when one or both sides decided they were getting too close for comfort. Somebody flinched, and a brief but deadly skirmish broke out between the CCW and TGE armadas. Fearing this could turn into a wider conflict, both side withdrew from the Splugorth territory, inadvertently sparing this Kingdom of Evil. The fact remains that Lord Rynncryyl is gone, having disappeared right when it looked like his Kingdom would be smashed to pieces by CCW and/or TGE might. Ever since, Rynncryyl's top lieutenants and advisors have been jointly running the Kingdom, certain that their cowardly lord indeed flew the coop, but fearful that if any one of them tries to

take over, he will either be killed by all of the other seconds in command, or by Lord Rynncryyl himself, if and when he returns from wherever he went.

This, more than anything else, is keeping the Kingdom of Rynncryyl fairly small and its operations contained. Though Splugorth Slavers routinely sortie forth from the Kingdom to raid outlying communities on the inner edge of the Halo, that is about the extent of the Kingdom's power at the moment. The leaders are too busy trying to make sure the secret of Lord Rynncryyl's absence never gets out, for if it did, then the legions of enemies who hate the Splugorth might seize upon the opportunity to destroy the severely weakened Kingdom once and for all.

Though the Kingdom is weak, it is recovering. Moreover, it is still Splugorth, and that means it is still a major player in just about any evil plot hatched within the Anvil Galaxy. Naturally, it does not make sense for the Splugorth to get involved in evil plots here, there and everywhere. They really should tend to their own teetering stability before mucking about with other worlds and civilizations, but, that is the Splugorth for you. They are compulsive evildoers who simply cannot get by without at least knowing that someway, somehow, they are making somebody's life miserable. And so, they continue to plot and interfere with the daily life of the Anvil Galaxy as best they can, knowing full well that every time they do so, they risk setting off a chain of events that could hurt them.

As a result of all this, the Kingdom's influence over galactic events is way out of proportion to its real power in terms of number of ships, soldiers, and financial capital. Rynncryyl spies and assassins can be expected to have a hand in many of the major political conspiracies ongoing in the Anvil Galaxy, especially if it is the sort of thing that might topple a government, cause a war, spark a widespread interplanetary panic, or have similar effect. As such, they have numerous contacts with the criminal superpowers of the CCW, they help foment rebellion among TGE worlds that have not yet joined the Free World Council, they feed information about the Free World Council back to the TGE, they help the Dark Covens of the UWW conduct their ark and evil practices, and so on.

At the forefront of all this plotting and double-dealing are the *Sunaj Assassins*, the Rynncryyl Kingdom's front line of terror and mayhem. Using the Sunaj as special forces operatives, the Rynncryyl lords routinely have them slay important members of various societies as well as cause other acts of mayhem. They also are the first people tapped to handle matters of espionage and global security. Meanwhile, slave rebellions within the Rynncryyl Kingdom is a problem that is getting worse and worse each day. It is as if the subjects know their leader is gone, and that is giving them the courage to throw off their chains and rebel. So it is that the Sunaj find themselves fighting desperately to crush any sign of revolt from without and within the Kingdom, lest it come apart completely, turning the once-proud Splugorth Kingdom into just another collection of Independent worlds populated by gleeful ex-slaves. Rynncryyl's assassins and spies keep an especially sharp eye out for agents of long time enemies such as the CCW and TGE, and deal with them quickly and ruthlessly.

Note: The **Rifts® Atlantis** World Book offers a ton of great details on how a "typical" Splugorth Kingdom might operate.

Keep in mind, Splynncryyth only controls a single continent. Rynncryyl's Kingdom controls 25 entire planets, so the scale of his forces would be many times that found on the Altantean continent of Rifts Earth. However, these are the same basic society, and any details one wishes to find for the Kingdom of Rynncryyl can be found within the indispensable **Rifts® Atlantis** book. Run, don't walk, to your nearest game or hobby shop and pick up a copy. You will *not* be sorry that you did.

Government

Like all Splugorth controlled worlds, these planets are ruled by an absolutist government, controlled by the Splugorth intelligences and their minions. The Kingdom of Rynncryyl was once controlled by Rynncryyl himself, but the big coward abdicated his throne when the CCW and TGE threatened to invade this Kingdom itself. Now, all of Rynncryyl's top advisors and second-hand men have formed an uneasy council through which they jointly run the Kingdom as if Rynncryyl were still around. Hey, the King is mad as a hatter, and it would not be out of the question for him to vanish like this just to test the loyalty of his minions. With that in mind, none of them have made the slightest move to take the throne for himself. Besides the certain death they would suffer at the hands of Rynncryyl's other top minions, the suffering inflicted by Rynncryyl himself should he decide to return would be far worse than death itself.

Military

The Kingdom maintains a formidable armada of warships as well as legions of soldiers hailing from the various conquered worlds and slave races. These include humans, Wulfen, Altara Warrior Women, Tattooed Men, Kittani, Kydians, Metzla, Gargoyles, and substantial numbers from the many other races commonly used by the Splugorth or found in the Three Galaxies. Atop this mess of slave-soldiers rules the standard Splugorth hierarchy of Slavers, Overlords, Powerlords, Conservators and High Lords. According to legend, this mob of firepower should be a nearly invincible fighting force. In truth, while devastatingly power, it is far from invincible. Since the defeat of their once powerful army, the Kingdom's forces have floundered with only basic training, equipment and resources abundantly available. Additionally, with their Splugorth Lord gone, there is no decisive leader willing to go out on a limb with many significant military incursions. Consequently, the current armed forces languish with little to challenge them. Furthermore, many of the starships and other equipment in use today are all left overs from the war against the CCW and the TGE. On top of that, the best leaders in the Kingdom are busy trying to pretend they are acting on Lord Rynncryyl's behalf in the hope of keeping the Kingdom together for next generation or two. As a result, second-rate (at best) leaders are left to control what passes for the military. To those in the know, it is a sad sight to see this once impressive military machine fall to such hard times and lack of spirit. The honest truth is that if another power bloc were to come in and wage total war right now, it is highly doubtful the Kingdom of Rynncryyl would survive the strain. Certainly if the CCW or TGE came in, they would shatter the Kingdom to dust, but that is not the greatest worry at the moment. No, the greatest worry are the other three Splugorth Kingdoms spread out through the Three Galaxies – two in the Corkscrew and one in the Thundercloud. The four Kingdoms have never really gotten along, and even for a Splugorth, Rynncryyl has a way of making enemies with *everybody*. If the other three Kingdoms ever realize how weak this Kingdom *really* is, they would waste no time taking it over or just destroying it outright. Against a much more organized, fleshed out, equipped Splugorth invasion, the Kingdom of Rynncryyl would fold like a piece of paper.

Then again, where is Lord Rynncryyl and what is he up to? Could he be hot on the trail of the Cosmic Forge? Could it or some other powerful weapon be within his grasp? Or is he hatching some new scheme or building a new secret army or alliance with some alien power in the Threshold, The Core or other part of the universe? It seems unlikely for him to be so frightened as to remain in hiding all these years. On the other hand, perhaps he met his doom trying to traverse the Threshold? Only time will tell.

Foreign Affairs

Consortium of Civilized Worlds: The Splugorth hate the CCW for their instrumental role in the Kingdom's defeat no so long ago. They already despised this civilization for its fairness, openness and embrace of liberty. The CCW stands or all the things the Splugorth do not, and so they long to destroy it.

Trans-Galactic Empire: The Splugorth also hate the TGE for its role in the Kingdom's defeat. They hate this society equally for its use of brute strength without appreciating the finer evils such strength can accomplish. In the arts of evil, the TGE are mindless thugs unworthy of the Splugorth's notice. That they lost a war to them really bothers the Splugorth.

United Worlds of Warlock: The UWW's condemnation of Splugorth Bio-Wizardry would be enough to get this magical society on the Splugorth's hit list if it weren't already there for its alliance with the CCW.

Naruni Enterprises: These sinister arms merchants are cut from the same cloth as the Splugorth, only they do not have the guts to enslave their clients outright. Their pretense of commerce disgusts the Splugorth, who feel that the Naruni are too soft in their ways and intentions, but annoying rivals nonetheless.

Hartigal Combine: The Splugorth see this organization as a prime target for one of its plots. Its youth makes it naive, and its breakaway status from the Naruni makes them reckless. Indeed, they shall feel the Splugorth sting soon enough...

Golgan Republik: The Kingdom of Rynncryyl fully intend to raid the hell out of the Golgan worlds just as they fall away from the Republik. In fact, the Golgan Republik is seen as the perfect target for "tuning up" its sluggish and flat military. It is also a safe target because they know Lord Rynncryyl had intended to raid, loot and conquer parts of the Rebublik and given their weak state, they make for a relatively soft target.

Altess Dynasty: The Kingdom is still smarting from the defeat the Altess handed them, unexpectedly. Though they lack the resources to make a full assault on the Altess, they would dearly love to. Sunaj assassins are being deployed in force to infiltrate their society so they might assassinate its leaders and sow dissent.

Central Alliance: These world are also excellent slaving targets because they are relatively poor and weak compared to giants like the CCW and the TGE. They also are right along the inner edge of the Halo, which makes them convenient to hit from the darkness of the Threshold. However, the Alliance has proven a worthy foe, and a society of cyborgs will not be victimized so easily.

Cosmo-Knights: Argh! These champions of justice are a constant thorn in the Splugorth's side. If they really knew how hurting the Kingdom of Rynncryyl was, they might descend upon it like jackals, destroying it completely, or so the current secret leadership believes. Indeed, if they massed their strength, the Cosmo-Knights could smash the Kingdom with relative ease.

Gene-Tech: The Splugorth occasionally deal with these merchants of misery. They are considering obtaining the Gene-Tech of the Threshold's secret armies of genetically augmented soldiers as a temporary solution to the Kingdom's military and manpower shortfalls.

Omegan Order: If the Splugorth could cross the Threshold easily themselves, they would certainly try to join forces with these admirably evil renegades. Surely, they have heard of the Splugorth, and on a few occasions, the Kingdom has received a few vaguely worded messages from the Omegans regarding a future partnership, but nothing has come of it as yet.

Xodian Collective: Like so many others in the galaxy, the Splugorth know little of the Xodians except that they are a super-powerful races capable of crossing space under their own power and acting as living weapons batteries. Word has it they are one of the few powers of the Core that is looking to cross the Threshold and colonize parts of the Halo for themselves.

K!ozn: These super-intelligent plotters and manipulators are both appreciated and despised by the Splugorth. On one hand, they admire their raw intellect and their ability to conduct simple manipulations behind the scenes to make the entire galaxy bend to the K!ozn will. They hate these aliens for just that ability, too, since the Splugorth dearly wish they had such influence, but do not. For that, they are jealous enough to kill.

Independent Worlds: The Splugorth consider small, cut off worlds to be prime targets for slave runs. If the world is inadequately protected, slave ships can take the place over, picking it clean of people before the CCW, TGE or Cosmo-Knights show up to investigate.

Society

The Splugorth dominated worlds tend to regard most mortals as lesser beings to be used, abused, enslaved, tortured, and, in some cases, even eaten by other supernatural creatures. As on might expect, the Splugorth and other powerful supernatural beings enjoy as many rights, freedoms and privileges as they can defend through raw strength and manipulation, while humans and other mortals languish in oppression and poverty. Humans and other races are in constant danger, and suffer the contempt and hostility of the monster races. The constant for most mortals

is a life of hard labor, servitude, and drudgery There is no justice for lesser beings, though there are laws and some semblance of order. Crimes committed by mortals upon other mortals may be ignored and go without punishment, or the there may be swift, brutal consequences from the so-called authorities; typically a beating. For a human or other lesser race to commit crime against a leader or greater supernatural beings, there can only be misery and death. There are only masters and slaves in this Kingdom, and if a slave dares to steal or harm his better, the slave may be struck down and beaten, tortured and/or slain, often on the spot. Masters enjoy absolute power over slaves, and they inflict whatever harm or "justice" they like upon their underlings. Slaves live in endless misery and humiliation as they serve their masters' every whim. All in all, there is no good side of life here. There is only those who give pain and those who receive it. Most receive it in some way or another.

Worlds of Interest

Gylcrdd: This world is the current throne planet for the Kingdom, home to Rynncryyl's top advisors and lieutenants. The world is supposed to be the great staging ground for a new invasion, but there are few soldiers here, and many of them are deployed to keep the peace in the streets. A monotonous and thankless job for soldiers who feel they should be out conquering the galaxy.

Ryythknn: This is the Sunaj headquarters, where they recruit, train and deploy their members. Huge Sunaj fortresses stand out in the open, almost daring enemies to strike if they dared. The Sunaj effectively govern the planet, since 90% of the population in some way serve the Sunaj. Word has it the leaders of the assassins here know that Rynncryyl is missing and are poised to make a move against all of the Kingdom's leaders, establishing Sunaj warriors in their stead until Rynncryyl comes back (whenever that might be).

Hhurigh: The Slave Market of Hhurigh is the largest of its kind on the Kingdom. On par with the Splynn Dimensional Market, the vendors here routinely jaunt between this world and Phase World in an effort to maintain two very busy financial fronts at once. The slavers here are very powerful and wealthy, and represent a powerful bloc within the society. Are they tough enough to help overthrow the government? Sure. Do they have the courage to do so? Not unless something drastic happens, no.

Alkasda: This world is in open revolt against its masters. The Splugorth have deployed a full Repression Fleet to exterminate the planetary population in the hopes of sending a dire message to all other potential rebels. Whether or not this fleet actually kills the bulk of the planet's population remains to be seen, since they are already getting messages about the attack and are secretly fleeing the world.

Skynnkyll: A renegade Splugorth Intelligence named *Blyythznn* is hiding on this otherwise unremarkable world because he made a few too many enemies in the other Splugorth Kingdoms of the Three Galaxies. He has learned that Rynncryyl is no longer on the throne here, and he is mulling over exactly how he might squirm his way to the seat of power. To get anything done, though, he needs to build a base of power, and to do that, he needs minions willing to fight and die for him.

Plthh: This world has also openly rebelled against their masters, only on this one, there have already been several large battles, and in each case, the slaves have won. Inept (non-Splugorth) leadership as well as the element of surprise on the rebel's part is largely determining the course of the rebellion. One or two more rebel victories, and the rest of the planet's population will rise up and kick out the Minions of Splugorth who dominate their planet. After that, Plthh will be as good as an Independent World.

Koliath: This is one of the few worlds where Lord Rynncryyl's Minions still have a fairly tight grip on the reins of power. Little do they know that a quartet of Cosmo-Knights have infiltrated the world posing as human slaves. They intend to topple the Splugorth's reign here, but to do that they will need to get the slaves themselves to rise up and fight for themselves. The four are debating whether they should just assume their super-powered forms and tear up the Splugorth until the locals take destiny into their own hands, or should they remain secret and act only once the locals have proven their intent to break away on their own.

Zaladast: This is where the last shots were fired in the CCW and TGE war. The Battle of Zaladast was the last TGE engagement, during which Empire warships bombarded the planet, slaughtering 90% of the population. Since then, the Splugorth have been desperately trying to re-colonize the world, but nobody will set foot there. Meanwhile, the 10% who survived the TGE bombardment are all on their own, building a piece meal society out of the scraps of the old order, wondering when somebody will come to give them some humanitarian aid.

Furego: Small harmonic disruptions are splitting this world apart, just as surely as a stonemason's hammer will eventually crack a great rock in two. The disruptions happen about every week or so, and many inhabitants will not leave until they are certain a big disruption will hit. For game purposes, consider the next disruption as having a 01-33% chance of splitting he world in half. Increase that chance by 2% for every week thereafter. Eventually, the world *will* break in half.

Nnyylld: Time has always been a bit unstable around this world, and a large force of Splugorth soldiers and scientists are trying to trigger a chronal distortion that will launch them far enough back in time so they might rewrite their terrible history, creating a win at the Battle of Zaladast and making sure the Kingdom's fortunes rose after that last war, not fell.

Threshold Gene-Tech

By Kevin Siembieda

Population: There are less than 2000 Gene-Tech in the Anvil Galaxy, and perhaps fewer than 10,000 throughout the Megaverse. The reasons for such low numbers remain a mystery, but leading theories suggest that either ancient space faring civilizations tried to wipe them out or that the Gene-Tech fell prey to a "designer virus" created to wipe them out. (As the story goes, the virus was created by one of their own, but nobody knows if this tale is true or not.) Since their near (self-inflicted?) genocide, they have sworn off microbe engineering and stick exclusively to modifying carbon-based hu-

manoids. Despite their low numbers, Gene-Tech still have a forceful presence in the Anvil Galaxy both as independent groups of mad scientists and, here in the Threshold, with armies of genetically altered warriors (total numbers estimated at nearly 300 million) mostly stored in enormous stasis lockers hidden throughout the Threshold.

Demographics: Monster X (10%), Cyborgs (20%), Warhounds (20%), Shapechangers (20%), Super-powered Beings (25%), Willing Slaves and fanatical Worshipers (5%; various races, most are not augmented or mutated). Roughly 900 Threshold Gene-Tech are responsible for this.

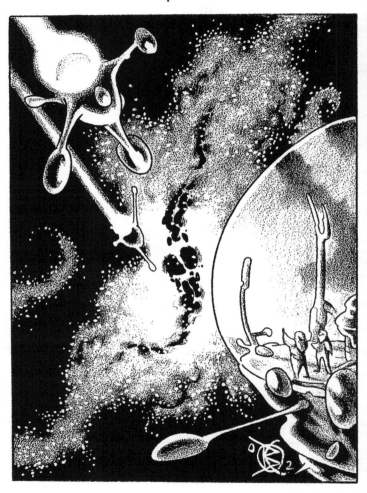

Overview: The Threshold Gene-Tech are typically referred to as "Gene-Threshers" or just "Threshers," to differentiate between them and the arguably more benign Gene-Tech gathered in small groups throughout the rest of the Three Galaxies and the universe (see the Aliens section earlier in this book for details). These mysterious geneticists are active throughout the Three Galaxies, but for reasons unknown, especially in the Anvil Galaxy. They have mastered the sciences of genetics and gene-engineering, surpassing even the Trans-Galactic Empire (a leader in genetic technology) and the Splugorth, and are easily on par with the near mythical and malevolent Gene-Splicers. In fact, the Gene-Tech's abilities to create and remake living beings is only matched by the magic of some of the most powerful ancient gods!

Many legends have grown around these strange "mad doctors." Some fanatics think that they are The First, newly returned to remake their children in their image. Some "believers" actually worship Gene-Tech and seek to serve them in any and every way possible. Only the Gene-Threshers usually take these fanatics up on their offer, and some even volunteer to be transformed and enslaved by the Threshers. Most other Gene-Tech find these deluded souls to be an annoyance. Fortunately, these are far and few between. On the other hand, some ancient writings suggest that the Gene-Tech might be related to, or descended from, "The One" (He who tried to pervert the Cosmic Forge untold millennia ago). Others mention a race of beings from another dimension who tried to use the creatures of the Three Galaxies as their playthings (as indeed the Gene-Tech do), and who were expelled or destroyed by the early Cosmo-Knights. The truth may be any or none of these.

One of the rumors popular among *non-humans* is that the entire human race is the creation of the Gene-Tech and that humans were merely dumb animals snatched out of the jungle by superior aliens, had a few choice genes rearranged to change and advance their evolution, and then let loose to see what happens. Now the aliens (the Gene-Tech, naturally) have returned to examine their handiwork, and perhaps to activate a certain command locked away in their subjects' genetic code that with a word, will make them all willing slaves of those who created them. Such rumors have caused entire civilizations to fear humans in this context. What if the stories were true? What if the Gene-Tech could simply hijack all of humanity with a single command? The consequences of such a thing are too horrible to consider. Of course, what makes this easier to deal with is that similar rumors float around connecting the Gene-Tech to every other race in the Three Galaxy, especially if they possess some special superhuman ability. These "puppet master" theories about the Gene-Tech taking are just stories designed to either scare people for fun or to besmirch the reputation of a particular race, often reflecting racial prejudice. Some, like the paranoid Golgans, actually wonder, though, and worry. Finding little comfort in the notion that if the Gene-Tech had this power, why haven't they used it to overrun and takeover the Three Galaxies? Perhaps they are just waiting for the right moment?

Gene-Tech normally operate in small groups of a dozen or less, usually only 1-4, and they travel in cruiser-sized starships. These vessels don't have the firepower of most war vessels in the Three Galaxies, but they can outrun all but the fastest known ships, and can travel galactic distances at incredible speeds using a warp-space system not yet developed by known civilizations. Their stealth systems also make them almost undetectable as well, so these villains can operate with relative impunity. They greatly fear Cosmo-Knights, Phase Adepts from Phase World, Second Stage Prometheans and beings of power such as gods, adult dragons and demon lords. In fact, they tend to avoid planets strong with magic as well as people who wield magic. At the same time they are fascinated by powerful beings, especially superhumans, godlings and supernatural creatures, and wish to map their genetic structures, perhaps out of some mad bid for power. It could be that these villains are so insane that they truly believe if they could master how to play with a dragon or god's genetic code, they could make themselves to be even more powerful than they. Actually, the most popular rumor contends they hope to learn how to make, and in so doing, enslave and command gods – raising the question, who is truly a god, the godlings or the ones who "make and command the gods?" It is a frightening and insane ambition, but one that

seems to fit the twisted psyche of the *Gene-Threshers* if not all Gene-Tech. The very fact that anyone could believe this could even be a real goal illustrates just how powerful, insane and dangerous the Gene-Tech really are.

Redrawing the Genetic Blueprint

Through genetic reconstruction, the Gene-Tech are able to move the building blocks of life around to make a completely new and different structure! They can do little things like change the color of an individual's eyes, hair or skin, grow new hair (by removing/fixing the gene for baldness), make the nose or ears smaller or larger, rounded or pointed, even add inches to one's height, take 20 years off one's appearance and eliminate genetic weaknesses in the body that might cause crippling disease. To these maniacal aliens, such advances are mere child's play.

Genetic changes can be an improvement or a disaster. The cruel aliens are just as likely to knock the building blocks apart or rearrange them to create monstrous structures. Frequently, they subject other life forms to strange and terrible things just because they can or for the purpose of scientific research – but then the Gene-Tech do almost everything, good and evil, in the name of science. Many Gene-Tech are sadistic and enjoy inflicting and studying physical and mental pain and trauma.

The entire record of evolution is recorded on each DNA molecule and the Gene-Tech know how to both read and rearrange the DNA codes on a molecular level. Thus, they can turn back the passage of time and explore every step of a creature's evolution, and rearrange the building blocks to explore evolutionary paths never taken. Along these lines, the Gene-Tech can reshape an individual to almost anything and instil their subjects with superhuman to animalistic powers and abilities. Whether there is any rhyme or reason to their insane creations, experiments and acts of torture is unknown (there doesn't seem to be any). They claim all they do is in the name of science, and many presume there is some secret agenda, but what it may be is unknown. The fact that the nefarious *Gene-Splicers* conduct similar experiments and exhibit the same callousness have suggested to some that these two races of mad scientist are locked in some sort of vile competition or seek the same answers to the same questions, though no one knows what they may be. With the rampant quest for the Cosmic Forge, some believe the Gene-Tech seek the location of the Cosmic Forge by searching for biological evidence and clues locked within all living creatures in the Three Galaxies. After all, the Cosmic Forge was used to create life long before it was used to destroy it.

Gene-Tech seem particularly fascinated by human beings and other carbon life forms, and spend a great deal of time experimenting on them. They often abduct or lure a subject into their clutches, work their scientific magic on them and release them. Sometimes the subject of experimentation is part of a long term study in which the individual is secretly observed, periodically recaptured, subjected to genetic adjustments or analysis, and released again. Just as frequently, test subjects are transformed and released never to be bothered by a Gene-Tech again.

The Threshers

The Threshold Gene-Tech are breaking all the normally accepted rules of Gene-Tech behavior. First, there are an estimated 900 of them working together. In some ways this is a bit misleading as the 900 Threshers are typically broken down into smaller groups of 6-30 working apart from most of the other groups. However, they do seem to be working toward the same cause: to create an army of super-powerful life forms. Not just lone individuals for the purpose of study or some twisted experiment, but have shifted their focus from random experimentation to mass production. Apparently, they have hit upon a few genetic "designs" they are very fond of, and have begun producing huge numbers of these creatures, but for what purpose no one can say.

Many claim they are creating and selling entire armies of pre-made genetic soldiers genetically programmed to loyally serve whomever they are sold to via an imprint mechanism that is burnt into the soldiers psyche the moment they awake from status and cast their eyes upon their superiors. (Not unlike a hatchling duck "imprinting" with the first living thing it sees believing it to be its "mother"whether it is actually the parent or something quite different). If so, the Threshers could be on the verge of creating an entirely new and terrible military market: Slave Soldiers completely loyal and willing to die for their leader/master/owner . Super powerful ones at that. This could change the entire balance of power, giving whomever who could afford to buy them, a decided edge in any conflict. Not to mention it gives the Gene-Threshers power because they ultimately chose whom to sell to and therefore help, bring into power or destroy. For example, selling millions of soldiers to the TGE could guarantee they could conquer the CCW, and vice versa. An interplanetary power could turn to the Threshers in a mad bid to destroy an enemy, conquer a world or extract bloody vengeance. This does not even being to take into account the *moral* ramifications of creating intelligent life for the sole purpose of combat, in effect creating a disposable army. Then, the Gene-Tech have never encumbered themselves with questions of morality, ethics or right and wrong.

Of course, nobody knows if this is what the Threshers have accomplished and plan to do, or not. Yes, it would explain why they have uncharacteristically banded together, and why so many millions of these mass produced life forms are locked in stasis, but it seems so unlike the Gene-Tech. These genetic engineers have never been interested in personal gain before, nor in the slave trade or mass market commerce. It *is* out of character. The main reason people have jumped to the conclusion that the Thresher are creating armies of super-soldiers for sale is because they sold one million to one of the Splugorth Kingdoms to quell an uprising. However, this has been the only sale and, knowing the Gene-Tech, it could have been nothing more than a "field test" or a game to frighten people and get a reaction.

For all anyone knows, they intend to create a super-army of their own, though that still leaves the question of *why?* To what end? Do they plan to conquer the Anvil Galaxy or one of the other Three Galaxies? Are they throwing in with one of the intergalactic powers? Are they preparing for an alien invasion from the Core? What do they know that the rest of the galactic community doesn't? Could they have the Cosmic Forge and have created an army to keep it? (Would they need such an army if they had the Forge?) More likely, they think they know where the Cosmic Forge is and are creating a giant army to seize it. Then again, the Gene-Tech have never shown much interest in acquiring the Cosmic Forge. Could it be they want to make

certain no one else does? Or will acquiring the Cosmic Forge enable them to become the all-powerful gods they have always dreamt of becoming, enabling them to remake the universe in their own twisted image? That's the problem with these mysterious beings, no one knows what's going through their minds or why they do anything.

Foreign Affairs

The Cosmo-Knights know the stories suggesting the Gene-Tech may be related to The First or The One are false, but they do not dispute that the Gene-Tech, particularly the Threshers, are one of the greatest threats to the Three Galaxies. Cosmo-Knights make it their business to keep an eye on these weird aliens and frequently interceded on the behalf of innocent victims in the Gene-Tech's clutches as well as spoiling Gen-Tech plots and machinations. The heroic Cosmo-Knights are at a loss as to what the Threshers may be up to, but they know it can't be anything good. A dozen are keeping a close watch on the situation and would dearly love to infiltrate the complex to learn more, but except for themselves and their creations, the Threshers' space complex is closed to outsiders. Breaching one of the "Cage" stations confirms that the Threshers have in stasis millions of warriors in cold storage.

Everyone else in the Anvil Galaxy. Most planets, systems and interstellar alliances in the Three Galaxies tolerate and put up with Gene-Tech, but only a few welcome or invite them. Some outlaw the aliens and either chase away or destroy them whenever Gene-Tech make their presence known. Inevitably, the appearance of a Gene-Tech individual or small group means trouble on some scale. Ultimately, the aliens are just too secretive, aloof, weird and spooky to make many friends in the intergalactic community (not that they seem to be looking for any). Thus, the Gene-Tech are the eternal outsiders ever floating around the fringe.

The Thresher's orbital complex and genetic army in the Threshold were only discovered recently, two years ago, by the Cosmo-Knights. Nobody knows what to make of it and all are worried, even the Splugorth and TGE who immediately consider ways how they might exploit and benefit from the situation, especially if the rumors are true about them creating super-armies for sale. The Golgan Republik is positively freaked out and have a thousand conspiracy theories on the unnerving discovery.

Worlds of Interest

Genesis Factory: This is the Gene-Threshers' base of operation. A giant, two-piece space station with an outer ring and a sphere suspended in the center. It is without question the Three Galaxies largest genetics engineering laboratory. A full half of the moon-sized facility is devoted to the creation, cloning, growing and conditioning of the Threshers' super-soldiers. A quarter is life support and infrastructure, and 22% is for manufacturing and maintenance. Only 3% is devoted to living space, laboratories and new research.

The Cage #1-7: Another gigantic space station type construct that is effectively the size of an artificial world or massive space station, only these are massive storage facilities that hold their mutant armies in stasis until . . . . whatever. Cage #7 is still under construction and yet to be "stocked." Cage #1-5 are filled and Cage #6 is at 81% capacity.

Worshipers and willing slaves are gathered in star ships and makeshift space stations all strung together to create something of a floating junkyard or parking lot floating in space. The Gene-Tech will not let them on the Genesis Factory or Cage Stations, so they gather in whatever they came in to be near the ones they have deemed to be gods. They beg the Gene-Threshers to utilize them to help or serve them in any way. The Gene-Threshers sometimes use them as pawns in genetic experiments and sometimes have them run errands for them or to do things for them like spying, information gathering and creating a diversion. However, these slaves and fanatical worshipers are always kept in the dark as to their masters' real plans and know nothing about the goings on in the Threshold or anything about the Gene-Tech or the Factory.

Gene-Splicing by the Gene-Tech

When one looks at all the myriad possibilities, there are millions of variations that can be explored! Add in gene-splicing, and the blending of one completely different life form with another, and the possibilities are virtually endless.

Gene-splicing is used to alter the genetic structure of one creature by combining it with several traits from two or three completely different aliens, monsters or animals. The "splicing" process allows the aliens to bond different animal parts into one monstrosity. Genetic reconstruction of the DNA code means there is no risk of the body rejecting any of its new parts or traits. The results can be staggering, combining incongruous and normally incompatible elements that defy natural evolution.

One of the frightening things about these genetic modifications its that because they are done on the most fundamental genetic level, frequently they can be passed on to offspring. Of course, the Gene-Tech usually control whether or not such "improvements" or "new variables" are hereditary or not. They can make a creation compatible or incompatible with his own (original) species or compatible or not with other creations like himself. Unfortunately for the victims of many genetic experiments, they are one-of-a-kind creations and completely alien.

The following are just a few notable traits/changes that the Gene-Tech can instill on humans and most other carbon life forms. While their genetic manipulation can produce an infinite variety of results, each alien race, monster or animal can only accommodate a certain range of changes. The following genetic modifications are those discovered by the Gene-Tech to work on 99% of all creatures encountered in the Anvil Galaxy (including many plants!). There are literally thousands of other modifications the Gene-Tech are capable of, providing their test subject has the right genetic make-up.

Note: Game Masters looking to craft a huge list of potential Gene-Tech modifications, check out the super abilities section of the **Heroes Unlimited, 2nd Ed. RPG** as well as the mutant and bionics sections. As for a wide range of animal mutants and animal powers you have to take a look at the **After the Bomb RPG**, with over a hundred different mutant animals. That having been said, we encourage G.M.s to use their imaginations and whip up their own genetic soup of mutants and super beings. Remember, Gene-Tech, Threshers included, may also combine bionics and cybernetics with their mutant creations.

Standard Genetic Modifications

Monster X: See the complete description in the Alien section of this book. Most (99%) Monster X are exclusively used by the Gene-Tech and never sold or traded away.

Cyborg soldiers: Typically partial cyborgs with one or two weapon arms and/or optics and sensors (occasionally built-in or detachable jet packs, bionic wings, modular weapons arms, bionic tentacles or extra pair of arms, bionic legs or machine lower body, lungs, etc.) built into a living humanoid genetically altered to better accept and compliment the artificial augmentation. Typically the bionic "elements" serve a specific function that goes hand in hand with a physical attribute, ability or power, including great physical endurance and Mega-Damage body (seldom more than 3D6x10+ 90).

Warhounds: Are humanoid soldiers that are built from predatory animals or given predatory instincts and abilities, often animal-like or feral. Typically S.D.C. creatures who require body armor or modest Mega-Damage beings (2D4x10 +P.E. attribute number in M.D.C. plus an additional 1D6 M.D.C. per level of experience). Warhounds often have a canine or wolfish appearance. Likes the taste of blood and likes to eat raw meat, may be a cannibal (01-50% chance).

Common Abilities (in addition to attribute and skill bonuses): +1 attack per melee round, +1D4 on initiative, +1D4 to strike, +1 to parry and dodge, +2 to disarm, +3 to pull punch, +2 to roll with punch, fall or impact, +1D6 to save vs Horror Factor, fatigues at one quarter the rate of humans and heals twice as fast, has perfect vision, keen sense of hearing and smell (which contribute to some of these bonuses).

Natural Weapons: Fangs for biting (typically does 3D6 S.D.C. damage), claws that may be retractable (typically does 3D6 S.D.C. damage plus P.S. damage bonus, or just does an extra 1D6 or 2D6 M.D. if also has Supernatural P.S.). May also have a prehensile tail or feet that can be used as an extra limb and/or weapon. May also have horns or antlers (typically capable of doing 2D6 or 3D6 points of damage).

Special abilities (pick three): Superhuman P.S. (robotic equivalent), Supernatural P.S. (counts as two choices), leaping (can leap three times his height in length and width), climbing (98% skill equivalent), swim (95% skill equivalent, plus can hold breath for 1D6+6 minutes), track by smell (60% +2% per level of experience, +10% to follow blood scent or other very strong scent), or prowl (75% skill equivalent). 10% may have one or two Minor Super Abilities from the *Heroes Unlimited™* RPG. See the *"Revised" Rifts® Conversion Book One* for **Rifts®** conversions.

Skills: Basic combat training including Hand to Hand: Expert or Martial Arts, 1D4+1 Weapon Proficiencies, Radio Basic, Military Etiquette, Land Navigation, Running or Body Building and 1D4 other very basic skills appropriate for a warrior. Most Warhounds are illiterate and don't know math or how to drive a vehicle.

Thresher Shapechangers: Typically an S.D.C. being with the power to transform into a different shape and form. This can be essentially a metamorphosis into any *humanoid* creature like a Changeling or one of the *Heroes Unlimited™ RPG* "Alter Physical Structure"(any) super abilities. See the *"Revised" Rifts® Conversion Book One* for Mega-Damage conversion for these and other powers (and lots of other useful stuff).

Thresher Super-Powered Beings: Typically a Mega-Damage humanoid with 5D6x10 M.D.C. +P.E. attribute number. Most are "space capable" meaning they are impervious to cold, can breathe without air for at least an hour at a time (some indefinitely), fly (Flight Wingless, 200 mph/321 speed), and one Minor or Major Super Ability of choice, typically a type of Energy Explusion – no Control Elemental Force power, nor Karmic Power or Lycanthropy. See the *Heroes Unlimited™ RPG* for complete description of super abilities (some conversion may be necessary). Also see the *"Revised" Rifts® Conversion Book One* for Mega-Damage conversion for many of powers from *Heroes Unlimited™* and lots of other useful stuff.

Other types of mutants & powers

The following are other types of powers and abilities commonly available from Gene-Tech.

- Reduce aging. Doubles the average life expectancy and the character always looks reasonably youthful.
- Stop aging. Actually the aging process is so dramatically reduced that he seems to have stopped aging entirely. Add 2D6 x 100 years to the character's normal life expectancy.
- Increase a creature's height and weight by as much as 100% or reduce it by as much as 50%.
- Increase human intelligence up to 30 but roll for one random insanity.
- Increase human aggression: +3 on initiative, +3 to strike and parry, +2 to save vs horror factor, +4D6 S.D.C.; tends to be hyper, short tempered, suspicious of others, competitive, loves combat and physical contests. Level of concentration is reduced; - 10% on skill performance and may have trouble sleeping.
- Add 2D4 psionic powers from any of the three lesser categories to minor psionics and double l.S.P.; add 3D4 psionic powers from any of the three lesser categories or four Super Psi-power to Major Psionics and double l.S.P.; or give ALL psionic powers of the Mind Melter or Mind Bleeders, and double l.S.P.
- Double the I.S.P., range and damage of a Burster's powers. Create the genetic equivalent of the following O.C.C.s: Burster, dog boy, crazy or juicer without artificial implants or drugs.
- Add one to four arms, tail (prehensile or not), wings and the capability to fly (may mean hollow bones and different size), horns, and others. Can also change physical features.
- Mega-Conversion! The test subject has been transformed into a light Mega-Damage creature To determine M.D.C., add together the test subjects hit points and S.D.C. And add 1D4x10. This goes up by 10 M.D.C. Per additional level of experience. 50% of the time, this transformation will also give the test subject supernatural P.S. (Although this P.S. Score will not increase).

Game Master Notes: How to use a Gene-Tech

One might think of Gene-Tech as a custom-design Monsters Factory as well as a reoccurring villain and story device. Using them as a story element, the Game Master can devise "one-of-a-kind" aliens, mutants and monsters, creating alternatives to the beings who populate the Three Galaxies. This can be useful in keeping players on their toes and guessing when an *unknown alien or monster* steps around the corner. Or they can be thrown for a curve when a familiar looking alien demonstrates some unusual power or ability.

The Gene-Tech is definitely restricted to *non-player characters* (NPCs). As arch-villains, they offer virtually limitless possibilities. BEWARE! Going crazy with the possibilities can unbalance your game or turn it into a monster-fest. Neither is desirable. To best use these characters, consider the following tips:

1. Gene-Tech should be used sparingly and in ways that are twisted, evil and dangerous. They are not benevolent beings, so they aren't going to create superhumans for the betterment of mankind and often have an ulterior motive, even if it is just to cause trouble or extract revenge. Nor are they likely to save a brilliant leader or hero from old age, disease or injury unless there's something in it for them, and the end result will always come with something negative – some cursed aspect, deformity or foul side-effect.

2. Not all monsters are ugly or alien looking. Evil is a state of mind and a way of life.

3. They have a twisted sense of amusement, humor and art, often turning heroes into grotesque monsters and monsters into beautiful or at least more attractive looking beings.

4. The creations of Gene-Tech monsters can be responsible for random acts of violence and intervention that could have little, medium level or great consequences to a particular person, place or event.

5. A Gene-Tech creation could become a major hero, misunderstood villain, an arch-villain, predator, slave, minion or just about anything. Whether or not a genetically reconstructed character is available as a player characters (and what his powers and penalties may be) is left entirely to the discretion of the Game Master.

6. Always think about the creations you allow in the game either as NPCs or player characters.

7. Gene-Tech can also make clones, duplicating perfectly any individual, even themselves. It is rumored that every Gene-Tech keeps several backup copies of themselves hidden away and attuned to the original person's brain waves. Then the brain signal from the original ceases, the nearest clone comes online and picks up where the original left off.

8. People can't usually tell the difference between a Gene-Tech "work of art" and an alien from another world.

9. Don't bee too vicious. Show some compassion.

10. Monsters and mutants created from the Three Galaxies don't have to adapt to a strange new environment. They already know the lay of the land and should be able to understand the languages, existing technology, laws, customs, routines, and so on, of the region. This strange familiarity can add to the mystery, suspense and tragedy of encounters with such beings.

Some Limitations

1. There are not many Gene-Tech throughout the Megaverse, let alone the Anvil Galaxy. At present, there are probably less than 1000 in the entire galaxy, and only a few times more throughout the Three Galaxies at large. Why there are so few of these creatures is a mystery, but not one most people are willing to question. For them, it is fortunate there are not more of these evil beings, so whatever has made them so scarce is something to be thankful for.

2. Although they can alter and evolve animals they usually spend most of their energy mutating humanoids and other intelligent life forms. One can only presume that the aliens get greater sadistic pleasure transforming creatures who will understand what horrors have befallen them and what their future may hold.

3. Remember, Gene-Tech are evil and they are motivated by cruelty and evil. They like to inflict misery on others through genetic reconstruction. They will seldom do anything to help anybody.

4. The creations of Gene-Tech are usually monstrous or deliberately flawed in some way. Remember, the majority are nothing more than genetic experiments. Like all experiments, some are more successful than others.

5. It takes 3D4 weeks to perform major genetic reconstruction, sometimes longer. However, simple genetic grafts, splicing and minor alterations can be accomplished in 6D6 hours, so can most bionic procedures.

6. Gene-Tech can quickly become hated and hunted monsters themselves. Many communities will try to find and destroy them, or at least chase them away. Indeed, the CCW, UWW and most Independent Worlds consider the aliens to be a plague that needs to be confronted wherever and whenever they rear their ugly heads.

7. Gene-Tech NEVER share their secrets! The TGE (and others) would pay or do just about anything to possess even a fraction of the Gene-Tech' knowledge of genetic reconstruction, but it will NEVER happen.

8. At least one third of their creations include cybernetic and bionic augmentation.

9. Energy beings, alien intelligences, androids, and most, true supernatural beings and creatures of magic cannot be genetically altered.

10. Lost limbs cannot (as a rule) be genetically regrown. However, new limbs of all kinds can be attached onto an individual from other creatures or clones.

The Core

To the inhabitants of the Halo section of the Anvil Galaxy, the Core is a region of nearly total mystery. Very few spacers ever make it there despite some heroic efforts, and even UWW operatives who can travel to the Core instantly by magic have done little exploration and even less diplomacy with the dazzling array of alien races living there.

What little is known about the Core is that it is a dense star field rich with worlds and rich with life. However, these worlds are totally incompatible with those of the Halo, so there is virtually no carbon-based life to be found. Any creatures in the Core are either of a totally different elemental strain (silicon-based, hydrogen-based, etc.) or they are carbon aliens who have somehow figured out the means to endure their strange and hostile environment.

The Core is commonly believed to be the resting place of the *Cosmic Forge*, but even if that were definitely the case (it may not be – the Cosmic Forge's location is not known by *anyone*), combing the Core for it would be no easy feat. It is still around three thousand light-years across, and the number of worlds and stars it contains is much denser than what might be found in the Halo. In terms of ground to cover, the Core is at least as "large" as the Halo, if not more so. Any search for the Cosmic Forge will be an extremely long and exhaustive process unless the searchers enlist the aid of local help, or if they somehow are attuned with the Cosmic Forge itself and use that to home in on it, or are just plain lucky.

Despite the ongoing efforts to learn more about the Core, it still remains a mystery, even to the Anvil Galaxy's top scientists, explorers, mystics and Cosmo-Knights. But as long as such a mystery exists, there will be people willing to risk their lives to explore it. One thing that might help facilitate the exploration of the Core is the army of Cosmo-Knights assembling on the Halo's border with the Threshold. For reasons they are not discussing with anyone outside of their order, the Cosmo-Knights are preparing an assault on the Threshold itself, perhaps to eliminate whatever it is that has been making it so tough for spaceships to cross it. If the Cosmo-Knights are successful in this regard (and they might very well be), then the Core shall be much more open to exploration, and the peoples of the Halo and the Core can meet and interact like never before. Who knows? Maybe this will bring about a new golden age for the Anvil Galaxy, with joint discovery and sharing of the Cosmic Forge to the mutual benefit of all! Or perhaps it is a colossal disaster waiting to happen as so many incompatible aliens get thrown in the mix together and learn that not only do they not understand each other, they do not trust each other, and they can not abide the other's presence. A kind of hatred that only leads to war.

Note: Since much of the Core remains a mystery, it will only receive a brief overview in this book. However, keep your eyes peeled for the upcoming **Cosmo-Knights** sourcebook, which will not only reveal more secrets about the Cosmo-Knights, but it will uncover much more about the Core of the Anvil Galaxy, the many exotic alien civilizations therein, and the impending Cosmo-Knight invasion which might push the Forge War to a whole new level.

The Powers That Be

Strangely enough, the alien races living in the Core seem to not be interested in the Cosmic Forge. From the very few contacts Halo explorers have had with Core aliens (mostly the *Xodian Collective* and the *K!ozn Continuum*), the Cosmic Forge does not have the same cultural significance that it does in the rest of the Three Galaxies. It is almost as if the peoples of the Core have lived in isolation for so long that they have fallen out of touch with what the rest of the Three Galaxies think and want. Of course, the irony of this is that among the Three Galaxies, there is a lot more territory like the Core than like the Halo, and it is the Halo nations that are in the minority, not the strange races found in the Three Galaxies' interiors.

Knowing that, Halo explorers try to be diplomatic and easy-going when encountering Core aliens, but most of the time, death and destruction result. For many years, it was just thought that the Core aliens were savages or relentlessly hostile. Now, it appears that a large group of Fallen Cosmo-Knights, the **Omegan Order**, have set up shop in the Core. Surely they have the ability to destroy Halo ships whenever they find them. Hating the Cosmo-Knights as they do, and probably on the search for the Cosmic Forge themselves, it makes sense that they would want to suppress any search for the Forge that does not directly benefit them.

There is also the enigmatic and powerful **Xodian Collective**, which as far as anybody from the Halo can tell, is a super-powered race of humanoids who have virtually no technology because they rely solely on their incredible natural abilities. Not quite on par with Cosmo-Knights in terms of raw strength or power, the sheer number of Xodians makes them at least as formidable a force in the galaxy as the Cosmo-Knights and even certain small or medium-sized power blocs. The Xodians do not appear to be overtly hostile, but they have been responsible for the destruction of several exploration vessels that made it to the Core. Scientists believe that the Xodians are merely mistaking these exploration ships as war vessels and are only attacking to defend themselves. If the Halo can figure out a way to tell the Xodians the truth, an ally in the Core might be in the making.

Finally, there is the **K!ozn (COT-zin) Continuum**. These aloof, super-intelligent aliens were quietly working on evolving their race to its next, god-like step when the Forge War kicked up over in the Halo. Now, like somebody disturbed right before he goes to sleep by the racket of kids across the street, the K!ozn have angrily put off their planned evolutionary ascension and sent some of their *junior members* (along with members of the K!ozn's warrior races) into the Halo to see exactly what the heck is going on. This gives the K!ozn reason enough to wage war against the people of the Halo, to keep them from establishing a base in the Core and bringing their hated Forge War into their sector of space.

These are just three out of hundreds of major races living in the Core, any number of which could have a reason for preventing Halo ships from visiting. Some might be overtly hostile to anything from beyond the Threshold. Others might be afraid that the carbon life forms will seek to transform the Core worlds into worlds more suitable for carbon habitation. Some might have a religious devotion to the Cosmic Forge itself, and have taken it upon themselves to deny any and all who are unworthy of the Forge (read: everyone but them) from obtaining access to it. Some might view the Halo aliens as barely evolved creatures no more worthy of the Cosmic Forge than a bug would be worthy of the secrets of space travel. Some might hold a grudge from some terrible conflict between the Halo and the Core long ago. Some might just think that the Core is *their* sovereign territory and they will be damned if they let some grubby little carbon life forms invade it uninvited. The upshot of all this is that for the moment, nobody knows what is going on in the Core, or how it might play into the phenomena of the Threshold and the larger implications of all this with the Forge War and life outside the Core. Until somebody learns something more, it will remain a tantalizing but unexplored part of the Anvil Galaxy, its secrets safe for now.

Omegan Order

Population: One billion sentient beings (estimated; this number could be extremely higher than originally projected).

Demographics: Fewer than 1,000 Fallen Cosmo-Knights form the leadership of this dark society. Supplementing them are an undetermined number of renegade Invincible Guardsmen from the TGE, and other super-powered beings. The rest of the Order's sentients consist of races found only in the Core, nearly all of which are unknown to the various power blocs in the Halo.

Overview: The dark side of the otherwise heroic and noble Cosmo-Knights is the sinister Omegan Order, a counter-society originally created by "fallen" knights – those who were granted powers by the Cosmic Forge to mete out justice throughout the Three Galaxies, but who could not keep from abusing their remarkable gifts. These individuals tried to take over worlds outright, committed acts of mass murder and/or genocide, and other vile deeds of abuse and tyranny. The Cosmic Forge is always watching its charges, and those who break its laws are always punished. They lose all but a fraction of their former abilities, and they must live forever more with the nagging memories of what it once was like to command such incredible power only to be returned to a lowly state.

Most of the time, Fallen Cosmo-Knights wander the galaxy, bitter and alone. Some kill themselves, some go mad, some lose themselves to a life of drink (or worse). All in all, theirs is a tragic case, but once one falls from grace, they rarely have the strength and conviction to continue their evil deeds. They just slowly dwindle away, like an ancient and dying star.

A small cadre of fallen knights somehow maintained their drive and vision, even after losing their cosmic powers. They banded together and swore that one day they, and their brethren, would return to the Halo and wreak havoc on it. They would rule the galaxy with an iron fist. They would see the Cosmo-Knights driven before them. And they would control ultimate power by finding and enslaving the very Cosmic Forge that once spurned them.

Over the last few decades, a growing number of Fallen Cosmo-Knights, calling themselves the **Omegan Order**, have slowly recruited other fallen knights into their ranks, as well as huge legions of thieves, killers, pirates, mercenaries, and any other interstellar cut throat willing to join this army of darkness. After the first ten years, the order gained momentum, and now virtually every Fallen Cosmo-Knight in the Anvil Galaxy has hooked up with the Omegan Order, bringing with them whatever lowly minions they could find.

In a wildly unexpected move, the Omegans also managed to recruit several dozen disaffected *Invincible Guardsmen* from the TGE. These are super-powered warriors close to being on par with Cosmo-Knights but supposedly fanatical devotees of the Kreeghor Emperor. How could the Omegans have gotten to these, the most dedicated loyalists of the Trans-Galactic Empire? Some think that maybe the Invincible Guardsmen are not so fanatical after all, and that some are unhappy with how the Empire is being run and how they, in particular, are being treated. Others think that the Guardsmen are susceptible to good and evil just like anybody, and that those whose moral centers failed them turned to the Omegans. Still others suspect that there is a larger, more sinister force at work, something that is corrupting good Cosmo-Knights and loyal Invincible Guardsmen alike. This force would be responsible for the alarmingly high number of fallen knights (their numbers have tripled in the last twenty years alone) as well as the Invincible Guardsmen insurrections occurring here and there in the TGE. If such a force is at work, then the civilized peoples of the Anvil Galaxy have a major problem on their hands. What could be so strong that it could corrupt the soul of the galaxy's purest champions and soldiers? So far, there is no answer, and quite honestly, there are those who would rather not find one for fear of learning what the Anvil Galaxy might be up against.

Whatever is providing the Omegan Order with its energy – be it a supernatural mystery force or simply the natural gathering of some really bad people – the Omegan Order is a force that must be stopped and destroyed entirely. They are in the Core already. They are looking for the Cosmic Forge, and as far as anybody can tell, they may be the closest to finding it. After all, is not even a Fallen Cosmo-Knight somehow linked to the Cosmic Forge? Can't they feel its energies?

If the Omegan Order wins control of the Forge, certainly they will *lose* it shortly thereafter (the Cosmic Forge does not like being a tool of evil), but before then, the Omegans would surely do something unspeakable with it. (Like extinguish all of the stars in the Anvil Galaxy, render themselves invincible and immortal, or any of a number of other horrific plans.) Nobody really knows how close the Omegans might or might not be to the Cosmic Forge, but the thought of them seriously searching for it is enough to send shivers down a Cosmo-Knight's spine. For the sake of the Cosmic Forge, the Anvil Galaxy, and the entire Megaverse, the Omegan Order must be destroyed *immediately*. It is for this reason that many military analysts believe the Cosmo-Knights and their allies are lining up on the edge of the Threshold, preparing for a big jump into the breach. Maybe they have decided the Omegans have had their fun long enough, and that it is finally time for this ultimate battle to join.

Omegan Order Rumor Mill

1) The alien races of the Core are far more likely to work with the Omegan Order than with any power bloc of the Halo.

2) The Omegan Order has developed a super-weapon that will more than offset any extra power the Cosmo-Knights might possess.

3) All Cosmo-Knights are destined to become fallen knights someday, and when they do, the Omegan Order will be there to accept them.

4) There can only be a certain number of Cosmo-Knights and/or fallen knights in the universe at the same time. The Omegan order is slowly boxing out the possibility for there to be new Cosmo-Knights by providing a place where all the bad guys can live in peace. With every fallen knight who stays alive while a crusading Cosmo-Knight dies, the number of bad outweighing the good increases by just a little bit more. Could it be tipping the scales of good and evil on a cosmic level, at least in the Three Galaxies?

5) The Omegan Order maintains its headquarters in the heart of a rogue moon somewhere along the Core's edge. The moon has a huge engine on it so the Omegans may actually pilot it from place to place. It is a huge floating fortress that dwarfs any of the Dominator planetoid fortresses.

6) If the Omegan Order finds the Cosmic Forge, they will all get their original power back. Perhaps even greater power than before.

7) The Omegan Order has within its capability, the means to destroy either the CCW or the TGE in a single stroke. They have not used it because they cannot decide on which civilization to snuff out.

8) The *real* reason why technology has not really progressed in the Anvil Galaxy the past fifty years is because the insidious Omegan Order has conspired to make it so. They have done this so that the technologies *they* are developing – starships, artificial intelligence, armor and shielding, prototype phase components – are well ahead of anything the Halo can produce.

9) Every hundred years, up to six Omegans regain their full powers as Cosmo-Knights, only any villainy they conduct afterwards does not result in the revocation of their powers. It is like the Cosmic Force has mistakenly granted these foul knights parole and fully reinstated them without thinking about what they would actually do with their restored power.

10) The worlds controlled by the Omegan Order are the closest thing to Earth-like habitats in the Core. If anybody from the Halo wishes to make an extended exploration of the galaxy, they will need a good base of operations. The only worlds that fit that bill are in Omegan hands.

11) Supposedly, there is one Fallen Cosmo-Knight locked in something like an undead state. He was defeated long ago by true Cosmo-Knights, but he never truly died. Instead, his corrupted life force lives on. It is said that any true knight who touches this slain traitor to the cause will in turn be corrupted, too. This single, unknown villain knight is thought to be the root of all fallen knights, and if his body were destroyed, all fallen knights would break free of their villainous mind set, and might possibly regain their once-cherished cosmic power.

12) Threshold Gene-Tech have sold untold *millions* of genetically modified soldiers to the Omegans, who intend to use them as expendable troops if and when the Cosmo-Knights and their allies invade the Threshold and the Core.

Actually, conflicting rumors suggest the Gene-Threshers are in league with the Omegans and create their army for them, while others say the Gene-Threshers create their army to battle and destroy the Omegans, either because they are rivals or because the Threshers have joined forces with the good Cosmo-Knights. Who knows what the Threshers are up to, or whether it has anything at all to do with the Omegan Order?

13) The Omegan Order secretly receives help, intelligence and assistance from its network of spies, which has agents in very high places in the CCW, TGE, Naruni Enterprises, the Altess Dynasty, and the Golgan Republik.

14) There is not a single non-human among the fallen Cosmo-Knights. Could it be that only humans are capable of falling from grace once they have been given the powers of a Cosmo-Knight?

15) Any Fallen Cosmo-Knight who is captured will never yield any useful information. Most are mentally conditioned so that it is impossible for them to talk about certain topics (secrets). Others have miniature nuclear or fusion bombs surgically implanted in their bodies and slaved to their heartbeat. The moment their heart stops, the bomb goes off.

16) Small strike teams of fallen Cosmo-Knights keep hitting the same 20 or 30 worlds in the CCW and the TGE. Investigators have been able to put no link between these worlds, and are at a loss for the fallen knights' motivations.

17) The Omegan Order is composed of secret followers of the *Tenth Heresy*, an unknown Heresy regarding the location of the Cosmic Forge and how to get it.

18) The Omegans already have found the Forge – only to discover that its power burned out long ago. There is nothing more to search for.

19) There has been a coup d'etat within the Omegan Order. Its leaders are dead, and a powerful faction within the Order wants to admit the Cosmo-Knights to their territory and clean house. The Cosmo-Knights must act quickly on this, lest the Omegan rebels lose their grip on power.

20) The Omegans already have the Cosmic Forge and with it, they have set into motion the chain of events that will *unmake* the Anvil Galaxy within the next ten years.

Xodian Collective

Population: Three trillion (unreliable estimate).

Demographics: Unknown.

Overview: At present there is an impressive body of rumor, speculation and hearsay that is circulating throughout the Halo regarding the Xodian Collective. Since the Xodians are seemingly involved in about 80% of the ship disappearances in the Threshold, the Halo power blocs have taken an acute interest in these aliens, even if they know next to nothing about them. The following is a breakdown of some of the most persistent nuggets of information about the Xodians. Some, all or none of them *may* be true. Until a scouting contingent from one of the Halo worlds makes meaningful contact with the Xodians and has a prolonged chance to converse with them and exchange information, the Xodians will remain just as mysterious as ever. Of course, the lack of knowledge about this race has not stopped the Halo's power blocs from all taking a stand on these creatures. The politicians and leaders of these major societies have all decided that they would rather take any stand regarding the Xodians – even if they abandon it later – than to take no stand at all. Taking a stand requires one to keep an eye on the Xodians and gather new information about them. All of them maintain at least a trace level of readiness if and when the Xodians swing into action. There is evidence that the Anvil Galaxy was invaded by the Xodians once before. It could always happen again.

136

Xodian Rumor Mill

1) The Xodian Collective is a collection of clone worlds where everybody is the same and the only thing separating one from the competition is your record of deeds. It is the ultimate meritocracy.

2) The Xodians are all tough customers, but when they pool their strength, they are invincible! Somehow, they can share the energies coursing within their bodies, creating an energy web capable of doing almost anything. This is how they have survived and remained independent, even now as the Forge War is heating up.

3) Xodians are notoriously neutral in all things. They do not like picking sides at all. Their involvement in the Threshold attacks is being done out of self-preservation. They believe they are under attack by the Halo ships for some reason.

4) Xodians are extremely long lived, but are unable to learn anything new or improve on what they already know or can do. The time for that comes during brief periods of intense activity once every few decades.

5) During their bursts of development, Xodians undergo a personality change and become independent, opinionated, and aligned. They adventure, carouse with others, and think for themselves for a while, strengthening themselves as much as possible. Then it ends and they return home to rejoin the Collective.

6) Xodians appear as giant-sized, armored humanoids, only their armor is really a kind of carapace that is resistant to all but the most powerful of weapons. A Xodian's carapace is grooved with intricate patterns of channels that all glow with energy whenever they prepare to use their powers.

7) There are four sub-species of Xodians – low-level grunt, a mid-level super-soldier, a high-level master planner, and a few ultra-powerful overlords who command the entire society, but are not above taking direct action in battles themselves.

8) The Xodians hate all carbon-based life because of a tenet in their religion or philosophy that brands carbon as the "element of sin."

9) A renegade fragment of the Collective was expelled long ago and it tried to colonize a portion of the Halo. It was destroyed after a long and costly war with the various power blocs in existence at that time.

10) The Xodians are a soldier race created specifically by the Cosmic Forge to protect it while it is in hiding. Xodian territory forms a big perimeter around the center of the galaxy, which obviously must be where the Forge is hidden.

11) Xodians are the "finished draft" of a super-race created by the Forge. The "rough draft" were the Cosmo-Knights, who lack the uniformity and incorruptibility of the Xodians.

12) The Xodians do not actually know of the Cosmic Forge's whereabouts, nor do they care. They are merely a huge society trying to expand its territory throughout the Core so they all have a place to live. The other Core aliens do not like the Xodians' relentless advance, and so they sow seeds of rumors about the Xodians being evil monsters in the Halo. They do this in the hopes that Halo power blocs will pick a fight with the Xodians, thus distracting them from their relentless pursuit of new living area.

13) The Xodians are really the dying remnants of the First! After the hiding of the Cosmic Forge and the near-obliteration of the race, they regressed to a primitive state and have stayed there ever since.

14) The Xodians have no use for technology, as they can fly through space and manipulate energy with their own natural abilities. They disdain anybody who must rely on machinery to survive, and by extension, feel that the entire Halo are nothing more than backward savages who should probably be wiped out for the betterment of the Anvil Galaxy.

15) The Xodians are a silent partner in the Cosmo-Knights' quest to bring peace and justice to the Anvil Galaxy. They are arranging to help bring the Cosmo-Knight invasion force across the Threshold so they may attack the Omegan Order in full strength.

16) Xodian "solos," those who have broken away from the Collective, are turning up in the Halo as independent adventurers, mercenaries and freebooters. Commanding remarkable power, they have no trouble finding jobs as super-soldiers in any of the galaxy's war zones.

17) The Xodians know of secret pathways and methods for crossing the Threshold safely. The Threshold is like a giant invisible maze made up of harmonic energies. Deviate from the safe courses through this maze, and suffer a harmonic disruption! This explains why so few ships make it through safely.

18) The Xodians are paranoid about Halo visitors learning too much about them, so they blank out the memory of visitors before teleporting them back to wherever they came from.

19) Each member of the Xodian Collective is himself a collective organism consisting of billions of intelligent, psychic microorganisms. These creatures come together and build a shared body out of pure psychic energy. This is what gives them their power.

20) Divergent thinkers from the Xodian planet of Nacene have introduced a dangerous and virulent concept into the Collective of the *Nacene Hierarchy*. It states that one's echelon should dictate one's position in society. For a society with no rank at all, this is a wild concept, and one that threatens to tear the Collective apart. Now, all Xodians are being forced to choose a side. Are they with the Nacene Hierarchy, or are they against it?

K!ozn Continuum

Population: Unknown.

Demographics: Unknown.

Overview: The K!ozn (pronounced "COT-zin") are a race of extraordinarily advanced and enlightened people who are on the verge of entering a new evolutionary phase, one in which they will transcend the mere physical and become god-like beings of pure energy. However, all of the ruckus in the Halo regarding the Forge War, and increasing numbers of visitors trying to cross the Threshold in search for the Cosmic Forge, has proven to be a great collective distraction to the K!ozn race. Until these conflicts are resolved, they will never be able to make their long-awaited Ascension. The K!ozn would much rather leave this turbulent galaxy far behind them, but for now they are still stuck here, and if they want to leave, they will have to either

help the searchers of the Cosmic Forge find what they are looking for, discourage them from looking any further, or destroy them outright.

The K!ozn must tread carefully, for if total war ignites over the Cosmic Forge, then the K!ozn can write off Ascension for at least another several centuries. However, there still is a chance that they might salvage their progress towards Ascension if this Forge situation can be controlled. Thus, the K!ozn are sending their most junior members to the Halo on a three-pronged mission to: 1) Gain intelligence on the origin, players, conditions, and likely outcomes of the Forge War, 2) Discern what it would take to bring about the most expedient end to the Forge War, and 3) Put plans in motion to bring about said expedient end. The Forge War must be stopped by any means necessary. That means if the K!ozn nuke an entire world to prevent the Forge War from flaring up in a particular sector, then that is perfectly fine by the K!ozn superiors.

It is assumed that K!ozn operatives in the Halo are keeping a very low profile, because none have ever been detected. Granted, there are a ton of different alien species in the Halo, many of which live on only one planet, so running into strange life forms is to be expected. In that regard, it is easy for a strange-looking alien to travel freely without gathering too much notice. However, the K!ozn are not carbon-based life forms. They are something else, and as such, they will be unable to handle *any* planetary environment in the Halo. While there are certain aliens who must wear full environmental protection at all times (the In'Valian Robo-Jockeys and the Lurgess are two good examples), such aliens are few and far between, making it all the more likely that somewhere, somehow, somebody will encounter a K!ozn. But that has not happened yet, leading some to wonder if maybe these aliens are just a figment of the galaxy's collective imagination.

K!ozn Rumor Mill

1) The K!ozn are remarkably humanoid in appearance for a non-carbon life form. They are tall, slender, have large heads, pointed ears, and purple skin. Their eyes are recessed deeply in their eye sockets, and they tend to wear long, flowing robes that conceal the features of their bodies.

2) Every K!ozn has a triple-lobed brain. At any given time, one of these lobes will be running as an independent brain, allowing the other two to rest. Every 8-10 hours, the K!ozn's primary lobe switches off and another switches on. This gives the K!ozn the ability to work non-stop without ever sleeping, but his personality will undergo minor changes as each lobe changes over.

3) The K!ozn do not even exist. They are the product of a Halo rumor mill that specializes in telling tall tales for the purpose of manipulating galactic events. The story of the K!ozn is to light a fire under the searchers for the Cosmic Forge. To make people in the Halo worried that some alien race in the Core is getting involved in the search and they might lose their chance to grab the Cosmic Forge if they do not take action quickly. With that kind of infectious incentive, the Forge War has begun and threatens to get even hotter still.

4) The K!ozn have not visited the Halo in force, but they do send a lot of FTL message pulses to the various power blocs looking for the Cosmic Forge. Usually, they are gloating messages decrying the search for the Forge as a fool's crusade, and an invitation to sure destruction. These messages also warn against any Halo ship trying to cross the Threshold, which is something they have been trying themselves to cross but without success.

5) Rather than risk members of their own race on dangerous missions, the K!ozn use members from one of a dozen different soldier races at their disposal. Many of these aliens live to die, and never really develop meaningful personalities.

6) The K!ozn do not really believe in the Cosmic Forge, but they do sense a great danger coming out of the Forge War, which is why they are trying so hard to direct the crisis from afar and from behind the scenes. They want to bring the war to an end, regardless of who thinks they have the Cosmic Forge.

7) The only reason why the K!ozn are so hellbent on Ascending is that when they do, each of them will have power comparable to that of the Cosmic Forge. They will become the rulers of the universe!

8) In one of the TGE's infamous Hellworld prisons, there is a K!ozn operative who knows everything that the K!ozn do. He can build their fabulous technology, he knows the truth behind the Forge mythos, he knows why ships can't cross the Threshold, everything. He is scheduled for execution tomorrow.

9) The K!ozn are masters of time travel, and the presence of chronal distortions throughout the Anvil Galaxy is just the wake of their own journeys through time. The K!ozn forbid themselves from changing the past, but they do jump into the future all the time to raid it for resources, technology, information, etc., and then they come back to their present, where they can use the stuff without fear of what might happen to the future time line (which may or may not happen anyway) that they took it from.

10) The K!ozn have mapped out every single star, planet, and sector of space in the Anvil Galaxy. For every moving object they have a trajectory course, and they even have a bead on 66% of all starships traveling through the galaxy, as well. It has taken them a thousand years to set up this monitoring network, but now that it is in place, there is no place in the galaxy they can not see.

11) According to K!ozn scientists, the center of the Anvil Galaxy is an enormous white hole, the reverse of a black hole. Entire star systems constantly spew forth from the hole, contributing to the Anvil Galaxy's gradual expansion across the Cosmos. One day, it shall grow large enough to incorporate the Corkscrew and Thundercloud Galaxies, forming a super-galaxy the likes of which the universe has never seen.

12) The K!ozn live in a Utopian supertech society where their every bit of machinery and technology is so radically advanced it makes the most cutting-edge Naruni prototypes look like a child's toy. They use super high-tech far beyond Naruni means.

13) The K!ozn know of Rifts Earth, have visited it a few times undetected, and have written it off as an unimportant backwater place of chaos. They find the Four Horsemen of the Apocalypse intriguing, however, and wonder what they might do once they lay waste to that world. Move on to other planets, perhaps?

14) Unbeknownst to the vast majority of people, the K!ozn were the secret power behind the building of Phase World. But the K!ozn no longer have any use for it, so they have set into motion a plan to destroy it.

15) The K!ozn were themselves created as a soldier race for an ancient master race. The K!ozn rebelled, killing their masters and seizing control of their own destinies. Now the K!ozn are waiting for their own slaves to kill them and complete the cycle, paving the way for the K!ozn's Ascension.

16) The K!ozn already control the Cosmic Forge and are merely toying with the people of the Halo by dropping clues here and there that make it seem like the Forge is still waiting to be discovered somewhere.

17) This race is composed of anti-matter and will explode with nuclear force the moment they come into contact with anything that is not anti-matter. They wear special containment suits so they can interact with other creatures, but one breach to these suits, and it's KA-BLAM!

18) For as long as there has been a CCW or a TGE, the K!ozn have been stealing their ships from interstellar space and storing them in a secret inter-dimensional pocket. The K!ozn have been especially ruthless about ship-grabbing in the Threshold, which is why so many ships disappear there. For what purpose the K!ozn are keeping these ships is unknown. Some think the K!ozn themselves are acting under mandate from an even higher power still.

19) The K!ozn and their many agents are the true champions of the Three Galaxies, and they are currently planning to launch a crusade that will rid the galaxy of all evil.

20) When the Cosmic Forge is eventually found, it shall be the K!ozn's job to destroy it. The K!ozn and the Forge are inextricably linked, as if they are two sides of the same force working throughout the universe. In this regard, the K!ozn are less of an alien species and more like an intelligent galactic phenomenon.

The World Builder's Toolbox

An essential part of space opera is exploring strange new worlds, and the **Phase World®** setting is no different. Even though this sourcebook details a large number of pre-made worlds, let's face it – part of the fun of running a campaign is creating things yourself! Making up worlds within the Anvil Galaxy (or any other outer space setting, really) can be a fun and immersive experience in which the creator can lavish as much detail on the planet as he or she wants, right down to the cultural intricacies of its inhabitants, fluctuations in local weather patterns, and so on. However, sometimes, one needs to whip up an alien world in just a few minutes, or one might be stuck for ideas. In either case, a *random generator* might do the trick. The series of random tables that follow just give the bare bones for creating an alien world. There are plenty of details left to the G.M., such as designing alien cultures, assigning monsters and animals, specific technologies, special magic, specific crises or ongoing dramas, etc. But, the World Builder's Toolbox should give you a good start. (**Note:** Because this book is an overview of the Anvil Galaxy, many of the worlds described elsewhere in this book could not include a lot of details about the actual planets themselves. They largely focus on their primary intelligent race, civilizations and ongoing crises or dramas. This set of tables, however, can be used to generate whatever details the G.M. feels one of his worlds might need.)

One more thing – astute Palladium fans might notice that the **Heroes Unlimited™ Galaxy Guide™** and **The Rifter® #18** also feature a random planet creation system. This section is not a reprint or expansion of those rules. It is merely *another way* of rolling up planets. The **Heroes Unlimited™** generator is designed to go hand in hand with that particular game's rules for creating Alien super heroes, but if you feel it might be fun to use for your **Anvil Galaxy™** or **Phase World®** campaign, be our guest. Heck, you can even combine the two (or three) systems if you want! The important thing is to have fun and explore the possibilities.

Solar System

These tables are just to give an overview of an entire solar system. If you only wish to create a *single planet*, please skip this section. Otherwise, just roll through it. When finished, there might be several different planets within the system. Roll through the rest of the generator for each world to get a full set of results.

Number of Stars

Like other galaxies, nearly half of all stars are part of a binary system. While this is not so unusual, some scientists contend that their arrangement within the galaxy is. Certain Anvil Galaxy researchers are mapping out the galaxy's entire stock of binary systems to see if those systems form any kind of special pattern. It is believed by these researchers that once the location of every binary system is known, the pattern of those systems will reveal the location of the Cosmic Forge. As a result, there

has been a recent rush of explorers trying to find binary systems and report the information back to the scientists willing to pay for such data. Needless to say, these mercenary explorers often are in tight competition with each other, and when running afoul of each other in deep space, vicious, dirty battles are the typical result as each side tries to prevent the other from stealing their payday.

01-50%: Solitaire. A single star in the center of the system. Most solar systems in the Anvil Galaxy are like this.

51-90%: Binary stars. The system is really a pair of solar system in tight formation. The planets of each star probably will not interlock their orbits, but sometimes that actually does happen. In such cases, the systems periodically "swap" the outermost planets of either system. Sometimes, this leads to planetary collisions that destroy both worlds and shower the rest of the solar system with deadly fragment.

91-97%: Trinary Stars. The solar system is actually a set of three stars. Like a binary system, only larger. These are really rare.

98-00%: Exotic Formation. The system might be a Quaternary System (four stars) or it might feature some other extremely unusual solar arrangement. Systems such as these are almost unheard of. When they are discovered, they become items of intense scientific interest, generating a kind of "gold rush" in which research vessels streak to the system so they might be the first to make a thorough examination of it. In such cases, the local civilizations of these systems sometimes do not know how to handle all of this sudden alien interest in their home, and troubles arise. These might range from mild cultural misunderstandings to all-out war.

Star Type

This is the *spectral class* of the star, or its basic type, size, diameter, and so on. In most space opera, this is more of a scientific detail that has no real importance on any of the dramas at hand. We include it here as something that might spark additional ideas for the worlds you are creating. An Earth-type world, for example, will turn out a lot differently orbiting a super-hot blue star than if it orbits a relatively mild yellow star (like our sun) or a cold white dwarf. There are no rules for these things; we are only offering them as fodder for your imagination.

01-05%: Blue Supergiant. These are blue stars with a surface temperature of over 25,000 Kelvin, which makes them the hottest standard star in the Anvil Galaxy. Blue super-giants stars have roughly 60 times the mass of a yellow dwarf (the Earth's Sun is a good example of a yellow star) and roughly 15 times the radius. They are almost 1.4 million times as bright as the Sun and they emit incredible amounts of radiation, rendering their solar system uninhabitable by the "standard" humanoid life forms that populate the Three Galaxies. Non-carbon life forms are known to live in blue supergiant star systems, however. Most times, they are dependent on the high levels of radiation they receive and therefore do not visit yellow, orange or red dwarf systems because the radiation drought might starve them.

06-10%: Blue Giant. These are blue stars with surface temperatures ranging from 11,000 to 25,000 K. They have 18 times more mass than the Sun, 7 times the radius, and are generally 2,000 times as bright. Though not as severe as a blue supergiant, blue giants are still pretty nasty for carbon life forms, and they are something to avoid, both because of their heat and radiation.

11-20%: Blue Sub-Giant. These are blue stars with surface temperatures ranging from 7,500 to 11,000 K. They have 3.2 times the Sun's mass, 2.5 times the radius, and are around 80 times as bright. Compared to their two "big brothers" mentioned above, blue sub-giants are the mildest of the purely blue stars. They are still dangerous to most forms of carbon life, and their systems are not eagerly sought for exploration or colonization. Interestingly, the closer one gets to the core of the Anvil Galaxy, the hotter and bluer the stars get, which explains why so many of the civilizations to be found are on the galactic edge, among the more yellow and red stars. Still, there are many civilizations to be discovered in the galaxy, living amid the hottest blue stars, strangely adapted to such environments.

21-35%: Blue Dwarf. These are blue-white stars with surface temperatures between 6,000 and 7,500 K. They have 1.7 times the mass of the Sun, roughly 1.3 times the radius, and are around six times as bright. For most carbon-based life forms, blue dwarves are on the upper edge of systems they are likely to inhabit. They are uncomfortably hot and bright, but they can be adapted to far more easily than the upper-class blue stars.

36-55%: Yellow Dwarf. These are white-yellow stars with surface temperatures between 5,000 and 6,000 K. The Sun is a yellow dwarf. Oddly enough, over 66% of the civilizations in the Anvil Galaxy are in systems with yellow dwarves. Most of the others inhabit systems with orange or red dwarves, described below.

56-75%: Orange Dwarf. These are orange-red stars with surface temperatures less than that of the Sun, only 3,500 to 5,000 K. They are also smaller than the Sun, having only 0.8 times the Sun's mass and 0.9 times the Sun's radius. They are also considerably less bright, having only 0.4 times the luminosity of the Sun. Orange dwarf systems are still fairly easy to inhabit, as evidenced time and time again by the many different communities on the outer edge of the Anvil Galaxy. While many aliens have evolved or adapted to live under orange dwarf conditions, many other species (including humans) find it difficult to exist here without some kind of assistance, be it a suit to keep warm, or genetic modification to compensate for the lower level of solar radiation. Orange dwarf-type aliens rarely have the same difficulties when visiting yellow dwarf systems, a fact that has always given "orange" aliens a bit of an edge in military campaigns, since they need not specially outfit their ships or personnel during raids or invasions of "yellow" territory.

76-00%: Red Dwarf. These are the most commonly encountered kind of star in the Anvil Galaxy. They are red stars with relatively cool surface temperatures (for a star, anyway) of under 3,500 Kelvin. They have only 0.3 times the mass of the Sun, 0.4 times the radius, and they are only 0.04 times as bright as the Sun. This makes them very faint. Aliens living under red dwarf conditions often find it impossible to tolerate living under anything brighter than a yellow dwarf unless they carry with them some kind of intense shielding; ranging from polarizing lenses to environmental exoskeletons that shield out all excess radiation.

Number of Planets

01-10%: Zero. But don't give up hope! There can always be artificial habitats (derelict spaceships, space stations, etc.) in the system. Or, some strange alien race might inhabit the sun itself. Ultimately, it is the G.M.'s call.

11-20%: One. Roll through the rest of the generator to see what features this world has.

21-30%: Two. Roll through the rest of the generator for each of the worlds in the system.

31-40%: Three. Roll through the rest of the generator for each of the worlds in the system.

41-50%: Four. Roll through the rest of the generator for each of the worlds in the system.

51-60%: Five. Roll through the rest of the generator for each of the worlds in the system.

61-70%: Six. Roll through the rest of the generator for each of the worlds in the system.

71-80%: Seven. Roll through the rest of the generator for each of the worlds in the system.

81-90%: Eight. Roll through the rest of the generator for each of the worlds in the system.

91-93%: Nine. Roll through the rest of the generator for each of the worlds in the system.

94-96%: Ten. Roll through the rest of the generator for each of the worlds in the system.

97-00%: Eleven or more. Roll through the rest of the generator for each of the worlds in the system. Chances are, all planets in this system will be fairly small because the planetary mass has been so spread out. Or, the system is simply gargantuan. G.M.'s call. Either way, solar systems in the Anvil Galaxy rarely have more than 15 worlds under any circumstances. Only three such systems are on record, and in each case, most of the worlds are merely large asteroids with nothing remarkable about them other than their high number.

Optional: When Stars Die

Stars, like organic life, grow old and die. They do so over incredible lengths of time, but they die all the same, and when they do so, they tend to have a massive effect on the planets that orbit them. For the purposes of running campaigns in the Anvil Galaxy, we offer the following tables for seeing if, a) the star of a randomly generated system is about to kick the bucket and, b) what it will do when it happens. This is not meant to be a strict science lesson. It is meant to be another source of ideas for adventures.

Imagine for a moment that the heroes are in a star system that is on the verge of turning into a red giant or going supernova. All of a sudden, life in the system becomes very dicey, doesn't it? Politics can turn upside down, military situations might be thrown on their head, local ley lines might surge uncontrollably, and all sorts of other turmoil could result. Likewise, a system whose star has become a brown or black dwarf might once have thrived with life, but now is a cold and dark place, home only to barren planets that are covered with the ruins of whatever civilizations once lived there. Such stellar graveyards could be fun places for explorers to poke through or opportunists to plunder for treasure and technology. Or, perhaps the system has been living under these conditions for a while now, and as a result, the societies there are really weird or bizarre, having adapted to life around a turbulent supergiant or a black hole in the making. The possibilities are endless, so throttle your imagination into overdrive and see what you come up with!

The life span of a star depends on its mass. Generally speaking, the more massive a star is, the shorter its life span. (This makes things a bit interesting in the core of the Anvil Galaxy, which has an awful lot of massive stars, most of which seem to teeter on the edge of their own demise – much to the concern of the alien civilizations living in those systems.) A yellow dwarf like the Sun has an estimated average life span of about 10 billion years, but a blue supergiant, for example, might only live for a few *million* years! Conversely, a red dwarf might live twice as long or longer than a yellow dwarf.

However long a star lives for, none of them are immortal. This is because all stars operate with a limited amount of fuel. The nuclear reactions that cause stars to burn will eventually deplete the star's internal fuel source. When that happens, the star enters its death cycle, and that is when some really cool things begin to go down. Some stars turn into brown or black dwarves. Some turn into neutron stars, and some turn into black holes. Whatever their fate, should you decide to incorporate a dying star into the system you are creating, be sure to exploit this unusual situation for all it is worth. Star death is a dramatic and unique occurrence. It is the perfect excuse to cut your imagination loose, so go for it!

If the G.M. wants to randomly determine if a star system is about to hit its death cycle, roll percentile dice. A roll of 01-02% means the star has begun its death cycle. To find out exactly where, roll on the appropriate table below. Chances are, these tables will radically alter the nature of the star, which is something the G.M. should consider regarding the planets in the system. The planets of a red giant system will be having a much hotter time than those of a planetary nebula or brown dwarf.

Small Stars

Yellow dwarves, orange dwarves and *red dwarves* all fall into this category. When stars of this size die, they first become *red giants*, then *planetary nebulae*, then *white dwarves*. Sometimes, when in their white dwarf phase, small stars will turn into *novas*. If not, they become *black dwarves*.

01-23%: Red Giant. Initially, stars burn their vast stockpiles of hydrogen as fuel. Well, they don't really "burn" hydrogen. They fuse hydrogen into helium. For roughly 99% of its lifetime, a star will burn hydrogen as its primary fuel. When the star eventually runs out of hydrogen, it begins burning helium. This changeover causes the star to expand to anywhere from 30 to 100 times its original size!

Despite this increase, the star's surface itself actually cools off somewhat (thereby becoming "red" and no longer yellow or orange). The star has now transformed into a *red giant*. When a star goes red giant, it poses a serious problem to the planets orbiting it. When the Earth's Sun goes red giant (in about five billion years, so don't worry), for example, it will completely engulf Mercury and Venus, and it will turn Earth into a great, big semi-molten slag pile. Mars' environment will heat up quite a bit, too. In other words, the entire environment of the solar system will be radically changed in a very short period of time. In the Anvil Galaxy, red giants in inhabited systems tend to create mass evacuations of the rest of the system. During these mad, panicked flights to safety, sometimes entire planetary infrastructures are left behind. Huge factories, industrial stockpiles, etc., all discarded for the sake of safety. Salvage operators generally view such places as great but risky targets, since much can be scrounged from them, but the original owners often return to pick up some of what they left behind. When these two forces butt heads, fireworks are sure to follow.

When red giants occur in uninhabited systems, they sometimes draw large numbers of visitors who are convinced the giant might be a manifestation of the Cosmic Forge. These visitors include pilgrims looking to worship the Forge, military ships looking to capture it, explorers seeking to study it, and adventurers looking to get involved in whatever trouble might arise. In the Anvil Galaxy, red giants do not last very long, only for about 1% of the star's previous life span (i.e., the time from the star's formation to when it turned into a red giant) before it exhausts the star's nuclear fuel and becomes a . . . .

24-46%: Planetary Nebula. Just as the star went through all of its hydrogen, the red giant will go through all of its helium, fusing it into carbon. For reasons too complicated to clutter up an RPG book with, small stars cannot burn carbon, so the core locks down. The nuclear fires of the star have no more fuel to burn, and the star itself condenses down to a diameter of only a few thousand miles/kilometers. However, the outer layers of the star that began expanding during the red giant phase will keep on expanding as a huge cloud of stellar gas, forming a *planetary nebula* (even though it really has nothing to do with planets).

In a game context, planetary nebulae are incredible resources to mine for raw materials. Advanced civilizations have made a practice of visiting planetary nebulae and scooping up all of that stellar material into huge *ram scoops*, where it is then compressed on a molecular level into solid elements. Those elements are then typically used as fuel, or in unusual situations, as building material or even as a form of monetary unit. Though it has remained largely unstudied, some scientists in the Three Galaxies are intensely interested in what happens to planets that are in the path of an expanding planetary nebula. Certain theories suggest that in some cases, the planetary nebulae from unusual stars have "coated" inhabited planets, effecting dramatic changes on the populace, ranging from freakish deformities, dramatic but inconsequential cosmetic changes (like a change in skin color), a major shortening or lengthening of individual life spans, the emergence of incredible super-powers, transformation into Mega-Beings, a total reversal of alignment, the development of magical or psionic powers, and other wild results. None of this has yet been proven, but there are plenty of scientists willing to give it a try.

47-69%: White Dwarf. After a star goes through the planetary nebula phase, it will have no nuclear fuel left, and it becomes a *white dwarf*. A faint reflection of its former self, the star is a fraction of its original size and is very cool. For billions of years, it will live out a twilight existence as it radiates the last of its heat into space. Though white dwarves are small and cold

(relative to other stars), they still give off considerable amounts of energy, and they tend to light up their surrounding planetary nebulae in a beautiful spectacle. Astronomers in the Anvil Galaxy often can spot white dwarves by sighting their surrounding planetary nebulae first.

White dwarves are also of interest to Anvil Galaxy scientists because they are so incredibly dense. Were the Earth's Sun to turn into a white dwarf, for example, a single teaspoon of it would weigh about *16 tons* once you got it back to Earth (or a planet of similar gravity)! For those who mine stellar material, planetary nebulae are nice, but the real payday are white dwarves. If one has a ship capable of withstanding the incredible gravity of a white dwarf (it exerts a force of nearly 100 million pounds/45 million kg), then one can actually begin cutting it apart and transporting the stellar material away as super-dense raw materials. Decompressing the stuff is a complicated process, and only a handful of organizations can do it, most notably, the CCW and the TGE, and even then only with limited success. A few advanced local powers in the Anvil Galaxy have had much more success with extracting and manipulating white dwarf material, which explains why, even though they command relatively few star systems, they have the material resources of an empire many times their size. This situation is slowly but surely making it impossible for the large governments of the CCW or the TGE to expand any further into the Anvil Galaxy. In fact, in time it will probably result in the currently "small" powers of the galaxies pushing these big powers into smaller and smaller corners of territory before ejecting them from the Anvil Galaxy altogether. Of course, this is a *highly speculative* situation, and one many generations down the road, but it is a situation that makes the farsighted CCW and the TGE a bit nervous. As a result, both powers have spies and scientists scrambling to figure out how to exploit white dwarves more effectively. This has turned the once-barren and discarded territory of the inner galaxy into white-hot interstellar real estate.

70-87%: Nova. If a white dwarf is part of a binary star system, then chances are it will turn into a *nova* at some point. When this occurs, the white dwarf suddenly increases in brightness by a factor of 2x to 20x. The brightness peaks over a period of five to twenty days, after which the star gradually dims back to its normal luminosity. This dimming can last for a couple of weeks to hundreds of days; every star's rate of decline is different.

Novas are interesting to astronomers on an academic level, but they are positively deadly to explorers and miners who are checking out a white dwarf when it undergoes this change. So far, Anvil Galaxy scientists have been unable to accurately predict when a nova candidate will actually go nova. This means that any of the wildcatters who are "mining" a white dwarf do so at the risk of getting caught at ground zero if and when a nova transformation occurs. There is no technology in the Anvil Galaxy that can withstand being right on top of a nova star. Those caught in the transformation are instantly destroyed. However, some theorists insist that on stars with any kind of ley line activity, a nova will not destroy those on or near the star, but instead transports them randomly across the Megaverse, to parts unknown. Given that nobody ever hears from those unfortunates caught in a nova transformation, there is really no way to tell if this "transportation" theory has any credibility. Yet.

One should note that as a white dwarf dims back to normal, it ejects a tremendous amount of gas from itself. If any white dwarf miners are in the area, this gas is of moderate value, somewhere between harvesting planetary nebula gas and harvesting actual white dwarf material. The problem with these gas jets is they are short lived, and prospectors tend to crowd in on each other to draw off the gas stream while it is around. This tends to promote "claim jumping" as rival miners push each other out of the gas stream. Tensions run high under situations like these, so everybody involved tends to get a little jumpy, and minor space battles between miners have been known to result.

88-00%: Black Dwarf. Once a white dwarf has expelled all of its heat, it truly dies, becoming a *black dwarf*. Black dwarves are fairly uncommon because white dwarves actually live for a really long time (billions of years, in fact), and the Anvil Galaxy is not all that old, astronomically speaking.

The chances of finding white dwarves is decent, but finding one that has finally died out is quite another story. To date, only 3 black dwarves have been reported in the entire Anvil Galaxy. Of course, there might be more that have gone undiscovered. And there are almost certainly some that have been discovered, but kept a secret from the rest of the galactic community. The reason why somebody would want to hide a black dwarf is because these dead stars are essentially huge lumps of highly compressed carbon and are *filled* with diamonds! And we're not talking about just measly one- or two-karat diamonds, either. These are huge, ranging from the *Hope Diamond* to diamonds the size of automobiles or houses. If mined and sold in the right markets, the "diamond harvest" from a black dwarf can produce unimaginable wealth (as a few local star systems have already done). This is a tricky operation, though. If the miners flood their local market too quickly, they will destroy the value of their diamonds, making them nearly worthless. Moreover, if news gets out of a black dwarf mine, certain parties will spare no expense to take over the mine for themselves. This means pirates, evil (or just plain greedy) corporations, alien marauders and cutthroat governments. Mining a black dwarf, an be extremely rewarding, and talking about it can be extremely deadly. Often the two end up going hand in hand, so those who stumble upon these treasures must tread carefully when they cash in on them.

Huge Stars

Huge stars include *blue dwarves* and *blue sub-giants*. When stars of this size die, they first become *red supergiants*, then go out with a bang by going *supernova*, and then became super-dense *neutron stars*.

01-34%: Red Supergiant. Much like their smaller cousins, the red giants, *red supergiants* are large stars that have begun burning helium instead of hydrogen. But, because these stars are so much bigger in the first place, their helium-burning reaction is much more dramatic. Red giants expand to the size of an entire solar system, spelling certain doom for whatever planets once orbited it. There is no escape – they all get engulfed by the star, a process which melts down the planets and leaves nothing behind later on. Red supergiants in the Anvil Galaxy develop very quickly, ballooning from their normal size to supergiant size in a period of 10-100 years. In inhabited systems, this leaves plenty of time for folks to clear out before their homes are destroyed. However, there have been examples in which people did not want to leave their system without resolving a few outstanding conflicts with their neighbors first, and what resulted was a system at war but under a time limit. These kinds of conflicts typically end with one or both parties falling prey to the system star as it overtakes them.

35-67%: Supernova. As a red supergiant burns, it transforms helium into carbon. These stars are so incredibly big and hot they can burn the carbon, too, fusing it into still heavier elements like oxygen and sodium. This keeps the red supergiant in business until it creates a stockpile of iron and begins burning it. Iron behaves differently from all of the elements the star had previously been using as fuel. In short, it halts the star's nuclear chain reaction and the star collapses under its own weight. The iron in the star absorbs the energy of this collapse, allowing the star to fall in on itself at tremendous speed. Then, like a tightly coiled spring, the star expands back outward again in a catastrophic explosion that leaves behind only the tiniest fragment of its former self. In this explosion, the star's temperature rises to several *trillion* degrees! This mega-explosion is a *supernova*, arguably the most powerful naturally occurring event in deep space.

Supernovas have their own importance in the Anvil Galaxy, of course. First, they will obliterate whatever is in their solar system at the time. Ships, space stations, asteroids, moons, planets, all of it destroyed. There is no known force that can withstand the blast of a supernova that close to ground zero. The minimum safe distance from a supernova depends on the size of the blast, but usually being in the next nearest star system is a safe bet. Like a white dwarf's nova, supernovas give little to no warning before they occur. The entire chain reaction that is a supernova takes just a few minutes, from beginning to end. In most cases, this is not even enough time for people to get to their spaceships and get out of town before the star explodes. Ships already in space might have a chance if they initiate their FTL protocols immediately, but even then, there is a decent chance those ships might not get away in time. The best bet to escape a supernova is some kind of teleportation or dimensional travel – something that will instantaneously remove one from harm's way. This might be one reason why so many conventional space travelers avoid red supergiants as a matter of course. Would *you* want to take a chance on having a supernova go off in your face? It might also account for why so many of the Anvil Galaxy's psychics and practitioners of magic feel comfortable around these stellar powder kegs. Reportedly, certain mystics and psychics can tell when a red supergiant is about to pop its cork, and they also have the means to blip out of the system with a mere 15 second's notice. No scientific study has been done of any mystic or psychic means of detecting an impending supernova, but nevertheless it remains an unwritten rule that to see a supernova coming, science alone will not get the job done.

On a darker note, there are also *rumors* that certain nefarious elements within the galaxy, notably renegade scientists and rogue governments, have been working on prototype weaponry that would somehow accelerate a large star's rate of decrepitude exponentially. The end result would be a device that could actually cause a huge star to enter its red supergiant phase in the span of a microsecond, and from there to go supernova a few seconds later. People have talked about "star killers" for eons, but so far, nobody has been able to create such a terrifying weapon. Recent fears hinge on the bizarre and disturbing "chain reaction" of supernovas several years ago in the southern sectors of the galactic core, when the stars of seven adjacent solar systems all went supernova in the span of a single 24 hour period. Some fear that the event was somebody "testing" a star killer weapon, but most believe it was a strange natural phenomenon or a massive coincidence – many stars at or near the core are fairly old and are entering their death cycles, despite the relative youth of the Anvil Galaxy itself. Despite such explanations, the rumors of a super-weapon being responsible for this event persist, and keep popping up in the galactic intelligence community like a persistent cold nobody seems able to stamp out. Whether or not any such weapon is being seriously researched by *anybody* or if this kind of weapon is even possible is something both the CCW and the TGE care not to discuss publicly. That stance only fuels the fires of speculation even more. The worry with most state intelligence officials is that even if this supposed super-weapon does not exist, the persistent discussion of one will eventually inspire rogue scientists to try to build one. Such technology, the CCW and the TGE feel, is best left undiscovered by everybody. On that, these two rival governments are in total agreement.

68-00%: Neutron Star. What happens after a supernova depends on the size of the red supergiant that blew up. If it was utterly huge, then it turns into a *black hole*, which is discussed in the next table. If it was smaller, like one of the stars in this category, then it turns into a *neutron star*. Just prior to the star's explosion, the materials of the collapsing star pile up at the center, and the star's remaining electrons and protons combine to form neutrons and neutrinos. The center of the star is now a pure ball of neutrons only ten miles (16 km) in diameter, but with most of the star's original matter packed into it, giving it simply incredible density. Neutron stars emit neutrinos all the time, like how a fire might emit warmth, or a light bulb emits illumination. Sometimes, neutron stars have "neutrino storms" – sharp bursts of radiation that even planets with marginal technology (by Phase World standards) can detect on radio telescopes. For many low-tech astronomers, this activity also gives neutrons the title of *pulsars*. But besides giving one type of star two different names, these neutrino storms and their spikes of radiation play an interesting role in the ongoing search for the Cosmic Forge. Various scientific organizations have noted that the galactic pattern of pulsar emission, when charted over an extremely long period of time (thousands upon thousands of years at the minimum), seems to fit a repeating pattern. The pulsar radiation spikes might very well be part of a huge kind of galactic morse code, but nobody has been able to discern if indeed these pulses are part of a code, and if so, what that code might be saying. Naturally, fingers point towards the Cosmic Forge, and that this is all a special means of locating the Forge, i.e. a trail left behind by the Cosmic Forge itself. Only advanced civilizations would be able to pick up such a subtle message, thereby ensuring that only an advanced civilization would find the Cosmic Forge! A nice theory, but it supposes that all pulsar activity is not natural, but manipulated into being by some outside force. Many scientists laugh off such a notion, but lest they become too arrogant, the Cosmic Forge itself is sure to have existed, and if that is the case, then anything is possible, even a galactic Easter egg in the form of a pulsar network steadily beaming out a message of where to find the most carefully hidden object in history.

Giant Stars

Giant stars include *blue giants* and *blue supergiants*. When stars of this size die, they first become *red supergiants*, then go *supernova*, and then they collapse and become the bogeyman of deep space, a dreaded (and revered) *black hole*.

01-34%: Red Supergiant. The transformation into a red supergiant is essentially the same for both huge stars and giant stars. For details on red supergiants, see the previous section. The only real difference is size – red supergiants of this class become much larger than even their entire solar system. In cases of binary stars, they might even reach the outermost planets of their neighboring solar system.

35-67%: Supernova. The supernova chain reaction is essentially the same for both huge stars and giant stars. For details on supernovas, see the previous section. The only real difference is magnitude – the effects of a supernova from this class can be felt even in adjacent star systems. This is especially true of binary star systems, in which the supernova of one star will lay waste to every planet orbiting the other star. In some cases, scientists have even recorded massive damage being done to the companion star, such that the star began its own transformation into a red supergiant and then into supernova almost immediately thereafter. In such instances, absolutely nothing is left of either solar system, and ships within 100 light years of the blasts can expect to receive heavy damage, if not outright destruction.

68-00%: Black Hole. Most of the time, after a star explodes into a supernova, it condenses into a *neutron star*. However, if that star were supermassive, like a blue giant or blue supergiant, then something different happens. After such stars go supernova, they condense and form a body of such incredible gravity that the very fabric of space and time warps infinitely, creating the ultimate in spatial phenomena: the *black hole*.

In the Anvil Galaxy, back holes are both a blessing and a curse. For ships not equipped with up to date navigational data, accidental encounters with black holes are not uncommon, especially the closer one gets to the galactic Core. If properly equipped with navigational coordinates, and if driven by an expert pilot, spaceships can navigate a black hole, skipping past its singularity (the point where the star has been condensed to a single point – not really a place one wants to be under any circumstance) and flying through the black hole. Once past the singularity, the pilot will see that black holes actually form *hyperspace tunnels* to other places! Sometimes these tunnels are to other spots in the Anvil Galaxy or the Three Galaxies, or sometimes they lead to alien worlds and dimensions far across the Megaverse. Sometimes a black hole's 'wormhole' wanders like a water hose without somebody to hold on to it, a tunnel that sends its travelers to a different destination every time. Other times, wormholes are fixed and can be used as a regular shortcut by interstellar travelers.

Wormholes are a relatively easy means of skipping across huge distances in no time at all, but such capabilities are tempting to galactic engineers, many of whom are currently hard at work at perfecting hypergravitic technology – machines that can artificially enhance gravity to such a point that an *artificial*

black hole might be made for travel purposes. Of course, certain scientists on such projects secretly fear this technology might be used as a weapon, and so they are actually willing to lie, cheat, steal and commit sabotage to see that their project does *not* always succeed, especially when their superiors come for peer review.

Planetology

Okay, so we know what kind of star we have and how many planets are in the system. Now is the time to hash out the details for every planet. This is where the real fun (and the real detail) begins. There are five basic categories to planetology: *type* (moon, asteroid, planet, etc.), *diameter* (relative to the norm for that planetary type), *gravity* (again, relative to the norm for that planetary type), *temperature*, and *special features* (moons, rings, etc.).

Type

01-15%: Asteroid. This entails any rocky body between 10 km and 1,000 km in diameter. Anything larger than that may be classified as a planet. Anything smaller than that is considered a meteorite. Asteroids generally do not have an atmosphere, standing water, or biosphere (plants and animals). However, there are always exceptions to the rule, such as an asteroid with some giant creature living inside of it, an asteroid with large ice plates on its surface or an asteroid with trace amounts of oxygen clinging to it. In these cases, however, such elements almost always are deposited on the asteroid by some external force. Throughout the Anvil Galaxy, there are many examples of how asteroids actually are attractive habitats for certain people. Mercenaries, pirates, and rebels all love to hide out in asteroid belts because the real estate is cheap and it is easy to lie low there. Miners like asteroids because they can make their home right on top of their workplace. Hermits like them because they can get some decent solitude. And adventurers like them, well because asteroids are just cool.

16-55%: Terrestrial Planet. Also known as "rocky" planets, worlds of this type are like Mercury, Venus, Mars and the Earth – relatively small rocky bodies that might or might not support atmospheres, water or life. They are different from gas giants in that they are more rock than gas. In any given solar system, terrestrial planets tend to be closer to the sun than any gas giants. They also tend to be the ones most likely to harbor some kind of life or civilization.

56-96%: Gas Giant. Gas giants typically have a relatively small rocky core the size of a terrestrial planet surrounded by an enormous atmosphere of some kind. Most gas giants have a radius many times that of even the largest terrestrial planet, effectively making them huge clouds of gas clinging to a rocky core and held in place by gravity and rotation. Gas giants may have life within them, but it is rarely of the "standard" humanoid, carbon-based type, and it is almost never technologically sophisticated. For that, a gas giant's best bet is if it has any moons. In many cases, gas giant moons are, in effect, small planets (Jupiter's Io, Europa, Ganymede and Callisto are fine examples) which might very well support life (as well as a trip through the Random Planet Generator if you feel like hashing out all of their details).

97-00%: Exotic. The planet is of a strange and nonstandard form. Examples might include a huge comet that somehow supports permanent life on its surface (or in its interior), a *ring habitat* (an artificial habitat maybe a few thousand miles/kilometers in width but with a radius of a planetary orbit, giving a huge surface environment), a *sphere habitat* (known as *Dyson Spheres* on Earth, they are like ring habitats except they enclose an entire orbital diameter; they are considered by most to be purely theoretical, but reports of sphere worlds from near the galactic core persist), a *rogue planet* (a world that belongs to no solar system and drifts freely), part of a *rosette* (several worlds all on fixed points on the same orbital track, like a string of pearls – almost always formed artificially by a super-advanced civilization) or some other odd type.

Diameter

This chart gauges how large the world is relative to its type. *Asteroids* typically range from 100 km to 1,000 km in diameter. *Terrestrial Worlds* typically range from 1,000 km to 25,000 km (with the average being around 12,000, which is the rough diameter of Earth). *Gas Giants* are always big, typically ranging from 75,000 km to 250,000 km in diameter. Exotic worlds have no typical range, so for them, anything goes.

01-05%: Microscopic. Well, not really, but worlds of this size *are* beyond 75% below the normal minimum size for their type. -66% on the Gravity table, below.

06-15%: Minuscule. As much as 75% below normal minimum size for its type. -50% on the Gravity table, below.

16-25%: Tiny. As much as 50% below the normal minimum size for its type. -33% on the Gravity table, below.

26-40%: Small. At the low end of the normal size range for its type. -25% on the Gravity table, below.

41-60%: Average. Right in the middle of the normal size range for its type.

61-75%: Large. At the high end of the normal size range for its type. +25% on the Gravity table, below.

76-85%: Huge. As much as four times larger than the normal maximum size for its type. +33% on the Gravity table, below.

86-95%: Enormous. As much as eight times larger than the normal maximum size for its type. +50% on the gravity table, below.

96-00%: Gargantuan. Beyond eight times larger than the normal maximum size for its type. +66% on the gravity table, below.

Gravity

The average gravity for most habitable worlds in the Anvil Galaxy is roughly equivalent to that of the Earth, so that will be the basis of comparison for this table.

01-10%: Minuscule. The world has only the slightest hint of gravity, similar to what one might find on a small asteroid or a tiny moon like Deimos or Phobos (both moons of Mars). On a world such as this, a human of average strength can throw a baseball into orbit! Or, if one threw parallel to the ground, the ball would eventually come back around and hit the thrower in the back of the head, if the world were small enough. Those with superhuman strength can perform mind-boggling feats of brawn on worlds such as this. In game terms, lifting and carrying capacity is increased by 100x (or more!), as is leaping distance (Careful — leaping into orbit isn't out of the question here!).

11-20%: Light. The world has a fairly light gravity, comparable to what we find on Earth's Moon. In game terms, lifting/carrying capacity and leaping distance are increased by 50x to 100x.

21-35%: Low. The world has a fairly low gravity, comparable to what we might find on Mars or one of Jupiter's planetary moons. In game terms, lifting/carrying capacity and leaping distance are increased by 10x to 50x.

36-55%: Average. The world has a gravity comparable to Earth's. This still covers a fairly wide range of gravity, and depending on how the G.M. designs this world, lifting/carrying capacity and leaping distance might still be increased by as much as 10x, or it might be decreased by as much as 25% due to higher-than-average gravity.

56-70%: High. The gravity is up to twice what one might find on Earth. As a result, lifting and carrying capacity and leaping distance are reduced by 50%. Also, one's endurance lasts only half as long, making hard physical labor a real hassle. Humanoids native to such a world typically have high P.S., P.E. and Spd.

71-80%: Heavy. The gravity is up to four times what one might find on Earth. As a result, lifting and carrying capacity and leaping distance are reduced by 75%. Also, one's endurance lasts only one-quarter as long, making hard physical labor utter torture. Humanoids native to such a world typically have superhuman P.S., P.E. and Spd.

81-90%: Extreme. The gravity is up to eight times what one might find on Earth. As a result, lifting and carrying capacity and leaping distance are reduced by 90%. Also, one's endurance lasts only one-eighth as long, making sustained physical labor virtually impossible without the aid of an exoskeleton, bionics, or some other form of mechanical enhancement. Humanoids native to such a world typically have superhuman or even supernatural P.S., P.E. and Spd.

91-00%: Punishing. The gravity is more than eight times what one might find on Earth. As a result, lifting and carrying capacity and leaping distance are reduced by 99%. Also, one's endurance lasts only one-sixteenth as long, making sustained physical labor impossible without using an exoskeleton, bionics, or other mechanical help. Most humanoids under such circumstances have to use a suit of environmental body armor all the time, since the gravity is so harsh one will have difficulty breathing otherwise. The only alternative is setting up habitats where artificially light gravity can be generated.

Temperature

The following temperatures are rated by how they might affect the "standard" carbon-based humanoids of the Anvil Galaxy. Most of these life forms live with temperatures roughly equivalent to what might be found in the Earth's solar system. For temperature gauges in a really hot or cold solar system, the G.M. is invited to extrapolate the following table accordingly.

01-10%: Frozen. The planet's surface temperature is below 40 Kelvin (-387.5 F/-233 C). Only non-carbon aliens are able to adapt to such cold. Carbon-based technology can still handle the cold, however, though it might suffer long-term adverse effects if not maintained properly.

11-20%: Freezing. The planet's surface temperature is roughly equivalent to Pluto, typically ranging between 40 K (-387.5 F/-233 C) and 60 K (-351.4 F/-213 C). Carbon-based life forms generally can not fully adapt to this environment. Technologically advanced humanoids can defeat the cold with a heavy environmental suit, or they might one day alter the environment through terra formation, but on their own, this cold will prove too much for them.

21-30%: Frigid. The planet's surface temperature is roughly equivalent to Neptune, typically ranging between 60 K (-351.4 F/-213 C) to 80 K (-315.4 F/-193 C). Carbon-based life forms can live here with heavy adaptation. For most humanoids, this means wearing heavy environmental suits or undergoing special genetic engineering.

31-40%: Cold. The planet's surface temperature is roughly equivalent to Uranus or Saturn, typically ranging between 80 K (-315.4 F/-193 C) and 100 K (-279.4 F/-173 C). Carbon-based life forms can live here with moderate adaptation. For humanoids, this means environmental suits or portable heating units in their uniforms.

41-50%: Cool. The planet's surface temperature is roughly equivalent to Jupiter (on the cold end) or Polar Mars (on the high end), typically ranging between 100 K (-279.4 F/-173 C) and 200 K (-99.4 F/-73 C). Carbon-based life forms can live here with minimal adaptation. For most humanoids, this means wearing really warm clothes.

51-60%: Temperate. The planet's surface temperature is roughly equivalent to Equatorial Mars or the Earth, typically ranging between 200 K (-99.4 F/-73 C) and 325 K (125.6 F/52 C). Carbon-based life forms can live here with no problems adapting.

61-70%: Warm. The planet's surface temperature is roughly equivalent to what Venus might be like without its greenhouse effect, typically ranging between 325 K (125.6 F/52 C) and 500 K (440.6 F/227 C). Carbon-based life forms can live here with moderate adaptation. For humanoids, this means environmental suits or portable cooling units in their uniforms.

71-80%: Hot. The planet's surface temperature is roughly equivalent to Mercury, and what Venus actually is like, typically ranging between 500 K (440.6 F/227 C) and 750 K (890.6 F/477 C). Carbon-based life forms can live here with heavy adaptation. For most humanoids, this means wearing heavy environmental suits or undergoing special genetic engineering.

81-90%: Scalding. The planet's surface temperature typically range between 750 K (809.6 F/477 C) and 1,000 K (1,340.6 F/727 C). Carbon-based life forms generally can not fully adapt to this environment. Technologically advanced humanoids can beat the heat with a heavy environmental suit, or they might one day alter the environment through terra-formation, but on their own, this heat will prove too much for them.

91-00%: Scorching. The planet's surface temperature is hotter than 1,000 K (1,340.6 F/727 C). Only non-carbon aliens are able to adapt to such heat. Carbon-based technology can still handle the heat, however, though it might suffer long-term adverse effects if not maintained properly.

Unusual/Special Features

Roll percentile dice for *each* of the following categories of "unusual" or "special" features. A roll of 01-20% means that the world has that particular special feature. It is possible for a world to have every kind of special feature listed here, and then some. Or a world might have none of these features at all.

Strange Orbit. The world's orbit might be elliptical, or it might intersect with the orbit of another planet (raising the possibility of a collision, or some other effect when the planets get too close to each other), or it might be degrading (with each orbit the world gets closer to its sun) or it might be increasing (with each orbit, the planet moves farther away from the sun), or it might be transphasic (parts of the orbital path take place in different dimensions, so the world really shares time in various different spots across the Megaverse), or it might have some other form of unusual orbit. Almost always, odd orbits put the world in harm's way, make its environment more challenging, or they make it possible for alien creatures to set up shop permanently, sometimes without the aid of technology.

Unusual Axis. The planet is basically tilted dramatically in one direction. This by itself is not so noteworthy, except in the Anvil Galaxy, planets have been known to undergo dramatic and spontaneous axis shift. It is as if an unseen hand slapped the world, sending it spinning into its new axis. Such events, while rare, can be catastrophic. They throw the world's entire environment out of whack, and the damage they inflict on the settled civilizations there often is mortal. Many civilizations can not adapt quickly enough to their stark new landscape, and they either leave the planet or they die out trying in vain to adapt to their new surroundings. Sometimes, planets with an unusual axis have equally unusual magnetic fields or their planetary axis and polar magnetic axis are out of whack. The end result is that such planets can be much more difficult to approach for landing, especially when a ship is decelerating from lightspeed. Depending on the nature of the axis difficulties, piloting and navigation skill rolls may be affected by as much as -25% during landing procedures. Such planets are often known as "spaceship graveyards" for being so tough to land on.

Odd Revolution. The planet takes an unusually long or an unusually short period of time to go once around its star. To some extent, this might be explained by the planet's proximity to the star (Mercury whips around the Sun a heck of a lot faster than Pluto), but for these worlds, something else is almost always afoot. The most common phenomenon accompanying this (in the Anvil Galaxy, anyway) is a corresponding effect on the life span of whoever lives on the planet. If it has an unusually long revolution, then life spans tend to be a lot longer than usual. Conversely, really short revolution times mean that inhabitants live far shorter than usual. There is no acceptable explanation for this, so far. Only a handful of planets – fewer than three dozen – exhibit these effects in the Anvil Galaxy.

On a related note, several teams of Xeno-sociologists have conducted exhaustive studies comparing planetary military history and planetary revolution. Though the two seemingly have nothing in common, it is a fact that in the Anvil Galaxy, planets with unusually long revolutions tend to be very difficult to invade and occupy. Likewise, planets with really fast revolutions often have terrible and recurrent civil wars. These studies have been debunked by many as a chronicle of coincidence made to fit the scientists' conclusions, but coincidence or not, these facts speak for themselves.

Weird Rotation. The planet has a strange rate of rotation. Perhaps it spins extremely fast, making several revolutions per day! Such worlds are notoriously difficult to land or take off from; -33% on all piloting and navigational skills. Or maybe the world periodically switches what direction it rotates in. Or maybe the planet does not rotate at all, or it rotates in synch with its rate of revolution, so one face always sees the sun and one face never does.

Moons. The planet has a number of satellites orbiting itself. Roll 1D20 to see how many moons the planet has. For determining the nature of these moons, feel free to roll again on these tables. Only subtract -50% to the rolls for Type, Diameter and Gravity, and do not roll on the Unusual/Special Features table.

Rings. The planet has some kind of orbital ring made up of ice particles and small rocks, the largest of which might classify as small asteroids. The ring may be really skinny and almost invisible, or it may be wide and majestic, like Saturn's rings – G.M.'s choice. Aside from being a nice spectacle, rings can provide crude shelter for spacecraft. In emergencies, lifeboats have often found a temporary refuge within rings, in which they could hide until their rescue. Pirates and smugglers also use rings as a hiding place, to jump out on unsuspecting prey, or to sneak past the authorities.

Craters. Somewhere, sometime the planet has been hit (and hit *hard*) by meteors, comets, and a few smaller things, too. Almost all planets have some kind of cratering on their surface, but planets in this case have really serious craters on them. The kind that came very close to shattering the planet (like the one on the Saturnian moon of Mimas). Worlds with active biospheres often turn these craters into spherical oceans or verdant valleys where unusually dense concentrations of plants and animals can be found. Worlds without biospheres often look like they have a big eye staring up into space, something which certain religious cults in the Anvil Galaxy and elsewhere consider a holy sign meaning that the presence of a deity is nearby, watching.

Special Energy Field. This can be any kind of strange energy emanating from the planet. It does not need to be overtly harmful, either. It could be that the planet emits especially powerful radio waves, making the world an astronomic beacon across the galaxy. (On a few such worlds, the inhabitants have figured out how to manipulate and accelerate such energies in order to speak instantaneously to any other planet in the Anvil Galaxy!) Or, the world could emit powerful levels of radiation, either of a kind people are already familiar with, or something strange, alien and new. Either way, the G.M. should determine if this energy being emitted is good or bad, and how it might affect the inhabitants of the planet.

Other. The G.M. is encouraged to come up with something really strange about the planet. It has varying speeds of rotation or revolution; it is actually hollow with people living inside; it is really a living organism; it is on the verge of exploding; it has no magnetic field whatsoever, it gets pummeled constantly by meteor showers; its core emits a sort of radiation that renders technology unusable, etc. The possibilities are wide open here, so run with it and have a ball. This is your blank check to make the world as bizarre as you care to.

Environment

Now that we have a basic idea of what the planet is like, let's consider what life on the actual surface might be like. There are four basic sections to this category: *atmosphere* (most life needs to breathe something, right?), *terrain* (what surprises do the ground and its associated climates hold?), *hydrosphere* (the amount of freestanding water on the planetary surface), and *biosphere* (the degree to which plants, animals and other life forms have developed on the world).

Note that none of these categories are necessarily prerequisites for each other. It is possible, for example, for a planet to have a massive biosphere but no atmosphere. In such an apparent contradiction, the G.M. is encouraged to figure out a reason for why this set of circumstances came about. Give it a try – you might find that the reasons you develop end up adding some great detail and mystery (and maybe even adventure hooks) to the world you are building. Or adjust accordingly.

Atmosphere

Another interesting coincidence uniting most of the humanoid races of the Anvil Galaxy is their need to breathe a more or less "Earth-like" atmosphere (one rich in oxygen and nitrogen). There are always exceptions, of course, but for the most part, the readily habitable worlds of the Anvil Galaxy are those sporting an atmosphere most humans would feel at home in.

01-10%: No Atmosphere. Like Earth's Moon, this world has no atmosphere whatsoever. This is most common of asteroids, moons and planets that are either very close or very far from their sun. In most cases, planets tend to have at least *some* kind of atmosphere. If the planet is a gas giant and No Atmosphere is rolled, either re-roll, or try to come up with an interesting reason for why this gas giant has lost its gas. Was it some kind of ancient battleground? Was the gas giant ignited somehow, and it burned off its atmosphere in a star-like blaze of glory? Did some weird galactic phenomenon blow the atmosphere away? Or did some advanced race deliberately alter the environment, losing the atmosphere in the process? (Rumor has it certain advanced cultures that have terribly polluted their home worlds will actually steal the atmosphere off a gas giant in order to replenish their own tainted air. For this to work, those aliens would have to have incredible technology not only to steal the gas, but to modify it so they could breathe it.)

11-20%: Trace Atmosphere. There is only the barest hint of an atmosphere on this world. For just about any life form that needs to breathe, there is not remotely enough atmosphere to sustain life. Certain kinds of plants and protists can thrive in such an environment, however. Full-enclosure atmosphere suits and pressurized habitats are required. Of course, worlds such as this can always have an atmosphere added to them by terra-formation. In fact, the more atmosphere there is, the easier terra-forming becomes, so for many planetary engineers, a Trace Atmosphere world is a more preferable target than a No Atmosphere world.

21-30%: Thin Atmosphere. There is definitely an atmosphere, but for breathing purposes, it is a little lacking. Most life forms that need to breathe can adapt to this environment. Indeed, there are many examples of plants and animals that thrive in thin atmospheres. For the first-time visitor, wearing some kind of breathing gear will be necessary, even if it is just a simple rebreather or oxygen mask. After a few weeks, depending on the visitor's biology and endurance, unassisted breathing should be possible. Those not used to a thin atmosphere should not overexert themselves, or they will become exhausted very quickly. All heavy labor and combat can be performed for 2D6x10 minutes before the person peters out.

31-50%: Normal (Earth-like) Atmosphere. The atmosphere is very similar to Earth's. The vast majority of space-faring folk can breathe the air here just fine, even if it is not the native atmosphere of their home. The funny thing about atmospheres like this is that they seem to be almost universally breathable. In the Anvil Galaxy, many of the aliens who breathe different atmospheres on their home world often have little difficulty adapting to a Normal Atmosphere, whereas those races (including humanity) that naturally require a Normal Atmosphere have a very difficult time adapting to any other atmosphere. Some races see this as a fortunate hedge against the forces of humanity from spreading out too far and taking over every corner of the Anvil Galaxy.

51-60%: Dense Atmosphere. While the atmosphere is similar to Earth's ,there is simply more of it. A *lot* more. In fact, the atmosphere is about twice as dense as the galactic norm for life-bearing worlds, which makes it really difficult to breathe here. (Too much of a good thing, huh?) Most humanoids will require some kind of breathing assistance, such as an air mask or filter. Humanoids and animals can adapt to such circumstances, however, and numerous Dense Atmosphere worlds have thriving native biospheres on them. Unfortunately for such life, visiting a Normal Atmosphere feels like a Thin Atmosphere world.

61-70%: Super-Dense Atmosphere. The atmosphere is just too dense to breathe. This is often the case with certain gas giants or with terrestrial planets whose atmospheres are so large that by the time one reaches the rocky surface of the planet, the atmospheric pressure is incredible. Breathing unassisted here is impossible for most humanoids, who will require air masks, filters, or best yet – environmental suits/armor. Native life can thrive on worlds such as this, but it is fairly uncommon. Planetary engineers find such worlds to be very easy to terra-form. All they have to do is rid the world of what they consider "excess atmosphere." A few firms have actually managed to skim off atmosphere from one world and basically transplant it elsewhere. Such operations are called "swap outs," and they are seen by some to be the new face of planetary reformation.

71-80%: Tainted Atmosphere. The atmosphere is close to Earth-like but contains enough of some noxious element to render it unsafe to breathe. With air filtration, the air can be made safe again, but breathing without a mask or filter of some kind is hazardous to one's health. The degree to which the atmosphere hurts non-native humanoids is up to the G.M. The effect can be insidious, building up a cumulative effect over several hours. Or, the effect can be almost instant, sending visitors scrambling for their air masks. With no more than moderate terra-forming, the atmosphere can be "scrubbed" clean, however.

81-90%: Hostile Atmosphere. The planet's atmosphere is patently unbreathable and would require extensive atmospheric processing to make it safe for most humanoids. Usually, the atmosphere simply has too much of a noxious element or not enough of a critical element. Pirates, smugglers and other sorts of underworld or renegade types love to set up their headquarters on such worlds because the risk of being discovered by snoopy colonists or planetary engineers is minimal.

91-00%: Exotic Atmosphere. The planet's atmosphere is strange, to say the least. It might very well be breathable, but it also has exotic qualities to it that make it alien. Exotic effects might include the presence of gravity-defying gas clouds, the tendency for the atmosphere to change the voice pitch of whoever breathes it, the equivalent effect of sleeping gas on certain species, etc.

Terrain

In planetology terms, "terrain" refers both to the topography land mass formation and climate(s) of a planet.

01-10%: Single Terrain. The world is dominated by a single kind of terrain. These are the classic "space opera" planets – a jungle world, a desert world, a frozen world, etc. The exact nature of this terrain is left to the G.M.'s discretion, but it covers virtually the entire planet. It can be something found on Earth, it can be an odd amalgam of Earth-like terrains, or it can be something entirely alien and unknown to Earth geologists.

11-20%: Two Terrains. The world has a primary and a secondary terrain. In most cases, the primary terrain covers 1D4x10+50% of the planetary surface (maximum 90%, never less than 60%) and the secondary terrain covers the rest.

21-30%: Three Terrains. The world has a primary, secondary and tertiary terrain. In most cases, the primary terrain covers 1D4x10%+30% of the planetary surface (max 70%), the secondary covers 1D4x10% of what is left over, and the tertiary terrain covers what is left to as little as 1%.

31-50%: Four+ Terrains. The world has four or more terrains. Usually, any given terrain covers roughly 1D4x10% of the planet's surface, with each terrain covering at least 10%.

51-60%: Exotic Terrain Present. Either the entire planet or 1D6x10% of it is some exotic terrain. This means it possesses some alien and dangerous characteristic not found on most inhabited worlds. This could include areas that run backward or parallel in time, spots that have unusual magnetic fields, spots that randomly teleport those who visit them, zones where gravity behaves differently, regions covered by forests of crystals, and so on. Or, the exotic terrain can be more climatic than actual terrain – arctic jungle of ice, mountainous swamps, etc.

61-70%: Hostile Terrain Present. At least one of the planet's terrains is hostile. This means it possess some alien characteristic not found on most inhabited worlds. This could include a field of needle-like rock stalactites that might easily pierce the feet of whoever walks through, areas of super-deadly quicksand, weird and devastating storms, areas that are bathed with deadly radiation during the day, and so on.

71-80%: Unusual Mineralogy. On, near and under the surface of this planet lie out of the ordinary mineral formations. Most of the time, given enough analysis, these minerals can be found to have some fairly valuable — if not at least interesting — properties. Entire fortunes can be made on finding such things, and indeed, mining interests in the Anvil Galaxy spend large sums of money sending survey teams into space so they might find those one or two systems with cold fusion diamonds, crystallized teelium 231, or some other wild mineral that represents millions, billions, or even trillions of credits in excavation potential.

81-90%: Unusual Seismology. The seismic nature of the planet is unusual, to say the least. At one extreme, the world might be seismically inert. There is no tectonic activity whatsoever. This means there can be no earthquakes. It also means that if there are any volcanoes on the planet, they will never stop growing. (A good example of this is on Mars, where one volcano, Olympus Mons, has grown to the size of Texas. No kidding.) At the other extreme, the planet might be one great big seismic event, with incredible earthquakes and volcanoes going off 24-7. (Jupiter's moon Io is a good example of this. Turned inside out by Jupiter's gravity field, Io is nothing but spewing volcanoes.)

91-00%: Unusual Geology. The rock formation of the world is eccentric. This can create a host of weird circumstances, such as: there might be huge pockets in the crust (perfect for civilizations to settle), the world might actually be hollow, the world might have no real core to speak of (so it loses heat), the planet may be covered with deep canals or canyons or pillars of stone, or it might be full of holes and tunnels like a block of Swiss cheese, the world might have a super-dense metallic core producing freaky magnetic fields, or the world's geo-formation might make it vulnerable to certain harmonic frequencies, which means that at any time, it might spontaneously explode.

Hydrosphere

01-10%: Dry. The planet is devoid of standing water. Trace amounts might be found in the soil, but not enough to support life.

11-20%: Desert. No large bodies of standing water. The occasional river or oasis, but that is it. There might be substantial amounts of water on the planet, but it is trapped somehow, either as ice at the poles, suspended in the rock and dirt, etc.

21-40%: Badlands. In select places there is enough water to sustain life. These are small rivers, isolated springs, etc. Besides such oases, the majority of the planet is fairly dry, making it a dangerous place to travel long distances unless one has copious amounts of water with them. This category also accounts for the surprisingly high number of worlds in the Anvil Galaxy that have abundant surface water but for some reason it is unfit for consumption. Excessive metal content, poisonous trace elements, microorganism contamination, you name it.

41-60%: Balanced. The world has a large amount of standing water on the surface. This means a small ocean and/or lakes, rivers, streams and ponds. There is still a lot more land than water, but the world is wet enough that deserts are now a minority form of territory.

61-80%: Moist. There is slightly more water on the planet than land, usually in the form of one or more large/small oceans, and numerous lakes, streams, rivers and ponds. Large and abundant aquatic biospheres are possible, as is underwater colonization.

81-90%: Soaking Wet. Mostly ocean. One major land mass, maximum. In some parts, the oceans get so deep that they might not be fully explored by the land-dwelling inhabitants. On more than one occasion, this has led to a nasty culture clash on worlds with two technologically advanced species, one on land, one at the bottom of the ocean. Eventually, these two peoples will butt heads, and sometimes, global warfare can result. In fact, more times than not, such encounters turn hostile and stay that way until one race leaves, is enslaved, or is destroyed.

91-00%: Water World. No major land masses, just water stretching endlessly to the horizon. Land dwellers might live on the surface, cruising around in houseboats and meeting in artificial atolls. But for the most part, this is a swimmers' world, and if there is any significant civilization to be hand, it will be underwater. Depending on the nature of the biosphere, these underwater dwellers might or might not be technologically proficient.

Biosphere

01-23%: Lifeless. The world either never developed life (like Mercury) or it once had life but it was exterminated. In the second situation, ruins might still exist, as do the ghosts of those who died in the world's final reckoning.

24-50%: Sparse. Few thriving species. Planet is either just developing life, or is on the verge of going totally extinct. There probably is not quite enough here to form a stable biosphere, so worlds like this are especially susceptible to outside tampering. Renegade genetic engineers just love finding worlds like this. To them, it is like a blank canvas on which they can create whatever their twisted minds desire. Bacteria may be the primary life form.

51-70%: Thin. This is the weakest form of stable biosphere likely to be found in the Anvil Galaxy. There are only two or three prominent species besides bacteria. Anything else plays a marginal role. For various reasons, the life forms here tend to be simple and show little signs of evolutionary specialization.

71-80%: Moderate. Varied thriving species. The planet has an established biosphere, but it is fairly simple and could be thrown out of whack easily if interfered with. There are plenty of specialized species, and it is on worlds like these that explorers often begin seeing some of the *really* strange monsters and animals known to lurk the galaxy.

81-90%: Dense. Numerous thriving species. The planet has a wide variety of life environments. Were one to crash, it would probably not take all others with it, but one can never tell. As a side effect of such an active biosphere, microorganisms often pose a problem to humanoids. In short, disease, infection, and all sorts of micro-contamination become likely. Unless one takes strenuous measures to keep clean of these buggers, any kind of long-term stay on the planet will probably be hazardous to one's health.

91-95%: Verdant. Many different plant and animals species, contributing to a robust and diverse biosphere. On the plus side, this means abundant crops, tons of pharmacologically beneficial life forms, and a treasure trove of genetic information awaiting the research team willing to collect it. On the down side, numerous predator species, strange species, and numerous ways for micro-creatures to get inside and kill somebody without their ever knowing it.

96-00%: Cornucopia. Massive numbers of thriving species. Only a sustained destruction of the global environment by disease, industrialization, war, or cosmic event (e.g., asteroid impact) would seriously upset the biosphere of this world. Such worlds are poor candidates for any kind of industrial development, since history shows that the environment *will* overgrow any transplanted buildings or machinery. For most organizations, colonizing or setting up shop on planets like this are not worth the effort, in the long run. So, they leave them alone. As a result, criminals, rebels and runaways of all kinds *love* to use such worlds as hideouts.

Civilization

Population

01-20%: Uninhabited. Nobody lives on this world. Yet.

21-30%: Skeleton Crew. The world is home to up to *100* people. In most cases, the inhabitants are either a shipwrecked crew, a small band of bandits, explorers, runaways, etc. Sometimes they are the skeleton crew of a larger contingent of people, like if most of the staff of a science outpost were called away and never came back for some reason. If the people are very self-sufficient and have adequate supplies, they can probably survive indefinitely barring any external threat like pirates landing or scary animals approaching.

31-40%: Outpost. The world is home to *1,000* or a few thousand people. This is the lower limit of most colonies. Outposts are usually populated by scientists, miners, explorers, and other hard-knock types. These places feel less like an actual town or village, and more like a great, big workstation (which is what they are). Outposts tend to have their own peculiar traditions and culture, and most resent it terribly when colonists show up and try to make a "model community" out of the place.

41-60%: Colony. The world is home to up to *100,000* people. This is the upper limit of most colonies. With any more people, the world is generally considered settled. That means it is no longer a mere outgrowth of its home society; it is now another full-fledged part of it. For a lot of space-faring societies, there is a distinct change in how life feels at a place such as this. Soon the old "frontier" mentality will give way to a more polished and urbane sense of things. A major transition is in the works, and those who were with the planet from the beginning will likely leave to make room for the new wave of immigrants who, as far as they are concerned, are just moving from one civilized place to another.

61-70%: Settled. The world is home to *1D4 million* people! There will be at least one large city, as well as numerous smaller cities, towns and villages. Population density is still fairly sparse, considering that there is roughly the population of a moderate pre-Rifts European country spread out over an entire planet.

71-80%: Busy. The world is home to *tens of millions* of people! The planet has at least a handful of large cities as well as a dense network of smaller cities, towns and villages.

81-90%: Crowded. The world is home to *hundreds of millions* of people! The planet most likely has numerous large cities, and countless smaller cities, towns and villages.

91-00%: Jammed. The world is home to *tens of billions* of people! Unless the world is very large, chances are the civilization will have had to build some kind of arcology network or underground warren just to accommodate everyone.

Technology

01-05%: No Technology! For some reason, the people here never developed any kind of tools. Most of the time, it is because the natives have not yet progressed to the point of understanding technology, much less building or inventing it for themselves, In rare cases, however, (and this seems to be the case more in the Anvil Galaxy than in either the Corkscrew Galaxy or the Thundercloud Galaxy) certain alien peoples will either forsake all technology or will have developed themselves beyond a need for it. Such people often have advanced magic, psychic or super-powers which obviate their needs for weapons, armor, vehicles and other associated gadgetry, even basic tools.

06-15%: Stone Age. This world has progressed to the Cro-Magnon level of technology. They understand basic things like using and building a simple shelter (hut or cave house), tools, keeping (making) fire, developing language, using clothing and basic weapons and tools, and so on. But these folks must still rely more on their purely natural abilities than on the tools they can build. To them, exposure to *any* technology from a higher technology level will seem like magic or the creation of the gods.

16-25%: Iron Age. The world's collective technology hovers somewhere between that of Ancient Rome and Medieval Europe. Tools are commonplace, but mass production, the key to

more advanced technologies, is not. Gunpowder or its equivalent may or may not be part of this picture (the G.M.'s call).

26-35%: Industrial Age. The world's collective technology hovers somewhere between the advent of Steam Power and the development of Atomic Power. Though most civilizations bridge this gap in a relatively short period of time, this period is a huge leap in technical capabilities, and it can be very stressful for civilizations not equipped to handle it.

36-55% Information Age. The world's collective technology hovers somewhere between the end of the Atomic Age and the beginning of a reach for the stars. During this time span, the world is likely to have developed massive computerization, networking, global production, and other marvels. However, pollution, resource depletion and overcrowding are all perils in waiting. For many civilizations, the answer to such problems is to find another world to live on. Hence, the beginnings of space colonization. The world has, at this point, successfully extended its reach to other planets, but not other stars. Still, the world might not yet have encountered other alien races. It might also still think it is alone in the universe. It certainly is unlikely to know of a larger intergalactic community to become part of.

56-80%: Stellar Age. The world has, at this point, successfully extended its reach to well beyond its own solar system. It is aware of the galactic community, the Three Galaxies, the Cosmic Forge, and all that such things entail. This civilization is ready, willing, and able to send explorers to the farthest corners of the galaxy, where they might establish friendly acquaintances and possible diplomatic connections. This is the level of technology most commonly encountered among the major powers of the Anvil Galaxy – the CCW, the TGE, Naruni Enterprises, etc. More advanced technology is available (as the next two entries show), but they are comparatively uncommon and mere adventurers will have a hard time getting their hands on it.

81-95%: Galactic Age. The world is home to an advanced star-faring culture, one that sees intergalactic travel (and not just between the Three Galaxies) as something no more dramatic than taking a monorail across town. Galactic Age planets are in short supply in the Anvil Galaxy, the result of endless warfare amongst their own people.

96-00%: Megaverse Age! The people of this world are beyond star-faring. They may have developed incredible magic, psionics, or some technological means of instantaneously casting themselves as far away as they like. Oftentimes, their travels include breaching the Megaversal fabric and going to other dimensions and even alternate versions of the Megaverse itself. Time travel is also a common technology to such cultures. Needless to say, precious few of these exist anywhere within the Three Galaxies. Those in the Anvil Galaxy tend to be near the core, in star systems beyond the scope of what most carbon-based humanoids consider to be habitable. Thankfully, Megaversal races often have reached a state of extreme evolution, and have either purged themselves of the need for conquest, or have developed their technology so much that they have no need to expand to other star systems. Otherwise, such societies would be running the Anvil Galaxy.

Economy

Roll on this table three times for each planet. The first roll determines the largest pillar of the world's economy, accounting for about 60% of all domestic production and income. The second roll determines the world's secondary economic pillar, accounting for about 30% of all domestic production and income. The third roll determined the world's tertiary economic pillar, accounting for only about 10% of the all domestic production and income.

01-25%: Agricultural. The growing of crops and the raising of livestock.

26-55%: Industrial. The manufacture and distribution of goods. Or, the performance of a particular service on a mass scale.

56-83%: Commercial. The mass buying and selling of goods. Or the transactions between manufacturer and retailer.

84-98%: Service & Information Technologies. 10% agricultural, 20% industrial & Commercial, and the rest of its business is service, communications, and information technologies. These people do not do a great deal of manufacturing but trade tons of services and information/technology and operate an advanced global (probably even an interplanetary) communications network. Information and communications is virtually everything.

99-00%: Exotic. Some weird fusion of any of the preceding categories. This might mean a kind of agricultural commercialism whereby there is a massive consumer economy but produce and livestock are used instead of actual money. Or, an agricultural industrial world in which components used for heavy machinery are actually produced organically, and therefore, must be farmed. That sort of thing. Feel free to get as strange as you can on this one. In fact, the stranger, the better!

Wealth

01-10%: Utter Squalor & Poverty. The world has nothing of value and its people live in the worst conditions imaginable for anything that might qualify as a civilization. Usually such poverty is only found in areas that have been devastated by war or natural disaster, populations being actively oppressed by invaders, or areas where some kind of total breakdown has occurred in the economy. Crime is oddly low only because there is nothing for crooks to take. Everybody has nothing. This is the very picture of misery. Unless the native people place no importance on money or material gain, that is. If that is the case then the squalor perceived by off-worlders might not be seen as such by the locals, who might be rather content to live their simple, uncluttered lives.

11-20%: Impoverished. The world has an economy teetering on the edge of total collapse. There is not enough of anything to go around. Shortages are common even for the most basic commodities. Luxuries of any sort are not to be found; what is considered luxurious is to get all the food, clothing and shelter one needs for a time.

21-30%: Poor. The world does not have much income at all. The majority of the people live hard and spare lives. They are not impoverished, but they definitely are lacking in many materials and in wealth, a condition the economy is just not large, strong or healthy enough to counter. Most often, poor conditions are created by government ineptitude, destruction of industries, inability to gain trading partners, population growth that exceeds economic growth, or any number of other factors.

31-40%: Depressed. The world is probably of an average or better economy but it has fallen on hard times and now things look pretty bleak. Unemployment and debt are high, as is crime of all sorts. This is generally a transitory state; if things get worse, the world will begin to slip into permanent poverty. If they get better, the world will jump up a notch or two in Wealth rating. However, it fell from grace once, it could always do so again.

41-50%: Average. The world has a stable and solid economy. It is diversified enough so that any minor or moderate problems can be ridden out with minimal disruption. Still, the world is no economic superpower, and the vast majority of its people live modest, "middle class" lives. These people do not want for basic necessities, but they hardly live luxury-laden lives, either.

51-60%: Prosperous. The world has a robust economy. Either it is an Average economy during a boom time, or the economy is just naturally strong and the people can afford to live high on the hog. Luxury items are commonplace, and the government usually has a great deal of resources at its disposal.

61-70%: Wealthy. The world is well above average in both resources and cash flow. Unemployment and crime is fairly low. There will always be some of both on this world, but there is little enough that the government can brush it under the carpet with minimal trouble.

71-80%: Rich. The world is simply rolling in dough. There might be class divisions in terms of wealth, but even the poor here have little to complain about compared to the truly destitute on other worlds. Here, being poor means not having as much as the richest have. Even the most impoverished person here has their basic needs more than taken care of. Crime is generally the product of those who will commit larceny or other outlaw activity no matter how well off they are.

81-90%: Super-Rich. The world has a stronger economy than 90% of the rest of the Anvil Galaxy. Typically, these worlds are massive trading powers, able to dictate prices for most commodities in the sector. They are capable of mass building or industrialization if they like, and their citizenry enjoy lives of ease and luxury. For this world, life is a great big bowl of cherries, and handling problems of any sort is simply dirty work that somebody else must take care of.

91-00%: Utopia! There are only a handful of worlds like this in the Anvil Galaxy, those with so much wealth that they have eliminated poverty altogether, and everybody lives by getting pretty much whatever they want, whenever they want. The funny thing is, with a life no longer defined by the scarcity of resources, the people quickly lose interest in material things and begin living life for intangibles such as love, hate, mastering skills or talents, and achievement.

Government

By this time, we have a rough idea of what kind of society inhabits this world. But no society is complete without rulership, and in the Anvil Galaxy, there are almost as many different examples of bizarre governments as there are alien races to run them. Rolling up a government has four main sections: its *type* (democracy, monarchy, etc.), its *law level* (or "crime and punishment index"), its *popularity* (do the governed accept their rulers?) and its *stability* (how likely are the governed to accept their rulers' authority?).

Like other tables in this generator, there can easily be some really strange or contradictory results, but as always, take it as an opportunity to make a really unique and memorable world for your adventurers to explore. Remember, this is the Anvil Galaxy. This is space opera. Not only are bizarre worlds to be expected, in some ways, they are the norm.

Type

01-05%: Anarchy. No government at all! This might result from a total breakdown in the government (tantamount to revolution or civil war), or the society might have progressed to such a point that it no longer needs a formal government. In such a case, all individuals take ultimate responsibility for their own lives in every way.

06-10%: Militocracy. Rule by the military. This is different from a mere junta or military coup d'etat regime in that a genuine militocracy succeeds itself over a period of administrations or regimes. In other words, a real militocracy can stand the test of time, and is not merely an interim government until something more palatable comes around. A good example of a militocracy is on *Keskis Alpha*, a world terribly beset by annual raids from the Star Hives. As an independent world, Keskis Alpha throws most of its resources into military defense. By default, military leaders are also governmental leaders. To do otherwise is mere redundancy.

11-15%: Autocracy. Rule by a single figure. Also known as *dictatorships*, autocracies make no pretensions to royalty, divinity or any other trappings of an immortal nature. They are simply governments set up by a single person who decided to take power for whatever reason. Somewhere along the line, this person got enough people to go along and in the end, the dictator ended up running things. There are, sadly, all too many examples of autocracies in the Anvil Galaxies, especially among Independent worlds. One particularly heartbreaking example is on *Paruvia*, in which a vile despot named *Orthus Kretch* overthrew a popular and democratically elected government simply because he, to quote Kretch directly, "needed a place in the galaxy where he could rape and kill whoever he wanted." In the 30 years since Kretch overthrew Paruvia, he has satisfied those very urges thousands and thousands of times, inflicting himself upon a populace too terrified to oppose him or his dreaded shock troopers, the *455 Legion*.

16-20%: Monarchy. Rule by a hereditary sovereign. Monarchies are the classic royal setup, typically with a king or queen presiding, though sometimes a prince, princess or regent might find themselves on the throne during unusual circumstances. Monarchies succeed themselves by bloodline, which makes marriage a very big deal to these people. There are a fair number of monarchies throughout the Anvil Galaxy, but the *Kingdom of Wex Kragaa* gains special notice because its sovereigns routinely duel their own heirs every five years for the right of premature ascension to the throne. If the sovereign loses, he or she is executed or enters exile. If the heir wins, they take control. One might think this would lead to an unstable monarchy, but the Kingdom has survived for over 1,000 years, probably because the Wexians themselves live for centuries, are extremely resilient to physical harm (bio-regeneration) and have up to 40 offspring in a single brood.

21-25%: Aristocracy. Rule by nobility. Similar to a monarchy, except instead of a single ruling sovereign, there is an entire group of them. Most often, this means a noble family or a coalition of noble families hold power. In the Anvil Galaxy, aristocracies almost always occur after a monarchy has crumbled or been overthrown by a large number of potential heirs-in-waiting who overthrew their monarch when he or she was weak. Aristocracies tend to be transitional governments; either a new monarch ascends from the ruling aristocrats or an heir to the deposed sovereign returns and reclaims the throne somehow, or the aristocracy evolves into something different. A notable example of an enduring aristocracy is the *Kangsreal*, a world that was once a monarchy, but turned into an aristocracy after a violent coup. Three centuries later, the ruling nobles have increased in number so that fully 65% of the population bears noble rank and the other 35% have enough money to pretend to be noble. Though things are running well now, the government is in shambles and is a revolution waiting to happen.

26-30%: Hierarchy. Rule by stratified layers of authority. This is fairly uncommon in the Anvil Galaxy, but a good example might be the *Strossian Fellowship*, which controls the *Paxares* system. The Strossians have nine different parliaments, each of whom have authority over the one below them and answer to the one above them. Only the ninth parliament answers to the first, making it a round robin government. Maybe not a strict hierarchy, as there is no bottom and top, but this does maintain the hierarchical spirit, as officials are constantly striving to advance in their parliamentary "level," and making it all the way around the circle is seen as a feat of considerable achievement.

31-35%: Confederacy. Rule by allied power blocs. The elements within a confederacy might actually be of varying governments, but adhering to the principle of a whole being greater than the sum of its parts, these elements come together in mutual accord and mutual governance. Most confederacies, or *federations* as they often like to call themselves, are fairly loose governments with few rules. The Consortium of Civilized Worlds is a fine example of a very large confederacy that has proven immensely successful.

36-40%: Democracy. Rule by popular accord. Many of the CCW's member states are democracies, a kind of government widely regarded as a high benchmark of civility and governmental maturity. That said, democracies are not infallible, and in the Anvil Galaxy, many have collapsed under their own weight. The most familiar scenario is when a democratic society gets too prosperous for its own good, which breeds apathy, which means nobody bothers to vote anymore, which means the government either falls apart into a mass of squabbling petty interests, or a dictator of some kind takes over, or the whole thing just melts into anarchy. In the sad case of *Tyhid II*, all three have occurred and keep occurring with regularity as the government goes through an odd cycle of boom, bust and self-destruction.

41-45%: Oligarchy. Rule by an elite. This elite might have nothing to do with government; it might be those who adhere to a particular philosophy, those who have achieved a certain task, those who are part of a certain ethnicity, race, breed, or profession, and so on. Oligarchies might best be thought of as a kind of dictatorship except instead of a single ruling autocrat, there is a whole gaggle of them who share power more or less equally. A notable oligarchy is the *Council of Longo*, whose lackluster rulership over the *Mucahle* system has kept these otherwise resource-rich worlds from becoming the local economic superpower they could be. The problem is, any time someone challenges the Oligarchy, the Oligarchy simply takes them into their ranks. Hence absolute power corrupts absolutely, and there is no further opposition for a while.

46-50%: Syndicracy. Rule by a group of syndics, or common business interests. In the Anvil Galaxy, this is an increasingly common form of government in which powerful businesses somehow wrest control from more traditional governments. Or, these businesses colonize worlds for economic gain and end up having to rule the place once colonists put down roots there. Syndicracies tend not to be very effective governments, since they are more attuned to maintaining a healthy profit margin than dealing in the more personal goals of good government. This is illustrated well in the case of *Tholos, LLC*, a huge multi-planetary company that bought numerous worlds outright with the hopes of setting up automated factories on them. They treated the native populations like trespassers, and after a while, the locals decided to revolt. In a wild turn of events, some of them hacked into the Tholos mainframe and transferred the company's stock to the native populations. They then sold the stock short in the Phase World bourse (stock exchange) and made a mint. Shortly thereafter, the company was dissolved by its shareholders, and the local natives lived in peace. Tholos operatives have vowed revenge, however, and might one day try to regain their former asset worlds.

51-55%: Plutocracy. Rule by the wealthy. There are few of these in the Anvil Galaxy, but those that do exist serve as a good counterpoint to the shortcomings of most syndicracies. Plutocracies generally work best when citizens are also shareholders, and the term "voting with your wallet" takes on a literal meaning. Citizens come and go to these societies more freely as they buy and sell their interest in the government. Strict controls keep such societies from selling citizenship to enemies of the state. As the cases of *Vurious III*, *Sketti Syl*, and *New Dahan* show, a plutocracy run with the shareholders in mind can actually be a stable and very profitable way of running a planet. Indeed, each of those three worlds possess higher standards of living than 90% of the rest of the Anvil Galaxy, and they have had no major political upheavals in over 250 years.

56-60%: Bureaucracy. Rule by bureaucrats. Strangely, nobody seems to know exactly how these redundant, inefficient and individual-smothering organizations ever get started. Lead theories suspect it is when large and complicated societies become too much of both and the government drowns itself in the details of running daily business. Soon, the forest gets lost for the trees, and the entire government spends 99% of its time and resources chasing its tail, crossing "T"s, dotting "I"s, and filling things out in triplicate. Some bureaucracies have become enormously powerful, however, as the massive fleets of the *Jjelong Collective* illustrate. Thankfully, their naval commanders must send request memos to over thirty different departments before gaining authorization to carry out anything purely offensive in nature, which keeps the society from invading their neighbors.

61-65%: Pedocracy. Rule by the learned. This is different from a *technocracy*, rule by the those who possess certain skills, in that pedocracies are usually run by scholars and academics, not applied experts. Pedocracies tend to exist in highly advanced, peaceful, and bountiful societies where external threats are minimal and most efforts are placed towards learning. Pedocracies rarely stir up trouble, but when they do, they do it in style. One example is the *Gautian Quorum*, a pedocracy made up of evil scientists who only wanted one thing: the extinction of all carbon-based life (including their own). Thankfully, the intervention of several unknown adventurers halted their most recent plot, but as long as a group like the Quorum has an entire planet's resources at its disposal, nothing good will ever come of their efforts.

66-70%: Theocracy. Rule by clergy. There seems to be little room for religion in the Anvil Galaxy outside of some kind of worship for the Cosmic Forge. Because passions run so hot regarding the varying interpretation of the Cosmic Forge legends, any government devoted to a particular religious tenet of the Forge often generates too many enemies and dies a quick death. However, there are a few enduring theocracies in the Anvil Galaxy. One in particular is the *Path of Light*, a militant cult that unified a system's worth of planets and imposed their ultra-harsh religious views on everybody under their control. Little more than a form of totalitarianism, the Path of Light exists only because news of it has not really reached the rest of the galaxy yet. When it does, a Cosmo-Knight or other noble crusaders will make sure the Path's days are numbered and that justice and tolerance might be replaced in the system.

71-75%: Mageocracy. Rule by magic-wielder. The means by which that magic wielder assumes power is varied; another roll on this table might be helpful. There is only one real major mageocracy in the Anvil Galaxy, and it is the United Worlds of

Warlock. Still, there are a few very small mageocracies among the independent worlds. They try to keep a low profile so they are not swallowed by their neighbors.

76-80%: Gerontocracy. Rule by those of a certain age. Basically, a kind of oligarchy wherein only people of a certain age are considered fit to govern. Some gerontocracies disqualify the young from government while some disqualify the old. The world of *Susk* prohibits anybody whose age is a multiple of three from governing, an odd stricture that has no apparent origin or aim other than to shake up the government once in a while.

81-85%: Gendocracy. Rule by those of a particular sex. Most of the time, governments such as this exclude either men or women from ruling. In a few alien societies, gendocracy gets more complicated among species that have more than two sexes. The unusual *Feereon* race, with their eleven distinct sexes, often resort to gendocracy to meet their political aims. In a society such as theirs, one's sex often determines what political party or faction they are likely to belong to.

86-90%: Technocracy. Rule by those possessing certain skills. In the Anvil Galaxy, this form of government comes about most often on highly economic worlds in which trade unions or guilds obtain serious political clout. Eventually, one of these trade groups takes over the government, and to make sure they remain in power, modify things so that only one from their guild or union may rule. The end result is a technocracy, which usually has little to do with the actual skill the technocrats in power possess. The world of *Pandehi* has been a technocracy for many years, only the skill sets that make one eligible for rulership change all the time. Given that most of the populace have datajacks in their heads into which they can slot memory cards that let them practice any skill, the technocratic rules of their government are fairly obsolete. But, despite all odds, they persist. Probably because no viable alternative has yet been offered.

91-95%: Mechocracy. Rule by machine. In some cases, a mechocracy may exist for a society of intelligent automatons, as was the case with the Machinists' Machine People long ago. In other cases, a carbon-based people might cede their political authority to a machine of some sort (a mega-computer comes to mind) to make their decisions for them. Mechocracies can work very well; the machines in charge are very efficient and get a lot done while their organic masters live lives of luxury. The only problem is dislodging the machines from power once they are there. Many machines do not see it as logical to return government to their carbon masters. More than a few wars have begun over that particular misunderstanding.

96-00%: Exotic. The planet has some kind of government not described above, and which might be best classified as...eccentric. With a setting as large as the Anvil Galaxy, there is room for just about any kind of political permutation one can think of. Most of the time, these eccentric governments are one of a kind, the product of unique geography, culture, economy and politics. So while there might be a lot of Exotic governments across the Anvil Galaxy, they also tend to be isolated political entities that one will not find elsewhere. Just one more thing to keep space travelers on their toes. Some of the more interesting examples of Exotic governments include:

Xenocracy, or rule by aliens. The *Kingdom of Aad* has long lived by such a government. Basically, nobody born on the planet may be eligible for any seat in government, and the monarchy must be made up of those outside the Aadian race.

Mutocracy, or rule by mutants. This can be found on the post-industrial wasteland planet of *Zerten VI*. Once the jewel of an ancient interstellar kingdom, it is now a Kreeghor dumping ground for all kinds of noxious pollutants. The planet is currently out of Kreeghor hands, and most of the population has undergone some kind of genetic change thanks to all of the radioactive, teratogenic, or otherwise mutagenic crap laying around. Thus, the Zerteni Parliament may only be populated by those who have a "true" feeling for what life on Zerten VI is like — and those folks would be the world's mutants, many of whom have actual super powers as well as grotesque deformities.

Chronocracy, or rule by those displaced by time. This can be found on *Ghuria Prime*, where a Temporal Raider took over years ago and sought to assure that only he and his kind would rule by decreeing that only those who can travel through time have the perspective needed to govern effectively. Since the native Ghurians have extremely short lives (only 1D4+1 years!), the long life span of a Temporal Raider, coupled with its ability to travel through the very medium which defines the Ghurian culture (time), makes the Raiders seem like gods. So who are the Ghurians to question that?

Criminiocracy, or rule by those who have broken the law. This is best seen on *Auriaon*, a world that is utterly fascinated by crime and punishment, and whose population is almost entirely comprised of lawyers, justices, law enforcement personnel and ex-cons. The Auriaon legal system is so complex and contradictory that it is almost impossible for somebody to *not* break the law over the course of their lifetime. (This is something many off-world visitors learn the hard way during their first visit.) In many sectors of the planet, folks ritually break the law as a rite of adulthood, and the years they spend in prison are considered a valuable part of their personal growth. As far as government is concerned, the idea is that one can not possibly understand how the Auriaon society works without having experienced firsthand its very foundation — its legal and penal systems. This type of government has been tried on a few other worlds, but usually they fail within a few years. Only Auriaon has been able to really make it work.

Ludocracy, or rule by games of chance. A famous ludocracy was established on *Haddlegun*, which historically had been locked in seemingly endless civil wars between its various nations. A brilliant general finally conquered all warring parties and established a unified government, keeping the peace for 100 years. In his old age, the despot-leader went a little wonky in the head, and developed an unhealthy love for any kind of game of chance. With no heirs or any other perceptible means of transferring power once he would be gone, the leader held a tournament of gaming to determine who would take over. The tournament not only proved to be a big hit with the people, but it also produced a successor who was actually pretty good at leading! Since then the Haddlegun Ludocracy has become a galactic oddity — a must-see for tourists and professional gamblers alike. This attention keeps the government in business (imagine if the casinos of Monaco or Las Vegas were really parliamentary factions!) and the Ludocracy has remained stable through seven successive transfers of power.

Mystocracy, or rule by unknown or anonymous figures. An example of this is *Tyrol Greva*, a world plagued by banditry and lawlessness of every kind until it was tamed by an unknown crusader some years ago. It was rumored that this unknown hero was really a Cosmo-Knight who chose to hide his identity. Be that as it may, a weird side effect of the planet's transformation from lawlessness is that in honor of their hero, all government heads hide their identities when on the job. This has its problems, though, like when rival politicians or meddling off-worlders impersonate standing leaders to cause unrest. Since everybody wears a hood or mask or otherwise obscures their identity, it is hard to tell who is the imposter and who is the real McCoy. It is an inefficient, awkward government, but it beats the non-government they had before.

Randocracy, or rule by random selection. Sharing traits with the Haddlegun Ludocracy, the *Randocracy of Sehesia* determines its president and congress by a four-year planetary lottery. The lottery is quite an affair, with months of build up and sub-lotteries for lesser offices. Though the government has worked well enough, it does have the unfortunate side effect of drafting lots of unwilling individuals into governmental posts of great importance. As a result, these folks often end up ceding most of their authority to friends, family, their cabinets, or they actually sell the position off to the highest bidder. As a result, about one in every six planetary lotteries ends up in some form of serious governmental crisis. In fact, this has already sparked two revolutions and a short-lived civil war. But the Sehesians, a profoundly philosophical and easy-going race, do not seem to mind it all that much (a Sehesian civil war is a far less bloody

thing than civil wars on most other worlds), and so their Randocracy works about as well as any other form of government might. And at least this way, there can be no blame on how people got into power. It has all been decided, in one way or another, by Lady Luck.

Law Level

01-10%: Lawless! This place is like Dodge City of the Old West with heavy energy weapons. In most cases, the world has suffered a total breakdown in law and order, either because of civil war, or some kind of economic, political or cultural meltdown. Such worlds are prime choices for heroes like Cosmo-Knights, noble mercenaries or other wandering champions to step in and do some good. On the other end of the spectrum, there are also lawless worlds that are the product of a culture so enlightened and advanced that it no longer needs laws of any kind. Its people can be trusted to always do the right thing and not hurt their fellow citizen. This does not mean these societies have no means to defend themselves – often times, as gentle as they are on their own citizens, they can be utterly brutal against off-worlders stirring up any kind of trouble.

11-20%: Minimal. There might be some kind of law enforcement present, but it in no way meets the local needs. In many cases, this might be a lonely sheriff or an outclassed police department up against overwhelming crime — like if Elliot Ness was all by himself in Prohibition Chicago. In most cases, worlds like this are unable to solve their crime problems. They need help, and in a big way. The big difference between a Minimal world and a Lawless! world is that on a Minimal world, the presence of at least a few good guys means they can get the word out that they need help. As a result, they tend to receive reinforcements faster. Even with extra help, though, taming worlds like this is an uphill battle.

21-40%: Moderate. The world has a well established legal system and law enforcement, but for some reason, it just is not quite getting the job done. Maybe the good guys are not funded well enough. Maybe the bad guys are just too powerful — led by a super-being of some sort or equipped with unusually tough hardware. Or maybe the good guys have corruption in the ranks which weakens them. Or perhaps they lack experience. Whatever the reason, crime has the upper hand on worlds such as this, though it is not yet a crisis situation, even if it feels like it to the people living here. Wandering champions might not receive such a warm welcome here, only because the lawmen of this world have the sense that things are not entirely out of control, and they could lay down the law if only people didn't get in their way. As a result, unless specifically asked for, wandering champions are seen more as a hindrance than a help.

41-60%: Lawful. The world has a good law system set up, and it keeps crime well in check. Best of all, it does so without trampling the civil liberties of its citizens. In a place as wild and wooly as the Anvil Galaxy, striking this balance can sometimes be really difficult. It helps if the world has a stable government, a culture not prone to lawlessness or barbarity, and a military that can keep away bandits, pirates, and other independent troublemakers. In general, such worlds welcome Cosmo-Knights and other champions of good as fellow peacekeepers, but they expect them to obey the local laws during their stay. Fellow lawman or not, the peace must be upheld, and if visiting champions must be asked to leave or put in the lockup for a night to do that, then such is the price to pay. Something to keep in mind is that on Lawful worlds, weapon possession may or may not be restricted. Some worlds allow their citizens to own any weapon they like, but they somehow have set up an environment where such ownership does not lead to anarchy. Likewise, other worlds restrict weapons ownership, but they do it in such a way that it does not foment resentment or rebellion among the people. For any world, the G.M. is at liberty to decide how much weapons restriction plays into the world's law level.

61-80%: Overbearing. This world forcefully keeps the peace through a "better safe than sorry" attitude. Crime is way down, but that's because the local peacekeepers are not adverse to stepping on some toes to do it. Civil liberties are seen as a luxury that the government does not want to take away, but it will the moment it feels such liberties are getting in the way of keeping the peace. Visitors especially must watch their step, lest they find themselves in lockup or facing stiff fines for breaking laws they did not know existed. On worlds such as this, criminal or sedition suspects are considered guilty until proven innocent, they may or may not have the right to remain silent, and the cops may or may not have the right to arbitrarily beat the hell out of them.

81-90%: Authoritarian. Crime? What crime? This world is a police state in which restrictions far outweigh freedoms. The government keeps a close eye on everything, and people generally are fearful that they might somehow get on the government's bad side. Such worlds have large police and military forces, and they have no problems suspending any or all civil liberties to maintain what it perceives as "order." A free press is a hypothetical concept here, and political dissent of any kind is strictly monitored and governed. Basically, one can not so much as sing on a street corner without getting a permit which itself has a three month waiting list. Get the picture?

91-00%: Totalitarian. Big Brother had the right idea, but he lacked the guts to do the job properly! Totalitarian governments enforce near-total control and oversight of the people's lives. There is no freedom or privacy, and any dissent is crushed without hesitation. Worlds such as this almost always have extraordinary police and/or military forces, as well as extensive surveillance *everywhere*. On the plus side (if there really is one), totalitarian worlds tend to have outstanding intelligence gathering abilities. This makes them very valuable when they take part in coalition military endeavors, though for freedom-loving societies, working with totalitarian regimes feels like making a deal with the Devil.

Popularity

01-10%: Hated. The people of this world utterly despise their government. Chances are good that the world's Stability rating is in a steady decline of some sort. No matter how much control a government might have, when its people hate it this much, some kind of uprising is bound to happen. Eventually, the government will be overthrown, or it will capitulate to the people and give them what they want.

11-20%: Angry. The people are out for blood, and are certainly experienced at rioting. If talk of revolution is not in the air, it will be soon. However, there is a sizeable portion of the population that either does not care about the current political troubles or is too scared/intimidated to do anything about it. On some worlds, this can lead to an unfortunate balance in which a world never stops being near a revolution.

21-40%: Unpopular. The government has a habit of getting on the people's bad side, but serious revolution is not yet a foreseeable possibility. More likely, there will be isolated pockets of resistance where terrorists (or freedom fighters, depending on one's perspective) strike at the existing establishment.

41-60%: Ambivalent. Things are fairly middle ground here. There are the usual grievances against the government, but things are good enough that the civilian populace does not really care about the state of their own world, much less anybody else's. In this state, the government can maintain power for a really long time, since the people are too busy with other things than to provide oversight to the military.

61-80%: Popular. The government is liked by the people, and though it has its detractors, on popularity alone, it is a successful and stable way to run a planet. Unless there is tremendous crime or a military emergency, armed police may or may not be seen on such worlds.

81-90%: Beloved. The government is the apple of the citizenry's eye, and as far as the common man is concerned, the government can do little wrong.

91-00%: Fanatical. The people are willing to lay down their lives for their rulership. Most commonly, this occurs when a cult takes control of the society, mass brainwashing has been conducted, some kind of technology effects mass personality control, or by other such means. Fanatical societies tend to be dangerous because they believe their way is the only way, and those that are different are enemies that must be destroyed. This applies to any culture, government, philosophy, whatever. In the Anvil Galaxy, fanaticism of any sort rarely is a good thing.

Stability

01-10%: Revolution/Civil War. Things don't get much more unstable than this. The planet's government is under direct attack. In the case of a revolution, the fighters want to overthrow or destroy the government, replacing it with one of their choosing. In the case of a civil war, the aim is more likely to be for a segment of the population to break away and form a government of their own. Either way, the potential for warfare, destruction and disruption is immense. In the Anvil Galaxy, there are entire solar systems embroiled in revolution or civil war for decades at a time.

11-20%: Rebellion. The government is under attack, but by a significantly smaller portion of the populace than in a revolution or civil war. Depending on how powerful the government (i.e., the chances of the rebels actually winning), the rebels might be considered to be mere criminals stirring up trouble. Still, life on the planet is being seriously disturbed by the ongoing rebellion, and until it ends, there can be no peace.

21-30%: Uprising. A small portion of the population are directly opposing the government, but they have little chance of succeeding. Or, a large number of people might be opposing the government, but they are not resolved to really wage war, so things can't be disrupted all that badly. Uprisings are an interesting crossroad of political disturbance: if things get worse, then the government is probably on a downward slope to revolution or civil war. If things get better, then the government can be pretty sure they will remain in power for the foreseeable future.

31-40%: Unrest. There is widespread grousing, and there might be the occasional terrorist or revolutionary stirring up trouble, but the planet is basically at peace, and the government will remain in place for the foreseeable future. That said, the populace has some pretty severe grievances that are not being addressed. This might lead to a less disruptive overthrow of the government, like a sweep in upcoming elections or some other peaceful transfer of power.

41-60%: Stable. The government is more or less liked and approved of by the populace. There might be the occasional scandal or cause for protest, but in the long run, things are working and should continue to do so. Terrorists and revolutionaries are very much in the minority, and are seen by most people as criminals, nut cases, or both.

61-70%: Solid. The government is either so popular that it is very unlikely to be replaced by its citizens for any reason, or the government might have so much power that even if the population wanted to replace it, they would have a very difficult time doing so. Either way, governments this stable are good in the short run, but in the long run they sometimes lead to either complacency among the citizenry, or tyranny within the government.

71-80%: Long-Standing. The government has a long tradition of stability, so much so, that the people can hardly imagine life without it. For a government of this kind to be overturned, circumstances would have to become radically different from what they are now.

81-90%: Dynastic. The government has been ruling in its current form for at least several generations now. Chances are good that the planet has a long history of dynastic government, although there is a first time for everything, even a governmental dynasty. The problem with dynasties is they can become very oppressive, corrupt and inefficient. Usually this is the case when you have a people who by culture, brainwashing or other means, simply can not conceive of changing the government themselves. Sometimes, this is because the people lack the power to change their government, and have come to live with it.

91-00%: Immortal. A most rare condition in the Anvil Galaxy, the government is almost impossible to change and can be expected to remain in place for thousands, if not tens of thousands, of years. A good example of this is the dracology of Llakancen, which has been ruled by Llakancen the Just, an immortal dragon from another dimension who rules his world with justice, nobility, and utter power.

World Building Template

Solar System
  Number of Stars:
  Star Type:
  Number of Planets:

Optional: When Stars Die
  Small Stars:
  Huge Stars:
  Giant Stars:

Planetology
  Type:
  Diameter:
  Gravity:
  Temperature:
  Special Features:

Environment:
  Atmosphere:
  Terrain:
  Hydrosphere:
  Biosphere:

Civilization
  Population:
  Technology:
  Economy:
  Wealth:

Government
  Type:
  Law Level:
  Popularity:
  Stability: